T0254250

Lecture Notes in Computer Science

Lecture Notes in Artificial Intelligence   **14692**

Founding Editor

Jörg Siekmann

Series Editors

Randy Goebel, *University of Alberta, Edmonton, Canada*
Wolfgang Wahlster, *DFKI, Berlin, Germany*
Zhi-Hua Zhou, *Nanjing University, Nanjing, China*

The series Lecture Notes in Artificial Intelligence (LNAI) was established in 1988 as a topical subseries of LNCS devoted to artificial intelligence.

The series publishes state-of-the-art research results at a high level. As with the LNCS mother series, the mission of the series is to serve the international R & D community by providing an invaluable service, mainly focused on the publication of conference and workshop proceedings and postproceedings.

Don Harris · Wen-Chin Li
Editors

Engineering Psychology and Cognitive Ergonomics

21st International Conference, EPCE 2024
Held as Part of the 26th HCI International Conference, HCII 2024
Washington, DC, USA, June 29 – July 4, 2024
Proceedings, Part I

 Springer

Editors
Don Harris
Coventry University
Coventry, UK

Wen-Chin Li
Cranfield University
Cranfield, UK

ISSN 0302-9743   ISSN 1611-3349 (electronic)
Lecture Notes in Artificial Intelligence
ISBN 978-3-031-60727-1   ISBN 978-3-031-60728-8 (eBook)
https://doi.org/10.1007/978-3-031-60728-8

LNCS Sublibrary: SL7 – Artificial Intelligence

This Springer imprint is published by the registered company Springer Nature Switzerland AG
The registered company address is: Gewerbestrasse 11, 6330 Cham, Switzerland

If disposing of this product, please recycle the paper.

Foreword

This year we celebrate 40 years since the establishment of the HCI International (HCII) Conference, which has been a hub for presenting groundbreaking research and novel ideas and collaboration for people from all over the world.

The HCII conference was founded in 1984 by Prof. Gavriel Salvendy (Purdue University, USA, Tsinghua University, P.R. China, and University of Central Florida, USA) and the first event of the series, "1st USA-Japan Conference on Human-Computer Interaction", was held in Honolulu, Hawaii, USA, 18–20 August. Since then, HCI International is held jointly with several Thematic Areas and Affiliated Conferences, with each one under the auspices of a distinguished international Program Board and under one management and one registration. Twenty-six HCI International Conferences have been organized so far (every two years until 2013, and annually thereafter).

Over the years, this conference has served as a platform for scholars, researchers, industry experts and students to exchange ideas, connect, and address challenges in the ever-evolving HCI field. Throughout these 40 years, the conference has evolved itself, adapting to new technologies and emerging trends, while staying committed to its core mission of advancing knowledge and driving change.

As we celebrate this milestone anniversary, we reflect on the contributions of its founding members and appreciate the commitment of its current and past Affiliated Conference Program Board Chairs and members. We are also thankful to all past conference attendees who have shaped this community into what it is today.

The 26th International Conference on Human-Computer Interaction, HCI International 2024 (HCII 2024), was held as a 'hybrid' event at the Washington Hilton Hotel, Washington, DC, USA, during 29 June – 4 July 2024. It incorporated the 21 thematic areas and affiliated conferences listed below.

A total of 5108 individuals from academia, research institutes, industry, and government agencies from 85 countries submitted contributions, and 1271 papers and 309 posters were included in the volumes of the proceedings that were published just before the start of the conference, these are listed below. The contributions thoroughly cover the entire field of human-computer interaction, addressing major advances in knowledge and effective use of computers in a variety of application areas. These papers provide academics, researchers, engineers, scientists, practitioners and students with state-of-the-art information on the most recent advances in HCI.

The HCI International (HCII) conference also offers the option of presenting 'Late Breaking Work', and this applies both for papers and posters, with corresponding volumes of proceedings that will be published after the conference. Full papers will be included in the 'HCII 2024 - Late Breaking Papers' volumes of the proceedings to be published in the Springer LNCS series, while 'Poster Extended Abstracts' will be included as short research papers in the 'HCII 2024 - Late Breaking Posters' volumes to be published in the Springer CCIS series.

I would like to thank the Program Board Chairs and the members of the Program Boards of all thematic areas and affiliated conferences for their contribution towards the high scientific quality and overall success of the HCI International 2024 conference. Their manifold support in terms of paper reviewing (single-blind review process, with a minimum of two reviews per submission), session organization and their willingness to act as goodwill ambassadors for the conference is most highly appreciated.

This conference would not have been possible without the continuous and unwavering support and advice of Gavriel Salvendy, founder, General Chair Emeritus, and Scientific Advisor. For his outstanding efforts, I would like to express my sincere appreciation to Abbas Moallem, Communications Chair and Editor of HCI International News.

July 2024   Constantine Stephanidis

HCI International 2024 Thematic Areas
and Affiliated Conferences

- HCI: Human-Computer Interaction Thematic Area
- HIMI: Human Interface and the Management of Information Thematic Area
- EPCE: 21st International Conference on Engineering Psychology and Cognitive Ergonomics
- AC: 18th International Conference on Augmented Cognition
- UAHCI: 18th International Conference on Universal Access in Human-Computer Interaction
- CCD: 16th International Conference on Cross-Cultural Design
- SCSM: 16th International Conference on Social Computing and Social Media
- VAMR: 16th International Conference on Virtual, Augmented and Mixed Reality
- DHM: 15th International Conference on Digital Human Modeling & Applications in Health, Safety, Ergonomics & Risk Management
- DUXU: 13th International Conference on Design, User Experience and Usability
- C&C: 12th International Conference on Culture and Computing
- DAPI: 12th International Conference on Distributed, Ambient and Pervasive Interactions
- HCIBGO: 11th International Conference on HCI in Business, Government and Organizations
- LCT: 11th International Conference on Learning and Collaboration Technologies
- ITAP: 10th International Conference on Human Aspects of IT for the Aged Population
- AIS: 6th International Conference on Adaptive Instructional Systems
- HCI-CPT: 6th International Conference on HCI for Cybersecurity, Privacy and Trust
- HCI-Games: 6th International Conference on HCI in Games
- MobiTAS: 6th International Conference on HCI in Mobility, Transport and Automotive Systems
- AI-HCI: 5th International Conference on Artificial Intelligence in HCI
- MOBILE: 5th International Conference on Human-Centered Design, Operation and Evaluation of Mobile Communications

List of Conference Proceedings Volumes Appearing Before the Conference

1. LNCS 14684, Human-Computer Interaction: Part I, edited by Masaaki Kurosu and Ayako Hashizume
2. LNCS 14685, Human-Computer Interaction: Part II, edited by Masaaki Kurosu and Ayako Hashizume
3. LNCS 14686, Human-Computer Interaction: Part III, edited by Masaaki Kurosu and Ayako Hashizume
4. LNCS 14687, Human-Computer Interaction: Part IV, edited by Masaaki Kurosu and Ayako Hashizume
5. LNCS 14688, Human-Computer Interaction: Part V, edited by Masaaki Kurosu and Ayako Hashizume
6. LNCS 14689, Human Interface and the Management of Information: Part I, edited by Hirohiko Mori and Yumi Asahi
7. LNCS 14690, Human Interface and the Management of Information: Part II, edited by Hirohiko Mori and Yumi Asahi
8. LNCS 14691, Human Interface and the Management of Information: Part III, edited by Hirohiko Mori and Yumi Asahi
9. LNAI 14692, Engineering Psychology and Cognitive Ergonomics: Part I, edited by Don Harris and Wen-Chin Li
10. LNAI 14693, Engineering Psychology and Cognitive Ergonomics: Part II, edited by Don Harris and Wen-Chin Li
11. LNAI 14694, Augmented Cognition, Part I, edited by Dylan D. Schmorrow and Cali M. Fidopiastis
12. LNAI 14695, Augmented Cognition, Part II, edited by Dylan D. Schmorrow and Cali M. Fidopiastis
13. LNCS 14696, Universal Access in Human-Computer Interaction: Part I, edited by Margherita Antona and Constantine Stephanidis
14. LNCS 14697, Universal Access in Human-Computer Interaction: Part II, edited by Margherita Antona and Constantine Stephanidis
15. LNCS 14698, Universal Access in Human-Computer Interaction: Part III, edited by Margherita Antona and Constantine Stephanidis
16. LNCS 14699, Cross-Cultural Design: Part I, edited by Pei-Luen Patrick Rau
17. LNCS 14700, Cross-Cultural Design: Part II, edited by Pei-Luen Patrick Rau
18. LNCS 14701, Cross-Cultural Design: Part III, edited by Pei-Luen Patrick Rau
19. LNCS 14702, Cross-Cultural Design: Part IV, edited by Pei-Luen Patrick Rau
20. LNCS 14703, Social Computing and Social Media: Part I, edited by Adela Coman and Simona Vasilache
21. LNCS 14704, Social Computing and Social Media: Part II, edited by Adela Coman and Simona Vasilache
22. LNCS 14705, Social Computing and Social Media: Part III, edited by Adela Coman and Simona Vasilache

47. LNCS 14730, HCI in Games: Part I, edited by Xiaowen Fang
48. LNCS 14731, HCI in Games: Part II, edited by Xiaowen Fang
49. LNCS 14732, HCI in Mobility, Transport and Automotive Systems: Part I, edited by Heidi Krömker
50. LNCS 14733, HCI in Mobility, Transport and Automotive Systems: Part II, edited by Heidi Krömker
51. LNAI 14734, Artificial Intelligence in HCI: Part I, edited by Helmut Degen and Stavroula Ntoa
52. LNAI 14735, Artificial Intelligence in HCI: Part II, edited by Helmut Degen and Stavroula Ntoa
53. LNAI 14736, Artificial Intelligence in HCI: Part III, edited by Helmut Degen and Stavroula Ntoa
54. LNCS 14737, Design, Operation and Evaluation of Mobile Communications: Part I, edited by June Wei and George Margetis
55. LNCS 14738, Design, Operation and Evaluation of Mobile Communications: Part II, edited by June Wei and George Margetis
56. CCIS 2114, HCI International 2024 Posters - Part I, edited by Constantine Stephanidis, Margherita Antona, Stavroula Ntoa and Gavriel Salvendy
57. CCIS 2115, HCI International 2024 Posters - Part II, edited by Constantine Stephanidis, Margherita Antona, Stavroula Ntoa and Gavriel Salvendy
58. CCIS 2116, HCI International 2024 Posters - Part III, edited by Constantine Stephanidis, Margherita Antona, Stavroula Ntoa and Gavriel Salvendy
59. CCIS 2117, HCI International 2024 Posters - Part IV, edited by Constantine Stephanidis, Margherita Antona, Stavroula Ntoa and Gavriel Salvendy
60. CCIS 2118, HCI International 2024 Posters - Part V, edited by Constantine Stephanidis, Margherita Antona, Stavroula Ntoa and Gavriel Salvendy
61. CCIS 2119, HCI International 2024 Posters - Part VI, edited by Constantine Stephanidis, Margherita Antona, Stavroula Ntoa and Gavriel Salvendy
62. CCIS 2120, HCI International 2024 Posters - Part VII, edited by Constantine Stephanidis, Margherita Antona, Stavroula Ntoa and Gavriel Salvendy

https://2024.hci.international/proceedings

Preface

The 21st International Conference on Engineering Psychology and Cognitive Ergonomics (EPCE 2024) is an affiliated conference of the HCI International Conference. The first EPCE conference was held in Stratford-upon-Avon, UK in 1996, and since 2001 EPCE has been an integral part of the HCI International conference series. Over the last 26 years, over 1,000 papers have been presented in this conference, which attracts a world-wide audience of scientists and human factors practitioners. The engineering psychology submissions describe advances in applied cognitive psychology that underpin the theory, measurement and methodologies behind the development of human-machine systems. Cognitive ergonomics describes advances in the design and development of user interfaces. Originally, these disciplines were driven by the requirements of high-risk, high-performance industries where safety was paramount, however the importance of good human factors is now understood by everyone in order to not only increase safety, but also enhance performance, productivity and revenues.

Two volumes of the HCII 2024 proceedings are dedicated to this year's edition of the EPCE conference.

The first volume centers around a diverse array of interconnected themes related to the interplay between human physiology, cognition, performance and assisted decision-making. From examining the impact of sleep deprivation and the impact of startle reflex on human performance and mood to evaluating the competence of pilots as well as workload and cognitive control, each paper sheds light on performance in demanding and high-stress environments. Furthermore, papers explore the effects of individual factors on working memory, the role of personality in errors, and the impact of stress on cognitive tasks. A considerable number of articles in this volume explore the complexities of decision-making, resource management and operation safety, while showcasing innovative systems to support and empower decision-making in complex situations. From adaptive pilot assistance and advisory systems, to resource management in remote and distributed teams, to task allocation in cooperative aviation operations, and multiple probability judgement, these systems are designed to enhance safety and efficiency in high-pressure environments.

The second volume offers a comprehensive exploration of the role of engineering psychology in user experience and the impact of human factors on aviation. Papers, through the lens of engineering psychology, provide insights to designers and engineers into users' cognitive processes, perceptual capabilities, and ergonomic preferences, allowing them to create solutions that are intuitive, efficient, and satisfying to use. The prominence of human factors in aviation is addressed in a number of papers, discussing research and case studies for a wide range of aviation systems, including ground operations, air traffic controllers, and piloting tasks, and exploring users' perceptions and perspectives. These works also deliberate on aspects of safety, automation, awareness, and efficiency, highlighting the importance of human factors, ensuring that technology, procedures, and personnel are aligned to support safe and effective flight operations.

The papers in these volumes were accepted for publication after a minimum of two single-blind reviews from the members of the EPCE Program Board or, in some cases, from members of the Program Boards of other affiliated conferences. We would like to thank all of them for their invaluable contribution, support and efforts.

July 2024

Don Harris
Wen-Chin Li

21st International Conference on Engineering Psychology and Cognitive Ergonomics (EPCE 2024)

Program Board Chairs: **Don Harris**, *Coventry University, UK*, and **Wen-Chin Li**, *Cranfield University, UK*

- James Blundell, *Cranfield University, UK*
- Mickael Causse, *ISAE-SUPAERO, France*
- Anna Chatzi, *University of Limerick, Ireland*
- Maik Friedrich, *German Aerospace Center (DLR), Germany*
- Hannes Griebel, *CGI, UK*
- Nektarios Karanikas, *Queensland University of Technology, Australia*
- Ting-Ting Lu, *Civil Aviation University of China, P.R. China*
- Maggie Ma, *Boeing, USA*
- Pete McCarthy, *Cathay Pacific Airways, UK*
- Brett Molesworth, *UNSW Sydney, Australia*
- Miwa Nakanishi, *Keio University, Japan*
- Anastasios Plioutsias, *Coventry University, UK*
- Tatiana Polishchuk, *Linköping University, Sweden*
- Dujuan Sevillian, *National Transportation Safety Board (NTSB), USA*
- Lei Wang, *Civil Aviation University of China, P.R. China*
- Jingyu Zhang, *Institute of Psychology, Chinese Academy of Sciences, P.R. China*
- Xiangling Zhuang, *Shaanxi Normal University, P.R. China*
- Dimitrios Ziakkas, *Purdue University, USA*

The full list with the Program Board Chairs and the members of the Program Boards of all thematic areas and affiliated conferences of HCII 2024 is available online at:

http://www.hci.international/board-members-2024.php

HCI International 2025 Conference

The 27th International Conference on Human-Computer Interaction, HCI International 2025, will be held jointly with the affiliated conferences at the Swedish Exhibition & Congress Centre and Gothia Towers Hotel, Gothenburg, Sweden, June 22–27, 2025. It will cover a broad spectrum of themes related to Human-Computer Interaction, including theoretical issues, methods, tools, processes, and case studies in HCI design, as well as novel interaction techniques, interfaces, and applications. The proceedings will be published by Springer. More information will become available on the conference website: https://2025.hci.international/.

General Chair
Prof. Constantine Stephanidis
University of Crete and ICS-FORTH
Heraklion, Crete, Greece
Email: general_chair@2025.hci.international

https://2025.hci.international/

Contents – Part I

Contents – Part II

Human Factors in Aviation

Cognitive Processes and Performance in High-Stress Environments

Speech Analysis

Malcolm Brenner[✉]

Chevy Chase, United States
malcolmbrenner@verizon.net

Abstract. With recent advances in computer memory, speech analysis is becoming practical for real-time workload monitoring. Speech analysis can potentially provide a remote measure of physiological stress, without the need to attach sensors to the speaker, providing workload evidence that is not readily recognized by the human ear. It is especially appropriate for remote CRM applications, potentially providing a continued monitoring of individual physiological responses that can be accessed in real-time.

This paper reviews recent evidence for three basic speech measures of stress/workload: fundamental frequency, speaking rate, and amplitude. It summarizes results from a laboratory experiment and from three real-life accident situations: a helicopter accident, a 1994 accident involving the Boeing 737, and the 2014 disappearance of Malaysia flight 370.

Keywords: Speech analysis · Remote CRM · Workload/stress assessment · Air crash investigation

1 Laboratory Experiment

A laboratory study examined whether speech analysis might prove useful for remote measurement of pilot workload.[1] The study monitored speech changes, along with heart rate changes, shown by college students performing the Jex task in which they used a joystick to try to stabilize a wildly moving cursor in the middle of a television monitor. Each trial ended whenever the cursor touched an anchor point on either the far right or far left side of the screen. A computer program controlled the randomness and violence of the cursor movement to systematically vary workload. For speech, each subject counted quickly from "90" to "100" every 10-s during the trial in response to an alert (thus providing a speech sample that was almost entirely voiced).

After a 40-min training session, in which the computer gradually raised the workload challenge, each subject participated in two paid trials: a "simple" trial at the low end of

M. Brenner—The author is a private consultant. He served for 26 years as a U.S. National Transportation Safety Board (NTSB) investigator and received the NTSB Chairman Award for technical excellence.

[1] . The study was funded by the U.S. Air Force. See: Brenner, M., Doherty, E. Thomas, and Shipp, T. (1994). Speech measures indicating workload demand. *Aviation, Space, and Environmental Medicine, 65*:21–6.

their practice performance, and a "difficult" trial close to their best practice performance. Subjects earned $2 for successfully performing the "simple" trial for 90 s (and all subjects succeeded on the first try). By comparison, they received $50 for successfully performing the "difficult" trial for 90 s (or $45, $40, and so forth for successively easier trials until they performed one successfully). Finally, following a 15-min rest, each subject provided a baseline trial in which they counted every 10-s without performing.

Subjects performed at two identical laboratory sessions separated by several days. The results were derived solely from the data at Session 2. Session 1 data were not analyzed, but were used to familiarize subjects with the task and the laboratory to reduce extraneous sources of stress.

As shown in Fig. 1, heart rate increased more than 10 beats per minute for the "difficult" trial compared to the "simple" trial or baseline (statistical significance: p < .01). Similar trends were shown for speech amplitude (p < .01), speech fundamental frequency (p < .01), and speaking rate (p = .05). Although easily determined by computer-analysis, and statistically significant, the differences in audible speech were so small that they would not be readily noticed in normal conversation (being about 2 db. Amplitude and 5 Hz. in fundamental frequency). Therefore, the computer was much better at scoring these aspects of stress than humans within this workload range (where we believe humans tend to judge stress by what the speaker says rather than speech characteristics). It should be noted that these three speech components are all basic aspects of screaming that are readily recognized as stress by all human listeners. One theory is that screaming, which is an innate biological response common to all mammals, may begin to affect speech at low levels of stress where the changes are not readily audible and then grow until they become clearly recognized at extreme stress. In any case, these speech changes are promising measures for CRM monitoring even while they are not readily noticed by the human ear.

This laboratory study also confirmed the presence of individual differences. One subject, out of 17, failed to show changes in heart rate across the three treatments (although, perhaps surprisingly, he did show the characteristic changes across the three treatments on speech measures). Similarly, there were subjects who failed to respond on each speech measure. We estimate that about 85% of subjects show consistent changes in speech measures. Therefore, in order to apply speech measures to CRM applications, it may be necessary to test individual subjects in advance to confirm their speech responses or, alternately, to design the application so a failure of some subjects to respond will not cause significant issues for the application.

This laboratory study confirmed all three speech measures as promising indicators of workload/stress. The next studies were based on aviation accidents, involving higher levels of stress than can normally be produced in a laboratory setting.

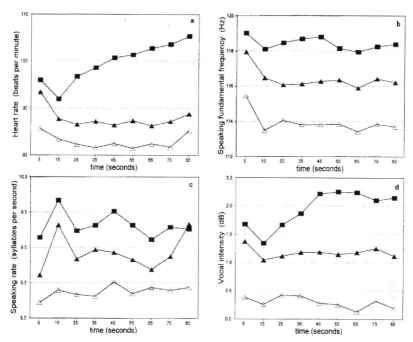

Fig. 1. Subject responses to workload variations on a laboratory task for heart rate, speaking fundamental frequency, speaking rate, and vocal intensity. The line with black squares represents a difficult trial on which subjects won $50; the line with black triangles represents an easy trial on which subjects won $2; and the line with white triangles represents a baseline in which subjects relaxed and did not perform the task.

2 Helicopter Accident

The next study was made from an air traffic recording of routine and emergency radio transmissions from a helicopter pilot involved in an accident.[2] The pilot of a military helicopter contacted air traffic control at a regional airport with a routine request to change his destination to this airport, confirming as well that appropriate fuel would be available on the ground. Seconds later, the pilot again contacted this air traffic facility to report an emergency involving a rotor failure. The pilot had the presence of mind to repeat important information, specifically his call sign, location, and name of the facility, thus allowing a direct comparison of speech aspects before and after the onset of the emergency for the same spoken phrase.

As shown in Fig. 2 and Table 1, several aspects of the pilot's speech changed significantly between the two radio transmissions. Fundamental frequency increased by 62% during emergency communications and, in this case, could be readily perceived as stressful accompanying the serious content of his message. Variability of fundamental frequency more than doubled, and the length of the statements shortened. Amplitude changes were not evaluated here (because of possible gain control in the microphone

---

[2] Provided by the U.S. Federal Aviation Administration for scientific purposes.

and potential differences in speaker-to-microphone distance and transmission quality). Speaking rate, in this case, remained steady. Speaking rate typically increases in response to stress, as in the laboratory study, but in this case the pilot appeared to have the presence of mind to enunciate the emergency information carefully without showing an increased rate. Speaking rate is the weakest measure of stress among the three speech measures examined and, perhaps, is the one most subject to conscious control. Fundamental frequency scores increased dramatically, however, and length of statements decreased, both common aspects of a speech response to high workload.

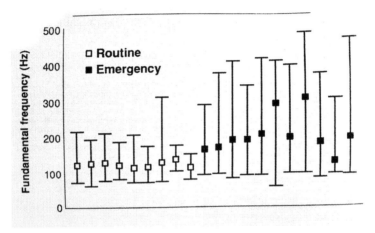

Fig. 2. Mean and range of speech fundamental frequency for a helicopter pilot speaking in routine and emergency conditions.

Table 1. Summary of speech measure changes observed in radio transmission from a helicopter pilot experiencing routine and emergency conditions.

Measure	Routine	Emergency	Significance
Fundamental frequency (Hz)	123.9	200.1	<.001
Range of fundamental frequencies (Hz)	124.2	297.3	<.0001
No. of syllables	11.7	6.7	=.054
Speaking rate (syllables per second)	5.3	4.4	n.s

3   Boeing B-737 Accident at Aliquippa PA

Another real-life study was provided by the cockpit voice recording (CVR) of a major airline accident. Shortly before sunset on September 8, 1994, USAir Flight 427, a Boeing B-737 airplane, crashed while maneuvering to land at Pittsburgh International Airport. The airplane encountered wake turbulence unexpectedly from a preceding flight and, in responding, entered an extended left bank from which it failed to recover.

Engineering analysis determined that the upset path of the airplane could be caused by only one control input: a full right rudder input maintained for at least 10 s. However, the rudder system examined in the wreckage was still functional and displayed no abnormalities. Therefore, the investigation focused on two possibilities: a human explanation involving an aggressive pilot rudder input for unknown reasons or, alternately, a hardware explanation involving some unknown transient abnormality of the rudder control system (allowing that the rudder system would return to good working order by the time the airplane impacted the ground). The resulting investigation was one of the longest in NTSB history.[3]

The human performance investigation examined and eliminated many potential human explanations based on details of the accident, such as potential medical impairments, deliberate action, and disorientation. Speech analysis was employed as a new technology to address another issue of the investigation: did a pilot panic and inadvertently input and hold full rudder?

Figure 3 displays a computer scoring of the fundamental frequency of the captain's speech. It shows that the frequency increased immediately after the initial encounter with wake turbulence ("sheeze"). The magnitude of fundamental frequency from this point to the end of the flight increased gradually and was significantly higher than during any previous period of the flight. However, as discussed below, the initial increase in fundamental frequency was relatively small and consistent with a constructive focusing of attention on an unexpected problem, as the captain was likely caught by surprise by the turbulence on a clear day and was concerned for passenger comfort. Contrary to panic, the captain's fundamental frequency did not show unusually high levels of stress around the time the full rudder input was entered (just after statement "whoa"). It was only as the emergency progressed, and normal control efforts failed, that the captain slowly progressed to higher levels of fundamental frequency associated with degraded performance. Therefore, the possibility of a panic explanation for rudder input did not appear consistent with speech evidence.

It may be noted that the captain's speech reduced immediately to very short exclamations, consistent with the reduction in number of syllables shown in the helicopter accident. The captain eliminated extraneous comments during the emergency and focused on simple phrases. Unfortunately, the captain's statements did not communicate any clear statement as to the exact nature of the problem (perhaps, in large part, because even as an experienced pilot he did not understand what was happening).

Speech amplitude was obtained in this case, as shown in Fig. 4. It was captured because the captain was wearing a boom microphone positioned close to his mouth that did not move (and was recorded by the onboard cockpit voice recorder). Valid amplitude measures are difficult to obtain in real-life situations but, with the use of the boom microphone, amplitude measurement showed a pattern similar to that of fundamental frequency. Amplitude, when it can be obtained, may be as good a measure of workload/stress as fundamental frequency.

---

[3] See: National Transportation Safety Board (1999). Aircraft Accident Report, NTSB/AAR-99/01, DCA-94-MA-076. Uncontrolled descent and collision with terrain, USAir Flight 427, Boeing 737–300, N513AU, near Aliquippa, Pennsylvania, September 8, 1994.

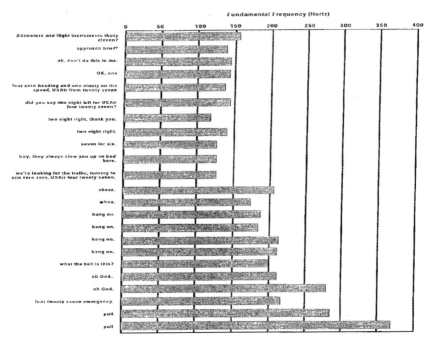

Fig. 3. Speech fundamental frequency for statements recorded on the cockpit voice recorder (CVR) for the Aliquippa airline captain during routine conditions and emergency conditions (beginning with the statement "sheeze"). The statements read from top to bottom in chronological order.

The first officer, who served as the flying pilot, was largely quiet throughout the emergency period so no comparable speech analysis could be conducted for him. However, speech analysis proved to be extremely helpful on an unexpected topic: grunting. The first officer betrayed two grunting sounds early in the upset period, a soft grunt followed by a louder and more protracted one. These sounds are unusual in normal cockpit activity, since control forces are designed to be used by pilots without the need for excessive force. The investigation was able to overlay these grunting sounds on what was known about control inputs to investigate any possible match. It was immediately determined that the grunting did not match column inputs or any tug-of-war with the captain (who was not using the controls at this point in the emergency period). Finally, late in the investigation, advanced mathematical analysis of the known flight path provided evidence on the likely inputs on other control variables of wheel and rudder input. It was found that the grunting sounds overlay perfectly with rudder data. Specifically, they occurred exactly about the time that the rudder went "hard over" to cause the accident, with a pilot fighting a rudder reversal (an abnormality that emerged as a possibility in the investigation in which the rudder pedal moves in a direction opposite to that commanded by the pilot). This is shown in Fig. 5. It overlays the first officer grunting sounds with a mathematical determination of when the rudder had to reverse for the airplane

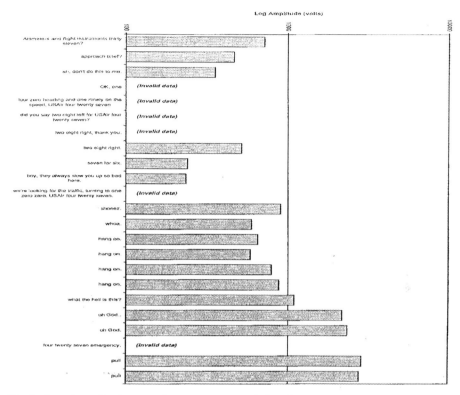

Log Amplitude (volts)

Fig. 4. Speech amplitude scores for statements recorded on the cockpit voice recorder (CVR) for the Aliquippa airline captain during routine conditions and emergency conditions (beginning with the statement "sheeze"). Data are invalid when the captain communicated to air traffic control via microphone rather than speaking naturally within the cockpit.

to reach the accident site.[4] The first grunting sound would likely be inadvertent, as the first officer's foot was pushed back unexpectedly by a rudder pedal moving upwards in opposition to his input. The second grunting sound would represent a determined and unsuccessful effort by the first officer to make the pedal comply with his demand to go down. The grunting sounds failed to correspond to any other command input so, as a result, speech evidence provided the most direct evidence of what the pilot was doing at the most critical time in the emergency. Speech evidence became a primary source of information for determining the probable cause of the accident. The Aliquippa accident led to a worldwide redesign of the Boeing 737 rudder control system that has successfully eliminated any repeat problems.

---

[4] NTSB (1999) DCA-94-MA-076 Crash of USAir Flight 427 Boeing 737 at Alequippa PA. Two figures prepared/shown at the public "sunshine" Board meeting, 1999: Overlay of CVR grunting sounds with reconstructed control inputs. Available on request from NTSB, Washington D.C.

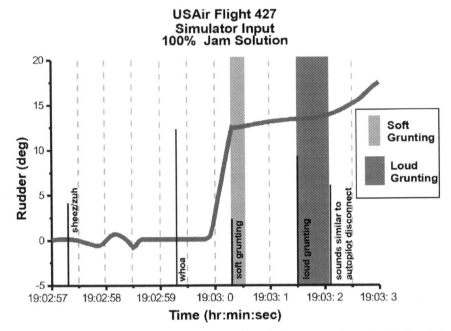

Fig. 5. Overlay of pilot grunting sounds on a mathematical reconstruction of rudder inputs for the airplane to reach the accident site of the Aliquippa accident.

4 Disappearance of Malaysia Flight 370 (MH370)

Speech analysis, finally, provides unique evidence on MH370, an airliner that disappeared from radar on 8 March 2014 shortly after takeoff from Kuala Lumpur, Malaysia. The official reason for the disappearance is currently not determined.[5]

Speech analysis was conducted on air traffic control recordings of radio communications with the flight during the brief period before its disappearance. The captain was serving as a check airman on the flight, evaluating the first officer's performance for future upgrade. It was the captain who completed all radio communications following takeoff. Figure 6 shows computer scorings of the nine statements identified as having been spoken by the captain. He displayed an average fundamental frequency overall of about 118 Hz., typical of male speech. However, this changed in his communication at 0107:56, about 12 min before the abrupt end of communications, where he displayed a fundamental frequency that was about 30 Hz. Higher than his other statements (statistical significance: $p < .05$). This unusual increase, consistent with an unusual increase in stress, was not reflected in the content of what he said which was a routine report that the airplane had reached its assigned altitude: "Malaysian ah…three seven zero maintaining level three five zero." But, surprisingly, the communication itself represented an error unusual for a management pilot conducting training. The controller had not requested the

---

[5] Safety Investigation Report, Malaysia Airlines Boeing B777-200ER (9M-MRO), 08 March 2014. By The Malaysian ICAO Annex 13 Safety Investigation Team for MH370, Issued on 02 July 2018, MH370/01/2018.

pilot to report reaching the altitude and, significantly, the captain had already reported this information several minutes before. The captain was displaying an unusual sign of stress or confusion, consistent with the high fundamental frequency of his voice, but inconsistent with the bland and unnecessary message.

As shown in Fig. 7, the MH370 captain also displayed evidence of stress in his final statement at 0119:30: "Good night ah Malaysia three seven zero." It was spoken significantly faster than all previous statements (p < .05). It also contained an operational error. In his haste, the captain failed to repeat the assigned new radio frequency. Like his preceding communication, this communication showed evidence of stress in both speech and operational error that was unrelated to the routine response. This communication was the also the final one transmitted from MH370. It was followed by the captain's greatest error: he never contacted the new controller as instructed, which would normally occur a few seconds later. Whatever went wrong with the flight began during these few seconds, and the captain was displaying surprising evidence of increased stress during the time approaching this point.

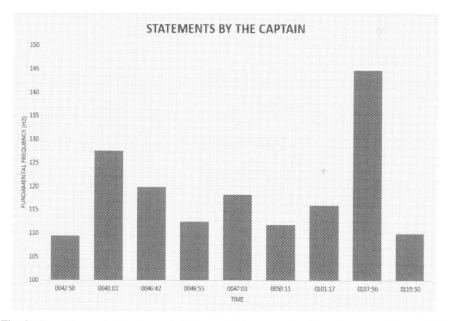

Fig. 6. Computer analysis of speech fundamental frequency in the radio transmissions of the MH370 captain.

The official investigation of the MH370 disappearance stated that it "found no evidence that there was any stress or anxiety" in the pilot transmissions when reviewed by a panel of clinical experts. By contrast, computer speech analysis found significant increases in fundamental frequency and speaking rate in the last two transmissions. These increases are consistent with unusual operational errors as prospective indicators of stress. Speech evidence provides secondary evidence of deliberate action, that the captain was aware that the airplane was about to disappear but that he made an effort to

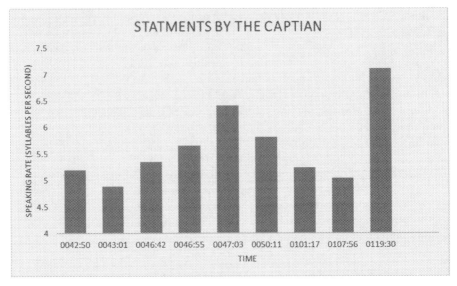

Fig. 7. Speaking rate analysis for the radio transmissions of the MH370 captain.

sound routine. Computer analysis provides insights on the captain's workload that are not readily available to the human listener.

5   Speech Analysis for CRM Applications

This paper provides evidence for three speech factors – fundamental frequency, amplitude, and speaking rate – as promising indicators for remote CRM applications through their ability to monitor the workload/stress experienced by a speaker.

Fundamental frequency is the most accessible measure and can potentially provide a real-time monitoring for CRM applications. With regard to workload and performance, it is commonly considered that stress/workload first improves performance at first but then can degrade performance as it reaches higher levels. If helpful, the following guidelines have been used in accident investigations. At low levels of workload/stress, when fundamental frequency increases to about 30% above baseline levels, performance improves. The speaker, alerted by some unusual situation, tends to focus attention on the immediate task. Communications are accurate, extraneous comments are dropped, and the performance shows no procedural errors. As stress increases, however, with fundamental frequency reaching 50% to 120% above baseline levels, the pilot's increasing "tunnel vision" tends to degrade performance. Speech is fast, strained, and brief. The pilot does not make gross mistakes, but the response is more focused on well-practiced actions and less likely to display novel thinking. The pilot can skip items on a checklist. Finally, if stress increases further, it can reach "panic" levels in which "tunnel vision" becomes extreme and speech is characterized by those things that dominate the speaker's thinking regardless of the situation. CRM applications seem likely to remain in the first two categories, when stress/workload can transition from helpful to degrading for performance, and computer scoring can provide invaluable insights to supplement human listening within CRM situations.

Fundamental frequency is a robust aspect of speech that can be derived from even less-than-optimal audio recordings. In principle, it can be monitored in real-time by computer analysis and is currently the most promising speech aspect for remote CRM applications. Since there are individual differences in the strength of speech responses, as is generally true for all physiological measures, it may be helpful to pre-test individual subjects in order to personalize the computer modeling for applications where remote monitoring must be carefully conducted on specific individuals.

Amplitude is a second speech measure that appears to respond to stress/workload. However, it is often a difficult measure to obtain in practical situations. Amplitude scores are affected by factors such as the speaker's distance from the microphone, the relative quality of the recording (as with successive radio transmissions from different origins), and whether the microphone has an automatic gain control feature (which automatically adjusts volume continuously based on the relative volume of speech and competing background noise). Valid measurements are possible, as in the Aliquippa example, by designing around these limitations with features such as a simple boom microphone located a fixed distance from the speaker's mouth. Laboratory and field evidence suggest that amplitude is effective for monitoring stress/workload, and a combination of this measure with fundamental frequency can in principle provide very effective real-time monitoring of the speaker's physiological state.

Speaking rate is the third speech measure tested here and, while promising, may not be appropriate at this time for real-time monitoring. This measure requires human input to score the number of syllables spoken and typically requires at least seven spoken syllables to be considered valid. It is also the weakest indicator of workload of the three measures studied and is probably the most affected by conscious control. Yet this measure can provide useful information on the speaker's state, and so adds valuable information for CRM monitoring whenever it can be integrated.

6 Conclusion

Speech analysis is rapidly becoming practical for real-time assessment of psychological stress, and I urge my colleagues to consider this type of analysis for use in remote CRM.

Multimodal Recognition of the Stress When Performing Cognitive Tasks Under Limited Time Conditions

Oleksandr Burov[1]([✉]) [ID], Evgeniy Lavrov[2] [ID], Svitlana Lytvynova[1] [ID],
Olha Pinchuk[1] [ID], Oleksii Tkachenko[3] [ID], Natalia Kovalenko[4] [ID], Yana Chybiriak[2] [ID],
and Yana Dolgikh[5] [ID]

[1] Institute for Digitalisation of Education, National Academy of Educational Sciences of
Ukraine, Kyiv, Ukraine
burov.alexander@gmail.com
[2] Sumy State University, Sumy, Ukraine
y.chibiryak@cs.sumdu.edu.ua
[3] Taras Shevchenko National University of Kyiv, Kyiv, Ukraine
otkachenko@knu.ua
[4] Sumy State Pedagogical University, Sumy, Ukraine
NatalyaKovalenko@i.ua
[5] Sumy National Agrarian University, Sumy, Ukraine

Abstract. In the usual human cognitive performance, the speed of the human-computer interaction is not critical, but in emergent technologies and in a high stream of information in a learning process, a human (learner) ability to process teaching tasks can be limited by the human abilities or lead to this human's stress as a physiological "cost" of his/her successful performance. The goal of the paper is to carry out the comparison analysis of the speed and reliability of cognitive activity by subjects performing computer tasks at a free and fixed pace, considering the physiological "cost" of such activities to reveal potential preliminary markers of stress. We have studied 4 group of indices of subjects' cognitive test performance: 1) operational - test performance including direct indices (rate of tasks solving, reliability) and their secondary indices including general productivity; 2) subjective test indices before and after test performance; 3) physiological support of activity by indices of the cardiovascular system; 4) indices of electropuncture diagnostics. Besides, to account external factors of possible influence on a human cognitive work, we used indices of the solar wind and geomagnetic field. The time limitations make a human more sensitive to external physical factors and influence his psychological state in addition to physiological regulation that can be considered as a stress condition of activity. This result has confirmed our guess that multimodal description is more effective to reveal a stress during cognitive activity of a simple nature.

Keywords: Cognitive Performance · Stress · Multimodality

© The Author(s), under exclusive license to Springer Nature Switzerland AG 2024
D. Harris and W.-C. Li (Eds.): HCII 2024, LNAI 14692, pp. 14–25, 2024.
https://doi.org/10.1007/978-3-031-60728-8_2

1 Introduction

The Future of Growth Report 2024 presented by The World Economic Forum in Davos (January 2024) has shown that the future of growth can be grounded by "four areas essential to driving more balanced growth: innovation, inclusion, environmental sustainability and systemic resilience" [1, p. 9]. Those areas can be structured in sub-systems and the high rank of them is a "Talent ecosystem". That notion was in line with outcomes of the WEF over the last 5 years.

It means that lifelong learning needs new skills and continues re-skilling [2], set new requirements to learners and workforce, especially because of appearance of the hybrid workforce as a new trend over last year's [3]. As a result, new requirements to modern schools have appeared [4] and are needed in both education [5] and research [6]. In addition, the digital transformation of the society is accompanied by the ICT evolution in all areas of a human life and activity [7].

A particularly striking explosion of interest in the last few years has been observed in the field of immersive technologies and artificial intelligence, both in education and in other areas. This led to a revision of the Milgram and Kishino's reality-virtuality (RV) continuum [8] and rethinking the ways and forms of human-Artificial Intelligence interaction [9]. To date, the RV continuum is considered more as unending and is often described as Extended Reality (XR). According to the authors of [10], today's view of the synthetic environment points to the increasing "role of XR in spatial perception, cognition, and behavior and *vice versa*. XR offers a plethora of opportunities to reveal new or unexplored dimensions of human interaction with environments". At the same time, user states in extended reality media experiences are still a very difficult problem without a clear solution and thus heavily worked upon [11].

New learning tools and technologies give new opportunities of learning. In particular, a new direction began to take shape more clearly - VARK, four sensory modalities (Visual, Aural, Read/write, and Kinesthetic) that are used for learning information and that can be associated with the students' and teachers' experiences [12]. It can be especially effective in the synthetic learning environment that extends a learner opportunity to use more sensory channels to get new information [13]. The methodological and instrumental basis for this direction is developing and improving very actively, because life is multimodal, and there are seldom instances where one mode is used or is sufficient [14]. Respectively, a multimodal learning looks like more effective. The highest popularity such an approach demonstrates by language teachers and researchers [15], but in general, it could be appropriate in other areas where flexibility of education can be provided, and the learning style can be essential and productive [16].

Multimodal teaching, learning, and training allows to increase motivation and efficiency of the learning process. But on the other hand, this increases the tension of the body's regulatory systems, involving more of them in the physiological support of learning activities and "imposing" a certain pace of information exchange between the learning environment and the learner. Although according to the authors [17], there is no evidence that associations between adolescents' digital technology engagement and mental health problems have increased, possible clinical consequences of innovative technologies should be evaluated *before* their implementation into the education process. Significant, but not always studied in innovative tools, functional deviations in the functioning of physiological support can manifest themselves at a subthreshold level. According to study of physiological response of volunteers' performed cognitive tests with different time limitations for a task [18], the analysis of the lipid metabolism has shown different changes in ratio of saturated and polyunsaturated fatty acids classifying subjects in 3 groups: high, medium and low adaptive ability. That finding can be used as preliminary sickness' indicator in conditions of regular repetitive workload in digital environment and a low stress associated with the cognitive task performance. It has been revealed that such an effect can be described for different subjects by different physiological indices and with different level of accuracy of assessment.

The goal of article is to carry out the comparison analysis of the speed and reliability of cognitive activity by subjects performing computer tasks at a free and fixed pace, considering the physiological "cost" of such activities to reveal potential preliminary markers of stress. We consider the "stress", but not the "distress" (after H.Selye).

2 Method

The research method used in this study was the development of the method used in our previous research of the psychophysiological maintenance of operator cognitive performance [19] and in applications to study learners' performance as operator-researchers [20]. The current modifications of the research method relate to the test performance and data analysis to achieve the research goal.

As in our previous research [20], 5 weeks experimental research was based on the use of a computer system to monitor the cognitive activity of subjects (15 MSc and PhD students, males). The survey includes test task performance (2 types of logical tasks, and test for functional mobility of nervous processes' assessment), blood pressure and heart rate (heart rate HR and blood pressure (systolic ADs, diastolic Add, by means of the digital blood pressure monitor Model LD11) every 20 min during the test performance, as well as electropuncture diagnostics (EPD) by Nakatani method (together with Mygal and Protasenko) was conducted after the test session for each subject [21].
The adjusted tests block included:

Self-assessment test T4. The subjective state assessment of subjects by means of the reduced variant of the test "General_state - Activity – Mood" (GsAM), test T4, at the beginning and at the ending of the test session (the indices of mood *mood*, serviceability *FfD*, attention *atten*, anxiety *anxiety*) prior to the beginning (index "0") estimated and upon finishing the tests performance.

Numbers permutation test (combinatorial) in ascending order. The test material: a sequence of numbers (from 0 to 9) which were not repeated and placed in a random order; the task was to rearrange the numbers in ascending order in a few steps, on each one could only change 2 adjacent numbers. Time for every task performance was free during the test session (the next task appeared just after entering the answer), "auto"-pace (test T6) or fixed one (time for every task was limited and fixed in each session, calculated as an averaged time plus 25%, after the training session, test T5). The time (TI) and accuracy of the task performance were measured.

Duration of every test session was 180 min, 5 sessions (the first one was training to adapt to the cognitive test and physiological indices measurement) were organized 1 time per week, at the same day of week and the same day time to eliminate infradian and circadian rhythms. Test T5 was used in the experiment sessions 3, 4 and 6 (E3...E6), test T6 was used in the session E5.

To check an influence of the external physical factors on the cognitive task performance the solar activity was studied as external factor possibly impacting a human performance. The data on influence of solar activity on a human health and some physiological systems are known, however results of study of cognitive activity associating with heliophysic parameters in different activities and different groups of subjects are known not enough in the scientific literature to date. In our preliminary pilot research, the precise connection between effectiveness of operator activity and parameters of a solar wind (SW) was revealed. With the purpose to study this phenomenon we registered indices of proton component of a solar wind - velocity SWsp (km/s) and density SWden (proton/sm^3) on the data from Internet site NASA [22], as well as parameters of the geomagnetic field (GMF) - planetary index Ks, index of "equivalent amplitude" A, as well as Wolf number of the solar spots.

Because the study involved human subjects, all subjects signed the informed consent of participants, their personal data were excluded from the database of research, their participation in this research was coordinated and approved by the university authority. In addition, it has been acquired the approval of the National Committee for bioethics of Ukraine in order to conduct the study.

3   Results and Discussion

The focus of our research is revealing some potential markers of stress at preliminary stages before the clinical changes of a human organism. It is possible to do if measuring functional changes in physiological indices as under influence of workload and external factors accounting "starting" (in the beginning of the cognitive performance) and the current functional state during work (test task performance in our study).

It is well-known that a human activity is modulated by a hierarchy of rhythms both internal and external. And their constellation influence reliability and efficiency of a human performance in specific elements and in general. The most known rhythms are circadian, infradian and lunar once. To eliminate their possible influence. Our research was carried out in the same day of a week, the same time of a day and one time per week for every subject to study a human performance and its physiological "cost" in similar conditions. The duration of every experimental session was 3 h and the dynamics of the test performance has been assessed by way of averaged data stored every 20 min smoothing out the effects of catecholamines (most of which have a period of 3.5 to 15 min) and averaging data of the whole test time.

One more important feature of our research is to compare free and fixed pace of tasks to be solved by way to adjust fixed time to every subject: an individual fixed "average" time was calculated by results of the first, training, session with the free pace. Because all subjects were well-motivated, they were in equal conditions and were compared not with one another, but with their inherent parameters of activity.

As it was revealed in our previous research, the analysis of this study has confirmed that time of tasks performance had individual dynamics and average time (M3, M4 and M5 respectively to experiments in the number of the research week) fluctuated and differed in the same fixed tempo from one week to another (see Fig. 1). Not only average level of tasks' time performance, but their inner regularity differed.

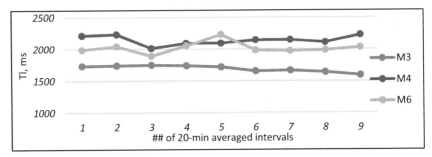

Fig. 1. An example of the dynamics of the tasks' performance time, one subject.

3.1 Test Performance Productivity

As it is possible to see from this example, variation of the task time performance can vary significantly from day to day for each person. One of questions in our study was whether a general tendency can be in the whole group of subjects, if to compare experiments' results in a month and the test tempo. The study was organized in such a way that all subjects underwent the next experiment in the same week. In other words, each number of the experiment corresponded to the same phase of the month.

One can see from the Table 1 that averaged time of the tasks performance (Tl) in the column 2 does not differ between experiments with the fixed pace (experiments E3, E4 and E6). But Tl in the experiment with free pace (E5) differs significantly, and the coefficient of variation (cv Tl) is twice higher than in fixed pace' experiments.

Table 1. Averaged results of tests performance by experiments.

# Experiment	Tl, s	cv Tl, %	W	UTR
E3	2.62	53	0.36	0.52
E4	2.61	60	0.45	0.45
E5	3.56	123	0.31	1.0
E6	2.50	66	0.50	0.39

It is expected that reliability and time of task performance can depends on the individual style of work. To avoid this difficulty, we calculated the productivity factor to accounting efficiency of the test performance as the ratio of reliability (ratio of correct solved tasks to the whole numbers) to Tl: W = R/Tl * 1000. This factor demonstrated a good usefulness in our previous research [20]. According to data in the Table 1, the productivity W5 in the test 5 does not differ from W3…W6 so significantly as Tl. It can be explained by the fact that the reliability in tests E3, E4 and E6 is lower than in E5 (in average, 0.87 vs. 0.98).

According to this finding, we can suppose that the fixed tempo (TT) of tasks performance mobilized subjects to work with some greater "tension" putting in more effort, though their fixed tempo was quite similar to their own tempo.

What could have further usefulness is a study what part of the "window" (exposition time) for the task performance was used by subjects actually and whether they could control their time for every task without loss of reliability. To answer that question, we calculated useful time utilization rate (UTR) as a factor UTR = TI/TT.

The Table 1 demonstrates that when subjects used more time and UTR was 0.52 (i.e., they used 52% of time available for task solution), their productivity was lower than in other cases. In fixed pace test, they used 100% of time, because the next task appeared just after entering the answer. One can assume that the lower productivity is a result of lack of a time reserve and lower reliability (it was the lowest in the experiment E3).

3.2 Physiological Support of the Test Performance

The physiological support of activity had an even more pronounced individual character by indices of blood pressure systolic (BPs) and diastolic (BPd) that was natural and well known from scientific publications. Their averaging does not have clinical reason but can be informative for analysis of the test performance changes and appropriate physiological support. The Fig. 2 demonstrates the dynamics of the systolic blood pressure (subjects averaged for 20-min intervals continuously, mmHg) by experiments sessions (E3, E4 and E6 as above).

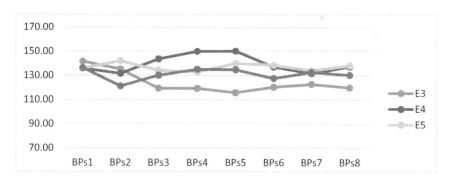

Fig. 2. Changes of BPs (subjects averaged) over the test session.

As one could expect, the main trends exist independently on inter-individual variation and differ for all three fixed pace tests, on one side, and free pace, on another one. The fixed pace tests are accompanied by clear decries of BPs in the beginning of the test performance (first 20 min) and its differed levels till the end of the second hour (measurement in point # 6). Afterwards, BPs has stabilized till the end of the session. At the same time, free tempo (experiment E5) is accompanied by some 1-h (three 20-min intervals) fluctuations of the BPs. This can be explained by a higher efforts of the subjects' mental work under "pressure" of the fixed time for tasks and needs of some additional physiological support of the neurohumoral system. The experiment E3 as the first one in the sessions' series required additional emotional mobilization of the subjects at the beginning of the research (an element of anticipation of a new type of activity), since they were all highly motivated and responsible.

But the diastolic blood pressure BPd has dynamics closer to free pace test in experiment E6 than in E3 and E4 (see Fig. 3). It can be assumed that this type of cognitive activity has become more common, and the regulation of the diastolic component of blood pressure may have a slightly different character than the systolic component. In our earlier studies of the influence of heliophysical factors on operator-type's cognitive activity, it was revealed that it was diastolic blood pressure that was more sensitive to such influence [23].

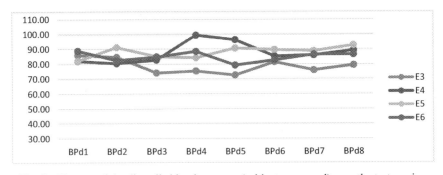

Fig. 3. Changes of the diastolic blood pressure (subjects averaged) over the test session.

It is necessary to note that the heart rate in all experiments has very similar dynamics and decreasing evenly from the start to the finish of test sessions from approximately 88 bit per minute to 70 bits.

Thus, a preliminary conclusion can be made that the cardiac respiratory system as a whole can carry information about the manifestation of stress changes, but its indicators change in different directions.

According to our previous research, electropuncture diagnostics' (EPD) indices can be informative in relation to some stress changes during cognitive work [20]. However, it is necessary to note that EPD is used in clinical goals, as a rule. The questions of its application for functional implementation is still under consideration, especially because of different tools and methods of measurement.

Since in 1950, the Japanese physician Y. Nakatani described the method of electropuncture diagnostics of the functional state of meridians, based on the measurement of electrocutaneous resistance (ECR) at representative acupuncture points, this approach has gained many supporters both for clinical purposes and as well as general diagnostics of the body's condition [24]. We have found in our joint research that EPD by Y. Nakatani method could be informative tool to study external influences and appearance of the stress during cognitive activity. Colleagues, G.Mygal and O.Protasenko, developed that technique in direction to use skin capacity indicators in wider applications

[21]. In this research, we used more traditional approach, measurement of skin resistance indicators, to analyze appearance of signs of stress during 3-h cognitive activity (classical 12-points measurements in representative meridians left Rl and right Rp).

If to compare the left (before the test session beginning, index "0") and right (after the test performance finishing, index "1") histograms at the Fig. 4, one can see some decries of points' resistance of many meridians.

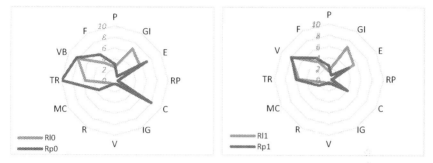

Fig. 4. Changes of skin resistance in acupuncture points by Y.Nakatani method before test performance (left) and afterwards (right). Example of one subject in E6.

But in the experiment with free pace of task performance (see Fig. 5), associated changes in the skin resistance have the opposite trend and resistance increased after the test performance, and its structure (the subjects' EPD 'portrait') is significantly different in comparison with the fixed pace tasks.

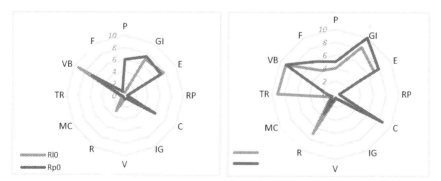

Fig. 5. Changes of skin resistance in acupuncture points by Y.Nakatani method before test performance (left) and afterwards (right). Example of the same subject in E5.

According to Nakatani, any changes in the internal organs are certainly reflected in the skin. It follows that the ryodoraku (meridians) act as sensitive indicators to these changes, signaling danger and, to a certain extent, its extent. Later it was recognized that the phenomenon of ryodoraku is noted not only in connection with the disease of the organ, but also reflects its physiological changes, therefore they began to distinguish between "pathological" and "physiological" ryodoraku. Some authors explain this phenomenon by the viscerocutaneous sympathetic reflex.

The physiological mechanisms of such changes are not the subject of study in this article; we are only looking for objective indicators that could be used in assessing the occurrence of a certain stress when a human performs cognitive tasks (even simple) with the computer and has more or less continuous interaction with it.

Though averaging of all subjects' physiological indices does not have ϕ semantic interpretation, practical usefulness of the EPD indices could be useful at pragmatic level, if some indices could have a general trend. So, we use not prompt meridians' indices (they differ from one subject to another), bur asymmetry factor AF (left-right hands and feet). It has been revealed that AF > 1 in all experiments excluding E3 (as in BPd). After experiments, all AF have normalized and approached 1, the higher balance was achieved in E5 (1.03). The biggest changes during the test sessions in the resistance value were registered for the right hand (all subjects used right-hand mouse).

It is possible to note that changes under influence of the cognitive test performance during 3 h in physiological response (by all meridians) were registered, as well as a difference in response to fixed and free tempo of workload in tests.

As a result, it is possible to consider some indices of the physiological support as indicators of the stress, but their predictive possibilities when using separately are questionable.

3.3   Multimodal Recognition of Stress in Test Performance

We have studied 4 group of indices of subjects' cognitive test performance: 1) operational - test performance including direct indices (rate of tasks solving, reliability) and their secondary indices including general productivity; 2) subjective test indices before and after test performance (the index "anxiety" decreased in E5 and E6 for 1/3 of subjects but increased for almost all subjects in E3 and E4); 3) physiological support of activity by indices of the cardiovascular system; 4) indices of electropuncture diagnostics. Besides, to account external factors of possible influence on a human cognitive work, we registered indices of the solar wind and geomagnetic field (described in p. 2) that were informative in relation to cognition after our previous research.

No one group of indices could not be enough strong indicator differentiated work with time limitations and without them. We believe that multimodal assessment could be more informative even with reduced number of indices but when they have synergetic effect. To confirm or to reject this notion, we used multiple regression analysis with the forward stepwise procedure (formal, used only mathematical criteria without participation of researchers) selecting the most informative index at every step. The criterial (outcome) index was the subject's productivity in the cognitive test performance. It was assessed by the model built by appropriate formal selection of indices from other group of indices.

Models for the index W were built separately for the test with the fixed pace (with some time "tension") and for auto (free) pace, accordingly, Wf and Wa.

The "optimal" Wf model included such indices: BPs2, Rl1, BPd6, BPs7, Ks and "rest" (subjective index of the feeling "rest – fatigue"). The structure of this model represented all group of indices: cardiovascular system (blood pressure at the 2nd, 6th and 7th 20-min intervals); EPD index (skin resistance of the left part of meridians after the test performance); external influence (Earth's magnetic field's index Ks). The multiple correlation coefficient was R = 0.71, p ≤ 0.001.

The "optimal" Wa model differ by its indices structure and included: BPs9, HR5, Rl1-Rl0 and BPd8 (R = 0.98, p ≤ 0.001). This model could describe the high productivity in the test performance by only physiological indices (blood pressure and EPD as changes in the skin resistance in left meridians over the test session).

The structure of models Wf (model for a normally stressed cognitive performance) and Wa (stressless performance) differ and demonstrated that the stress involves more complex mechanisms of regulation and depends on both internal and external factors.

4   Conclusion

These results argue that cognitive activity of such a type can be described only with physiological parameters in conditions of free pace (natural and comfort for a human) of the tasks stream. But the time limitations make a human more sensitive to external physical factors and influence his psychological state in addition to physiological regulation that can be considered as a stress condition of activity.

This result has confirmed our guess that multimodal description is more effective to reveal a stress during cognitive activity of a simple nature.

The results can be applied to optimize a human and digital system interaction accounting a human cognitive and psychophysiological limitations in interaction pace. The optimization goal can be to adjust their interaction pace to avoid stress appearance and to achieve maximal general performance in short- and long-term perspective by using models for prediction of student ability to effective learning [25], as well as in designing working environment as an element of the ensuring automated systems [26].

Further research: study a possible cumulative effect and long-term consequences of repetitive and/or prolonged even "low" stress when working in the digital environment.

Acknowledgments. This research has been supported by the Institute of Information Technologies of the National Academy of Pedagogic Science, as well as the National Aerospace University "KhAI", Kharkiv.

References

1. The Future of Growth Report 2024: World Economic Forum 2024. https://www3.weforum.org/docs/WEF_Future_of_Growth_Report_2024.pdf. Accessed 28 Jan 2024
2. Kim, J., Park, C.-Y.: Education, skill training, and lifelong learning in the era of technological revolution. Asian Development Bank, Economics Working Paper Series, no. 606, January 2020
3. Gratton, L.: An emerging landscape of skills for all. MIT Sloan Manag. Rev. (2021). https://sloanreview.mit.edu/article/an-emerging-landscape-of-skills-for-all/. Accessed 28 Jan 2024
4. Schools of the Future: Defining New Models of Education for the Fourth Industrial Revolution. Report. World Economic Forum 2020. https://www.weforum.org/reports/schools-of-the-future-defining-new-models-of-education-for-the-fourth-industrial-revolution. Accessed 28 Jan 2024

5. EU4Digital: Connecting Research and Education Communities (EaPConnect). https://euford igital.eu/discover-eu/eap-connect/. Accessed 28 Jan2024
6. Kozák, S., Ružický, E., Štefanovič, J., Schindler, F.: Research and education for industry 4.0: present development. In: Cybernetics & Informatics (K&I), pp. 1–8 (2018)
7. Burov, O., Bykov, V., Lytvynova, S.: ICT evolution: from single computational tasks to modeling of life. In: Proceedings of the 16th International Conference on ICT in Education, Research and Industrial Applications. Integration, Harmonization and Knowledge Transfer. Volume II: Workshops, Kharkiv, Ukraine, 06–10 October 2020. Volume 2732 of CEUR Workshop Proceedings, pp. 583–590. CEUR-WS.org (2020)
8. Skarbez, R., Smith, M., Whitton, M.C.: Revisiting Milgram and Kishino's reality-virtuality continuum. Front. Virtual Real. **2**, 647997 (2021). https://doi.org/10.3389/frvir.2021.647997
9. Stratton, J.: The future of work starts with trust: How can we close the AI trust gap? World Economic Forum, 15 January 2024. https://www.weforum.org/agenda/2024/01/why-there-is-an-ai-trust-gap-in-the-workplace/. Accessed 28 Jan 2024
10. Zhao, J., Riecke, B.E., Kelly, J.W., Stefanucci, J., Klippel, A.: Editorial: human spatial perception, cognition, and behaviour in extended reality. Front. Virtual Real. **4**, 1257230 (2023). https://doi.org/10.3389/frvir.2023.1257230
11. Lopes, P., Voigt-Antons, J.-N., Garcia, J., Melhart, D.: Editorial: user states in extended reality media experiences for entertainment games. Front. Virtual Real. **4**, 1235004 (2023). https://doi.org/10.3389/frvir.2023.1235004
12. Kress, G., Selander, S.: Multimodal design, learning and cultures of recognition. Internet High. Educ. **15**(1), 265–268 (2012)
13. Philippe, S., et al.: Multimodal teaching, learning and training in virtual reality: a review and case study. Virtual Real. Intell. Hardw. **2**(5), 421–442 (2020). https://doi.org/10.1016/j.vrih. 2020.07.008
14. VARK Modalities: What do Visual, Aural, Read/write & Kinesthetic really mean? Horizon Europe Guide. https://vark-learn.com/introduction-to-vark/the-vark-modalities/#google_vig nette. Accessed 29 Jan 2024 (2024)
15. Kessler, M.: Multimodality. ELT J. **76**(4), 551–554 (2022). https://doi.org/10.1093/elt/cca c028
16. Glazunova, O., et al.: Learning style identification system: design and data analysis. In: Proceedings of the 16th International Conference on ICT in Education, Research and Industrial Applications. Integration, Harmonization and Knowledge Transfer. Volume II: Workshops, Kharkiv, Ukraine, 06–10 October 2020, pp. 793–807 (2020). https://ceur-ws.org/Vol-2732/
17. Vuorre, M., Orben, A., Przybylski, Andrew, K.: There is no evidence that associations between adolescents' digital technology engagement and mental health problems have increased. Clin. Psychol. Sci. (2021). https://doi.org/10.1177/2167702621994549
18. Pinchuk, O., et al.: VR in education: ergonomic features and cybersickness. In: Nazir, S., Ahram, T., Karwowski, W. (eds.) AHFE 2020. AISC, vol. 1211, pp. 350–355. Springer, Cham (2020). https://doi.org/10.1007/978-3-030-50896-8_50
19. Burov, O., et al.: Cognitive performance degradation in high school students as the response to the psychophysiological changes. In: Ayaz, H., Asgher, U. (eds.) AHFE 2020. AISC, vol. 1201, pp. 83–88. Springer, Cham (2021). https://doi.org/10.1007/978-3-030-51041-1_12
20. Burov, O., et al.: On the way to hybrid intelligence: influence of the human-system interaction rate on the human cognitive performance. In: Ahram, T., Taiar, R. (eds.) Human Interaction and Emerging Technologies (IHIET-AI 2023): Artificial Intelligence and Future Applications. AHFE (2023) International Conference. AHFE Open Access, vol. 70. AHFE International, USA (2023). https://doi.org/10.54941/ahfe1002925
21. Mygal, G.V., Protasenko, O.F.: Functional state of the human-operator as a source of monitoring information. «ХАИ», Kharkiv, no. 40, pp. 187–193 (2008). https://dspace.library.khai. edu/xmlui/bitstream/handle/123456789/4491/Migal5.pdf?sequence=1

22. SEC's Anonymous FTP Server (Solar-Geophysical Data). http://sec.noaa.gov/ftpmenu/lists/ace2.html
23. Burov, O.Yu., Pinchuk, O.P., Pertsev, M.A., Vasylchenko, Y.V.: Use of learners' state indices for design of adaptive learning systems. In: Information Technologies and Learning Tools, vol. 68, no. 6, pp. 20–32 (2018)
24. Ahn, A.C., et al.: Electrical properties of acupuncture points and meridians: a systematic review. Bioelectromagnetics **29**(4), 245–56 (2008)
25. Spirin, O., Burov, O.: Models and applied tools for prediction of student ability to effective learning. In: 14th International Conference on ICT in Education, Research and Industrial Applications. Integration, Harmonization and Knowledge Transfer, vol. 2104, pp. 404–411. CEUR-WS (2018)
26. Lavrov, E., Pasko, N., Siryk, O.: Information technology for assessing the operators working environment as an element of the ensuring automated systems ergonomics and reliability. In: IEEE 15th International Conference on Advanced Trends in Radioelectronics, Telecommunications and Computer Engineering (TCSET), Lviv-Slavske, Ukraine, pp. 570–575 (2020). https://doi.org/10.1109/TCSET49122.2020.235497

Evaluating Cause-Effect Relationships in Accident Investigation Using HFACS-DEMATEL

Wesley Tsz-Kin Chan$^{(\boxtimes)}$ ⓘ, Wen-Chin Li ⓘ, Arthur Nichanian ⓘ,
and Elizabeth Manikath ⓘ

Safety and Accident Investigation Centre, School of Aerospace, Transport and Manufacturing,
Cranfield University, Cranfield, UK
`wesley.chan@cranfield.ac.uk`

Abstract. This paper addresses the 'routes to failure' in the causal chain of events as categorized using the Human Factors Analysis and Classification System (HFACS) framework. By using the Decision-Making Trial and Evaluation Laboratory (DEMATEL) method to evaluate the comparative influence of each HFACS category on other categories, the present research aims to classify each HFACS category as either an overall 'cause' or an overall 'effect' factor, and to give each HFACS category a comparable statistical value of their overall level of influence. Analysis of N = 30 responses from aviation safety experts identified that frontline perception faults had the potential to influence higher-level preconditions, and that 'Environmental Factors' were found to have the highest overall influence amongst HFACS categories at levels 1 and 2. The findings support the use of the DEMATEL method in the selection and direction of safety interventions. Safety remedies focusing on 'cause' factors are likely to have additional second-order benefits on associated 'effects', and more influential categories are likely to be more effective in influencing overall system safety. The methodology can assist safety managers in selecting and prioritizing safety initiatives, especially when faced with issues such as monetary or time constraints in the industrial context.

Keywords: Human Factors Analysis and Classification System (HFACS) ·
Human Factors Interventions · Safety Management Systems

1 Introduction

The investigation and analysis of accidents and incidents form the basis for safety management objectives and human factors interventions. Contemporary investigation processes typically utilize a wide range of information sources, such as flight data and psychometric assessments, to ensure the objectiveness of the findings [1]. Yet, the collection, interpretation, and projection of these sources by accident investigators are known to be affected by subjective demographic and cultural factors [2], and investigative taxonomies often fail to sufficiently account for human contexts behind decisions and behaviors [3]. To illustrate, expert pilots may choose to accept minor deviations (that are within a certain

© The Author(s), under exclusive license to Springer Nature Switzerland AG 2024
D. Harris and W.-C. Li (Eds.): HCII 2024, LNAI 14692, pp. 26–35, 2024.
https://doi.org/10.1007/978-3-031-60728-8_3

safety margin) to free up mental capacity for other tasks. As most investigative methods are still exceedance-based, i.e., focus on deviation from acceptable performance and do not primarily focus on everyday performance, these deviations are typically considered as performance deficiencies and different investigators will attribute these deficiencies to different causes. Moreover, latent conditions are not inherently visible from an airline's flight safety perspective (e.g., through Flight Data Monitoring and Air Safety Reports) [4]. By failing to understand how underlying human contexts interact with latent conditions in the causal sequence of events, investigative processes are like "focusing on a fever without understanding the underlying illness that is causing it" [5].

1.1   The Human Factors Analysis and Classification System

To improve the objectivity of accident investigations, Wiegmann & Shappell (2003) developed the Human Factors Analysis and Classification System (HFACS) to provide investigators with a taxonomy of latent and active failures implicated in the causal sequence of events. By providing a system-wide taxonomy, the HFACS encourages investigators to associate human factors deficiencies to latent conditions originating from across multiple organizational levels, rather than simply attributing faults to acts committed by frontline crew members.

Human factors deficiencies can be attributed to failure modes across four levels representing different parts of the organizational hierarchy (Table 1). The HFACS has been widely used for safety investigation purposes across multiple domains including aviation, maritime, rail, nuclear, and medical fields. More recent applications of HFACS suggested the integration of failure modes at the 'Preconditions for Unsafe Acts' level (L2) into three underlying categories (i.e., 'Environmental Factors', 'Condition of Operators', and 'Personnel Factors' categories) [6]. Notably, whilst the four error and violation types at the 'Unsafe Acts of Operators' level (L1) can also be simply integrated into the two categories of errors and violations, previous research indicated that this was not desirable if the data contained sufficient detail, in order to provide a level of granularity required for accident investigation purposes [5].

As HFACS was developed on the basis of Reason's (1990) Swiss Cheese model of accident causation, the framework has an implicit assumption of cause-effect directionality with each "slice" of cheese considered to influence the "slice" at the next lower level [5]. 'Routes to failure' are considered to flow in a top-down direction within the organizational hierarchy [8]. For example, in relation to the interaction between cabin crew and cockpit crew, psychological and physical barriers complicate communication which affects flight safety [9]. A prominent example of missing communication between cabin and cockpit crew is the Air Ontario Flight 1363 accident in Dryden, Canada, which crashed shortly after take-off as it was unable to attain sufficient terrain clearance due to ice accretion on the wing [10]. Although the cabin crew noticed ice build-up on the wings prior to take-off they did not inform the cockpit crew. In this case, historical 'Organizational Influences' (HFACS level 4) were found to have created psychological barriers between cabin and cockpit crew members, resulting in the lack of communication and teamwork (representative of 'Personnel Factors' at level 2) in the incident.

Table 1. Levels and categories of the Human Factors Analysis and Classification System (HFACS).

Level		Categories
L4	Organisational Influences	1. Resource Management 2. Organizational Climate 3. Organizational Process
L3	Unsafe Supervision	4. Inadequate Supervision 5. Planned Inappropriate Operations 6. Failed to Correct a Known Problem 7. Supervisory Violations

L2	Preconditions for Unsafe Acts	8. Environmental Factors
		  • Physical Environment
		  • Technological Environment
		9. Condition of Operators
		  • Adverse States
		  • Adverse Physiological States
		  • Physical/Mental Limitations
		10. Personnel Factors
		  • Crew Resource Management
		  • Personal Readiness

L1	Unsafe Acts of Operators	11. Decision Errors 12. Skill Based Errors 13. Perceptual Errors 14. Violations

1.2 Directionality of Associative Pathways

There is a research gap as previous studies do not adequately address the possibility that converse, bottom-up relationships may also exist within the HFACS. To illustrate, it is logical to conceive how aircraft control errors at the lowest, frontline level can cause the loss of situation awareness. The loss of situation awareness can then be considered, in effect, as a 'Condition of Operators' deficiency at HFACS level 2, which may in turn play a part in subsequent events.

Aside from the directionality of relationships, other studies have found that each error or unsafe act can be associated with more than one precursor in a 'many-to-one' concept [8]. It has been argued that remedial safety actions will be most effective if they can be aimed at categories which share the greatest number of associations with other concomitant precursors [11]. However, the problem is that when each category is associated with multiple others, then amongst the numerous 'routes to failure', the category in question can on the one hand be the cause of failure for some 'routes' and on the other hand be the consequential effect in other 'routes'. Similarly, some categories may be heavily influenced by other factors yet exert little influence over the wider system, whereas other categories may be resilient to external influences but nevertheless exert a _strong influence onto others. A wider perspective looking into comparative influences at the whole-system level from a cause-effect perspective can paint a clearer picture of how factors in each category function and compare as a net 'cause' or 'effect' in the wider safety system.

Based on the literature review, the goals of the present research were to investigate cause-effect relationships amongst HFACS categories and to identify the comparative influence of each category as part of the wider system. Firstly, the results will be useful for safety managers in directing future safety actions to net 'cause' factors, which can help to ensure that remedial actions will rectify system-level root causes. Secondly, the ranking of relative influence amongst the various categories will enable safety managers to select more influential categories on which to spend precious resources.

2 Method

2.1 Participants

Responses from $N = 30$ subject matter experts in aviation safety were included in the present analysis. Participation was voluntary, no identifying information was collected, and participants had the right to terminate their participation at any time. Ethics approval was provided by the Cranfield University Research Ethics System (CURES/20576/2023).

2.2 Research Design

Interrelations amongst categories of human factors conditions at HFACS level 1 ('Unsafe Acts of Operators') and level 2 ('Preconditions for Unsafe Acts') were assessed using the Decision-Making Trial and Evaluation Laboratory method (DEMATEL: Fontela & Gabus, 1972).

HFACS Categories and Failure Modes. In the aviation environment, social and physical distances between frontline and back-office workplaces (pilots and cabin crew do not work in airline headquarters) are known to create a level of separation between operational personnel and conditions at higher supervisory and organizational levels [13]. It was suspected that bottom-up relationships will mostly be amongst HFACS levels 1 and 2, as these categories are within the remit of operations personnel. Thus, HFACS categories in this study included four error and violation types at HFACS level 1 ('Decision Errors', 'Skill-Based Errors', 'Perceptual Errors', and 'Violations') and three categories at HFACS level 2 ('Environmental Factors', 'Personnel Factors', and 'Conditions of Operators').

DEMATEL Method. The DEMATEL method operates by pitting human factors categories against each other, comparing each category's contribution to the system (net given influence: R_i) against the effects that the other categories exert on them (net accepted influence: C_i). A category is considered as a 'cause' if its net given influence is greater than its net accepted influence (Ri – Ci > 0), whereas a category is consid-ered as an 'effect' if its net accepted influence exceeds its net given influence (Ri – Ci < 0) [14].

Data collection was done by an online survey. The survey was designed to quantify the degree of interaction between HFACS categories as perceived by the participants. For DEMATEL calculations, all seven categories at HFACS levels 1 and 2 (Table 1) were listed both horizontally and vertically into a 7 × 7 matrix (Table 2). The survey items pits the row elements in the matrix with the column elements by asking participants to quantify the degree of interaction between exemplars of each element on 4-point scales ranging from 'no' (0) to 'high' (4) influence. For example, to quantify the level of influence that 'Environmental Factors' (L2-1) has over 'Personnel Factors' (L2-2), the survey item asks: "In your opinion, does physical or technological environment (e.g., lighting, ventilation, equipment design) influence crew resource management or personal preparation for duty?". Thus, for a 7 × 7 matrix, the survey had a total of 42 items.

2.3 Statistical Analysis

Statistical analysis was conducted using Microsoft Excel (version 2312). Following the steps of DEMATEL [12], survey responses from all N = 30 participants were (1) averaged and combined into a Direct-Influence Matrix which shows the strength of interaction that each row element has on each column element (Table 2); (2) Items in the Direct-Influence Matrix were normalized to adjust the data to a common scale, enabling the comparison of each element bi-directionally in terms of cause and effect; (3) The normalized matrix was multiplied with an identity matrix (where all the elements on the main diagonal are 1, and all other elements are 0), to generate a Total Relation Matrix where the row total represents the Net Given Influence (Ri) by the respective horizontal element category, and the column total represents the Net Accepted Influence (Ci) received by the vertical element category; (4) For each element, simple arithmetic deduction of the Net Accepted Influence (Ci) values from The Net Given Influence (Ri) values were calculated to find the directionality and strength of influence. The Net Accepted Influence (Ri), Net Given Influence (Ri), and 'cause' (Ri – Ci > 0) or 'effect' (Ri – Ci < 0) identity values for each HFACS category are presented in Table 3.

Table 2. The Direct Influence Matrix, based on N = 30 responses, presenting the degree of interaction from 'no influence' (0) to 'high influence' (4) that each row element has on the column element.

Direct Influence Matrix	L2-1 Environmental Factors	L2-2 Personnel Factors	L2-3 Conditions of Operators	L1-1 Decision Errors	L1-2 Skill-Based Errors	L1-3 Perceptual Errors	L1-4 Violations
L2-1 Environmental Factors		3.14	3.33	3.19	3.14	3.57	2.81
L2-2 Personnel Factors	1.86		2.95	3.48	3.43	2.81	2.95
L2-3 Conditions of Operators	2.05	3.43		3.67	3.71	3.29	3.29
L1-1 Decision Errors	1.81	2.57	2.57		2.76	2.62	3.38
L1-2 Skill-Based Errors	1.75	3.14	3.00	3.50		3.14	3.33
L1-3 Perceptual Errors	2.10	2.67	3.00	3.71	3.52		3.33
L1-4 Violations	2.24	3.00	2.71	3.48	2.90	2.62	

3 Results and Discussion

3.1 Active Failures as the Cause of Human Factors Preconditions

Notably, 'Perceptual Errors' at HFACS level 1 functioned as a net 'cause' factor, and the 'Personnel Factors' category at level 2 was found to be an 'effect' factor (Table 3). The finding of 'Perceptual Errors' as a 'cause' factor is contrary to the accepted knowledge where categories at HFACS level 1 were considered as the 'bottom-level' final manifestation of the causal sequence. The finding of 'Personnel Factors' as an 'effect' factor was also unexpected, as within the HFACS framework the second level of 'Preconditions for Unsafe Acts' were conventionally presumed to be 'higher-level' preconditional causes.

A review into the failure modes associated within each category provides an explanation for the present findings. The 'Personnel Factors' (L2) category encompasses the failure modes of Crew Resource Management (e.g., teamwork, communication, etc.) and Personal Readiness (e.g., individual training and risk judgement) (Table 1). A possible explanation could be that 'Perceptual Errors' (L1) conferred amongst individual crew members a deluged "perception of the world [which] differs to reality" [5], in turn instigating a breakdown of crew resource management and risk judgement when this deluged individual has to work with others within multi-crew environments.

For safety management, fixes on 'effect' factors are likely to be limited to first-order conditions. Contrarily, interventions on 'cause' factors are likely to also rectify second-order 'effects' and may therefore be comparatively more effective. The present results provide evidence for the existence of multi-directional 'routes to failure', with bottom-up pathways likely to exist. In the future, a more encompassing perspective with the

Table 3. DEMATEL output of the Net Accepted (Ri) and Given (Ci) influence for each category, and the identity values (Ri – Ci) for each category as a cause or effect factor.

Category	Ri	Ci	Ri-Ci	Identity
L2-1 Environmental Factors	5.81	3.75	2.06	Cause
L2-2 Personnel Factors	5.32	5.45	−0.13	Effect
L2-3 Conditions of Operators	5.84	5.33	0.51	Cause
L1-1 Decision Errors	4.85	6.30	−1.45	Effect
L1-2 Skill-Based Errors	5.42	5.86	−0.44	Effect
L1-3 Perceptual Errors	5.54	5.44	0.10	Cause
L1-4 Violations	5.18	5.81	−0.64	Effect

consideration of how 'Unsafe Acts of Operators' at level 1 can possibly create second-order influences at higher system levels can possibly assist safety managers in selecting safety recommendations and interventions with broader applicability.

3.2   Selecting System-Wide Remedial Actions

Although the finding of a 'cause' factor at level 1 and an 'effect' factor at level 2 suggests that a new, more inclusive interpretation of the direction of causal sequences within HFACS is desired, a review of cause-effect values (Ri – Ci) across the board nonetheless suggests that the conventional top-down direction is most dominant. The majority of level 2 categories were 'causes', and the majority of level 1 categories were 'effects'. As presented in Fig. 1, cause-effect values for level 2 factors were leaning towards the 'cause' side, whereas three out of four level 1 factors were leaning towards the opposite 'effect' side. To an extent, this confirms previous assumptions of top-down 'routes to failure', with active failures at level 1 for the most part a manifestation of higher-level 'causes' in the sequence of events.

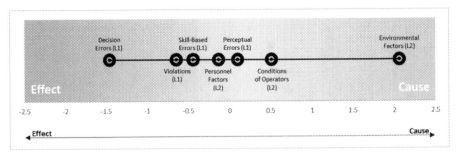

Fig. 1. Cause-effect values of categories at HFACS levels 1 and 2. Positive values signify that the category is an overall 'cause', and negative values signify an overall 'effect'.

In the present results it was notable that amongst the four 'effect' categories in HFACS levels 1 and 2, the level 1 categories of 'Decision Errors' (Ri – Ci = −1.45), 'Skill-Based Errors' (−0.44), and 'Violations' (−0.64) were comparatively stronger 'effects' (leaning further towards the left in Fig. 1), than the level 2 category of 'Personnel Factors' (−0.13). In conventional safety management, the mindset was that safety actions should simply be directed at 'cause' categories which are associated with a high number of concomitant categories [11]. The present finding of comparative differences amongst the categories on the cause-effect spectrum showcases the need for user-centered design adaptations. Rather than focusing solely on the quantity of cause-effect relationships emancipating from each category, safety managers will be wise to also consider the comparative, 'qualitative' influence of each category on the basis of their strength as a cause or an effect factor. A comparison of the cause-effect (Ri – Ci) value can highlight categories which are stronger 'causes' as contributors to the overall system safety. Remedial actions focusing on these stronger 'causes' are likely to be more effective or have a stronger effect on system-wide outcomes.

3.3 Selecting Categories Within Levels

According to the Standards and Recommended Practices of ICAO Annex 13, safety recommendations suggested as part of accident investigation processes are typically directed to specific addressees [15]. This means that consequential remedial actions are likely to be constrained to specific levels within the organizational hierarchy. However, within each level of the organizational hierarchy, there are typically multiple ways to remedy any given scenario.

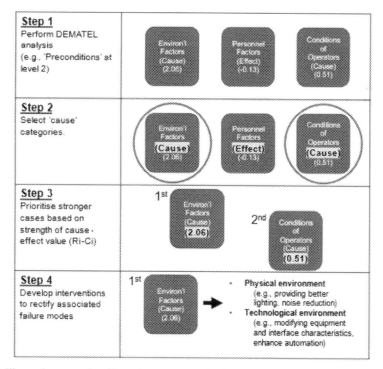

Fig. 2. Illustrative example of how the present methodology can be utilized by safety managers in selecting safety interventions for human factors preconditions at HFACS level 2.

The present finding of the co-existence of both 'cause' and 'effect' categories at each level can assist in the selection of more effective human factors intervention strategies within each level. To illustrate, consider a situation where the Annex 13 investigation addresses improvements to 'Preconditions for Unsafe Acts', or HFACS level 2 (Fig. 2). Step 1: safety managers can conduct a DEMATEL analysis including the HFACS level 2 categories. Step 2: they can consider the cause-effect polarity of the various categories and select the 'causes', which in this example will direct them to focus on 'Environmental Factors' and 'Conditions of Operators'. Step 3: a comparison of the strength of the cause-effect $(Ri - Ci)$ value between these two 'causes' will suggest a prioritization on modifying 'Environmental Factors' $(Ri - Ci = 2.06)$ as it has an overall stronger causal effect than 'Conditions of Operators' $(Ri - Ci = 0.51)$. If resources are limited, then prioritize improving the work environment over rectifying operator conditions. Step 4: create and incorporate 'Environmental Factors' interventions into the safety management system. As resources such as time and money are generally limited in the aviation industry, the process can assist safety managers in making more informed decisions related to the development and selection of remedial safety interventions.

4   Conclusion

For the improvement of safety, remedial actions and human factors interventions are often dictated by safety recommendations from accident investigations. However, the investigation process can be affected by subjective cultural factors amongst accident investigators, and existing models such as the Human Factors Analysis and Classification System (HFACS) do not sufficiently capture decision-making contexts and frontline effects on preconditions at higher levels in the system hierarchy. The present research was an attempt to determine whether frontline-level deficiencies can affect higher-level conditions, and to evaluate how each category comparatively influences or is influenced by other factors in the wider system in a cause-effect spectrum. Analysis of $N = 30$ responses from aviation safety experts using the Decision-Making Trial and Evaluation Laboratory (DEMATEL) method found that frontline errors related to perceptual faults functioned as a 'cause' factor. Also, despite its designation as a 'preconditional' factor, personnel factors associated with crew resource management and risk judgement were found to be an overall 'effect', influenced in the second-order by other factors within the system. Evaluating human factors conditions using the DEMATEL method can assist safety managers in directing remedial actions to 'cause' categories with greater comparative influence, in this case, 'Environmental Factors' and 'Conditions of Operators', to achieve the most effective safety intervention outcomes.

Disclosure of Interests.   The authors have no competing interests to declare that are relevant to the content of this article.

References

1. Wang, Y., Yang, L., Korek, W.T., Zhao, Y., Li, W.-C.: The evaluations of the impact of the pilot's visual behaviours on the landing performance by using eye tracking technology, pp. 143–153 (2023)

2. Chan, W.T.-K., Li, W.-C.: Training for future investigators: understanding cultural effects on standardisation and international cooperation. In: ISASI Forum - Air Saf. Through Investig., vol. 55, no. 3, pp. 8–15 (2022)

3. McCarthy, P.: The application of safety II in commercial aviation – the operational learning review (OLR), pp. 368–383 (2020)

4. Nichanian, A., Li, W.-C.: Analysis of airline pilots' risk perception while flying during COVID-19 through flight data monitoring and air safety reports, pp. 150–162 (2023)

5. Wiegmann, D.A., Shappell, S.A.: A Human Error Approach to Aviation Accident Analysis. Routledge, New York (2003)

6. Salmon, P.M., Stanton, N.A., Lenné, M., Jenkins, D.P., Rafferty, L., Walker, G.H.: Human Factors Methods and Accident Analysis. CRC Press, Boca Raton (2017)

7. Reason, J.: Human error (1990)

8. Li, W.-C., Harris, D., Yu, C.-S.: Routes to failure: analysis of 41 civil aviation accidents from the Republic of China using the human factors analysis and classification system. Accid. Anal. Prev. **40**(2), 426–434 (2008). https://doi.org/10.1016/j.aap.2007.07.011

9. Chute, R.D., Wiener, E.L.: Cockpit-cabin communication: I. A tale of two cultures. Int. J. Aviat. Psychol. (1995). https://doi.org/10.1207/s15327108ijap0503_2

10. Ford, J., Henderson, R., O'Hare, D.: Barriers to intra-aircraft communication and safety: the perspective of the flight attendants. Int. J. Aviat. Psychol. **23**(4), 368–387 (2013). https://doi.org/10.1080/10508414.2013.834167

11. Li, W.-C., Harris, D.: Pilot error and its relationship with higher organizational levels: HFACS analysis of 523 accidents. Aviat. Space Environ. Med. **77**(10), 1056–1061 (2006). https://www.ingentaconnect.com/contentone/asma/asem/2006/00000077/00000010/art00009

12. Fontela, E., Gabus, A.: World problems an invitation to further thought within the framework of DEMATEL, Geneva (1972)

13. Chan, W.T.-K., Li, W.-C.: Investigating professional values among pilots, cabin crew, ground staff, and managers to develop aviation safety management systems. Int. J. Ind. Ergon. **92**, 103370 (2022). https://doi.org/10.1016/j.ergon.2022.103370

14. Liou, J.J.H., Yen, L., Tzeng, G.-H.: Building an effective safety management system for airlines. J. Air Transp. Manag. **14**(1), 20–26 (2008). https://doi.org/10.1016/j.jairtraman.2007.10.002

15. ICAO: Annex 13 to the Convention on International Civil Aviation - Aircraft Accident and Incident Investigation, 12th edn., Montreal, Quebec (2020)

Impact of Startle Reflex on Cognitive Performance, Face Temperature and Brain Activity

Jonathan Deniel[(✉)], Jens Neubert, Flora Schwartz, and Mickaël Causse

ISAE-SUPAERO, Université de Toulouse, 10 Av. Edouard Belin, Toulouse 31400, France
jonathan.deniel@univ-jfc.fr, flora.schwartz@isae-supaero.fr,
mickael.causse@isae.fr

Abstract. Human performance is of paramount importance in aircraft piloting. The ability to perform the required flying tasks under stressful conditions is critical. However, unexpected or threatening events have the potential to trigger a startle reflex, a phenomenon that can lead to cognitive incapacitation and potentially catastrophic accidents. Few studies have examined brain activity following a startle reflex, especially during a complex cognitive task. We conducted an experiment in which we induced a startle reflex using loud acoustic stimuli while participants were engaged in the Toulouse n-back task (engaging memory processes and mental calculation). During the task, brain measures were obtained using functional near-infrared spectroscopy (fNIRS) and facial temperature was recorded using a thermal camera. Our initial findings reveal that the startle reflex has been successfully induced, as demonstrated by the observable behavioral reactions captured in the camera recordings. After experiencing the startle reflex, participants showed a brief decrease in task performance, suggesting a momentary disruption of cognitive processes, highlighting the potential implications of the startle reflex for aviation safety. The integration of multimodal physiological techniques will allow us to comprehensively investigate both cerebral and peripheral physiological responses during the startle reflex. Our research will contribute to the understanding of how startle responses can affect cognitive performance and shed light on the potential cognitive incapacitation that may result from this phenomenon.

Keywords: Startle reflex · Aviation · Cognitive Incapacitation · Thermal imaging · fNIRS

1 Introduction

Maintaining optimal cognitive functioning even under stressful conditions is necessary for pilots. However, unexpected or threatening events can be a source of startle reactions, which can potentially disrupt current actions, train of thought, increase stress level and lead to errors. Several incidents, and even catastrophic accidents such as the

---

J. Neubert, F. Schwartz and M. Causse—These authors contributed equally to this work.

D. Harris and W.-C. Li (Eds.): HCII 2024, LNAI 14692, pp. 36–50, 2024.
https://doi.org/10.1007/978-3-031-60728-8_4

West Caribbean Airways Flight 708 [1] or the Colgan Air Flight 3407 [2] have been associated to startle reactions. The present study focuses on the neurophysiological and cognitive consequences of the startle reflex during the performance of a task generating a high cognitive engagement, such as those encountered in the cockpit.

1.1   The Startle Reflex

The startle reflex is an innate, unconscious and protective response to brutal or sudden stimuli such as fast uprising loud auditory alarms [3]. It is a widespread behavior among animals including mammals, birds, reptiles and amphibians [4,5]. It involves a very rapid reaction that has been reported to start as early as 14 ms after the stimuli onset [6] and usually lasts for 0.3 s to 1.5 s [7]. Body startle reaction is an evolutionary selected and stereotyped reflex that consists in eyes closure, shoulders forward elevation, head retraction and neck dorsiflexion [6,8]. It is commonly followed by attention related movement towards the threatening stimulus (i.e., head orientation). Neural pathways of startle have been extensively studied and were summarised by LeDoux [9]. He describes two neural routes of startling stimulus processing in the brain. Sensory inputs from the afferent neurons first reach the sensory thalamus before being split in two parallels routes. The slower one, called "processing route", or "thalamo-cortico-amygdala pathway", passes by sensory cortical areas where evaluations of threat and significance of the stimulus are computed. It usually takes about 500 ms of processing and ends in the basolateral amygdala. On the opposite, the so-called "quick and dirty route", or "thalamo-amygdala pathway", simply consists in a fast track going straight from the thalamus to the basolateral amygdala in a shorter amount of time (i.e., 14 ms). Based on that, output signal emerges from the central amygdala towards numerous efferent pathways (e.g., periaqueductal grey) [10]. Amygdala, especially it's central region, has been shown to play a key role in fear related reactions learning such as conditioned startle [11] and fear potentiated startle. Intensity of startle reactions is also under the influence of several factors. It was showed that startle reactions are highly variable among participants [12] and that emotional context was a modulating factor of startle reaction intensity [13]. Startle reactions are influenced by personality dimensions such as harm avoidance tendency, extraversion and neuroticism [14]. Sensitivity to reward and punishment as well as sex have also been shown to be associated with the modulation of startle reflex [15]. Moreover, startle reflex intensity have also been found to be affected by psychopathologies such as phobia [16], psychopathy [17], anxiety or post traumatic stress disorders [18]. A common type of startle modulation is fear-potentiation [11] in which the startle reaction is augmented by a fear prone context. Such variability in the intensity of startle reaction especially when considering emotional context leads to consider that startle may evolve from simple aversive reflex to a more intense startle/surprise reaction that involves the activation of the sympathetic nervous system as well as the endocrinal system, thus affecting heart rate, blood pressure, or respiratory rate. More elaborated behavioural consequences such as attentive freezing or flight behaviour also develop [10], even leading to 'confusion' and/or delays in information processing when occurring in highly demanding cognitive tasks situations like aircraft piloting [7].

1.2   Central Executive and Salience Networks

Highly demanding cognitive activities such as piloting require high levels cognitive processes that are supported and managed by a large-scale brain network involving the coordination of the activity in several brain regions: the Executive Control Network (ECN). The ECN has been shown to be important for managing cognitive load, executive functions, and intrinsic, goal-driven attention [19–22]. The ECN solicits resources from the lateral and medial parts of the dorsal prefrontal cortex (DLPFC and DMPFC, respectively), dorsal posterior parietal cortex (DPPC), and frontal eye fields [23,24].

The ECN activity has been shown to interact with other brain networks. Indeed, when facing a stressful and potentially aversive stimuli another network, namely the Salience Network (SN) [25] has been found to be involved, and sometimes at the expense of the ECN. The SN involves activity patterns from cortical areas such as frontoinsular, dorsal anterior cingulate, inferotemporal and temporoparietal areas as well as subcortical ones like the amygdala, the thalamus, the hypothalamus, and other midbrain regions [26]. Some studies like [24] found that in highly engaging situations, acute social stress despite not impairing performance, resulted in increased levels of HbO_2 concentration in ECN's bilateral pre-frontal and parietal cortical regions. Similar results were also found by Causse et al. [22] in an fMRI experiment involving an adapted N-back task (i.e., Toulouse N-back task) completed while exposed to unpleasant and stressful sounds (e.g., blackboard and plate scratching, dentist's drill, etc.). The authors found a maintenance of the overall performance thanks to an increased activity in ECN related areas, and also evidenced inhibitions of auditory signal processing. These results likely translates emotional regulation mechanisms at play in order to maintain an acceptable level of performance. In our study, we focus on another type of stressful situations that are the acoustic startling stimuli.

1.3   Physiological Measurements of the Startle Reflex

Functional infrared thermal imaging (fITI) is a non-invasive and contact-less technique measuring the spontaneously emitted electromagnetic radiation from body surface (i.e., face) varying depending on the blood flow. The temperature of the cutaneous surface, controlled through the vessel irrigating the skin by the automatic nervous system, depends on the current state of the body [27,28]. Previous research has shown the advantages of this non-intrusive, passive observation method allowing the monitored subject maximal comfort and concentration on the performed task [29]. Earlier investigations have reported a connection between the facial skin temperature and the bodily state, although the direction of this effect seems to depend on the specific region of the face. More precisely, a negative correlation between mental workload elevation and temperature decrease in the nasal area was found [27,30]. Moreover, the study of temperature variation of the periorbital region has provided contrasted results about its sensitivity to startle and stressful events. Initially, Pavlidis et al. found evidence for thermal reaction to startle in these regions of the face [31–33] but later work did not replicate these results [34,35]. On the other hand, Hong et al. [36], also found that the forehead region was likely to be reactive to startle and stressful stimuli even more than fever and physical exercise. Such heterogenous data leave room for further exploration especially with the use of recent deep learning applied to facial recognition techniques.

The functional near-infrared spectroscopy (fNIRS) allows for the monitoring of cerebral blood oxy- and deoxy-genation levels during mental tasks to observe brain activity alternations between phases of rest versus phases of mental stimulation [37–39]. In comparison to functional magnetic resonance imaging (fMRI), fNIRS has an inferior capacity to study the brain in terms of penetration depth, sensitivity, signal-to-noise ratio and spatial resolution, but it offers several practical advantages including higher temporal resolution, better cost efficiency, and more tolerence to head movements [40,41]. Photons emitted by the source optodes travel through the skin, skull, and the cerebrospinal fluid (CSF) before entering the brain. The detector receives a light intensity strongly influenced by the *"large difference in absorption spectra of oxy-hemoglobin and deoxy-hemoglobin"* [40] in the outer layer of brain tissue. Numerous ECN regions (e.g., fronto-temporal and parietal cortex) likely affected by startle reactions are accessible to fNIRS imagery technique [24], and as its sensitivity to possible movement induced by the startle reaction is lower than fMRI, it is good candidate for brain activity measurement in this context.

1.4   Research Question and Objectives

Despite its importance to safety, there is a lack of literature investigating brain activity associated with the startle reflex during the performance of cognitively demanding tasks, particularly using functional near-infrared spectroscopy (fNIRS). In addition, the relationship between the intensity of the startle reflex and the performance decrement is not well understood. The same applies to the influence of personality on startle responses consequences. Thus, this study aimed to address these gaps by investigating the impact of the startle reflex on cognitive performance and brain activity taking into account personality dimensions related to emotions and anxiety. Facial temperature was also collected as this is a promising contactless indicator of emotional arousal.

Our aim was to elicit startle responses during a demanding cognitive task under laboratory conditions. The specific goals of this study were (1) to identify the neural correlates of the startle reflex during a challenging cognitive task. It was hypothesised that variations in activity in the central executive network may play a critical role in the performance decrement following a startle response. (2) To identify facial temperature correlates of the startle reflex. It was hypothesised that nose temperature may vary due to the startle reflex and a deeper investigation of the sensitivity of periorbital and nasal regions is required to clarify the literature contrasted results. (3) To investigate the potential relationships between startle reflex intensity, transient cognitive decrement and personality dimensions (i.e., emotion management, anxiety). The general hypothesis is that certain personality traits may predispose people to a more intense startle response. In this article we present the ongoing protocol and its associated preliminary results.

2   Method

2.1   Participants

To date 4 healthy volunteers (mean age = 28.5 yo; 3 females) were recruited for the study through local advertising. All were students at ISAE-SUPAERO in Toulouse, France. An exclusion criterion was the wearing of corrective glasses, as this would interfere with the functionality of the thermal camera by masking the periorbital face region. None reported an affective or anxiety disorder, neurological or cardiovascular disease. None were taking any medication that could affect brain or autonomic function. All subjects reported normal hearing and vision. All participants gave written informed consent in accordance with the local ethics committee (CER number: 00011835 – 2023 – 0918 – 681).

2.2   Personality Questionnaires

To evaluate personality dimension and other potential modulating factors of startle, several questionnaires were filled out by the participants. The first one was dedicated to the use of different substances (i.e. coffee, tea, drugs, etc.) as well as physical activity and sleep during the last 24 h. The second one was dedicated to the assessment of emotional reactivity and regulation: the multidimensional emotion questionnaire (MEQ) [42]. Also, a short version of the Big Five Personality Inventory (BFI 10) [43], aimed to evaluate the participants' personality positioning on the dimensions of openness, conscientiousness, extraversion, agreeableness and neuroticism. The fourth one was the State Anxiety Inventory - Trait and State (STAI) questionnaire [44]. Finally, the fifth and last questionnaire was the Perceived Stress Scale (PSS-14), it estimated how participants perceive stress [45].

2.3   Mental Arithmetic N-Back Task (Toulouse N-Back Task)

Participants were administered with a modified n-back task, called Toulouse N-back task (TNT) [46,47]. The task was implemented in Matlab (*MathWorks*) using the Psychophysics Toolbox (*Psychtoolbox 3*, [48–50]). It combines a classical n-back task with mental arithmetic operations (Fig. 1). Instead of memorising and comparing single items, as in the classical n-back task, in the TNT participants have to memorise and compare the results of arithmetic operations calculated beforehand. On each block trial, participants had to compute the result and compare it either to a fixed number (50 in the 0-back condition) or to the result obtained 2 (2-back) trials earlier. The arithmetic operations were additions or substations where all operands were multiples of 5 (e.g., $15 + 40$, $90 - 35$). Therefore, memory load varied between 2 difficulty conditions, with the 2-back task producing the highest load. Participants response were provided with a 2-button Cedrus response pad (RB-740, *Cedrus Corporation, San Pedro, CA*). They were asked to press either a green button if the result matched the target number or a red button if not. Participants had to give their response as quickly as possible. Operations remained on screen until the end of the response window, any response after the 2 s delay was classified as a "miss". During rest periods, participants were presented with

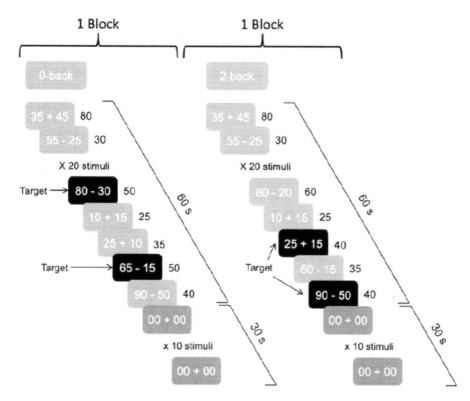

Fig. 1. TNT-Task protocol used in this experiment: Condition blocks each lasting 60 s and containing 20 mental calculations. Each condition is followed by a rest period of 30 s before the commencement of the next block

"00 + 00" operations and subjects were not required to make a response. Operations were displayed for 2 s in the centre of the screen, with an inter-stimulus interval of 1 s.

2.4   Acoustic Startling Stimuli

Startle reflex was induced by unpredictable loud sounds, triggered independently from task performance. Two acoustic startle stimuli were selected from an initial pool of six stimuli, based on their effectiveness at eliciting a startle reflex. This was determined thanks to pretests involving visual observation of the participants' physical responses. These stimuli consisted of a white noise and a recording of a metal bar falling to the ground. We also used a third stimulus as a control condition. This was a classic soft beep sound. This additional stimulus allows us to distinguish between a simple attentional capture effect, which is generated by the beep, and the impact of the startle stimulus. The three acoustic stimuli lasted 1000 ms and were presented through DT 770 Pro 80 Ω headphones (*Beyerdynamic GmbH & Co. KG, Heilbronn, Germany*). The intensity of the startle stimuli was set to 95 dB, measured at the output of the headphones. The intensity of the control tone was set to 65 dB.

2.5   fNIRS Measurements

Neurophysiological data were obtained via the NIRScout system (*NIRx Medical Technologies, LLC. Los Angeles, California*) equipped with 16 optodes, including 8 sources and 8 detectors. The source-receptor distance was set at 3 cm for adjacent optodes. The 16 optodes were placed on the head cap according to the 10-10 international system positioning. 15 Optodes were used to create 12 channels, focused on prefrontal and parietal cortices, part of the the Executive Control Network (Fig. 2). Eight channels (made of 5 sources and 4 detectors) were located over the prefrontal region and 7 channels (made of 3 sources and 3 detectors) were located over the parietal cortical area. Additional 8 short distance channels were used to control the superficial confounding signals (i.e., scalp perfusion, respiration, Meyer waves, cardiac). This was achieved using the remaining detector to receive the signal from the short channels. The system emitted 2-wavelength of infrared light (760 nm and 850 nm) at a sampling rate of 7.8125 Hz to measure the oxy- and deoxy-genated blood concentration. Acquisition were performed using NIRStar 14.3 software (*NIRx Medical Technologies, LLC. Los Angeles, California*). fNIRS data was preprocessed to clean the signal using processing steps: spike and motion artefact correction, drift removal functions, band pass filtering, and channel signal quality checks. The change in oxy- and desoxyhemoglobin on the 12 channels were calculated via the modified Beer-Lambert Law.

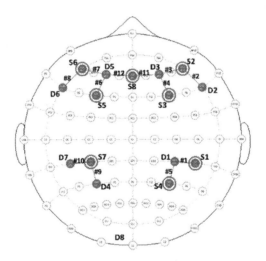

Fig. 2. 12-channel NIRS head cap setup according to the 10-10 positioning system used in the experiment. Sources are red with blue circles indicating the additional short channels, detectors are blue, and the channels are indicated by a "#" with the corresponding channel number. In the anterior part of the head representation, sources and detectors over the frontal brain areas are seen in the positions AF8 (S2), F4 (S3), F3 (S5), AF7 (S6), and AFz (S8) and F8 (D2), AF4 (D3), AF3 (D5), F7 (D6), respectively. In the posterior part, sources and detectors over left and right parietal regions are seen positioned in CP6 (S1), P4 (S4), and CP3 (S7) and CP4 (D1), P3 (D4), and CP5 (D7), D8 is reserved for short channels

2.6 Thermal Measures of the Face

Face temperature data was acquired via an Optris *Xi*400 infrared camera (*Optris Infrared Sensing LLC, Portsmouth, USA*), with an optical resolution of 382×288 *pixels*, a temperature range from $-20\,°C$ to $900\,°C$, a thermal sensitivity of 80 mK, and a sampling rate of 80 Hz. The recorded data was organised in the form of a matrix for each timestamp, assigning a temperature value to each pixel. For analysis, the thermal image were divided into several "Regions-of-Interest" (ROI). They consist of the nasal, cheek, chin, and periorbital areas. The upper part of the forehead could not be analysed because it was covered by the fNIRS head cap. Temperature data were averaged in the corresponding ROIs for both task difficulty conditions. All data (behavioural, fNIRS, thermal) were synchronised using Lab Streaming Layer [51].

2.7 Procedure

Participants were invited to take place in front of the computer screen and were given brief instructions about the task and the types of measurements that were performed. Information about the occurrence of startle sounds was not disclosed to the participants to avoid expectations effects. Then, participants were requested to fill numerical versions of the personality and emotion regulation questionnaires (i.e., BFI-10, PSS-14, STAI state and trait, MEQ and previous 24 h psychoactive substances consumption). After that, participants were given more detailed instructions about the TNT task and they were offered to familiarise with it during a 6 min training session consisting of one 0-back and one 2-back block. Once trained, the participants were equipped with the fNIRS cap, optodes were manually adjusted on the scalp. Headphones were positioned over the fNIRS cap so that any conflict with optodes could be detected beforehand. Calibrations were made for fNIRS and the IR camera once the participant was fully equipped. Recordings were launched and the participant was invited to complete the TNT task.

During the TNT session, each participants performed a set of 14 TNT blocks, alternating between 0-back and 2-back. Half of the participants were randomly assigned to begin with 0-back while the other half started with the 2-back condition. Each of the 14 blocks contained 20 operations and lasted 60 seconds in total, which was sufficient to allow the hemodynamic and thermal responses to be produced by the task and to go back to normality before the beginning of the next block. Figure 1 shows the structure of each type of n-back blocks. The two startling stimuli and the control sound (beep) were each presented three times in a random and different order (i.e., a total of 6 startling stimuli and three control sounds were delivered). Each type of sound was randomly played during 0-back and 2-back blocks, so that each sound was necessary played during each level of difficulty. An illustration of the arrangement of blocks and startling stimuli presentation can be found in Fig. 3. To minimise possible expectation and habituation effects, a second randomisation level was used inside each of the blocks for which a sound was affected. The sounds appeared randomly in the time interval between seconds 7 and 30 after the beginning of a block. Thus, no sound was presented during the first two operations (which did not require a response in the 2-back

condition) and the block continued for at least another 30 s after the stimulus presentation, leaving enough time to observe the startle reaction and behavioural consequences.
To ensure that any effect of the startling stimuli would be captured in the performance
data, the first 6 s were free of sounds as the first two operations of the 2-back condition only require memorisation and no response. Finally, each experimental block was
followed by a 30 s rest period (i.e., 00 + 00), so that physiological parameters could go
back to their normal values before the beginning of the next block.

Once the TNT task completed, the participants were invited to fill 4 NASA TLX
questionnaires and were dedicated to the evaluation of subjective workload for each of
the experimental conditions (i.e., 0-back, 2-back, startle and no startle). Finally, more
extensive explanations were given to the participants about the goals and the means of
the protocol and the reasons of the startling sounds.

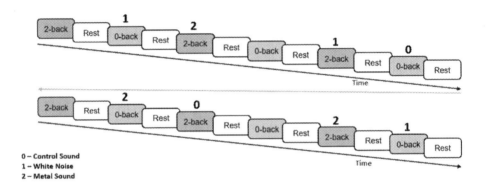

Fig. 3. Illustration of block and startling stimuli order arrangement.

3   Results

Over the 4 participants for which data have been acquired, 3 of them showed clear signs
of startle for the starting sound and no startling reactions to the control sound. Results
about performances to the TNT show possible trends that still have to be confirmed
and for which proper statistical analysis will be required once data will be acquired
for all participants. To evaluate participants' performance, the number of missed trials
(i.e., no response after two seconds) was computed and averaged for each block for
the 4 operations directly following the startle stimuli and for the equivalent periods of
time in the no-sound blocks. For these same periods of time, the percentage of correct responses and the reaction times were also computed and averaged for trials that
participants responded to. Preliminary results, as illustrated in Figs. 4, 5 and 6 show a
probable effect of the difficulty level manifesting by an increase in the number of missed
response, a decreased percentage of correct responses and increased reaction times. No
clear effect of startle sounds on the number of missed responses can be drown from the
current data, excepted for the 0-back condition during which a slight increase in missed

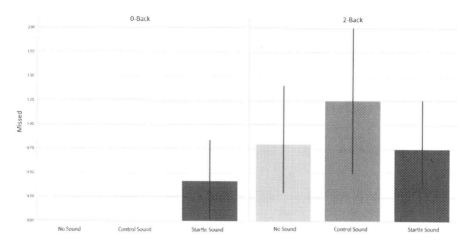

Fig. 4. Box plot of the number of missed responses according to the level of difficulty and the type of sound (i.e., no-sound vs control sound vs startle sound

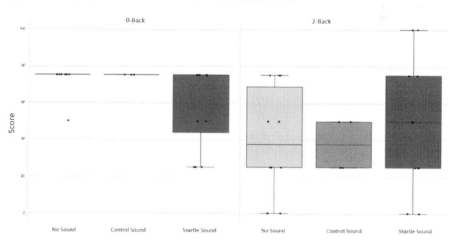

Fig. 5. Box plot of the percentage of correct responses (i.e., accuracy) according to the level of difficulty and the type of sound (i.e., no-sound vs control sound vs startle sound

response was visible. The presence of the startle sound seems to affect the percentage of correct responses only for the 0-back level of difficulty. Finally, the reaction time is affected in a contrasted way as the average reaction time increases in the 0-back condition while it decreases in the 2-back one. Note that the variability is not negligible, which implies that data from more participants needs to be collected.

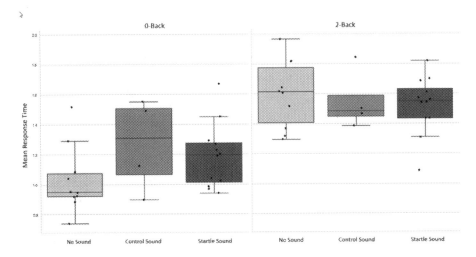

Fig. 6. Box plot of the reaction time according to the level of difficulty and the type of sound (i.e., no-sound vs control sound vs startle sound

4   Discussion

Our study confirmed the effectiveness of acoustic stimuli in inducing a startle reflex during the performance of a cognitively demanding task. Three participants out of four showed a typical and clearly visible startle response. It is noteworthy that our preliminary behavioural results indicate a decline in task performance immediately following the startle stimuli. In particular during the 0-back condition, the number of missed responses increased and the accuracy decreased following the startle sound. The results are less clear during the 2-back condition. More participants are needed to consolidate these findings. As we continue to analyse the fNIRS and thermal data, as well as correlating personality questionnaire responses with startle intensity, we expect to gain a more complete understanding of the neurophysiological and psychological dimensions of the startle reflex. We are targeting approximately 30 participants to ensure the reliability and validity of our findings. In terms of the neural mechanisms associated with the startle reflex, we expect to observe a shift in the executive control network, characterised by reduced activity following the startle reflex.

Declarations

- Funding: Agence Nationale de la recherche ANR-19-ASMA-0009
- Conflict of interest/Competing interests: Authors confirm the absence of conflicts of interests.
- Ethics approval: CER number 00011835 − 2023 − 0918 − 681
- Consent for publication: Authors provide their consent for publication

References

1. Bolivariano, G.: Rapport final West Caribbean Airways DC-9-82 (MD-82) Immatricule HK4374X Machiques, Venezuela 16 AOÛT 2005. Accident report JIAAC-9-058-2005, Ministerio del Poder Popular para Transporte y Comunicaciones (2005). https://bea.aero/docspa/2005/hk-x050816/pdf/hk-x050816.pdf. Accessed 26 Jan 2024
2. NTSB: Loss of Control on Approach Colgan Air, Inc. Operating as Continental Connection Flight 3407. Accident report NTSB/AAR-10/01 PB2010-910401, National Transportation Safety Board, 490 L'Enfant Plaza, S.W.Washington, D.C. 20594 (2010). https://www.ntsb.gov/investigations/accidentreports/reports/aar1001.pdf. Accessed 21 Jan 2024
3. Blumenthal, T.D., Goode, C.T.: The startle eyeblink response to low intensity acoustic stimuli. Psychophysiology **28**(3), 296–306 (1991). https://doi.org/10.1111/j.1469-8986.1991.tb02198.x. https://onlinelibrary.wiley.com/doi/pdf/10.1111/j.1469-8986.1991.tb02198.x. Accessed 25 Jan 2024
4. Eaton, R.C.: Neural Mechanisms of Startle Behavior. Springer, Heidelberg (2013)
5. Simons, R.C.: Boo!: Culture, Experience, and the Startle Reflex. Oxford University Press, Oxford (1996)
6. Yeomans, J.S., Frankland, P.W.: The acoustic startle reflex: neurons and connections. Brain Res. Rev. **21**(3), 301–314 (1995). https://doi.org/10.1016/0165-0173(96)00004-5. Accessed 2024-01-24
7. Martin, W.L., Murray, P.S., Bates, P.R.: The effects of startle on pilots during critical events: a case study analysis. In: Proceedings of 30th EAAP Conference: Aviation Psychology & Applied Human Factors, pp. 387–394 (2012)
8. Landis, C., Hunt, W.A.: The startle pattern. J. Mental Sci. **85**(357), 808–809 (1939). https://doi.org/10.1192/bjp.85.357.808-b. Accessed 26 Jan 2024
9. LeDoux, J.E.: The Emotional Brain: The Mysterious Underpinnings of Emotional Life, p. 384. Simon & Schuster, New York (1996)
10. Hamm, A.O.: Fear-potentiated startle. In: Wright, J.D. (ed.) International Encyclopedia of the Social & Behavioral Sciences, 2nd edn., pp. 860-867. Elsevier, Oxford (2015). https://doi.org/10.1016/B978-0-08-097086-8.55023-5. https://www.sciencedirect.com/science/article/pii/B9780080970868550235
11. Asli, O., Flaten, M.A.: In the blink of an eye: investigating the role of awareness in fear responding by measuring the latency of startle potentiation. Brain Sci. **2**(1), 61–84 (2012). https://doi.org/10.3390/brainsci2010061. Accessed 25 Jan 2024
12. Thackray, R.I.: Performance recovery following startle: a laboratory approach to the study of behavioral response to sudden aircraft emergencies: (586272011–001). American Psychological Association (1988). https://doi.org/10.1037/e586272011-001. http://doi.apa.org/get-pe-doi.cfm?doi=10.1037/e586272011-001. Accessed 03 Aug 2022
13. Lang, P.J., Bradley, M.M., Cuthbert, B.N.: Emotion, attention, and the startle reflex. Psychol. Rev. **97**(3), 377–395 (1990). https://doi.org/10.1037/0033-295X.97.3.377
14. Corr, P.J., et al.: Personality and affective modulation of the startle reflex. Pers. Individ. Differ. **19**(4), 543–553 (1995). https://doi.org/10.1016/0191-8869(95)00059-F. Accessed 25 Jan 2024
15. Blanch, A., Lucas, I., Balada, F., Blanco, E., Aluja, A.: Sex differences and personality in the modulation of the acoustic startle reflex. Physiol. Behav. **195**, 20–27 (2018). https://doi.org/10.1016/j.physbeh.2018.07.020. Accessed 25 Jan 2024
16. Hamm, A.O., Cuthbert, B.N., Globisch, J., Vaitl, D.: Fear and the startle reflex: Blink modulation and autonomic response patterns in animal and mutilation fearful subjects. Psychophysiology **34**(1), 97–107 (1997) https://doi.org/10.1111/j.1469-8986.1997.tb02420.x. https://onlinelibrary.wiley.com/doi/pdf/10.1111/j.1469-8986.1997.tb02420.x. Accessed 26 Jan 2024

17. Oskarsson, S., Patrick, C.J., Siponen, R., Bertoldi, B.M., Evans, B., Tuvblad, C.: The startle reflex as an indicator of psychopathic personality from childhood to adulthood: a systematic review. Acta Psychologica **220**, 103427 (2021). https://doi.org/10.1016/j.actpsy.2021.103427. Accessed 25 Jan 2024

18. Grillon, C., Baas, J.: A review of the modulation of the startle reflex by affective states and its application in psychiatry. Clin. Neurophysiol. **114**(9), 1557–1579 (2003). https://doi.org/10.1016/S1388-2457(03)00202-5. Accessed 25 Jan 2024

19. Corbetta, M., Shulman, G.L.: Control of goal-directed and stimulus-driven attention in the brain. Nat. Rev. Neurosci. **3**(3), 201–215 (2002). https://doi.org/10.1038/nrn755. Accessed 29 Jan 2024

20. Niendam, T.A., Laird, A.R., Ray, K.L., Dean, Y.M., Glahn, D.C., Carter, C.S.: Metaanalytic evidence for a superordinate cognitive control network subserving diverse executive functions. Cogn. Affect. Behav. Neurosci. **12**(2), 241–268 (2012). https://doi.org/10.3758/s13415-011-0083-5. Accessed 26 Jan 2024

21. Shen, K.-K., et al.: Structural core of the executive control network: A high angular resolution diffusion MRI study. Human Brain Mapp. **41**(5), 1226–1236 (2020). https://doi.org/10.1002/hbm.24870. https://onlinelibrary.wiley.com/doi/pdf/10.1002/hbm.24870. Accessed 26 Jan 2024

22. Causse, M., et al.: Facing successfully high mental workload and stressors: an fMRI study. Hum. Brain Mapp. **43**(3), 1–21 (2021). https://doi.org/10.1002/hbm.25703. Accessed 29 Jan 2024

23. Hermans, E.J., Henckens, M.J.A.G., Joëls, M., Fernández, G.: Dynamic adaptation of large-scale brain networks in response to acute stressors. Trends Neurosci. **37**(6), 304–314 (2014). https://doi.org/10.1016/j.tins.2014.03.006. Accessed 26 Jan 2024

24. Causse, M., Mouratille, D., Rouillard, Y., El Yagoubi, R., Matton, N., Hidalgo, A.: How a pilot's brain copes with stress and mental load? insights from the executive control network, Rochester, NY (2023). https://doi.org/10.2139/ssrn.4392279. https://papers.ssrn.com/abstract=4392279 Accessed 29 Jan 2024

25. Arnsten, A.F.T.: Stress signalling pathways that impair prefrontal cortex structure and function. Nat. Rev. Neurosci. **10**(6), 410–422 (2009). https://doi.org/10.1038/nrn2648. Accessed 29 Jan 2024

26. Hermans, E.J., et al.: Stress-related noradrenergic activity prompts large-scale neural network reconfiguration. Science **334**(6059), 1151–1153 (2011). https://doi.org/10.1126/science.1209603. Accessed 29 Jan 2024

27. Shastri, D., Merla, A., Tsiamyrtzis, P., Pavlidis, I.: Imaging facial signs of neurophysiological responses. IEEE Trans. Biomed. Eng. **56**(2), 477–484 (2009). https://doi.org/10.1109/TBME.2008.2003265. Accessed 30 Jan 2024

28. Dzedzickis, A., Kaklauskas, A., Bucinskas, V.: Human emotion recognition: review of sensors and methods. Sensors **20**(3), 592 (2020). https://doi.org/10.3390/s20030592. Accessed 30 Jan 2024

29. Stemberger, J., Allison, R.S., Schnell, T.: Thermal imaging as a way to classify cognitive workload. In: 2010 Canadian Conference on Computer and Robot Vision, pp. 231–238 (2010). https://doi.org/10.1109/CRV.2010.37. https://ieeexplore.ieee.org/abstract/document/5479180. Accessed 30 Jan 2024

30. Hassoumi, A., Peysakhovich, V., Coz, A.L., Hurter, C., Causse, M.: Thermal imaging of the face: mental workload detection in flight simulator. In: Neuroergonomics and Cognitive Engineering, vol. 42. AHFE Open Access (2022). https://doi.org/10.54941/ahfe1001822. https://openaccess.cms-conferences.org/publications/book/978-1-958651-18-6/article/978-1-958651-18-610. ISSN: 27710718 Issue: 42. Accessed 30 Jan 2024

31. Pavlidis, I., Levine, J., Baukol, P.: Thermal imaging for anxiety detection. In: Proceedings IEEE Workshop on Computer Vision Beyond the Visible Spectrum: Methods and Applications (Cat. No.PR00640), pp. 104–109 (2000). https://doi.org/10.1109/CVBVS.2000.855255. https://ieeexplore.ieee.org/abstract/document/855255. Accessed 30 Jan 2024

32. Levine, J.A., Pavlidis, I., Cooper, M.: The face of fear. Lancet **357**(9270), 1757 (2001). https://doi.org/10.1016/S0140-6736(00)04936-9. Accessed 30 Jan 2024

33. Pavlidis, I., Levine, J.: Thermal image analysis for polygraph testing. IEEE Eng. Med. Biol. Maga. **21**(6), 56–64 (2002). https://doi.org/10.1109/MEMB.2002.1175139. Accessed 30 Jan 2024

34. Gane, L., Power, S., Kushki, A., Chau, T.: Thermal imaging of the periorbital regions during the presentation of an auditory startle stimulus. PLoS ONE **6**(11), 27268 (2011). https://doi.org/10.1371/journal.pone.0027268. Accessed 29 Jan 2024

35. Lohn, S. V.: Evaluating Physiological Responses during the Startle Response Using Thermal-Sensitive Goggles. PhD thesis, Northcentral University (2011). https://www.proquest.com/openview/d86955a543aaa96eb2442b226e6ec11f/1?cbl=18750&pq-origsite=gscholar&parentSessionId=6fyCvPL287RClxkYFjMPw2Z1FuCf2r2BO7tceabyXRw%3D. Accessed 30 Jan 2024

36. Hong, K., et al.: Detection and classification of stress using thermal imaging technique. In: Optics and Photonics for Counterterrorism and Crime Fighting, vol. 7486, pp. 140–148. SPIE (2009). https://doi.org/10.1117/12.830496. https://www.spiedigitallibrary.org/conferenceproceedings-of-spie/7486/74860I/Detection-and-classification-of-stress-usingthermal-imaging-technique/10.1117/12.830496.full. Accessed 30 Jan 2024

37. Durantin, G., Gagnon, J.-F., Tremblay, S., Dehais, F.: Using near infrared spectroscopy and heart rate variability to detect mental overload. Behav. Brain Res. **259**, 16–23 (2014). https://doi.org/10.1016/j.bbr.2013.10.042. Accessed 30 Jan 2024

38. Causse, M., Chua, Z., Peysakhovich, V., Del Campo, N., Matton, N.: Mental workload and neural efficiency quantified in the prefrontal cortex using fNIRS. Sci. Rep. **7**(1), 5222 (2017). https://doi.org/10.1038/s41598-017-05378-x. Accessed 30 Jan 2024

39. Causse, M., Chua, Z.K., Rémy, F.: Influences of age, mental workload, and flight experience on cognitive performance and prefrontal activity in private pilots: a fNIRS study. Sci. Rep. **9**(1), 7688 (2019). https://doi.org/10.1038/s41598-019-44082-w. Accessed 30 Jan 2024

40. Cui, X., Bray, S., Bryant, D.M., Glover, G.H., Reiss, A.L.: A quantitative comparison of NIRS and fMRI across multiple cognitive tasks. Neuroimage **54**(4), 2808–2821 (2011). https://doi.org/10.1016/j.neuroimage.2010.10.069. Accessed 2024-01-30

41. Santosa, H., Fishburn, F., Zhai, X., Huppert, T.J.: Investigation of the sensitivityspecificity of canonical- and deconvolution-based linear models in evoked functional near-infrared spectroscopy. Neurophotonics **6**(2), 025009 (2019). https://doi.org/10.1117/1.NPh.6.2.025009. Accessed 30 Jan 2024

42. Klonsky, E.D., Victor, S.E., Hibbert, A.S., Hajcak, G.: The multidimensional emotion questionnaire (MEQ): rationale and initial psychometric properties. J. Psychopathol. Behav. Assess. **41**(3), 409–424 (2019). https://doi.org/10.1007/s10862-019-09741-2. Accessed 31 Jan 2024

43. Courtois, R., et al.: Validation franc, aise du Big Five Inventory 'a 10 items (BFI-10). L'Encéphale **46**(6), 455–462 (2020) https://doi.org/10.1016/j.encep.2020.02.006. Accessed 31 Jan 2024

44. Spielberger, C.D.: State-trait anxiety inventory for adults. American Psychological Association (2012). https://doi.org/10.1037/t06496-000. http://doi.apa.org/getdoi.cfm?doi=10.1037/t06496-000. Accessed 31 Jan 2024

45. Cohen, S., Kamarck, T., Mermelstein, R.: A global measure of perceived stress. J. Health Soc. Behav. **24**(4), 385–396 (1983) https://doi.org/10.2307/2136404. Accessed 31 Jan 2024

46. Mandrick, K., Peysakhovich, V., Rémy, F., Lepron, E., Causse, M.: Neural and psychophysiological correlates of human performance under stress and high mental workload. Biol. Psychol. **121**, 62–73 (2016). https://doi.org/10.1016/j.biopsycho.2016.10.002. Accessed 31 Jan 2024

47. Causse, M., Peysakhovich, V., Mandrick, K.: Eliciting sustained mental effort using the toulouse N-back task: prefrontal cortex and pupillary responses. In: Hale, K.S., Stanney, K.M. (eds.) Advances in Neuroergonomics and Cognitive Engineering. Advances in Intelligent Systems and Computing, pp. 185–193. Springer, Cham (2017). https://doi.org/10.1007/978-3-319-41691-5_16

48. Brainard, D.H.: The psychophysics toolbox. Spat. Vision **10**(4), 433–436 (1997). https://doi.org/10.1163/156856897X00357. Accessed 30 Jan 2024

49. Pelli, D.G.: The VideoToolbox software for visual psychophysics: transforming numbers into movies. Spat. Vision **10**(4), 437–442 (1997). https://doi.org/10.1163/156856897x00366. Accessed 30 Jan 2024

50. Kleiner, M., Brainard, D., Pelli, D., Ingling, A., Murray, R., Broussard, C.: What's new in psychtoolbox-3. Perception **36**(14), 1–16 (2007)

51. Kothe, C.: Labstreaminglayer. Swartz Center for Computational Neuroscience. originaldate: 2018-02-28T10:50:12Z (2013). https://github.com/sccn/labstreaminglayer Accessed 31 Jan 2024

A Measurement Tool of Airline Transport Pilot's Psychological Competency and Its Application

Ruiyuan Hong⏺, Qiyu Yang⏺, and Lei Wang$^{(\boxtimes)}$⏺

College of Safety Science and Engineering, Civil Aviation University of China, Tianjin, China
wanglei0564@hotmail.com

Abstract. Certain inherent psychological risks in pilots pose challenges that are difficult to tackle using low-cost flight training. Evaluating the psychological competence of pilots or aspiring flight students is crucial, and this study introduces a pilot's psychological competency measurement tool and its application. The measurement framework and method for evaluating airline transport pilot's psychological competency were developed based on the professional characteristics of airline transport pilots and the requirements of implementing pilots' Professionalism Lifecycle Management (PLM) system proposed by the Civil Aviation Administration of China (CAAC). The evaluation tool, grounded in occupational adaptability psychology and mental health considerations, focused on six dimensions: general cognitive ability, operational and professional ability, social-interpersonal ability, personality traits and attitude, mental quality, and mental state. To measure general cognitive ability and operational and professional ability, a combination of flight control sticks, a computer, and a tablet was employed. Social-interpersonal ability, personality traits and attitude, mental quality, and mental state were assessed using a tablet. Collaborating with various airlines and flight academies, the data collection phase was executed in March, July, and October of 2023. Robust and valid psychological competency data were collected from a diverse pool, including 22 airline pilots (average age 27.23 ± 3.32 years), 169 ab initio pilots (average age 24.57 ± 1.52 years), and 130 flight students (average age 22.38 ± 0.791 years). The findings from this comprehensive analysis illuminated some distinctions among ab initio pilots, airline pilots, and flight students. Notably, flight students showcased exceptional performance in the dimension of general cognitive abilities, demonstrating their cognitive prowess. On the other hand, airline pilots exhibited superior skills in flight operational capabilities, highlighting their expertise in psychomotor skills. However, a noteworthy concern emerged regarding flight students, revealing a higher prevalence of personality disorders and dangerous attitudes. Additionally, flight students exhibited a more intense negative mental health state, raising critical considerations about their overall psychological well-being. In contrast, airline pilots and ab initio pilots displayed more positive psychological health overall. In conclusion, this research initiative goes beyond the mere introduction of a valuable psychological competency measurement tool; it delves into a comprehensive analysis of its practical application. The collaborative endeavors with airlines and flight academies, paired with the meticulous collection and analysis of data, not only vividly showcase the user-friendliness and practical applicability of the tool but also significantly contribute to the ongoing discourse on the optimization of pilot training programs.

© The Author(s), under exclusive license to Springer Nature Switzerland AG 2024
D. Harris and W.-C. Li (Eds.): HCII 2024, LNAI 14692, pp. 51–60, 2024.
https://doi.org/10.1007/978-3-031-60728-8_5

Keywords: Psychological Competency · Measurement Method · Pilot Selection

1 Introduction

1.1 Background of Research

Safety plays a crucial role in the development of the civil aviation industry. Human error has long been considered a major cause of unsafe events. It was found that aircraft handling (37%) had the highest percentage of causal factors in undesired aircraft states [1]." Humans have a limited operational envelope and require specific information to do their job. They are limited in memory, endurance, and other abilities such as computation [2]. If the human is required to perform outside of this envelope or without sufficient information, they will fail [3]. Hence, pilots need to be equipped with high psychological competency to ensure civil aviation safety. Regarding the ability pilots need to be equipped, the International Civil Aviation Organization (ICAO) proposed eight categories of pilot capabilities (application of procedures and compliance with regulations, communication, flight path management, flight path management control, leadership and teamwork, problem-solving and decision-making, situation awareness and management of information, workload management) [4]. European Aviation Safety Agency (EASA) listed "knowledge" as the ninth competency [5]. Worldwide, psychological testing is becoming a prerequisite for selecting and training pilots [6]. EASA suggested that psychological assessments cover cognitive abilities, personality traits, operational and professional competencies, and social competencies following the crew resource management principles [5]. Six categories—English language proficiency, basic ability, composite abilities, operational abilities, social-interpersonal abilities, and personality traits—were put forth in the Guidance Material and Best Practices for Pilot Aptitude Testing (PAT) created by the International Air Transport Association [7]. The Professionalism Lifecycle Management System (PLM) was put forth by the Civil Aviation Administration of China (CAAC) in 2020 as a recommended course of action to enhance the post-competency of Chinese civil aviation pilots, and pilot competency and mental health are two essential parts in psychological competency dimension [4]. Currently, numerous studies have been conducted to address issues related to pilot competency indicators and assessment methods. However, due to the continuous advancement of technology, the demands on pilot capabilities also need to advance with the times. Ongoing exploration and research are essential to keep pace with these changes.

Combining with professional characteristics of airline transport pilots and the requirements of PLM, we established a measurement framework, specifying the measurement metrics [8]. In that study, a floating iceberg model of pilots' psychological competence was proposed. In the iceberg model, the observable performance and a portion of the mental health state of pilots are akin to the visible part of an iceberg floating on the water's surface. Beneath the surface lie concealed aspects, encompassing the pilots' professional adaptability (based on professional competence, cognitive abilities, personality traits, and social competence) and another segment of their mental health status. The state of the iceberg is susceptible to external influences, including organizational culture and work environment. The volume of the iceberg symbolizes an individual's overall psychological energy, while a stronger cohesiveness indicates higher levels of occupational adaptability psychology. The buoyancy of the iceberg reflects the stability of the pilots' mental health status, with weaker buoyancy suggesting more stability. Within each level of the iceberg model, there are small pathways. Flow factors move through these pathways, causing changes in the iceberg's form. The iceberg model indicates that mental health fluctuates between the surface and beneath the water, displaying variability. A hierarchical quality-state model has been established to elucidate this relationship [9]. Mental health can be divided into mental quality and mental state. Mental quality forms the foundation of individual mental health and tends to be more implicit and relatively static. On the other hand, mental state tends to be more explicit and relatively dynamic. The mental state represents the outward manifestations of an individual's mental health condition, resulting from the interaction between individual mental quality and external environmental factors. There is a mutual influence between the two, giving rise to dynamic changes in individual mental health. Specifically, when individuals encounter negative influencing factors (such as adverse life events) or positive influencing factors (such as social support), these environmental factors initially impact the individual's mental quality, leading to changes in the individual's mental state. A long-term sustained mental state, in turn, influences and shapes the individual's mental quality. Under the guidance of the iceberg model, based on literature review and analysis in the field of aviation psychology, and combined with PLM system requirements, pilots' professional adaptability indices were confirmed. Including 4 dimensions: general cognitive ability, operational and professional ability, social-interpersonal ability, and personality traits and attitude [8]. Meanwhile, combined with the quality-state model, pilots' mental health indices consisted of mental quality and mental state. Hence, the pilot's psychological competency would focus on both professional adaptability and mental health, with 6 indices.

Considering the need for pilot training and selection, several research have looked at the structure of basic cognitive abilities and flight ability evaluation. However, there is a lack of tools to measure and integrate the data on both the ability, personality, and mental health at the same time. Wang et al. [10] provided a complete process and algorithm for a psychological competency evaluation. Based on the process and algorithm, a pilot's psychological competency measurement tool was designed and developed with supporting software and hardware. The evaluation tool, grounded in occupational adaptability psychology and mental health considerations, focused on six dimensions: general cognitive ability, operational and professional ability, social-interpersonal ability, personality traits and attitude, mental quality, and mental state. It has certain applicability and can be widely applied.

1.2   Research Aim

Constantly updating and improvement of pilots' selection and training methods will be almost inevitable, considering the importance of human factors in maintaining flight safety and automatization of operational circumstances of transport aircraft. Professional adaptability evaluation has the potential to enable pilots to be more efficient and adaptive for flight operations in combination with mental health evaluation. This study applied a pilot's psychological competency measurement tool, combined professional adaptability with mental health, to comprehensively evaluate pilots' psychological competency. It mainly aims to seek to validate the applicability of the assessment tool employed by the pilots. Simultaneously, it investigates the differences in psychological competency among flight students, ab initio pilots, and airline pilots.

2 Methods

2.1 Participants

Collaborating with various airlines and flight academies, the data collection phase was executed in March, July, and October of 2023. Robust and valid psychological competency data were collected from a diverse pool, including 22 airline pilots (average age 27.23 ± 3.32 years), 169 ab initio pilots (average age 24.57 ± 1.52 years), and 130 flight students (average age 22.38 ± 0.79 years). Due to private reasons, three flight students and 1 ab initio pilot were unable to complete the psychomotor ability assessment and mental health evaluation, respectively. Consequently, these three flight students' scores for operational and professional ability and the ab initio pilot's scores for mental health and their overall performance were not included in the analysis.

2.2 Measures

Basic information(age, flight hours, aircraft type, and flight grade) and psychological competency data(general cognitive ability, operational and professional ability, social-interpersonal ability, personality traits and attitude, mental state, and mental quality) of pilots would be collected. A higher score in a particular module indicates better performance by the participant in that specific module.

General Cognitive Ability. The cognitive ability that pilots generally need to complete all mental activities is called general cognitive ability in this study, that is, the ability of individuals to process complex information, including reaction ability, memory ability, attention ability, judgment ability, decision-making ability, etc.

Operational and Professional Ability. To ensure the smooth takeoff and landing of a flight, pilots must make accurate judgments and decisions regarding the aircraft's flight status, trajectory direction, and deviation angles. They are required to execute corresponding tasks throughout the entire flight process, which occurs in a three-dimensional space. The nature of this work places a high demand on a pilot's spatial awareness and psychomotor skills. Therefore, the assessment of flight operational and professional abilities will primarily focus on evaluating abilities such as spatial orientation ability, spatial representation ability, hand-eye coordination ability, bimanual coordination ability, etc.

Social-Interpersonal Ability. Social-interpersonal ability includes teamwork ability and communication ability, which mainly assess the accuracy of information understanding, the effectiveness of expression, and the intention and performance of the pilot to achieve the common goal in interpersonal interaction.

Personality Traits and Attitude. Personality traits and attitude module not only focuses on the personality components and possible personality disorders of pilots but also analyzes the risky personality and dangerous attitudes of pilots.

Mental State. Psychological states can be divided into negative states and positive states. Negative states are evaluated from the perspectives of anxiety, depression, somatization, obsessive symptoms, interpersonal sensitivity, hostility, self-injury, suicidal tendencies, alcohol and drug dependence, etc. Meanwhile, the positive state mainly measured the subjective well-being of pilots.

Mental Quality. Self-orientation and adaptive ability are selected as the evaluation dimensions of psychological quality. Self-orientation mainly involves individual self-evaluation, self-control, and other personality elements, while adaptive ability mainly refers to the relevant ability of an individual to adapt to the social or external environment. These two dimensions can better fit with the connotation of mental health and can reflect the psychological quality of an individual more comprehensively.

2.3 Apparatus

A pilot's psychological competency measurement tool was used to collect data. As shown in Fig. 1, the tool consists of a combination of 5 modules that assess 6 indices (general cognitive ability, operational and professional ability, social-interpersonal ability, personality traits and attitude, mental state, and mental quality), mental state and mental quality are combined as one module. Most of the tests can be done on a tablet, to efficiently evaluate pilots' psychomotor ability (including operational and professional ability), a combination of flight control sticks and a computer was employed.

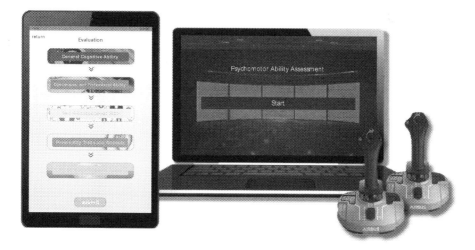

Fig. 1. Measurement tool of psychological competency

2.4 Procedure

Before the experiment, the experimental procedures were explained to pilots, and they signed the informed consent form and the ethical review form for the scientific experiment to allow their data to be used for academic research. Subsequently, the basic information of the pilots (such as flight hours, aircraft type, flight grade, etc.) was investigated. After the participants reported that they were ready, the experiment officially began. The pilot is required to complete evaluations of general cognitive ability, operational and professional ability, social-interpersonal ability, personality traits and attitude, mental state, and mental quality in order. For psychomotor ability evaluation, to ensure pilots could follow the rules of games on the computer, we set a 3-min-long practice session for each game.

2.5 Data Analysis

Due to variations in the score ranges across different modules, rendering direct comparisons challenging, normalization was applied to standardize scores within each module. We categorized the data into three groups based on their identity (Airline Pilot, Ab initio Pilot, and Flight Student), and tested descriptive data concerning different modules.

3 Results

3.1 Descriptive Analysis

Based on Table 1 and Fig. 2, it is evident that starting with the dimension of professional adaptability, flight students exhibit the highest performance in general cognitive ability, while airline pilots demonstrate the lowest performance. In terms of operational and professional ability, airline pilots perform the best, while ab initio pilots and flight students show relatively lower performance. Regarding social-interpersonal ability, flight students exhibit the strongest capabilities, followed closely by airline pilots and ab initio pilots. Finally, in the personality traits and attitude module, airline pilots and ab initio pilots demonstrate similar scores, with flight students scoring the lowest.

From the perspective of mental health, flight students have relatively lower scores in both mental state and mental quality, while airline pilots and ab initio pilots show similar performance in this dimension.

Table 1. The scores for different modules from different groups

Module	Group	N	Mean	SD
General Cognitive Ability	Airline Pilot	22	0.52	0.13
	Ab Initio Pilot	169	0.59	0.14
	Flight Student	130	0.63	0.18
Operational and Professional Ability	Airline Pilot	22	0.59	0.06
	Ab Initio Pilot	169	0.57	0.07
	Flight Student	127	0.57	0.120
Social-interpersonal Ability	Airline Pilot	22	0.22	0.13
	Ab Initio Pilot	169	0.28	0.21
	Flight Student	130	0.46	0.26
Personality Traits and Attitude	Airline Pilot	22	0.53	0.09
	Ab Initio Pilot	169	0.53	0.12
	Flight Student	130	0.51	0.17
Mental State	Airline Pilot	22	0.40	0.06
	Ab Initio Pilot	168	0.40	0.06
	Flight Student	130	0.39	0.10
Mental Quality	Airline Pilot	22	0.60	0.12
	Ab Initio Pilot	168	0.60	0.15
	Flight Student	130	0.57	0.18
Overall	Airline Pilot	22	0.52	0.05
	Ab Initio Pilot	168	0.54	0.08
	Flight Student	127	0.52	0.13

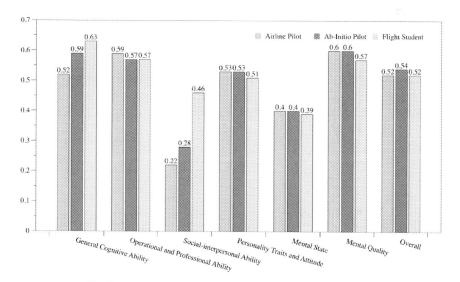

Fig. 2. The scores for different modules from different groups

4   Discussion

The main aim of the present study was to examine the availability of a pilot's psychological competency measurement tool. Meanwhile, This study also analyzed the scores for different modules in a pilot's psychological competency measurement tool from three groups (airline pilot, ab initio pilot, and flight student). The research showed that the tool is available and easy to use, besides, it can be used for a wide range of psychological competency assessments. Meanwhile, combined with the data analysis, airline pilots scored the highest in the operational and professional evaluation, while flight students and ab initio pilots fared nearly the same. Airlines have the highest operational and professional performance, while ab initio pilots and flight students perform at comparatively lower levels. Flight students are the most adept at social-interpersonal skills, closely followed by airline pilots and ab initio pilots. Besides, flight students receive the lowest results in the personality traits and attitude module, whereas airline pilots and ab initio pilots exhibit comparable scores. Ultimately, regarding mental health, airline pilots and ab initio pilots perform similarly in this area, however, flight students had comparatively lower ratings in both mental state and mental quality.

4.1   Availability Analysis

This tool has ease of use and quite an acceptance. On the one hand, this tool has been tested in many airlines and flight academies, except for the cases where it could not be completed due to human reasons, in other cases, multi-source data (audio data, behavioral data, questionnaire data, etc.) are accurately and effectively stored in the system background. At the same time, most pilots can complete the tests in turn under the guidance of the system instructions and would not misunderstand questions or rules. Besides, the application of this tool in different groups can effectively find some phenomena or problems existing in single or multiple groups, which could provide ideas for the further development of pilot selection and training programs.

4.2   Psychological Competency Comparison Among Groups

Flight students performed best in general cognitive ability and social-interpersonal ability, while airline pilots performed the least. This may be affected by age, with the average age of airline pilots, ab initio pilots, and flight students decreasing in turn. Some studies have shown that age affects pilots' cognitive abilities. Tucker-Drob noted that most cognitive abilities increase in level during childhood development, peak during late adolescence/early adulthood, and decrease in level across adulthood [11]. Causse, et al. noted that the performance of older relative to younger pilots was impaired in cognitive performance [12]. Liang and Sun investigated pilots' cognitive abilities and found a negative effect of age on cognitive ability [13]. Deary and Der illustrated that simple and choice reaction times become slower and more variable with age [14]. Meanwhile, with typical aging, communication skills change subtly at least in part because of changes in physical health, depression, and cognitive decline [15].

Airline pilots got the highest score in the operational and professional evaluation, while ab initio pilots and flight students performed about the same. Flight experience might contribute to this result. Ebbatson, et al. found that recent flying experience would positively affect pilots' manual flying skills [16]. Bazargan and Guzhva, meanwhile, noted that more experienced pilots were less likely to be involved in an accident caused by pilot error [17]. You, et al. found that flight experience had a significantly positive effect on safety operation behavior [18]. That is, due to the lack of experience operating transport aircraft, the operational and professional abilities of ab initio pilots and flight students might be inferior to those of airline pilots.

Flight students scored the lowest in the personality traits and attitude module, mental state module, and mental quality module. This suggests that flight students' mental health is worse, and they might suffer from greater personality disorders. One possible reason is stress. On the one hand, Kirschner, et al. illustrated that upper-class flight students would perceive lower pressure, and would use different methods to deal with stress levels than first-year students [19]. Pilots, compared with flight students, would be more mature to tackle difficulties, and more familiar with the flight environment. Therefore, their scores are higher than flight students in the relevant module. On the other hand, Görlich and Stadelmann noted that employees of airlines showed significant positive correlations between fear of job loss with depression, anxiety, and stress during COVID-19 [20]. Airline pilots and ab initio pilots have been hired, but flight students still need to face employment pressure and study pressure, especially because their study efficiency and employment rate might be disturbed by that epidemic. Hence, they might worry about whether their company would employ them, which might cause worse mental health and stronger personality disorder. Stress may be just one cause, there are many other causes that we need to study further. The poor mental health of pilots will affect pilots' career development and flight safety. Hence it is essential to be concerned about the mental health issues of flight students.

5   Conclusion

Research findings suggest that the pilot psychological competency measurement tool is user-friendliness and practical applicability. Meanwhile, by collaborating with airlines and flight academies, and analyzing collected data, we found the differences in pilot psychological competency, which might contribute to the ongoing discourse on the optimization of pilot training programs.

Acknowledgments. We would like to acknowledge financial support from the Civil Aviation Safety Capacity Building Project (Grant 2022231).

References

1. International Air Transport Association: 2021 Safety Report. International Air Transport Association, Montreal, p. 208 (2022)
2. Baddeley, A.: Human Memory: Theory and Practice, revised edn. Allyn and Bacon, Boston (1998)
3. Schutte, P.C., Goodrich, K.H., Cox, D.E., et al.: The naturalistic flight deck system: an integrated system concept for improved single-pilot operations (2007)

4. Civil Aviation Administration of China (CAAC): Roadmap for the Construction and Implementation of the Airline Transport Pilots Professionalism Lifecycle Management System in China (2020). (in Chinese)
5. European Aviation Safety Agency (EASA): AMC1 CAT. GEN. MPA. 175 (b) Endangering Safety. Annex III to ED Decision 2018/012/R (2018)
6. Bor, R., Eriksen, C., Hubbard, T., King, R.E. (eds.): Pilot Selection Psychological Principles and Practice. CRC Press, London (2019)
7. International Air Transport Association (IATA): Pilot Aptitude Testing, Guidance Material and Best Practices, 3rd edn. (2019)
8. Zhang, M., Wang, L., Zou, Y., Peng, J., Cai, Y., Li, S.: Preliminary research on evaluation index of professional adaptability for airline transport pilot. In: Harris, D., Li, W.C. (eds.) HCII 2022. LNCS, vol. 13307, pp. 473–487. Springer, Cham (2022). https://doi.org/10.1007/978-3-031-06086-1_37
9. Wang, L., Zou, T., Zhang, M., et al.: Construction of evaluation index system of airline pilots' mental health based on quality-state dual level model. J. Nanjing Univ. Aeronaut. Astronaut. (Soc. Sci.) 25(04), 96–104 (2023)
10. Wang, L., Peng, J., Zou, Y., Zhang, M., Li, D.: A measurement framework and method on airline transport pilot's psychological competency. In: Harris, D., Li, W.C. (eds.) HCII 2023. LNCS, vol. 14017, pp. 276-285. Springer, Cham (2023). https://doi.org/10.1007/978-3-031-35392-5_22
11. Tucker-Drob, E.M.: Differentiation of cognitive abilities across the life span. Dev. Psychol. 45(4), 1097–1118 (2009)
12. Causse, M., Chua, Z.K., Rémy, F.: Influences of age, mental workload, and flight experience on cognitive performance and prefrontal activity in private pilots: a FNIRS study. Sci. Rep. 9(1), 7688 (2019)
13. Liang, W., Sun, R.: Investigation and analysis on cognitive ability of airline pilots. J. Saf. Sci. Technol. 8(8), 106–110 (2012). (in Chinese)
14. Deary, I.J., Der, G.: Reaction time, age, and cognitive ability: longitudinal findings from age 16 to 63 years in representative population samples. Aging Neuropsychol. Cognit. 12(2), 187–215 (2005)
15. Yorkston, K.M., Bourgeois, M.S., Baylor, C.R.: Communication and aging. Phys. Med. Rehabil. Clin. 21(2), 309–319 (2010)
16. Ebbatson, M., Harris, D., Huddlestone, J., et al.: The relationship between manual handling performance and recent flying experience in air transport pilots. Ergonomics 53(2), 268–277 (2010)
17. Bazargan, M., Guzhva, V.S.: Impact of gender, age and experience of pilots on general aviation accidents. Accid. Anal. Prev. 43(3), 962–970 (2011)
18. You, X., Ji, M., Han, H.: The effects of risk perception and flight experience on airline pilots' locus of control with regard to safety operation behaviors. Accid. Anal. Prev. 57C, 131–139 (2013)
19. Kirschner, J., Young, J., Fanjoy, R.: Stress and coping as a function of experience level in collegiate flight students. J. Aviat. Technol. Eng. 3(2), 14 (2014)
20. Görlich, Y., Stadelmann, D.: Mental health of flying cabin crews: depression, anxiety, and stress before and during the COVID-19 pandemic. Front. Psychol. 11, 581496 (2020)

A Method for Estimating Human Respiratory Rate and Heart Rate Using Sparse Spectrum Analysis

Xiaoguang Lu, Chenhao Suo, Xiao Ma, and Zhe Zhang(✉)

College of Electronic Information and Automation, Civil Aviation University of China,
Tianjin 300300, China
cauc_2012@163.com

Abstract. Monitoring human health conditions has always been a significant concern, especially in the operational safety industry, such as civil aviation. Traditional contact-based methods can accurately measure human heartbeat and other vital sign information but have certain limitations for the users have to wear devices or sensors. Therefore, research has recently been increasingly attracted to non-contact methods such as optical cameras, infrared thermography, and millimeter wave radar. This paper uses Linear Frequency Modulated Continuous Wave (FMCW) mm-wave radar for non-contact measurement of vital signs. Considering the time-varying and frequency-domain sparse characteristics of vital sign signals and the low-sampling number limitation that will be faced in realistic scenarios, the Sparse Iterative Covariance-based Estimation (SPICE) is utilized to estimate the vital sign signals. The SPICE method demonstrated outstanding performance compared to the non-sparsity methods, including Fast Fourier Transform (FFT) or Chirp Z-Transform (CZT), for estimating the human respiratory and heart rates accurately in simulations and experiments, especially under short sampling time and low-sampling number conditions.

Keywords: Vital Signs Monitoring · FMCW Mm-wave Radar · Sparse Spectrum Analysis · SPICE

1 Introduction

Common vital signs detection methods in the medical field include electrocardiograph (ECG) [1] and photoplethysmography (PPG) [2], etc. However, these contact detection methods are not applicable in some exceptional cases: the presence of burns, infectious diseases, and psychiatric disorders in the person being measured. Millimeter-wave radar is a non-contact measurement method with high detection accuracy, and good penetration depth for clothes [3, 4]. In recent years, radar has become an active research field in vital signs detection, especially for respiratory and heartbeat rates estimation [5–7], in various application scenarios, including sleep monitoring of adults and newborns [8, 9], infant and child monitoring [10], human fall detection [11, 12], and detection of vital signs in post-earthquake rubble [13].

© The Author(s), under exclusive license to Springer Nature Switzerland AG 2024
D. Harris and W.-C. Li (Eds.): HCII 2024, LNAI 14692, pp. 61–78, 2024.
https://doi.org/10.1007/978-3-031-60728-8_6

In 1971, Caro et al. of the Royal School of Mines first applied radar to detect respiratory heartbeat signals in the biomedical field [14]. In 1980, Frank's team at the University of Sheffield successfully measured the specific parameters of children's respiratory heartbeat using radar technology [15]. In 2011, Zeng et al. utilized millimeter-wave radar to extract the characteristics of periodic motion features successfully through classical signal processing methods, such as the Fourier Transform and time-frequency analysis [16]. However, the classical Fourier Transform method was deficient in estimation accuracy. In 2014, Hu Wei et al. designed a Doppler radar non-contact vital signs detection system to accurately measure heart respiratory rates using short-time Fourier Transform and spectral interpolation [17]. However, since the human respiratory heartbeat fluctuates from time to time, determining a suitable window length for the STFT method is challenging, and the frequency resolution is affected by the selected time window. In 2022, Pan Haipeng et al. introduced a spectrum refinement algorithm based on the Chirp Z-Transform (CZT) for estimating the real-time heart rate, which realizes a fast and accurate estimation of the heart rate and solves the problem of the lack of spectral resolution under a short time window [18]. However, this method is highly dependent on the number of sampling numbers of the signal.

With the development of sparse signal representation and compressed perception, the problems of insufficient spectral resolution and high sampling numbers requirements of traditional spectral estimation methods have been solved [19]. Most sparse estimation methods require choosing the appropriate hyper-parameters in the trade-off between data fitting and sparsity, which is generally a challenging step and often relies on experience or extensive testing. In contrast, there is a kind of sparse estimation methods that only require the parameters to be estimated to satisfy the weak assumption of sparsity to achieve parameter estimation, such as the Sparse Iterative Covariance-based Estimation (SPICE) method based on a weighted covariance fitting criterion proposed by Stoica et al. in 2011 [20–22]. This method does not need to select hyper-parameters, has high resolution and global convergence, and can obtain more accurate results when parameter estimation is performed on data under low sampling conditions.

In this paper, the SPICE method is applied for the respiration and heartbeat frequencies of millimeter-wave radar echo signals, which is suitable for short sampling time and low-sampling number scenarios. The simulated and measured signals are processed using this method, and results show that the method can effectively obtain accurate estimation of respiration and heartbeat frequencies. The estimation results are consistent with the values suggested by the commercial contact wristband.

2   Principles of FMCW Radar Vital Signs Signal Detection

The FMCW radar has the advantages of low average transmit power, simple structure, and being without range ambiguity. The frequency of the transmitted signal of the FMCW radar increases linearly with time, and its transmitted signal $x_T(t)$ can be expressed as:

$$x_T(t) = A_{TX} \cos(2\pi f_C t + \pi \frac{B}{T_C} t^2 + \varphi(t)) \tag{1}$$

where, B is the bandwidth, f_c is the starting frequency of the linear FM signal, A_{TX} is the amplitude of the transmitted signal, T_c is the linear FM signal pulse width, $p(t)$ is the phase noise, t is the time dependent variable.

Let the distance from the human chest cavity to the radar be $x(t)$, then we have $x(t) = R(t) + d_0$, where d_0 is the distance between the human body and the radar, and $R(t)$ is the chest wall motion displacement. The transmitted signal $x_{T(t)}$ travels through the distance d_0 to the radar receiver with a time delay $t_d = 2R(t)/c$, where c is the speed of light. The received signal $x_R(t)$ can be expressed as:

$$x_R(t) = A_{RX}[\cos(2\pi f_c(t - t_d)) + \pi \frac{B}{T_c}(t - t_d)^2 + \varphi(t - t_d)] \qquad (2)$$

where, $\varphi(t - t_d)$ is the phase of the time delay t_d, A_{RX} is the amplitude of the received signal. After mixing the transmitted and received signals, the IF signal can be obtained, which is:

$$S_{IF}(t) = A_{TX}A_{RX}\exp(j(2\pi f_{IF}t + \psi(t))) \qquad (3)$$

where, $f_{IF} = \frac{2Bd_0}{cT_c}$ is the frequency of the IF signal, $\psi(t) = \frac{4\pi(R(t)+d_0)}{\lambda}$ is the instantaneous phase of the IF signal, λ is the wavelength of the signal, and j denotes a complex number.

Due to the slow motion of the human chest, $R(t)$ is very small in a single chirp, which can be approximated as a constant. Therefore, multiple chirps can be sent sequentially for sampling $R(t)$ to achieve the goal of measuring changes in thoracic displacement. Sending l chirps continuously, the sampling interval is T_m (i.e. frame period), when $T_m \geqslant T_c$, $R(t)$ appearing in the phase corresponding to the subject distance unit, the time delay t_d is changed to:

$$t_d = 2(d_0 + R(lT_c + t))/c \qquad (4)$$

where, $R(lT_c+t)$ denotes the change in distance. The displacement due to chest expansion can be expressed in the form of a sinusoidal signal [23], which $R(lT_c + t) = R(lT_c)$ is easily known from the periodicity of sinusoidal signals. Substituting t_d into $S_{IF}(t)$, it obtained:

$$S_{IF}(lT_c + nT_m) = A_{TX}A_{RX}\exp(j(2\pi f_{IF}nT_m + \psi_l)) \qquad (5)$$

$$\psi_l = 4\pi(R(lT_c) + d_0)/\lambda \qquad (6)$$

where, T_m is the sampling period of the IF signal; n is the number of sampling points. It denotes that the vibration caused by the human vital signals ($R(lT_c)$) is encoded in the phase ψ_l. Therefore, the position of the human body can be estimated from the IF signal f_{IF}, and the vibration frequency caused by the vital signals can be estimated from ψ_l.

The flow of human vital signs signal detection is shown in Fig. 1.

The FMCW millimeter wave radar collects the human vital signs signal through echoes and then obtains the IF signal. A/D conversion is then applied to the IF signal to determine the valid range bin containing corresponding vital sign information encoded phase signals. The proposed method is applied in the vital signal extraction step to obtain the respiratory and heart rates. The non-sparse approaches FFT and CZT are also applied in the vital signal separation and extraction step for performance comparison.

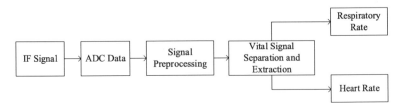

Fig. 1. The detection process of human vital sign signals

3 Respiration and Heartbeat Rate Detection

3.1 Radar Signal Preprocessing

The signal preprocessing steps include range FFT, phase extraction, phase unwrapping, and phase differencing. The radar signal obtained from the measurement contains M chirps, and range FFT processing is applied along the chirp dimension to obtain M spectrograms. Since the frequency corresponds to the subject distance, the distance spectrogram can be obtained by converting the frequency to the distance and determining the range bin where the human body is located.

Non-coherent accumulation of the processed signal is performed, and the range bin with the maximum energy is obtained, corresponding to the position of the measured human target. Under the condition that the human target remains stationary during the measurement, the small movements of the chest cavity caused by respiration and heartbeat are encoded in the phase information within the determined range bin. Then, the phase can be extracted using the arctangent demodulation method [24].

Phase unwrapping step is introduced to obtain phases within the range of $[-\pi, \pi]$. And for removing the constant phase offset corresponding to the fixed distance between the human target and the radar, phase differential operation is applied among the unwrapped phases of neighboring chirps.

Frequency estimation is performed on the phase difference signals at the same range bin to obtain the Doppler frequency, which corresponds to the respiratory and heart rates of the human target. The radar frame period is 25 ms in the experiment radar setup, and the number of chirps per frame is 16. Thus the sampling rate for all the chirps in the same range bin is 640 Hz. The respiratory and heartbeat signals are time-varying in practice. If estimating a signal with a longer collection time, usually only the average respiratory and heart rates can be obtained. To estimate instantaneous frequency, it usually has to process the signal within a short period of time. The frequency of respiration and heartbeat is usually within the range of 0–2 Hz. However, traditional estimation methods are often fed by insufficient samples to provide the required spectral resolution for distinguishing respiration and heartbeat under short-term sampling conditions.

Traditional estimation algorithms such as FFT and CZT can achieve satisfying spectrum estimations with sufficient sampling rates and sampling numbers. On the contrary, the FFT method's minimum resolvable spectral interval, which is inversely proportional to the spectrum resolution, increases when the sampling numbers decrease. The CZT method is essentially a spectral zooming approach of the FFT method, so they share the same spectrum resolution. Section 4.1 demonstrates more details. A method that can achieve high spectrum resolution with low sampling numbers is required to address this issue.

Thanks to the sparsity of the respiration and heartbeat signals, sparse methods can be applied to estimate respiration and heartbeat frequencies with high spectrum resolution dealing with low-sampling-number data. The energy of the signals is mainly concentrated in the low-frequency end of the spectrum due to the periodicity of the respiration and heartbeat signals. And the energy in the high-frequency end is so small that it can be neglected, so the respiration and heartbeat signals are sparse in the frequency domain. That, there are only few low frequency components with large amplitudes in the whole spectrum and most of the frequency components are close to zero. Therefore, the SPICE method is utilized to estimate respiratory and heartbeat frequencies under the condition of low sampling numbers.

3.2 Sparse Iterative Covariance-Based Estimation

The harmonic model is:

$$
y(n) = \sum_{k=1}^{K} a_k e^{if_k n} + \varepsilon(n); \; n = 1, 2, ..., N \tag{7}
$$

where, $y(n)$ is the observed data, $\varepsilon(n)$ is the additive noise, N is the number of samples, K is the number of harmonic components, f_k is the kth frequency, and a_k is the kth complex amplitude.

The complex form of the expression is:

$$
y(n) = \sum_{c=0}^{C-1} u_c e^{i\omega_c n} + \varepsilon(n); \; n = 1, 2, ..., N \tag{8}
$$

where, C is the number of grids, $\omega_c = 2\pi c / C$ is the frequency of the cth grid, and u_c is the complex amplitude of the cth grid. When the number of grids C is sufficiently large, i.e. $C \gg K$, the frequency parameter f_k in (7) could match a certain ω_c on the grid in model (8), the power a_k^2 corresponds to a value u_c on the grid in model (8).

The matrix form of Eq. (8) is:

$$
\begin{bmatrix} y(1) \\ y(2) \\ \vdots \\ y(N) \end{bmatrix} = \begin{bmatrix} 1 & e^{i\omega_1} & \cdots & e^{i\omega_{C-1}} \\ 1 & e^{i\omega_1 2} & \cdots & e^{i\omega_{C-1} 2} \\ \vdots & \vdots & \ddots & \vdots \\ 1 & e^{i\omega_1 n} & \cdots & e^{i\omega_{C-1} n} \end{bmatrix} \begin{bmatrix} u_0 \\ u_1 \\ \vdots \\ u_{C-1} \end{bmatrix} + \begin{bmatrix} \varepsilon(1) \\ \varepsilon(2) \\ \vdots \\ \varepsilon(N) \end{bmatrix} \tag{9}
$$

Its covariance matrix is:

$$
R = E\{yy*\} = BPB * + \sigma^2 I_N \tag{10}
$$

$$R = [B, I_N] \begin{bmatrix} p_0 & 0 & \cdots & \cdots\cdots\cdots & 0 \\ 0 & p_1 & 0 & \cdots\cdots\cdots & 0 \\ \vdots & 0 & p_{C-1} & \vdots & \vdots & \vdots & \vdots \\ 0 & \cdots & \cdots & \ddots\cdots\cdots & 0 \\ 0 & \cdots & \cdots & \cdots\,\sigma^2\,\cdots & 0 \\ \vdots & \vdots & \vdots & \vdots & \vdots & \ddots & \vdots \\ 0 & \cdots & \cdots & \cdots\cdots\cdots & \sigma^2 \end{bmatrix} [B, I_N]^* \tag{11}$$

The covariance matrix R can be further expressed as.

$$R \triangleq B_1 P_1 B_1* \tag{12}$$

where,

$P_1 = diag\{p_0, p_1, ..., p_{C-1}, \sigma^2, ..., \sigma^2\} \triangleq diag\{p_0, p_1, ..., p_{C-1}, p_C, ..., p_{C+N-1}\}$,
$B_1 = [B, I_N] \triangleq [b_0, b_1, ..., b_{C-1}, b_C, ..., b_{C+N-1}]$.

The following covariance fitting criterion for the parameters estimation of SPICE algorithm is:

$$\min_{\{p_c\}} ||R^{-1/2}(\hat{R} - R)||_F^2 \tag{13}$$

where, $c = 1, \ldots, C+N+1$, $||\cdot||_F$ represents the Frobenius norm, $(\cdot)^{-1/2}$ denotes the Hermitian positive definite square root of the matrix, and the sample covariance matrix $\hat{R} = yy^*$.

It can be expressed as the following optimization problem:

$$\min_{\{p_c\}} \left\{ -2||y||^2 + ||y||^2 y^* R^{-1} y + tr(R) \right\} \tag{14}$$

where, $tr(R) = E\{||y||^2\} = \sum_{c=0}^{C+N-1} ||b_c||^2 p_c$, $tr(\cdot)$ denotes the trace of the matrix, $||\cdot||$ denotes the Euclidean norm. Therefore, this optimization problem can be transformed into:

$$\min_{\{p_c\}} y^* R^{-1} y + \sum_{c=0}^{C+N-1} d_c p_c \tag{15}$$

where, $d_c = ||b_c||^2/||y||^2$. Since $tr(R) = E\{||y||^2\} = \sum_{c=0}^{C+N-1} ||b_c||^2 p_c$, then $||y||^2$ is the unbiased consistent estimate of $\sum_{c=0}^{C+N-1} ||b_c||^2 p_c$, then the Eq. (15) can be expressed as the following constrained minimization problem:

$$\min_{x, \{p_c\}} y^* R^{-1} y$$
$$s.t. \sum_{c=0}^{C+N-1} d_c p_c = 1 \tag{16}$$

Define $\beta = pB^*R^{-1}y = [\beta_0, \beta_1, \cdots, \beta_{C+N-1}]$, Eq. (16) can be expressed as:

$$\min_{x,\{p_c\}} \sum_{c=0}^{C+N-1} \frac{|\beta_c|^2}{p_c}$$
$$s.t. \sum_{c=0}^{C+N-1} d_c p_c = 1 \tag{17}$$

The overall flow of the SPICE algorithm is shown in Fig. 2, calculate the iteration result for p_c and then the estimation results can be obtained.

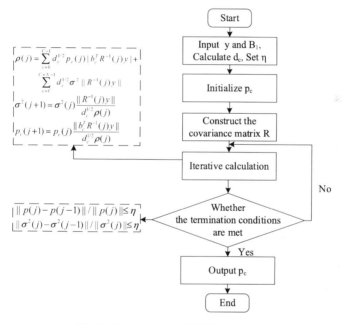

Fig. 2. The process of SPICE algorithm

4 Experiments and Results Analysis

4.1 Simulations

Signal Modeling. Simulated signals are used to evaluate the performance of the SPICE method applied to spectral estimation of respiratory and heartbeat signals. The motion of the human chest wall is modeled as a sinusoidal signal [25]:

$$x_b = A_b \sin(2\pi f_b t + \theta_1) \tag{18}$$

$$x_h = A_h \sin(2\pi f_h t + \theta_2) \tag{19}$$

where, x_b, x_h are the respiratory and heartbeat signals respectively. $A_b = 1.0\,\text{mm}$, $f_b = 0.3\,\text{Hz}$ are the amplitude and frequency of the respiratory signal, $A_h = 0.2\,\text{mm}$, $f_h = 1.3\,\text{Hz}$ are the amplitude and frequency of the heartbeat, and, θ_1, θ_2 are the initial phase. The mixed motion signal y can be obtained by superimposing the respiratory and heartbeat signals:

$$y = x_b + x_h \tag{20}$$

The signal is plotted in Fig. 3.

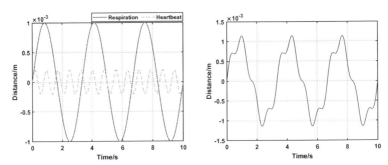

(a) Respiratory and heartbeat analog signals (b) Mixed respiratory and heartbeat signals

Fig. 3. The displacement model of respiration and heartbeat

Frequency Estimation for Simulated Signals. The simulation experiment firstly verifies the frequency estimation results of the measurement with sufficient sampling rate and sampling number. Therefore, the simulation uses FFT, CZT, and SPICE methods to estimate the frequency of the simulated signal with a sampling rate of 640 Hz and a sampling time of 20 s. Results are shown in Fig. 4.

These results suggest that all the three methods can successfully estimate the frequency when the sampling rate is high enough and the samples are adequate. With the sampling time unchanged and the sampling rate reduced to 4 Hz, the experimental results are shown in Fig. 5.

The results show that although the sampling rate is reduced, the three methods can still estimate the frequency of the simulated signal since the sampling time is long enough and the number of sampling points is sufficient. When the sampling time is reduced to 2 s with the same sampling rate of 4 Hz, the results are shown in Fig. 6.

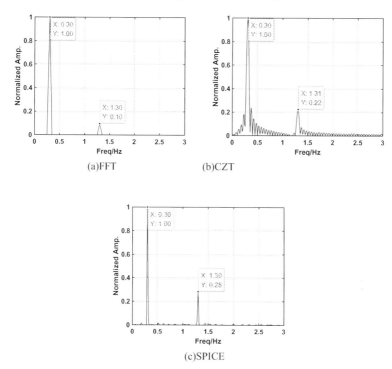

Fig. 4. The estimation results with a sufficient sampling rate and sampling number of FFT, CZT and SPICE

Figure 6 suggests that the FFT and CZT methods demonstrate large estimation errors when the sampling number is insufficient for the desired spectrum resolution for respiration and heartbeat rates. However, the estimation results of the SPICE algorithm are consistent with the predefined simulation parameters. In order to further investigate the frequency estimation performance of the algorithms, the root mean square errors of the three methods are calculated under different signal-to-noise ratios (SNR) and the same number of sampling points, as well as the same SNR with two different numbers of sampling points, respectively. 100 Monte Carlo simulations are performed under each condition and the results are shown in Fig. 7.

Figure 7 corresponds to the signal sampling rate of 4 Hz for the three methods. The sampling numbers of the data that feed to FFT and CZT are identical to the numbers of grids applied for the SPICE method. And the results shown in Fig. 7(a) suggest that the SPICE method has the lowest RMSEs for all SNR scenarios among the three methods. While Fig. 7(b) shows that the SPICE method has lower RMSEs for each identical number of sampling than FFT and CZT have.

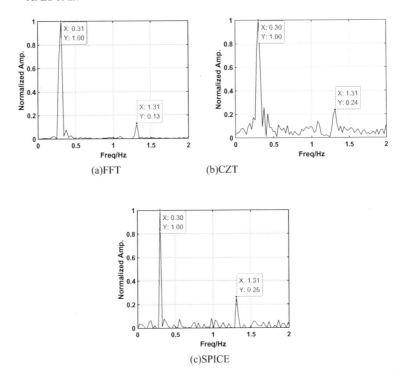

Fig. 5. The estimation results with a reduced sampling rate of FFT, CZT and SPICE

4.2 Experimental Measurements

Experiment Setup. The experiment uses TI's evaluation kit of IWR6843ISK and DCA1000. The radar operating parameters are set for experiments as start frequency at 60 GHz, FM slope at 70 MHz/μs, chirp signal period at 56 μs, 16 chirps per frame, frame duration at 25 ms, number of chirp signal samples at 200, the sampling rate for each chirp at 4MHz, and the total sampling duration at 20 s.

In all experiments, experimental subjects were sitting 0.6 m away in front of the radar. The position and height of the radar antennas were adjusted aiming directly to their chest on the same height. The subjects are required to keep as still as possible and breathed normally during the experiments. At the same time, every subject wore a contact wristband to synchronize the measurement and recording of the experimental data. The experimental setup is shown in Fig. 8.

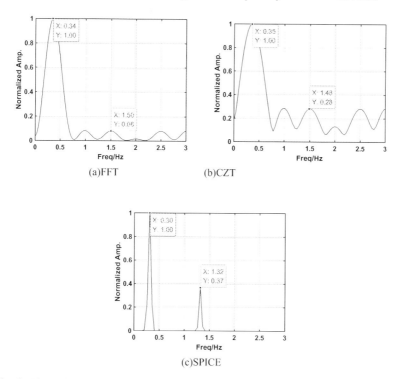

Fig. 6. The estimation results with a reduced sampling number of FFT, CZT and SPICE

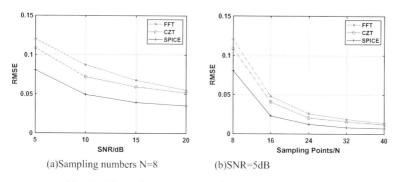

Fig. 7. The performance comparison of three algorithms

Results and Analysis. *Human Body Position Determination and Phase Information Extraction.* A typical range FFT result of the acquired radar signal is shown in Fig. 9(a), which can initially retrieve the experimental subject's position. Non-coherent accumulation is applied along the chirp dimension to determine the corresponding range bin of the experimental subject. This distance estimation is shown in Fig. 9(b). The wrapped phase information can be extracted from the obtained range bin using arctangent demodulation,

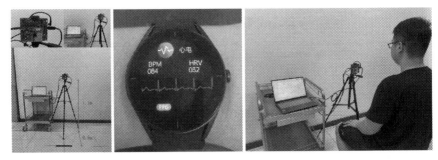

Fig. 8. Radar hardware, experimental environment, and signal acquisition scenarios

as shown in Fig. 9(c). The phase information will then be unwrapped and differentiated to prepare for respiratory and heartbeat estimation, as shown in Figs. 9(d) and 9(e).

Estimation of Respiratory and Heartbeat Frequency. The SPICE method is utilized to estimate the respiration and heartbeat rates under the condition of short sampling time with an insufficient sampling data volume which originally required by non-sparse methods. A typical phase segment with short sampling period of 2 s at sampling rate of 4 Hz is shown in Fig. 10.

The SPICE, FFT, and CZT algorithms are applied to the phase data segments, and the results are shown in Fig. 11.

The reference values obtained by the wristband for this period are 36 breaths/min and 89 heartbeats/min. The estimation results of respiratory rate by SPICE, FFT, and CZT shown in Fig. 11 are 34 breaths/min, 32 breaths/min, and 31 breaths/min, respectively, with similar estimation results and tolerable error levels. However, the estimation of heartbeat rate by FFT and CZT is far beyond the error tolerance. In contrast, the estimation result of heart rate by SPICE is 86 beats/min, which has a small error compared with the reference value. Moreover, from the processing results, it can be seen that, for the same data segment, the estimation spectrum of SPICE is narrower than those of FFT or CZT, proving that the SPICE method has an outstanding estimation performance.

Several further experiments were also conducted on different experimental subjects, with results shown in Fig. 12.

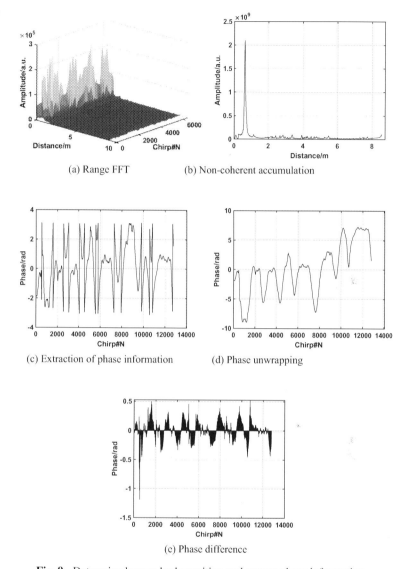

(a) Range FFT   (b) Non-coherent accumulation

(c) Extraction of phase information   (d) Phase unwrapping

(e) Phase difference

Fig. 9. Determine human body position and extract phase information

The FFT and CZT methods can achieve accurate spectrum estimation results of a single frequency signal or one of its integer harmonics with sufficient sampling numbers. However, the human vital signs signals collected in a short period in this experiment usually do not meet such conditions. The estimation results of heartbeat frequency of FFT and CZT in Fig. 12 (a)(b)(c) deviate from their reference values due to spectral leakage. Furthermore, the spectral leakage of FFT and CZT methods shown in Fig. 12 (d) even leads to substantial interference between the frequencies of respiratory and

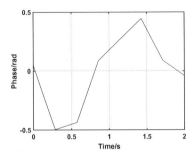

Fig. 10. Phase data to be processed for estimation with a short sampling period

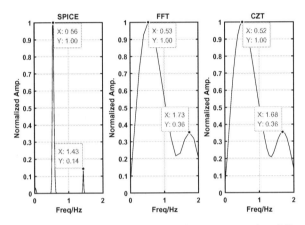

Fig. 11. The estimation results for the same phase data segment using different algorithms

heartbeat rates. However, the results of the SPICE method in Fig. 12 (d) appear to be unaffected by such adversity due to the intrinsic sparse nature of the SPICE method.

The summary of the measurement results and errors shown in Tables 1 and 2 suggest that the SPICE algorithm can estimate the respiratory and heartbeat rate frequencies with a much lower error level than the FFT or CZT method.

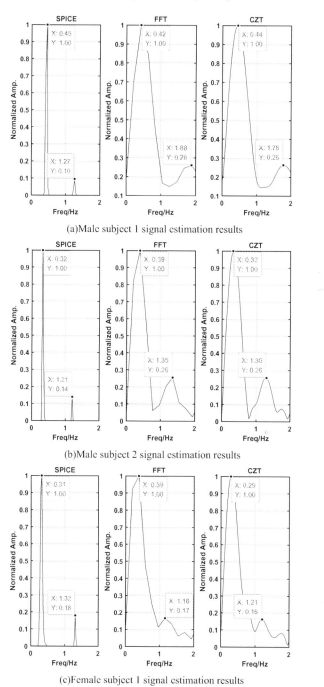

(a)Male subject 1 signal estimation results

(b)Male subject 2 signal estimation results

(c)Female subject 1 signal estimation results

Fig. 12. More estimation results of different methods on different experimental subjects

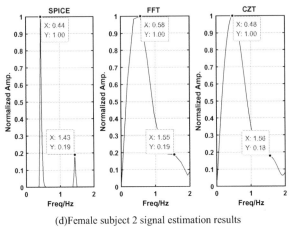

(d)Female subject 2 signal estimation results

Fig. 12. (*continued*)

Table 1. The estimation results on different experimental subjects

Experimental Subject		FFT	CZT	SPICE	Unit: times/min
					Wristband
Male #1	Respiratory Rate	25	26	27	28
	Heart Rate	113	107	76	79
Male #2	Respiratory Rate	23	19	19	17
	Heart Rate	81	78	73	71
Female #1	Respiratory Rate	23	17	19	20
	Heart Rate	70	73	79	83
Female #2	Respiratory Rate	35	29	26	27
	Heart Rate	93	94	86	83

Table 2. Summary of estimation errors in 50 groups of different experimental subjects

Estimation Method		RMSE	Min Error%	Max Error%	Mean Error %
Respiration	FFT	6.2	10.7	35.3	22.7
	CZT	5.4	7.1	27.6	15.4
	SPICE	2.5	2.8	7.6	3.8
Heartbeat	FFT	8.3	12.0	43.0	28.4
	CZT	6.7	7.4	35.4	17.7
	SPICE	2.9	3.6	11.8	6.2

5   Conclusion

This paper uses the SPICE method to estimate respiration and heartbeat frequencies of human vital signals collected by FMCW millimeter wave radar. The performance advantages of the SPICE method over traditional FFT and CZT spectral estimation methods are analyzed through simulation. The estimation results of the measured data demonstrate that the SPICE method can effectively estimate the respiratory rate and heart rate when data segments with a smaller sampling number than required by the FFT or CZT method. The SPICE's estimation results are consistent with reference values measured by the contact wristband.

Acknowledgments. This study was funded by Graduate Research Innovation Program of Civil Aviation University of China (grant number 2015/1455001024).

Disclosure of Interests.   The authors have no competing interests to declare that are relevant to the content of this article.

References

1. Varon, C., Caicedo, A., Testelmans, D., Buyse, B., Van Huffel, S.: A novel algorithm for the automatic detection of sleep apnea from single-lead ECG. IEEE Trans. Biomed. Eng. **62**(9), 2269–2278 (2015)
2. Bhattacharyya, S., Mukherjee, A., Bhaumik, H., Das, S., Yoshida, K.: Motion artifact reduction from finger photoplethysmogram using discrete wavelet transform. [Adv. Intell. Syst. Comput.] Recent Trends Sig. Image Process. **727**(10), 89–98 (2019)
3. Bakhtiari, S., Liao, S., Elmer, T., Sami Gopalsami, N., Raptis, A.C.: A real-time heart rate analysis for a remote millimeter wave I-Q sensor. IEEE Trans. Biomed. Eng. **58**(6), 1839–1845 (2011)
4. Zhang, H., Lei, B.: The millimeter-wave detective technology and target-searching fuses. Chin. J. Sens. Actuat. **2**, 184–186 (2003). (in Chinese)
5. Li, C., Cummings, J., Lam, J., Graves, E., Wu, W.: Radar remote monitoring of vital signs. IEEE Microwave Mag. **10**(1), 47–56 (2009)
6. Islam, S.M.M., Fioranelli, F., Lubecke, V.M.: Can radar remote life sensing technology help combat COVID-19? Front. Comms. Net. **2** (2021)
7. Paterniani, G., et al.: Radar-based monitoring of vital signs: a tutorial overview. IEEE Proc. **111**(3), 277–317 (2023)
8. Li, C., Lin, J., Xiao, Y.: Robust overnight monitoring of human vital signs by a non-contact respiration and heartbeat detector. In: 2006 International Conference of the IEEE Engineering in Medicine and Biology Society, pp. 2235–2238 (2006)
9. Kim, J.-Y., Park, J.-H., Jang, S.-Y., Yang, J.-R.: Peak detection algorithm for vital sign detection using doppler radar sensors. Sensors **19**(7), 1575 (2019)
10. Hafner, N., Mostafanezhad, I., Lubecke, V.M., Boric-Lubecke, O., Host-Madsen, A.: Non-contact cardiopulmonary sensing with a baby monitor. In: 29th Annual International Conference of the IEEE Engineering in Medicine and Biology Society, pp. 2300–2302 (2007)
11. Mercuri, M., et al.: Analysis of an indoor biomedical radar-based system for health monitoring. IEEE Trans. Microw. Theory Tech. **61**(5), 2061–2068 (2013)
12. Su, B.Y., Ho, K.C., Rantz, M.J., Skubic, M.: Doppler radar fall activity detection using the wavelet transform. IEEE Trans. Biomed. Eng. **62**(3), 865–875 (2015)

13. Droitcour, A., Lubecke, V., Jenshan, L., Boric-Lubecke, O.: A microwave radio for Doppler radar sensing of vital signs. In: 2001 IEEE MTT-S International Microwave Symposium Digest (Cat. No.01CH37157), pp. 175–178 (2001)

14. Caro, C.G., Bloice, J.A.: Contactless apnoea detector based on radar. Lancet **298**(7731), 959–961 (1971)

15. Franks, C.I., Watson, J.B.G., Brown, B.H., et al.: Respiratory patterns and risk of sudden unexpected death in infancy. Arch. Dis. Child. **55**(8), 595–599 (1980)

16. Zeng, Z.F., Sun, J.G., Li, J., et al.: The Analysis of TWI data for human being's periodic motions. In: 2011 IEEE International Geoscience and Remote Sensing Symposium, pp. 862–865 (2011)

17. Hu, W.: Non-contact Vital Sign Detection Based on Doppler Radar. University of Science and Technology of China (2014). (in Chinese)

18. Pan, H., Zhou, Y., Gu, M.: Noncontact accurate heartbeat detection using 77 GHz millimeter-eave radar. Chin. J. Sens. Actuat. **35**(02), 277–284 (2022). (in Chinese)

19. Zheng, J., Kaveh, M.: Sparse spatial spectral estimation: a covariance fitting algorithm, performance and regularization. IEEE Trans. Sig. Process. **61**(11), 2767–2777 (2013)

20. Stoica, P., Babu, P., Li, J.: SPICE: a sparse covariance-based estimation method for array processing. IEEE Trans. Sig. Process. **59**(2), 629–638 (2011)

21. Stoica, P., Babu, P., Li, J.: New method of sparse parameter estimation in separable models and its use for spectral analysis of irregularly sampled data. IEEE Trans. Sig. Process. **59**(1), 35–47 (2011)

22. Rojas, C.R., Katselis, D., Hjalmarsson, H.: A note on the SPICE method. IEEE Trans. Sig. Process. **61**(18), 4545–4551 (2013)

23. Fan, T., Li, W., Guo, W.: Method for separating life characteristic signals based on time-frequency filtering in the terahertz frequency band. J. Air Force Early Warn. Acad. **32**(01), 25–30 (2018). (in Chinese)

24. Wang, G., Gu, C., Inoue, T., Li, C.: A hybrid FMCW-interferometry radar for indoor precise positioning and versatile life activity monitoring. IEEE Trans. Microw. Theory Tech. **62**(11), 2812–2822 (2014)

25. Lee, H., Kim, B.-H., Yook, J.-G.: Path loss compensation method for multiple target vital sign detection with 24-GHz FMCW radar. In: 2018 IEEE Asia-Pacific Conference on Antennas and Propagation (APCAP), pp. 100–101 (2018)

Competency Evaluation of Chinese Pilots Based on Human Factors Analysis Model

Min Luo[✉], Yanqiu Chen, and Yuan Zhang

Academy of Civil Aviation Science and Technology (Engineering and Technical Research Center of Civil Aviation Safety Analysis and Prevention of Beijing), Beijing, China
luomin@sina.com, {Chenqanqiu,zhangyuan}@mail.castc.org.cn

Abstract. Pilot competencies are used to effectively predict and evaluate the level of pilot performance, which can be manifested and observed through the use of relevant knowledge, skills and attitudes to perform activities or tasks under specific conditions. This study (Supported by the Fundamental Research Funds of CASTC(X242060302102)) optimized the Human Factor Analysis and Classification System (HFACS), and then established the corresponding relationship between the three competencies of pilots and the dimensions of model analysis. Finally, the study used the optimized HFCAS model to analyze the typical occurrences of China in the past five years. In the end, the common concrete manifestations of the three major competency deficiencies are obtained to provide data support for industry risk identification and flight training direction.

Keywords: Core competency · psychological competency · Style competency · Optimized HFACS

1 Background

According to Professor Eric Hollnagel's theory [1, 2], we usually think of safety by reference to its opposite, the absence of safety. This traditional view of safety called Safety-I has consequently been defined by the absence of accidents and incidents, or as the "freedom from unacceptable risk". As a result, the focus of safety research and safety management has usually been on unsafe system operation rather than on safe operation. In contrast to the traditional view, resilience engineering maintains that "things go wrong" and "things go right" for the same basic reasons. This corresponds to a view of safety, called Safety-II, which defines safety as the ability to succeed under varying conditions. The understanding of everyday functioning is therefore a necessary prerequisite for the understanding of the safety performance of an organization. Therefore, Modern civil aviation puts forward the concept of competency.

Pilot competencies are some important dimensions used to effectively predict and evaluate the level of pilot performance, which can be manifested and observed through the use of relevant knowledge, skills and attitudes to perform activities or tasks under specific conditions.

In December 2020, The Civil Aviation Administration of China issued the China Civil Aviation Professionalism Lifecycle Management System Construction and Implementation Roadmap [3]. The framework of post competency (shown in Fig. 1) is put forward innovatively. Post competency includes not only the core competency that has been successfully practiced in the world [4, 5], but also the style competency and psychological competency that have not yet formed a mature system in the world.

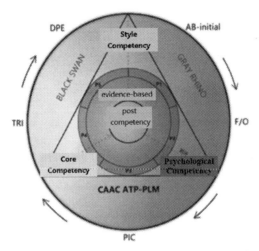

Fig. 1. Pilot post competency developed by CAAC

According to the roadmap, **Style competency** mainly refers to the stable attitude and behavior shown by the pilot in the safe operation, especially the internal identification and external response to the various behavioral norms that limit and guide the safe operation, and the conformity with the requirements of the post competency. **Psychological competency** refers to the conformity of the pilot's mental health state and occupational adaptability psychology with the requirements of post competency, which is formed on the basis of heredity and under the influence of education and environment through the subject practice training. **Core competency** mainly refers to a group of related behaviors, based on task requirements, which describe how to effectively perform a task. They describe what proficient performance looks like. They (shown in Fig. 2) include the name of the competency, a description, and a list of behavioral indicators [6].

However, in the construction of the three major competencies of civil aviation pilots of China, style competency and psychological competency are still in the process of screening evaluation indicators and establishing evaluation methods, while core competency indicators and evaluation methods are relatively mature. The core competency framework defined by ICAO, so the evaluation framework and indicators are relatively clear. It mainly through the reasonable design of simulator training scene, through the assessment way to find and improve the short board competency.

To this end, this study intends to dig out the types and specific manifestations of pilots' overall competency deficiency by analyzing the actual incidents in civil aviation of China in the past three years. The research results can not only give a favorable

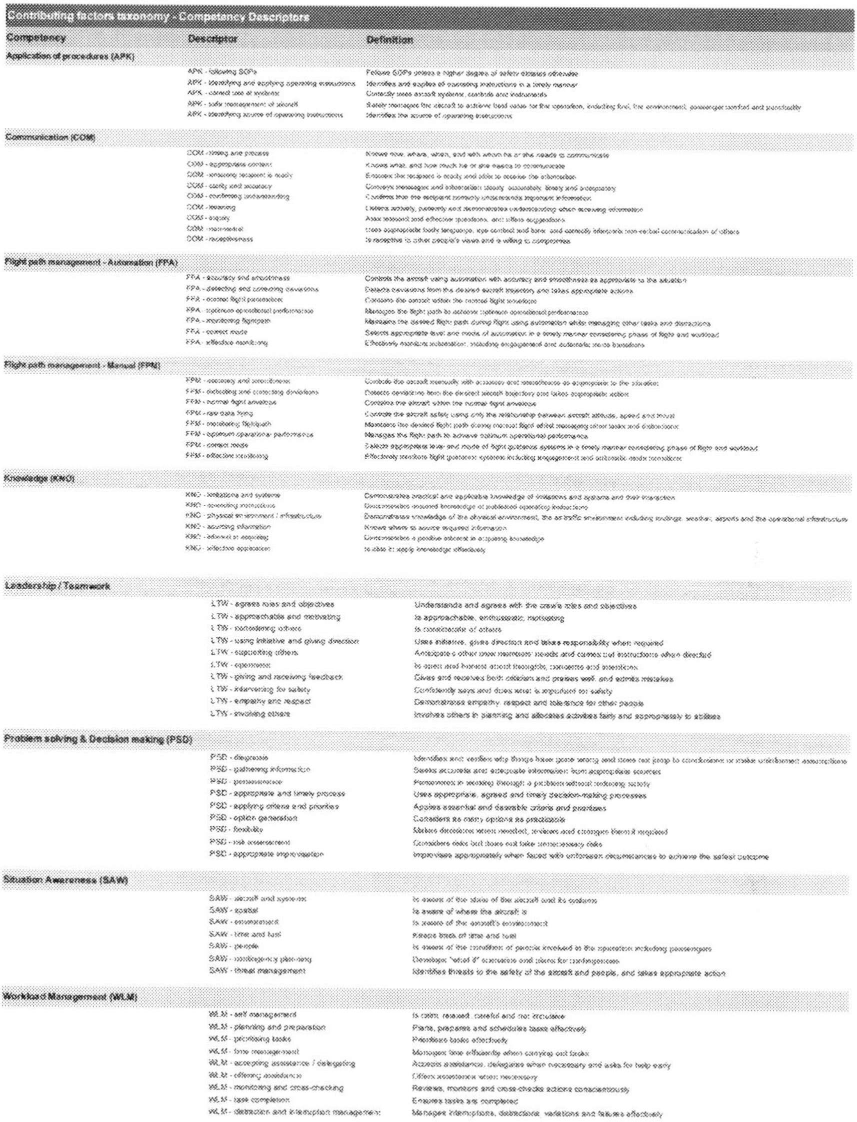

Contributing factors taxonomy - Competency Descriptors

Competency	Descriptor	Definition
Application of procedures (APK)		
Communication (COM)		
Flight path management - Automation (FPA)		
Flight path management - Manual (FPM)		
Knowledge (KNO)		
Leadership / Teamwork		
Problem solving & Decision making (PSD)		
Situation Awareness (SAW)		
Workload Management (WLM)		

Fig. 2. Core Competency of Pilots by IATA

reference for the three competencies construction, but also provide data support for industry risk identification and flight training direction.

2 Research Methods

Optimized HFACS Dimensions. To analyze unsafe events, it is necessary to understand the classical human factor analysis model. According to the human Factor Analysis and

Classification System (HFACS) model [7, 8], unsafe behaviors can be further divided into violation and error, and the error can be further divided into technological error, decision-making error and cognitive error. In this study, the HFCAS model was first optimized, especially the analysis dimensions and items applicable to China's civil aviation in terms of "unsafe behavior" (as shown in Fig. 3) and "preconditions for unsafe behavior" (as shown in Fig. 4).

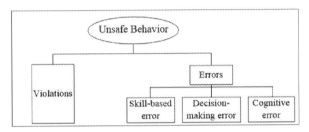

Fig. 3. The Classification of unsafe behavior in optimized HFCAS

"Unsafe behavior" refers to the frontline operator' behavior that violates the objective laws of safe operation during the work process, and lead to occurrence directly. In the optimized HFCAS model, "unsafe behavior" can be classified into two categories: violations and errors. Violations represent the willful disregard for the rules and regulations that ensure the safety of flight. Errors represent the mental or physical activities of individuals that fail to achieve their intended outcome. It can be classified into three categories: skill-based error, decision-making error and cognitive error. Skill-based error is best described as "stick-and-rudder" and other basic skills that occur without significant conscious; Decision-making error is an intentional behavior that proceeds as intended, yet the plan proves inadequate or inappropriate for the situation; Cognitive error happens when one's perception of the world differs from reality.

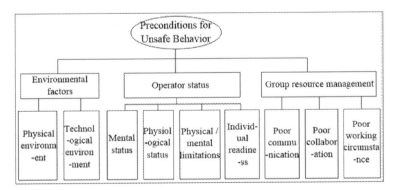

Fig. 4. The Classification of Precondition for unsafe behavior in optimized HFCAS

"Precondition for unsafe behavior" is the adverse objective and subjective conditions which cause the unsafe behavior. In the optimized HFCAS model, it can be classified into three categories: "environmental factors", "operator status" and "group resource management". "Environmental factors" refers to the physical and technological environment which reduces the operator's performance or lead to unsafe behavior. "Operator status" is the personal condition which may reduce the operator's performance, including "mental status", "physiological status", "physical/mental limitations", and "individual readiness". Besides, "Group resource management" refers to the poor communication or collaboration among the operator and their group which may lead to the occurrence, including "poor communication", "poor collaboration" and "poor working circumstance".

Obviously, "unsafe behaviors" and some part of "precondition for unsafe behavior" of the flight crew are directly related to the three competencies. In this study, corresponding relationship between optimized HFACS dimensions and pilot competencies needs to explore more.

Corresponding Relationship Between Optimized HFACS Dimensions and Pilot Competencies. This study establishes the corresponding relationship between the three competencies of pilots and the dimensions of model analysis, as shown in Table 1. Pilots' mental state is a direct reflection of their lack of psychological competency. Pilots' knowledge level, team resource management problems, and errors are direct manifestations of their lack of core competency, while violations are direct manifestations of their lack of certain style competency.

Table 1. Corresponding Relationship

Optimized HFACS Dimensions	Competency
Precondition for unsafe behaviors—Condition of operators—Adverse mental state	Psychological competency
Precondition for unsafe behaviors—Condition of operators—Physical/Mental limitations	Core competency—Knowledge
Precondition for unsafe behaviors—Crew resource management—Ineffective communication	Core competency—Communication
Precondition for unsafe behaviors—Crew resource management—Not working as a team	Core competency—Leadership / Teamwork
Precondition for unsafe behaviors—Crew resource management—Inadequate coordination	Core competency—Workload Management
Unsafe behaviors—Errors—Decision errors—Procedure option error	Core competency—Application of procedures
Unsafe behaviors—Errors—Skill-based errors	Core competency—Automation
Unsafe behaviors—Errors—Skill-based errors	Core competency—Manual
Unsafe behaviors—Errors—Decision errors—Operation decision errors	Core competency—Problem solving & Decision making
Unsafe behaviors—Errors—Perceptual errors Unsafe behaviors—Violations	Core competency—Situation Awareness Style competency

3   Data Analysis

This study collected and analyzed 41 incidents caused by air crew in civil aviation of China from 2020 to 2023.

Analysis of Post Competency. The study used the optimized HFCAS model to analyze these incidents to find "unsafe behavior "and "precondition for unsafe behavior". And then, it used the corresponding relationship which shown in Table 1 to classify the behavior.

The results showed that 199 behaviors can be observed totally. Table 2 showed the number of observed behaviors for each competency, and ratio between the observed behaviors and incidents.

Table 2. Descriptive statistics of post competency

Post Competency	N(observed behaviors)	Ratio (Observed behaviors: Incidents)
Core Competency	155	4:1
Psychological Competency	11	1:4
Style Competency	33	5:6

According to statistics, 155 behaviors related to lack of core competency can be observed in the above incidents. That is about 4 behaviors related to lack of core competency will occur in every incident. 11 behaviors reflecting poor mental state are observed, that means 1 out of every 4 incidents directly indicated psychological problems; In addition, 33 typical violations can be observed, which are the embodiment of the lack of style competency, that is 5 violations acts can be observed in every 6 incidents.

Through the classification of behavioral performance analyzed by the incident investigation report, it can be seen that the pilot's competency deficiency is mainly in the core competency. The most difficult to observe is the lack of psychological competence, which is related to the depth of the incident investigation and the difficulty of recovering the mental state at that time.

Analysis of Core Competency. The descriptive statistics of the core competency are presented in Table 3. It is demonstrated that the number of observed behaviors and corresponding proportion.

As can be seen from the table above, there are 155 behaviors observed for loss of core competency. Among them,

The first three skills that are most likely to cause problems are manual control, leadership / teamwork, and situational awareness. To be specific, in manual control, weak bias correction ability and rough action are the most common manifestations. In leadership and teamwork, inadequate preparation before flight is the most common cause. The "tunnel effect" is a common reason that causes pilots to lose situational awareness and make wrong decisions. The "tunnel effect" [9] mentioned here means that people lose the ability of rational judgment when carrying out decisive thinking,

Table 3. Descriptive statistics of core competency

Core Competency	N	Proportion
Core competency—Manual	31	20%
Core competency—Leadership / Teamwork	29	18.7%
Core competency—Situation Awareness	27	17.4%
Core competency—Problem solving & Decision making	17	11%
Core competency—Application of procedures	17	11%
Core competency—Communication	16	10.3%
Core competency—Knowledge	8	5.1%
Core competency—Workload Management	6	3.9%
Core competency—Automation	4	2.6%

Table 4. Descriptive statistics of psychological competency

Psychological competency	N
Fluke mentality	4
Recklessness	3
Anxious	1
Depression	1
Nervousness	1
Carelessness	1

and their thinking is like entering a long pipeline, tending to consider problems in a straight line according to a single mode, and they cannot properly adjust their thinking and behavior patterns when making decisions due to differences in time, place and emotion. If the pilot's mental activity enters this invisible "tunnel", he will focus on what he wants to do. The reminders of other crew members, the stimulation of external reference objects, the comprehensive information of airborne instruments, and the sound and light warnings of near-ground warning equipment are often ignored and turned a deaf ear. Proper concentration is the quality of normal life and work must have, but this excessive concentration will lead to unsafe incidents. In the 2002 Air China Busan crash, the pilot continued to approach despite repeated warnings from the co-pilot. On Helios Airways Flight 522 in 2005, two crew members were so obsessed with the so-called take-off warning horn that they ignored the aircraft's cabin altitude and the passengers' oxygen mask release lights.

Secondly, deficiencies in decision making, application of procedures, and communication capability are easier to attribute. Specifically, underestimating the complexity of weather is common in decision-making. In the application of procedures, it is common not to make targeted brief. The lack of communication caused by the authority gradient in the cockpit has been a common problem that is difficult to solve.

Finally, the three capability of knowledge, workload management, and automation are less frequent. Since the lack of knowledge application is different, all kinds of theoretical and practical knowledge deficiency occur. Workload mismanagement is mainly reflected in changing situations, such as temporary replacement of runways. Besides, the lack of automation is mainly due to the improper use of radar.

Analysis of Psychological Competency. The most common manifestation of poor mental competency in unsafe incidents is the pilot's fluke mentality and recklessness during the approach and landing phase. Of the 11 observable behaviors, 7 were associated with it (as shown in the Table 4). In addition, there was one incident in which the pilot was constantly criticized by the captain during the flight, and the mood was always in an extremely tense and depressed state, resulting in hyperventilation symptoms, reflecting the fragility of some pilots' psychological resistance to pressure.

However, it is worth explaining that the poor mental state reflected in the flight is only the tip of the iceberg, and psychological competency should be comprehensively evaluated from the long-term mental health status and occupational adaptability of pilots.

Analysis of Style Competency. The lack of style competency in the unsafe incident is mainly reflected in the failure to operate in accordance with the rules and procedures, which is a number of significant violations. This study conducted preliminary statistics on 33 violations, crew violations of standard operating procedure (SOP) are most common, as shown in the Fig. 5. Such as failure to cross check, failure to comply with the required standard communication, etc.

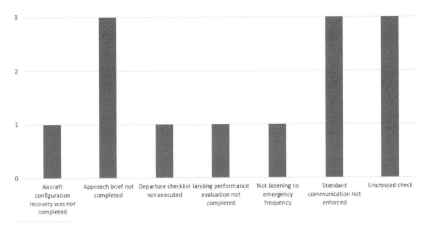

Fig. 5. The crew violations of SOP

In addition, there are some professionals spirts failures can be found, such as chatting during the critical phase of the flight, technical fraud, and failure to notify ATC in time after the incident.

Therefore, in addition to the incident investigation can be found, the style competency more should be reasonably evaluated in the daily management of pilots.

4   Conclusions

Through theoretical methods and data analysis, this study draws the following conclusions.

- There is a significant correspondence between the optimized HFCAS model and the competency model.
- Through the investigation of unsafe incidents, it is found that among pilots' core competency, psychological competency and style competency, the lack of core competency is the most significant and common.
- In the core competency, the most likely capability failure to cause problems are manual control, leadership/teamwork, and situational awareness. This is followed by deficiencies in decision making, application of procedures, and communication. Finally, knowledge, workload management, and automation are less frequent.
- In flight operation, fluke mentality and recklessness are the most intuitive manifestation of lack of psychological competency.
- Various violations of SOP can best reflect the problem of style competency in flight operation.

To this end, this study will continue collecting and analyzing more incidents to dig out the types and specific manifestations of pilots' overall competency deficiency. On this basis, it will provide data support for industry risk identification and flight training direction.

References

1. Hollnagel, E.: Safety-I and Safety-II: The Past and Future of Safety Management. Ashgate, Farnham, UK (2014)
2. Hollnagel, E.: Safety-II in practice. Routledge, Abingdon, Oxon, UK (2017)
3. Civil Aviation Administration of China (CAAC): China Civil Aviation Professionalism Lifecycle Management System Construction and Implementation Roadmap (2020)
4. The International Air Transport Association (IATA): EBT Data Report (2021)
5. The International Air Transport Association (IATA): Evidence-Based Training Implementation Guide Edition 2 (2024)
6. Civil Aviation Administration of China (CAAC): Evidence-Based Training (EBT) Implementation Method (AC-121-QS-138R1) (2023)
7. Shappell, S.A., Wingman, D.A.: The Human Factors Analysis and Classification System-HFACS DOT/FAA/AM-00/7. US Department of Transportation, Federal Aviation Administration, Washington (2000)

8. Douglas, A.W., Scott, A.S.: A Human Error Analysis of Cortical Aviation Accidents Using the Human Factors Analysis and Classification System (HFACS) DOT/FAA/AM-01/3. US Department of Transportation, Federal Aviation Administration, Washinton (2001)
9. Liu, Q.: Beware of "tunnel effect" in flight. News. carnoc.com/list/201/201713.html (2011)
10. AIR ACCIDENT INVESTIGATION & AVIATION SAFETY BOARD (AAIASB): Microsoft Word - FINAL REPORT 5B-DBY aa.doc (aaiu.ie) (2006)

Diagnosing Cognitive Control with Eye-Tracking Metrics in a Multitasking Environment

Sophie-Marie Stasch(✉) 🆔 and Wolfgang Mack 🆔

Universität der Bundeswehr München, Werner-Heisenberg-Weg 39, 85579 Neubiberg, Germany
sophie-marie.stasch@unibw.de

Abstract. In multitasking environments, such as military flight missions, effective task prioritization is crucial to ensure overall flight safety. Cognitive control plays a vital role in this process, balancing stability for goal pursuit and flexibility for reacting to unexpected events. This can be challenging, since cognitive stability is also associated with more difficult task switching and cognitive flexibility is linked to distractedness. This study explores the use of eye-tracking metrics to diagnose the cognitive control state of operators within an adaptive assistance system in a multitasking environment. Three studies, involving 144 participants, manipulated control modes using a task prioritization strategy in a low-fidelity flight simulator. Eye movement data was recorded at 1000 Hz. The study employed eight supervised machine learning algorithms for binary classification, namely random forest, k-nearest neighbors, support vector machines, naïve bayes, decision trees, logistic regression, linear discriminant analysis, and XGBoost. The average accuracy of 0.89 demonstrates that the recognition of the cognitive control mode via eye-tracking is feasible. The findings suggest the potential integration of eye-tracking metrics into real-time user state diagnosis for adaptive assistance systems, especially in safety-critical human-machine systems. However, further research is needed to validate the classifier in more realistic flight environments with an expert sample.

Keywords: Adaptive Assistance · MATB · Eye-Tracking · Safety-critical Systems · Cognitive Control · Multitasking

1 Multitasking, Task Prioritization and Cognitive Control in the Cockpit

1.1 Multitasking and Task Prioritization in the Cockpit

In highly demanding multitasking environments, such as flight missions, military tasks must be managed alongside with aircraft operations. Different cognitive theories try to explain and predict multitasking behavior in this working environment. For instance, the concept of multiple resources [1] assumes that simultaneous task processing is possible as long as both tasks do not rely on the same resource. Based on this theory, listening to radio messages from air traffic control while simultaneously scanning the environment for potential threats should be possible without task interference. Contrary, Oberauer and

Kliegel [2] argue that parallel task processing as a form of multitasking is possible, as long as task requirements do not exceed working memory capacity. Salvucci and Taatgen [3] propose in their theory of threaded cognition an integrated framework assuming that every task is represented by a thread. These threads are coordinated by a serial procedural resource, can act in parallel but are also constrained by available resources. However, no supervisory executive process controlling this process is needed.

Even if the precise mechanism leading to increased multitasking costs and higher error rates while multitasking in the cockpit [4–6] is not entirely clarified yet, all theories agree that multitasking costs arise at a certain point in time when executing multiple tasks simultaneously. As a consequence, unlimited task processing is not possible for the majority of people [7]. Pilots must therefore be able to deal with these limits of human information processing to be able to control the aircraft safely, also in mental overload situations.

One possibility of doing so is the adherence to the A-N-C-M axiom (Aviate-Navigate-Communicate-Manage), a task prioritization strategy that dictates the prioritization of the most safety-critical aviate task in emergencies. The strategy proposes that only if resources are left, less-safety critical tasks, like responding to radio messages, should be completed. The relevance of the correct task prioritization is also made apparent by the fact that task misprioritization is one of the nanocodes of the subcategory "decision errors" of the Human Factors Analysis and Classification System (HFCAS) used by Kelly and Efthymiou [8]. The authors analyzed 50 controlled flights into terrain aviation accidents from the military, commercial, and general aviation domains and could identify the nanocode "task misprioritization" 19 times within the report's analysis. Also Chou et al. [9] investigated cockpit task management errors in flight accidents and found that task prioritization made up 30% of all cockpit task management errors, including distraction by weather and traffic watches.

Cognitive control is key for the context-sensitive direction of attention to maintain situational awareness in multitasking situations. Focusing on the correct flight parameters in emergencies while simultaneously ignoring the less relevant radio messages is just one example for this phenomenon.

1.2 Stability-Flexibility-Dilemma of Cognitive Control

Effective task prioritization relies heavily on cognitive control [10–12], which enables efficient allocation of attention to pursuing task-relevant goals while resisting distractions. However, cognitive control is not a one-size-fits-all concept. It is subject to the stability-flexibility dilemma [13–16], encompassing opposing demands on cognitive control. On the one hand, cognitive stability is necessary for efficient goal pursuit and to mentally block out irrelevant distractions. However, too high levels of cognitive stability can lead to deteriorated task switches. On the other hand, cognitive flexibility is necessary to quickly react to unexpected events by flexibly alternating action tendencies. Similar to cognitive stability, cognitive flexibility is also accompanied by demerits: Too high levels of cognitive flexibility lead to distractibility and worsen the pursuit of goals. While it has been demonstrated that performance and workload level differ between a stable and a flexible control state in a low-fidelity flight simulator [17], it remains to be explored how an adaptive assistance system could consider the cognitive control mode of operators in order to compensate for the associated disadvantages of each mental state.

2 Adaptive Assistance Systems

2.1 User State Diagnosis

Adaptive assistance systems can autonomously adjust their behavior to meet the dynamic needs of users within a human-machine system [18]. Based on the "perceive – select – act" cycle [19], information systems and sensors initially perceive and assess the entire system's context, including the state of the system, the external environment, the task, and the operator's state. Based on this context assessment, an adaptations manager can select suitable adaptations. These adaptations are then executed by the automation system and the human-machine interface, which in turn can influence the operator's state, closing the "perceive – select – act" cycle (see Fig. 1).

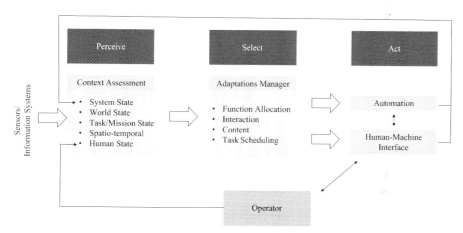

Fig. 1. Diagram of a generic adaptive joint human-machine system according to [18], based on the "perceive – select – act" – [19].

To ensure that this loop also leads to improved human-machine performance, the first step is to correctly determine the current user state. Schwarz et al. [20] describe in the multidimensional user state assessment six critical user states (workload, engagement, situation awareness, attention, fatigue, emotional state) that can lead to performance decrements in human-machine systems. In their generic model of the user state, the authors argue that the current user state can be influenced by the work environment, including the task, physical conditions, the context, the technical system, objectives, and events. Individual short-term factors, like sleep and general well-being as well as long-term factors, like ability, skills, and experience are also considered to interact with the current user state. If a critical user state occurs, for instance, a mental overload situation in a dynamic multitasking scenario, this leads on the one hand to a change in information processing. On the other hand, such a critical user state is also accompanied by behavioral reactions, like a change in facial expressions. Physiological reactions, like a change in pupil dilation or heart rate, are correlates of a critical user state, too. These critical user states can be assessed through performance measures, self-rating, behavioral measures, state modeling, and physiological measures.

Liu et al. [21] apply the concept of adaptive assistance systems in the Cognitive Pilot Aircraft Interface (CPAI). The CPAI architecture model consists of a sensing module, that tries to estimate a pilot's physiological condition by collecting data from the nervous system (e.g., brain waves), circulatory system (e.g., heart rate), respiratory system (e.g., respiratory rate) and sensory system (e.g., blink rate). Environmental conditions, like the weather and the terrain, as well as operational conditions, like a certain flight phase, are used to estimate external conditions. Based on this data, the estimation module can estimate in real-time the cognitive state of the pilot as well as the mental demands that are associated with upcoming tasks. Finally, the reconfiguration module can trigger adaptive automation, for instance by making the task manager redistribute tasks between the pilot and the automation system. Furthermore, an adaptive interface can influence the amount of displayed information to the pilot. Finally, an adaptive alerting system has the opportunity to modify caution and warning flags according to the current pilot's user state.

In general, physiological measures offer the distinct advantage, over for instance self-ratings, to be able to continuously and unobtrusively assess the user state in real-time due to the high temporal resolution of physiological reactions and sensors assessing those. Since operating an aircraft is a highly visual task, the use of eye-tracking technology is particularly suitable to assess a pilot's distribution of attention or other aspects relevant to the assessment of critical user states.

2.2   Use of Eye-Tracking in Adaptive Assistance Systems in the Cockpit

Different eye-tracking metrics have been intensively researched and linked to different performance outcomes in the aviation sector [22, 23]. To integrate eye-tracking technology into the cockpit, Peysakhovich [24] describe a four-stage process to assess the pilot's attentional distribution and underlying decisional processes. Stage I includes the analysis and recording of eye-tracking and performance data from pilot training on the ground. The eye and flight data are recorded in Stage II in the cockpit, forming a visual behavior database. This database serves to improve pilot training (Stage I) and verify the coherence of visual behavior within the flight context. If inconsistencies are detected, adaptation can be employed on the flight deck (Stage III), encompassing warning and alerting systems. Stage IV envisions gaze-based aircraft adaptation, involving the aircraft taking authority.

Given the interconnectedness of cognitive control and attention [10, 25], it is worthwhile to explore which eye-tracking metrics could be employed for real-time diagnosis of pilots' cognitive control mode.

Table 1 gives a selective overview of potential eye-tracking metrics and their associated cognitive correlates that might be relevant to diagnosing the cognitive control mode of pilots as part of a real-time cognitive condition estimation model. The table contains a selection of Area-of-Interest (AOI)-specific metrics, like the number of fixations and the fixation duration on a certain AOI, as well as AOI-independent or general eye-tracking metrics. The latter category includes metrics like the saccade-fixation-ratio, the coefficient K, the number of task switches, as well as stationary and transition entropy.

In the following, the total number of fixations relates to the total number of fixations on an AOI. The fixation duration means the mean duration of a fixation on an AOI. The Saccade-Fixation-Ratio is calculated by dividing the time spent on fixations (processing) by the time spent on saccades (searching) [26]. A task switch is identified when a fixation changes from AOI to another AOI. In the following, an AOI is to be equated with a task (see Fig. 2). The coefficient K is calculated based on the mean difference between z-transformed saccade amplitudes (a_{i+1}) and the processing i^{th} fixation duration (d_i):

$$K_i = \frac{d_i - \mu_d}{\sigma_d} - \frac{a_{i+1} - \mu_a}{\sigma_a}$$

[27]
such that:

$$K = \frac{1}{n} \sum_n K_i$$

where:
μ_d = mean fixation duration
μ_a = mean saccade amplitude
σ_d = standard deviation of fixation
σ_a = standard deviation of saccade amplitude
The calculation of stationary and transition entropy is based on Shannon's entropy equation, which refers to the average information or uncertainty associated with choice:

$$H(x) = -\sum_{i=1}^{n} (p_i) \log_2 (p_i)$$

[28]
where:
$H(x)$ = entropy value of sequence x
i = indexes of the individual states
n = length of x
p_i = proportion of each state within x
The interested reader is advised to consult Krejtz et al. [29] for details on the calculation of transition and stationary entropy.

Therefore, the following study tries to explore if eye-tracking metrics could be used to diagnose the cognitive control state of an operator in a multitasking environment. If this is feasible, the control mode could be incorporated into the "perceive" stage of a future adaptive assistance system for pilots.

Table 1. AOI-specific and general eye-tracking metrics potentially relevant for user state diagnosis of the cognitive control mode in the cockpit.

Metrics	Association
Number of Fixations	↑ increased information processing [30], increased task difficulty [31]
Fixation Duration	↑ deeper cognitive processing [32, 33]
Saccade-Fixation-Ratio	↑ more visual processing and less searching [26]
Task switches	↑ flexible control mode, ↓ stable control mode [15]
Coefficient K	Positive values → ambient processing; negative values → focal processing [27]
Stationary entropy	↑ Exploratory mode of visual attention, ↓ focal mode of visual attention [34]
Transition entropy	↑ complex pattern of sequential scanning behavior ↓ predictable scanning sequence with fewer fixation transitions between fewer AOI [34]

3 Method

3.1 Ethics

To address this question, two pilot studies and one experimental study (ethics approval number: EK UniBw M 23-16) were conducted. In total, 144 participants from the Universität der Bundeswehr München were tested and included in the dataset. Subjects participated in the experiments in exchange for student lab tokens prior to giving informed consent to all experiments. Data was recorded anonymously and processed in accordance with Art. 6 Abs. 1 lit. a EU-DSGVO.

3.2 Experimental Set-Up

The open Multi-Attribute Task Battery (MATB [35]) served as a multitasking environment, simulating four flight tasks that needed to be operated simultaneously. The respective task prioritization strategy was reinforced via a gamification method [36], which, among other things, provided participants with a feedback score varying between 0 and 100. The score reflected how well participants followed the instructions on task prioritization. No task prioritization was related to a flexible control state, and the prioritization of the tracking task was related to a stable control state. The experiments differed according to how the feedback score was calculated; the experimental instructions on task prioritization remained the same, though.

Two types of scenarios (A and B) were tested with either a flexible or a stable instruction, resulting in four conditions. This procedure was adopted to rule out the possibility that possible effects are only due to the design of the task. Conditions were counterbalanced between participants to control for sequence effects. One condition consisted of five trials, which were 90 s long. Eye movement data was recorded with the SR Research Eye-Link 1000 at 1000 Hz in a head-fixed position.

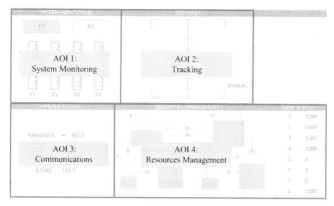

Fig. 2. The openMATB has four subtasks: System-Monitoring, Tracking, Communications and Resource Management. See [35] for details. Each subtask was defined as an AOI.

3.3 Data Pre-processing

Fixations and saccades were exported using the EyeLink Data Viewer software package (SR Research Ltd., version 4.3.1). Individual 90-second trials were utilized instead of averaged condition values, given the aim of incorporating the control mode of pilots into the real-time user state diagnosis. To ensure adherence to task prioritization instructions, only trials with a feedback score of 50 or above were included in the subsequent analysis. In total, 890 trials of the flexible condition and 646 trials of the stable condition were present in the dataset after pre-processing.

The eye-tracking metrics described in Table 1 served as features. The cognitive control mode served as the outcome variable. The data pre-processing workflow is based on recommendations for reporting machine learning results [37]. On average, 2.99% of the data was missing per selected feature. Data imputation on the missing values was performed to avoid data loss. Additionally, min-max normalization was performed to ensure scale independence and to support algorithm convergence. The subsequent analysis comprised two main steps: feature selection of eye-tracking metrics and supervised classification.

4 Results

4.1 Feature Selection

Eye-tracking metrics were selected based on correlations between each MATB subtask performance and the corresponding eye-tracking metrics. Those eye-tracking metrics demonstrating a correlation with performance indicators with at least substantial evidence ($BF10 \geq 3$) [38] were selected as input variables for different supervised machine algorithms. To distinguish relevant eye-tracking metrics, that will be considered as features in the models, correlations between the single MATB performance indices and the eye-tracking metrics per condition were performed. Detailed results can be found in this repository (https://osf.io/p6nu5/).

4.2   Supervised Classification

Train and test data were split in an 80/20 ratio. 10-fold cross-validation was used to obtain a more reliable estimate of each model's performance and to prevent overfitting. The employed algorithms include random forest, k-nearest neighbors, support vector machines, naïve bayes, decision trees, logistic regression, linear discriminant analysis, and XGBoost. The scikit-learn package Version 1.3.0 [39] in Python (Version 3.10.9) was used in the subsequent analysis. Each algorithm was evaluated based on accuracy, precision, recall, F1-scores, and Cohen's kappa. Table 2 demonstrates these performance metrics for these algorithms.

Table 2. Performance metrics of the tested algorithms.

Classifier	Accuracy	Precision	Recall	F1-Score	Cohen's Kappa
Random Forest	0.92	0.94	0.87	0.90	0.83
K-Nearest Neighbor	0.89	0.89	0.84	0.87	0.77
Support Vector Machine	0.89	0.91	0.83	0.87	0.77
Naïve Bayes	0.85	0.93	0.70	0.80	0.68
Decision Tree	0.89	0.87	0.88	0.87	0.78
Logistic Regression	0.92	0.94	0.87	0.91	0.84
Linear Discriminant Analysis	0.90	0.94	0.82	0.88	0.79
XGBoost	0.91	0.94	0.86	0.90	0.83
Average of all algorithms	0.89	0.92	0.83	0.88	0.79

Considering the accuracy value, the random forest algorithm as well as the logistic regression algorithm demonstrated the best performance with a value of 0.92. Regarding precision, the random forest, the logistic regression, the linear discriminant analysis, as well as the XGBoost algorithm showed the highest values of 0.94. The decision tree achieved the highest recall value of 0.88. Concerning the F1-Score, the logistic regression showed the highest value of 0.91. The highest Kappa value was also achieved by the logistic regression with a value of 0.84. ROC and precision-recall curves additionally visualize performance of each algorithm and allow for a visual comparison between the different algorithms (see Fig. 3).

Since all algorithms performed comparably well on performance metrics, Fig. 4 takes the example of the XGBoost algorithm to demonstrate the importance of each feature. With an F-Score of 136.0, the saccade-fixation-ratio is the feature with the highest importance. The fixation duration of the resource management task is ranked second with a F-Score of 134 follows. The fixation duration of the system monitoring task obtained an F-Score of 126. Stationary entropy is ranked with an F-Score of 118. The fixation duration of the tracking task is ranked with an F-Score of 115, and the

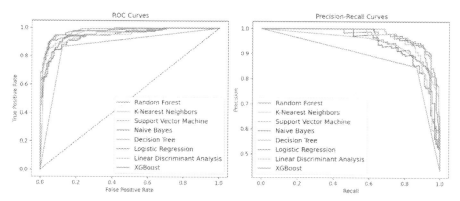

Fig. 3. Left: Receiver-Operating-Characteristic (ROC) curves demonstrate the relationship between the true positive rate and the false positive rate for each algorithm. *Right:* The Precision-Recall curves show the tradeoff between precision and recall for different thresholds.

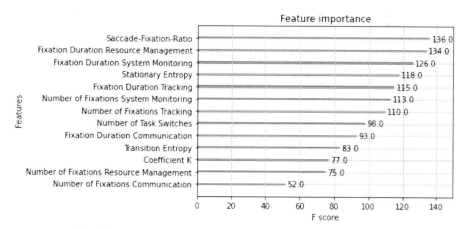

Fig. 4. Feature Importance of each feature of the XGBoost-Classifier.

number of fixations on the system monitoring task is ranked with an F-Score of 113. The number of fixations on the tracking task obtained an F-Score of 110. The number of task switches has an F-Score of 98 and the fixation duration on the communication task has an F-Score of 93. Transition entropy is ranked with an F-Score of 83. The coefficient K has an F-Score of 77. The number of fixations on the resource management task is ranked as second least important with a F-Score of 75. The number of fixations on the communication task is ranked as least important with an F-Score of 52. Table 3 shows the accuracy performance for each of the 10 folds of the XGBoost-Classifier, resulting in an average accuracy value of 0.91.

Table 3. Accuracy performance of the XGBoost-Classifier for each of the 10 folds.

	1	2	3	4	5	6	7	8	9	10	Ø
Accuracy	0.93	0.86	0.93	0.90	0.93	0.94	0.91	0.90	0.89	0.91	0.91

5   Discussion

5.1   Findings and Results

The present study investigated which eye-tracking metrics could be suitable as features in the user state diagnosis of the cognitive control modes in the cockpit. Potentially, the cognitive control mode could be included in the "perceive"- part of an adaptive assistance system. For this purpose, the eye movements of participants were evaluated at 90-second intervals in three experiments. The experiments manipulated the cognitive control mode via task prioritization instructions and a gamification method [36]. Eight algorithms were tested to predict a stable control or a flexible control mode based on 13 different eye-tracking features. Results reveal that the cognitive control mode can be predicted with an accuracy range of 0.85–0.92, with an average accuracy of 0.89. This means that on average, 89% of the predictions were made correctly. The use of 10-fold cross-validation further strengthens the robustness of the models and contributes to a stable performance estimate. Precision values range from 0.87 to 0.94 with an average of 0.92, providing a good value for the accuracy of the positive predictions. Recall values range from 0.7 to 0.88, with an average value of 0.83. The F1-Scores as well as the Kappa values are in line with the precision and recall values. Although the dataset is only slightly unbalanced (flexible: 58%, stable: 42%), the precision and recall values as well as the F1-Score were investigated.

At the current point in time, the costs of false negatives and false positives are considered to be more or less the same. Both types of control modes can be suitable or unsuitable according to the current context, since adaptive assistance is supposed to compensate for the associated disadvantages in information processing. For instance, a too flexible control mode is linked to an increased chance of distraction, potentially leading to deteriorated goal pursuit. A too stable control mode is associated with hampered task-switching. It is argued, therefore, that the prediction of both modes is equally important, and the interpretation of precision and recall values should be accorded equal importance.

5.2   Limitations, Future Research and Implications for the Design of Adaptive Systems

The good performance of the tested algorithms underscores the potential significance and feasibility of integrating eye-tracking metrics into the user-state diagnosis of the cognitive control mode. The use of 90-second intervals allows for a potential real-time assessment in the development of adaptive assistance systems. However, it should be taken into consideration that the current dataset is based on data from a low-fidelity flight simulator. The MATB does not reflect the entire complexity of an aircraft cockpit, including the variety of flight tasks that pilots face during a flight. Furthermore, the instruments in a cockpit are also arranged differently compared to the MATB. Future research should explore the extent to which the proposed classification approach is also applicable to different flight phases in a high-fidelity flight simulator. Furthermore, the tested sample consisted of university students with little to no flight experience. Previous research has shown that visual scanning techniques differ between novices and experts [40–42]. Since the saccade-fixation-ratio is grouped into the category of scanpath metrics [26] and has the highest feature importance in the example of the XGBoost algorithm, future research needs to investigate if the proposed metrics are also suitable to detect the control mode of experienced pilots in the cockpit with real-world scenarios. The current studies recorded the eye movements in a head-fixed position; a high-fidelity flight simulator would further add noise since head movements cannot be controlled. Consequently, future studies testing pilots with differing expertise will strengthen the external validity of the proposed classification approach.

The study of the eye movements of pilots on the ground is also the first stage of the proposed framework to integrate eye movements into the cockpit [24]. Feigh et al. [18] identify four primary ways of an adaptation system to influence human-machine performance (see Fig. 1). First, the modification of function allocation relates to who is executing a task (operator or machine) based on the current context assessment. For instance, additional tasks could be automated in case the operator is in a stable control mode and has a reduced ability to switch to other tasks. In the case of modification of scheduling, the system dynamically changes the timing, prioritization, and duration of a task to be performed. A task manager could, for instance, schedule activities with equal priority to be performed in close temporal succession if an operator is in a flexible control mode because task switches are associated with reduced cost compared to a stable control mode. Modifications of interactions relate to the layout of an interface and with which modality information is perceived. In the case of a stable control mode, warning signals could be increased in intensity (visual and auditory) to ensure that the operator is indeed processing the relevant information. Lastly, the modification of context relates to what information is presented to the user at a varying level of detail. Taking again the example of a flexible control mode, the interface could include less details that are not relevant to the pilots' current goals in order to avoid distraction by less task-relevant information.

Other applications in safety-critical human-machine systems are also conceivable. These include the user-state diagnosis of operators in power plants, in which adaptive assistance systems are highly important in emergency situations [43], railway transportation [44] or maritime operations [45].

Systems with a high degree of supervisory control, like those for air traffic control, could also benefit from an integration of the cognitive control mode. The "Vigilance and Attention Controller" [46] system assesses in real-time the vigilance level of the air traffic controller by electroencephalography (EEG) and eye-tracking and adapt the level of automation based on this assessment. The integration of the cognitive control mode could further enhance the overall human-machine performance by compensating for the associated disadvantages and preventing safety-critical "out-of-the-loop" situations. To achieve this, further research is needed under the aforementioned aspects.

6 Conclusion

The presented paper successfully demonstrated that the cognitive control mode can be diagnosed by the means of eye-tracking metrics in a multitasking flight environment. Results from eight binary classification algorithms demonstrate the feasibility of classifying the control mode with an average accuracy of 0.89 using the proposed features. This study marks a crucial step toward integrating the cognitive control mode of pilots into the "perceive"-stage of an adaptive assistance system. However, more studies are needed to strengthen the applicability and generalizability of these findings. Future research should explore the feasibility of the proposed classification algorithms in a high-fidelity simulator including a sample containing novice and expert pilots. Ultimately, the application has the potential to further enhance safety and human-machine performance in demanding multitasking scenarios.

Acknowledgments. This research is funded by dtec.bw – Digitalization and Technology Research Center of the Bundeswehr (project MissionLab). Dtec.bw is funded by the European Union – NextGenerationEU.

Disclosure of Interests. The authors have no competing interests to declare that are relevant to the content of this article.

References

1. Wickens, C.D.: The structure of attentional resources. In: Nickerson, R. (ed.) Attention and Performance, pp. 239–257. Erlbaum, Hillsdale, NJ (1980)
2. Oberauer, K., Kliegl R.: A formal model of capacity limits in working memory. J. Memory Lang. **55**(4), 601–626 (2006). https://www.sciencedirect.com/science/article/pii/S0749596X06000982
3. Salvucci, D.D., Taatgen, N.A.: Threaded cognition: an integrated theory of concurrent multitasking. Psychol. Rev. **115**(1), 101–130 (2008)
4. Wickens, C.D., Goh, J., Helleberg, J., Horrey, W.J., Talleur, D.A.: Attentional models of multitask pilot performance using advanced display technology. In: Human Error in Aviation, pp. 155–175 (2017)
5. Chérif, L., Wood, V., Marois, A., Labonté, K., Vachon, F.: Multitasking in the military: cognitive consequences and potential solutions. Appl. Cogn. Psychol. **32**(4), 429–439 (2018)
6. Loukopoulos, L.D., Dismukes, R.K., Barshi, I.: The Multitasking Myth: Handling Complexity in Real-World Operations. Routledge, London (2016)
7. Watson, J.M., Strayer, D.L.: Supertaskers: profiles in extraordinary multitasking ability. Psychon. Bull. Rev. **17**, 479–485 (2010)
8. Kelly, D., Efthymiou, M.: An analysis of human factors in fifty controlled flight into terrain aviation accidents from 2007 to 2017. J. Safety Res. **69**, 155–165 (2019)
9. Chou, C.C., Madhavan, D., Funk, K.: Studies of cockpit task management errors. Int. J. Aviat. Psychol. **6**(4), 307–320 (1996)
10. Mackie, M.A., van Dam, N.T., Fan, J.: Cognitive control and attentional functions. Brain Cogn. **82**(3), 301–312 (2013)
11. Liegel, N., Schneider, D., Wascher, E., Arnau, S.: Task prioritization modulates alpha, theta and beta EEG dynamics reflecting proactive cognitive control. Sci. Rep. **12**(1), 15072 (2022)

12. Fischer, R., Gottschalk, C., Dreisbach, G.: Context-sensitive adjustment of cognitive control in dual-task performance. J. Exp. Psychol. Learn. Mem. Cogn. **40**(2), 399–416 (2014)
13. Goschke, T., Bolte, A.: Emotional modulation of control dilemmas: the role of positive affect, reward, and dopamine in cognitive stability and flexibility. Neuropsychologia **62**, 403–423 (2014). https://www.sciencedirect.com/science/article/pii/S0028393214002358
14. Musslick, S., Jang, S.J., Shvartsman, M., Shenhav, A., Cohen, J.D.: Constraints associated with cognitive control and the stability-flexibility dilemma. In: Cognitive Science (2018). https://api.semanticscholar.org/CorpusID:117726732
15. Dreisbach, G., Fröber, K.: On How to Be Flexible (or Not): modulation of the stability-flexibility balance. Curr. Dir. Psychol. Sci. **28**(1), 3–9 (2019)
16. Nassar, M.R., Troiani, V.: The stability flexibility tradeoff and the dark side of detail. Cogn. Affect. Behav. Neurosci. **21**(3), 607–623 (2021)
17. Stasch, S., Mack, W.: Why the stability-flexibility-dilemma should be taken into consideration when studying pilots multitasking behaviour. In: Praetorius, G., Sellberg, C., Patriarca, R. (eds.) Human Factors in Transportation. AHFE International Conference. AHFE Open Access, vol. 95. AHFE International, USA (2023). https://doi.org/10.54941/ahfe1003846
18. Feigh, K.M., Dorneich, M.C., Hayes, C.C.: Toward a characterization of adaptive systems: a framework for researchers and system designers. Hum. Factors **54**(6), 1008–1024 (2012)
19. Wickens, C.D.: Engineering Psychology and Human Performance, 2nd edn. HarperCollins Publishers, New York (1992)
20. Schwarz, J., Fuchs, S., Flemisch, F.: Towards a more holistic view on user state assessment in adaptive human-computer interaction. In: 2014 IEEE International Conference on Systems, Man, and Cybernetics (SMC), pp. 1228–1234. IEEE (2014)
21. Liu, J., Gardi, A., Ramasamy, S., Lim, Y., Sabatini, R.: Cognitive pilot-aircraft interface for single-pilot operations. Knowl.-Based Syst. **112**, 37–53 (2016)
22. Di Stasi, L.L., Diaz-Piedra, C.: Re-examining the pioneering studies on eye movements in aviation: connecting the past to the present. Int. J. Aerosp. Psychol. **31**(2), 122–134 (2021)
23. Peißl, S., Wickens, C.D., Baruah, R.: Eye-tracking measures in aviation: a selective literature review. Int. J. Aerosp. Psychol. **28**(3–4), 98–112 (2018)
24. Peysakhovich, V., Lefrançois, O., Dehais, F., Causse, M.: The neuroergonomics of aircraft cockpits: the four stages of eye-tracking integration to enhance flight safety. Safety **4**(1), 8 (2018)
25. Lavie, N., Hirst, A., Fockert, J.W., Viding, E.: Load theory of selective attention and cognitive control. J. Exp. Psychol. Gen. **133**(3), 339–354 (2004)
26. Joseph, A.W., Murugesh, R.: Potential eye tracking metrics and indicators to measure cognitive load. Hum.-Comput. Interact. Res. **64**(01), 168–175 (2020)
27. Krejtz, K., Duchowski, A., Krejtz, I., Szarkowska, A., Kopacz, A.: Discerning ambient/focal attention with coefficient K. ACM Trans. Appl. Percept. **13**(3), 1–20 (2016)
28. Shannon, C.E.: A mathematical theory of communication. Bell Syst. Tech. J. **27**(3), 379–423 (1948)
29. Krejtz, K., et al.: Gaze transition entropy. ACM Trans. Appl. Percept. **13**(1), 1–20 (2015)
30. Yarbus, A.L.: Eye Movements and Vision. Springer, Cham (2013). https://doi.org/10.1007/978-1-4899-5379-7
31. Young, A.H., Hulleman, J.: Eye movements reveal how task difficulty moulds visual search. J. Exp. Psychol. Hum. Percept. Perform. **39**(1), 168 (2013)
32. Rayner, K.: Eye movements in reading and information processing. Psychol. Bull. **85**(3), 618 (1978)
33. Salthouse, T.A., Ellis, C.L.: Determinants of eye-fixation duration. Am. J. Psychol. **93**, 207–234 (1978)
34. Shiferaw, B., Downey, L., Crewther, D.: A review of gaze entropy as a measure of visual scanning efficiency. Neurosci. Biobehav. Rev. **96**, 353–366 (2019)

35. Cegarra, J., Valéry, B., Avril, E., Calmettes, C., Navarro, J.: OpenMATB: a multi-attribute task battery promoting task customization, software extensibility and experiment replicability. Behav. Res. Methods **52**(5), 1980–1990 (2020)

36. Stasch, S., Mack, W.: A new experimental method to investigate multitasking strategies in flight environments via the use of gamification. In: Proceedings of the Human Factors and Ergonomics Society Europe Chapter 2023 Annual Conference, pp. 23–33 (2023). http://hfes-europe.org

37. Stevens, L.M., Mortazavi, B.J., Deo, R.C., Curtis, L., Kao, D.P.: Recommendations for reporting machine learning analyses in clinical research. Circ. Cardiovasc. Qual. Outcomes **13**(10), 006556 (2020)

38. Jeffreys, H.: Theory of Probability. Clarendon Press, Oxford (1939)

39. Pedregosa, F., et al.: Scikit-learn: machine learning in Python. J. Mach. Learn. Res. **12**, 2825–2830 (2011)

40. Yang, J.H., Kennedy, Q., Sullivan, J., Fricker, R.D.: Pilot performance: assessing how scan patterns & navigational assessments vary by flight expertise. Aviat. Space Environ. Med. **84**(2), 116–124 (2013)

41. Robinski, M., Stein, M.: Tracking visual scanning techniques in training simulation for helicopter landing. JEMR **6**(2) (2013)

42. Kirby, C.E., Kennedy, Q., Yang, J.H.: Helicopter pilot scan techniques during low-altitude high-speed flight. Aviat. Space Environ. Med. **85**(7), 740–744 (2014)

43. Seong, P.H., Kang, H.G., Na, M.G., Kim, J.H., Heo, G., Jung, Y.: Advanced MMIS toward substantial reduction in human errors in NPPs. Nucl. Eng. Technol. **45**(2), 125–140 (2013)

44. Enjalbert, S., Gandini, L.M., Pereda Baños, A., Ricci, S., Vanderhaegen, F.: Human-machine interface in transport systems: an industrial overview for more extended rail applications. Machines **9**(2), 36 (2021)

45. Liu, C., et al.: Human–machine cooperation research for navigation of maritime autonomous surface ships: a review and consideration. Ocean Eng. **246**, 110555 (2022)

46. Di Flumeri, G., et al.: Brain-computer interface-based adaptive automation to prevent out-of-the-loop phenomenon in air traffic controllers dealing with highly automated systems. Front. Hum. Neurosci. **13**, 296 (2019)

Pilots' Workload in the Cockpit with Onboard Tangible Information System

Wei Tan[1,2] (ORCID), Yuan Sun[1(✉)] (ORCID), and Wenqing Wang[1(✉)] (ORCID)

[1] College of Safety Science and Engineering, Civil Aviation University of China, Tianjin, China
sunyuan_sy@163.com, 15263681730@163.com
[2] Key Laboratory of Artificial Intelligence of Civil Aviation Airlines, Guangzhou, China

Abstract. With the improvement of aircraft's cockpit automation level, human-computer interaction is becoming increasingly important. Nowadays, the display of flight instruments is highly integrated, and pilots' workload is also increasing. Improper handling of workload by the flight crew during the execution of flight missions is one of the important reasons for human errors. In the rapid development of intelligent technology, we need adaptive, intelligent, personalized, and higher-level automation technology systems. The intelligent onboard tangible information system (OTIS) adopted by this research was used to replace electronic flight bag (EFB). Different from step-by-step troubleshooting against operating procedures, this system can communicate in real-time with aircraft systems, quickly locate aircraft faults, help pilots quickly execute programs, reduce the time of interaction information with the system, and improve search efficiency.

This study conducted a comparative simulation flight experiment based on the A320 simulator to explore the differences in workload levels between pilots using traditional EFB and OTIS. The experiment used physiological indicators, NASA-TLX (NASA-Task Load Index) ratings, and task performed time to characterize the workload of pilots. Firstly, a difference test was conducted to explore whether there were significant differences in objective and subjective indicators of pilots handling the same abnormal scenario under EFB and OTIS; Secondly, the data were compared to further determine the levels of pilots' workload. The reduction of pilots' workload can preliminarily verify the rationality of OTIS. It proves that OTIS can effectively reduce pilots' workload. This study can provide a reference for the design of OTIS for the future cockpit.

Keywords: Pilots' Workload · Information System · Physiological Indicators · NASA-TLX

1 Introduction

For a long time, human factors scientists have been interested in the relationship between workload and human performance. The workload of operators can lead to frustration, discomfort, and fatigue, resulting in decreased accuracy and awareness of the surrounding environment. Conversely, individuals with insufficient workload may also experience the same problems. When operators fail to allocate attention properly and become complacent, less workload can result in a higher level of error rates, frustration, fatigue, and situation awareness [1]. Human errors are responsible for 75% of aviation accidents, with mental workload and fatigue being the primary causes [2].

Cockpit design has undergone a significant shift since the 1950s, moving towards a reduction in crewmembers, also known as 'de-crewing' [3]. From a five-crewmember to the current two-crewmember, taking advances in aircraft automation systems have allowed two pilots to perform all the tasks instead of a larger team previously [4]. This trend of reducing crewmembers is expected to be continued. This reduction in pilots leads to an increased workload obviously, however the improved level of automation can help to enhance pilots' performance and reduce workload [5]. While the technology of automation has reduced the physical workload of pilots, it has increased their mental workload and changed the human-machine interaction and flight operations in the cockpit [6]. Nowadays artificial intelligence technology is developed rapidly, the cockpit design requires adaptive, intelligent, and personalized technology systems with a higher level of automation. To address the challenges associated with automation, it is recommended to adopt a human-centered automation design approach, developing effective automation interfaces for human-machine interaction, and optimizing system design [7–9]. Intelligent onboard systems based on intelligent technology in aircraft may help overcome the limitations of current automation technology [10]. AI, and more specifically the machine learning field of AI, is bringing an enormous potential for developing applications that would not have been possible with the development techniques that have been used so far [11].

There are mainly three methods to measure workload: subjective measurement, performance measurement, and physiological measurement [12]. Performance measurement focuses on operators' performance objectively [1]. The most direct performance measurement technique is to measure the speed and/or accuracy of operators performing tasks. Subjective workload measurement requires operators to describe the workload they experienced while performing tasks. Workload scales mainly include the Instant Self-Assessment (ISA) technique, NASA Task Load Index (TLX) measurement technique, Bedford Workload Scale, Subjective Workload Dominance (SWORD) technique, and so on. The most widely used among them is the NASA-TLX, which is a multidimensional scale where participants subjectively rate workload based on six dimensions. NASA-TLX is used to obtain self-evaluation of operators' workload immediately upon or after performing tasks [13]. Subjective measurement alone cannot provide a continuous measurement that usually needs to be combined with physiological indicators for a comprehensive evaluation of workload [14–21]. Physiological measurement methods attempt to associate physiological changes with workload levels. Common physiological indicators include heart rate (HR), heart rate variability (HRV), electroencephalogram (EEG), and so on.

Alaimo et al. [16] examined the workload of pilots during simulated flight by analyzing objective indicators of heart rate variability (HRV) to predict pilots' mental workload. They compared these indicators with subjective evaluation data from the NASA-TLX to demonstrate that changes in cardiac activity may be associated with heightened mental demands or fatigue, as corroborated by subjective data. Zheng et al. [17] conducted a study to predict pilots' workload using eye-tracking data, heart rate, and respiratory rate, along with the NASA-TLX and HR-D (difference between real-time HR and baseline HR). The results indicated that flight scenarios and environment had a significant impact on NASA-TLX, eye-tracking data, and heart rate. However, respiratory rate was found not to be a reliable and long-term predictor of workload. Mohanavelu et al. [18] demonstrated a correlation between physiological workload measurement (HRV) and pilot performance through experiments and validated it using self-assessment (NASA-TLX). Alaimo et al. [19] used the NASA-TLX and HRV to assess workload and introduced the Maneuver Error Index (MEI) as a performance measure. This study aims to investigate the differences in workload among pilots using EFB and OTIS to handle an abnormal scenario and to indicate pilots' workload using HR, HRV, NASA-TLX, and task performed time.

2   Methodology

Subjective Measurement. NASA-TLX was proposed by Sandra in 1988 for subjective workload measurement [22]. This scale is widely used as a subjective evaluation scale for assessing operators' workload after performing the tasks that is commonly applied both in aerospace and aviation. The astronauts and pilots have to involve in the operations to process a large amount of information in their work and make accurate decisions in various tasks or unexpected situations. The mental workload on these groups can significantly impact work performance and flight safety. Using this scale as an evaluation tool for the workload of the participants in this experiment can effectively assess the workload of pilots using the onboard tangible information system, which makes a great significance for the real-time detection of pilots' stress and the improvement of psychological health. Furthermore, the scale has only 6 contents, which is convenient to complete and has high usability.

Physiological Measurement. Physiological measurements in this experiment relied on Mean HR and HRV indicators. Researches indicate that the sympathetic and parasympathetic nervous systems influence changes in heart rate. The sympathetic nervous system accelerates heart rate, while the parasympathetic nervous system slows it down. The person's heart rate constantly fluctuates in a calm and conscious state, with a high frequency of change. When he or she is tired, the heart rate will decrease. When the workload increases, the heart rate increases. Individual factors influence heart rate, and there are significant variations among individuals. The HRV indicators include Mean IBI (Mean Inter-Beat Interval), SDNN (The standard deviation of the interval difference between adjacent RR), RMSSD (Root mean square of the difference between adjacent RR intervals), LF (Low-frequency power), HF (High-frequency power), and LF/HF (The ratio of low frequency to high frequency). Related studies have shown that as fatigue increases, heart rate variability, standard deviation and mean of RR interval significantly increase, while RMSSD increases and LF/HF ratio decreases. As workload increases, HRV will decrease, while SDNN, RMSSD, and LF will decrease.

Performance Measurement. The task performed time was used in this experiment to indicate the task performance of pilots, mainly referring to the task execution time from the occurrence of malfunction to the end of trouble-shooting, which can reflect the efficiency of pilots in executing actions. When the pilots are tired, the task performance will relatively deteriorate.

Human-in-the-Loop Simulation. Simulations always require human is in the test loop, reacting to inputs from other components in the simulation, and generating outputs that affect the results of the simulation [23]. User test is a method to identify deficiencies in product design and provide a basis for product optimization by assigning tasks to users during their execution. This is also the main method adopted in this experiment, which involves users to identify the shortcomings of the onboard tangible information system and making improvements.

3 Experiments

3.1 User Tests

Twenty-four airlines pilots were invited to participate in the experiment using the simulator, include 2 airlines instructors, 7 captains, and 15 first officers, with abundant flight experiences. The experiment used the flight cockpit human-machine interaction simulation system and physiological measurement instruments. The simulation system can achieve a level A320 FTD which is divided into four parts: the flight and environmental simulation system, the simulated aircraft cockpit hardware system, the malfunction simulation and the instructor system, and the visual system in different scenarios. The physiological measurement instruments support the flexible combination of wearable sensors, biosensors, and other types, and can collect physiological data including electrodermal activity (EDA), HR, electromyography (EMG), and other data.

Each pilot needed to use EFB and OTIS for two rounds of simulated flight with normal scenarios and an abnormal scenario of Engine Failure. The wearable physiological measurement device called photoplethysmography (PPG) was used in this experiment to record pilots' HR and HRV. All the pilots were trained to use OTIS familiarly in the simulator before the experiment began. After each simulated flight, the time to complete the task was recorded as the performance indicator, and the pilot was required to fill out the NASA-TLX.

3.2 Results

The indicators are used as shown in Table 1. Mean HR, LF/HF, NASA-TLX ratings, and task performed time will decrease as the workload decreases, while Mean IBI, SDNN, SDSD, pNN50, and pNN20 will increase as the workload decreases. After conducting normality tests on the data, Paired Samples t-Test is used for data that conforms to a normal distribution, and Wilcoxon Signed Ranks Test is used for difference testing on data that does not conform to a normal distribution.

The results of the comparison test showed that there were significant differences in NASA-TLX ratings, Mean HR, Mean IBI, pNN50, pNN20, and task performed time when using EFB (represented by V1) and OTIS (represented by V2) to deal with Engine

Table 1. A summary of used indicators and their expected effects due to the decreased pilots' workload.

Name	Description	Expected effect
Mean HR	The average of Heart Rate	Decrease
Mean IBI	The interval measurement between two successive R peaks	Increase
SDNN	The standard deviation of "regular" RR intervals	Increase
SDSD	The standard deviation of the successive difference of RR intervals	Increase
pNN50	Percentage of NN50 intervals	Increase
pNN20	Percentage of NN20 intervals	Increase
LF/HF	Ratio between LF & HF	Decrease
NASA-TLX ratings	Subjective workload ratings	Decrease
Task performed time	The time taken by pilots to handle Engine Failure	Decrease

Table 2. Paired Samples t-Test results

Pair	t	Degree of freedom	Significance (2-tailed)
V1 Mean HR-V2 Mean HR	3.328	23	0.003
V1 pNN20-V2 pNN20	−4.097	23	0.000
V1 TLX-V2 TLX	0.416	23	0.000

Table 3. Wilcoxon Signed Ranks Test results

Pair	Z	Significance (2-tailed)
V1 Mean IBI-V2 Mean IBI	−2.571	0.010
V1 SDNN-V2 SDNN	−1.229	0.219
V1 SDSD-V2 SDSD	−0.971	0.331
V1 pNN50-V2 pNN50	−2.914	0.004
V1 LF/HF-V2 LF/HF	0.000	1.000
V1 Time-V2 Time	−4.114	0.000

Failure, while there is no significant difference in other data. The results of the Paired Samples t-Test and Wilcoxon Signed Ranks Test are shown in Tables 2 and 3.

Figures 1, 2, 3 and 4 show the results obtained from the sample of 24 pilots in terms of physiological indicators, NASA-TLX ratings, and task performed time. Analyzing the median values of the sample, Mean HR, LF/HF, and subjective workload are manifested as EFB>OTIS. The values of Mean IBI, SDNN, SDSD, pNN50, and pNN20 are the opposite. Both NASA-TLX ratings and task performed time using OTIS are reduced compared to those using EFB.

Changes in all physiological indicators indicate a decrease in the pilots' workload, as shown in Figs. 1 and 2.

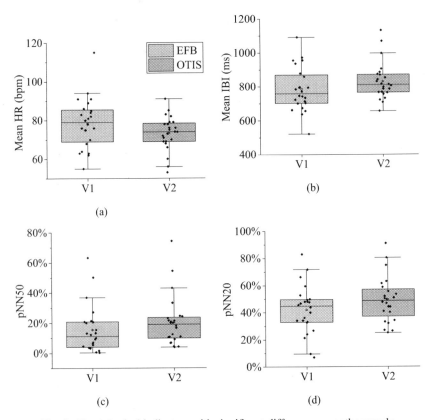

Fig. 1. Physiological indicators with significant differences over the sample

Figure 1 shows the physiological indicators with significant differences, including Mean HR, Mean IBI, pNN50, and pNN20.

Although there is no significant difference in SDNN, SDSD, and LF/HF, they still indicate a trend toward lower workload, as is shown in Fig. 2.

The result of NASA-TLX ratings indicates that the subjective workload of pilots is decreased when OTIS is used instead of EFB, as shown in Fig. 3.

The result of task performed time indirectly indicates that the objective workload of pilots is decreased, as shown in Fig. 4.

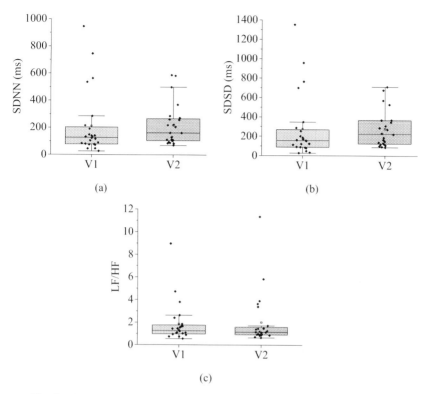

Fig. 2. Physiological indicators with no significant difference over the sample

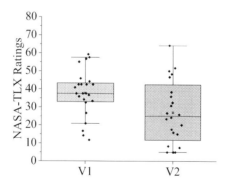

Fig. 3. NASA-TLX ratings over the sample

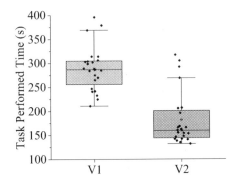

Fig. 4. Task performed time over the sample

4 Discussion

This study conducted a simulated flight experiment to measure the workload of pilots in the scenario of Engine Failure using EFB and OTIS. Three measurements were selected, including subjective questionnaire measurement, physiological measurement, and performance measurement. The results show significant differences in workload among pilots using two different information systems.

To measure the workload of pilots, NASA-TLX was used as a subjective workload measurement tool. This widely used scale allows pilots to rate their workload based on six dimensions after completing the flight tasks. The NASA-TLX ratings reveal that pilots experienced reduced subjective workload when using OTIS instead of EFB. However, the ratings of pilots using OTIS to deal with Engine Failure are more scattered compared to those using EFB, with a larger maximum rating value and range. It is suggested that pilots may not be as familiar with the intelligent system and may need to expend more time to understand and use it, resulting in a higher subjective load rating.

In terms of physiological measurement, Mean HR and HRV indicators were used in this study. HR stands for the average heart rate, which increases as pilots' workload increases. HRV, on the other hand, refers to the variation in the differences between heart rate cycles. Six HRV indicators were utilized in this study: Mean IBI, SDNN, SDSD, pNN50, pNN20, and LF/HF. As workload increases, HRV decreases, and LF/HF increases.

The results indicate significant differences in certain physiological indicators when pilots use two different information systems to deal with Engine Failure. Mean HR, Mean IBI, pNN50, and pNN20 with significant differences indicate that pilots' objective workload is also reduced. There is no significant differences in the values of SDNN, SDSD, and LF/HF. Even though the medians of these data are not the same when pilots use two systems. The average values are very similar. As a result, these three indicators have little significance.

As an indicator of performance measurement, task performed time can reflect the speed and efficiency with which the pilot performs the task. It refers to the time taken by pilots to perform tasks from the occurrence of malfunctions to the end of trouble-shooting. When pilots are fatigued, their performance will deteriorate, and the time taken to perform tasks will increase. This is the basic performance measurement for assessing pilots' workload. The results indirectly prove that using OTIS can reduce pilots' workload and improve efficiency of tasks to save time.

In summary, the intelligent onboard tangible information system in this research can significantly reduce the workload of pilots. The NASA-TLX ratings, Mean HR, Mean IBI, pNN50, pNN20, and task performed time in this study are valid data and have a certain reference value. However, SDNN, SDSD, and LF/HF may not have the same level of validity. The Mean IBI, pNN50, and pNN20 will increase as the pilot's workload decreases, while NASA-TLX ratings, Mean HR, and task performed time will decrease. The results demonstrate that utilizing OTIS reduces pilots' workload.

5 Conclusion

This study conducted a comparative simulated flight experiment using an A320 simulator to analyze the workload of pilots when using EFB and OTIS to handle Engine Failure. Objective and subjective data were collected. Performance measurement, such as task performed time, and subjective data, like NASA-TLX ratings can effectively characterize pilot workload. Among the seven physiological indicators, four can effectively characterize pilot workload, namely Mean HR, Mean IBI, pNN50, and pNN20.

The difference tests demonstrate that the implementation of OTIS has a significant impact on pilots' workload. Further analyses confirm that OTIS can effectively reduce pilots' workload.

This study emphasizes on comparing and analyzing the workload of pilots when using different information systems and provides preliminary evidence of the effectiveness of OTIS. However, the analysis of pilots' subjective workload indicates that some pilots report relatively high workload. Furthermore, researches can be done to optimize the interface and functions of the intelligent system through usability methods and other indicators like EMG and EDA, to enhance the general applicability of the system.

Acknowledgments. Thanks to all pilots who participated in experiments with their time and great feedback to the research: This study was funded by Tianjin Graduate Science and Innovation Research Project (grant number 2022SKY160).

References

1. Casner, S.M., Gore, B.F.: Measuring and evaluating workload: a primer. NASA Tech. Memo. **216395**, 2010 (2010)
2. Kharoufah, H., Murray, J., Baxter, G., Wild, G.: A review of human factors causations in commercial air transport accidents and incidents: from to 2000–2016. Prog. Aerosp. Sci. **99**, 1–13 (2018)
3. Harris, D.: A human-centred design agenda for the development of single crew operated commercial aircraft. Aircr. Eng. Aerosp. Technol. **79**(5), 518–526 (2007)
4. Comerford, D., et al.: NASA's single-pilot operations technical interchange meeting: proceedings and findings. In: Technical Interchange Meeting (No. ARC-E-DAA-TN8313) (2013)

5. Onnasch, L., Wickens, C.D., Li, H., Manzey, D.: Human performance consequences of stages and levels of automation: an integrated meta-analysis. Hum. Factors **56**(3), 476–488 (2014)

6. Wei, X.: A psychological study of human-automation system interaction in the cockpit of automated aircraft. J. Psychol. Sci. **26**(3), 523–524 (2003)

7. Billings, C.E.: Aviation Automation: The Search for a Human-Centered Approach. CRC Press, Florida (1996)

8. Wei, X.: Identifying problems and generating recommendations for enhancing complex systems: applying the abstraction hierarchy framework as an analytical tool. Hum. Factors **49**(6), 975–994 (2007)

9. Wei, X.: User-Centered Design (V): from automation to the autonomy and autonomous vehicles in the intelligence era. Chin. J. Appl. Psychol. **26**(2), 108–128 (2020)

10. Wei, X.: User-Centered Design (VII): from automated to intelligent flight deck. Chin. J. Appl. Psychol. **28**(4), 291–313 (2022)

11. European Union Aviation Safety Agency (EASA): Artificial Intelligence Roadmap 2.0 Human-centric approach to AI in aviation, May 2023

12. Kantowitz, B.H., Campbell, J.L.: Pilot Workload and flightdeck automation. In: Automation and Human Performance, pp. 117–136. CRC Press, Florida (2018)

13. Hart, S.G.: NASA-task load index (NASA-TLX); 20 years later. In: Proceedings of the Human Factors and Ergonomics Society Annual Meeting, pp. 904–908. Sage Publications, Los Angeles (2006)

14. Yeh, Y.Y., Wickens, C.D.: Dissociation of performance and subjective measures of workload. Hum. Factors **30**(1), 111–120 (1988)

15. Wei, Z., Zhuang, D., Wanyan, X., Liu, C., Zhuang, H.: A model for discrimination and prediction of mental workload of aircraft cockpit display interface. Chin. J. Aeronaut. **27**(5), 1070–1077 (2014)

16. Alaimo, A., Esposito, A., Orlando, C., Tesoriere, G.: A pilot mental workload case study in a full flight simulator. Aerotecnica Missili Spazio **97**, 27–33 (2018)

17. Zheng, Y., Lu, Y., Jie, Y., Fu, S.: Predicting workload experienced in a flight test by measuring workload in a flight simulator. Aerosp. Med. Hum. Perform. **90**(7), 618–623 (2019)

18. Mohanavelu, K., et al.: Cognitive workload analysis of fighter aircraft pilots in flight simulator environment **70**(2), 131–139 (2020)

19. Alaimo, A., Esposito, A., Orlando, C., Simoncini, A.: Aircraft pilots workload analysis: heart rate variability objective measures and NASA-task load index subjective evaluation. Aerospace **7**(9), 137 (2020)

20. Socha, V., Socha, L., Hanakova, L., Valenta, V., Kusmirek, S., Lalis, A.: Pilots' performance and workload assessment: transition from analogue to glass-cockpit. Appl. Sci. **10**(15), 5211 (2020)

21. Li, W., Li, R., Xie, X., Chang, Y.: Evaluating mental workload during multitasking in simulated flight. Brain Behav. **12**(4), e2489 (2022)

22. Hart, S.G., Staveland, L.E.: Development of NASA-TLX (Task Load Index): results of empirical and theoretical research. In: Advances in Psychology, vol. 52, pp. 139–183. Elsevier, North-Holland (1988)

23. Folds, D.J.: Human in the loop simulation. In: Loper, M.L. (eds.) Modeling and Simulation in the Systems Engineering Life Cycle: Core Concepts and Accompanying Lectures, pp. 175–183. Springer, London (2015). https://doi.org/10.1007/978-1-4471-5634-5_15

Sleep Deprivation-Induced Alterations in Mood States Correlate with Changes in Spontaneous Brain Activity

Jiatao Wang[1,2], Qianxiang Zhou[1,2(✉)], and Zhongqi Liu[1,2]

[1] School of Biological Science and Medical Engineering, Beihang University,
Beijing 100191, China
zqxg@buaa.edu.cn
[2] Beijing Advanced Innovation Centre for Biomedical Engineering, Beihang University,
Beijing 102402, China

Abstract. Modern warfare places soldiers under unique conditions, requiring them to operate on irregular schedules in extreme environments, resulting in unprecedented physical and psychological challenges. Prolonged duty, nighttime operations, intense combat, and dynamic work demands often reduce sleep duration and quality. Additionally, battlefield noise and harsh environmental conditions contribute to difficulty falling asleep and maintaining sleep. Consequently, numerous soldiers endure severe sleep deprivation; some even develop sleep disorders. Within military training, sleep deprivation can engender many adverse consequences, with mood variability being one of the prominent outcomes. Soldiers frequently manifest sensations of profound fatigue, heightened irritability, acute anxiety, and pronounced despondency, all of which correlate with insufficient sleep. Sleep insufficiency undermines mood stability and diminishes the capacity to cope effectively with conflicts and stressors, constituting a latent threat to soldiers' psychological well-being and work performance. Sleep is crucial in mood regulation and its impact on psychological health. In-depth research into the mechanisms underlying the relationship between sleep deprivation and mood can offer profound insights into improving soldiers' mood states and work efficiency. Furthermore, it can provide valuable data support for human-computer interaction design. This study aimed to investigate the impact of sleep deprivation on the mood states of healthy participants and the correlational relationship between alterations in mood states under the influence of sleep deprivation and spontaneous electroencephalographic (EEG) activity. The research involved a 36-h complete sleep deprivation experiment conducted on 30 male participants aged between 19 and 30. Mood states were assessed at baseline, 24 h into sleep deprivation, and 36 h into sleep deprivation using the Profile of Mood States (POMS) questionnaire, and concurrent resting-state EEG data were recorded. Statistical analysis was conducted on various mood factors assessed by the POMS questionnaire and the relative power of spontaneous brainwave rhythms, exploring the degree of association between mood states and spontaneous brainwave rhythms under sleep deprivation. The results of the POMS questionnaire showed significant differences ($p < 0.05$) in CB, AH, FI, and VA scores between the sleep deprivation group and the baseline group. Moreover, post-hoc comparisons revealed remarkable variations ($p < 0.001$) in CB, AH, FI, and VA scores at 24 h and 36 h of complete

© The Author(s), under exclusive license to Springer Nature Switzerland AG 2024
D. Harris and W.-C. Li (Eds.): HCII 2024, LNAI 14692, pp. 113–124, 2024.
https://doi.org/10.1007/978-3-031-60728-8_10

sleep deprivation compared to the baseline. Additionally, there were no meaningful differences in CB, AH, and FI levels between 24 and 36 h of complete sleep deprivation. In terms of the relative power of spontaneous EEG, theta (θ) and alpha (α) waves showed notable changes ($p < 0.05$) in various brain regions compared to baseline, indicating a marked influence of sleep deprivation on these brainwave frequencies. Moreover, gamma (γ) wave activity in the frontal and parietal lobes also exhibited significant changes ($p < 0.05$). However, delta (δ) and beta (β) wave frequencies did not show material impact in various brain regions. These findings emphasize the differential impact of sleep deprivation on different EEG rhythms, contributing to a more comprehensive understanding of the effects of sleep deprivation on brainwave activity. Correlation analysis revealed a certain degree of association between alterations in mood states and specific brainwave activities in particular brain regions. Under the conditions of 24 h of sleep deprivation for negative mood, CB exhibited a substantial positive correlation with the relative power of theta frequency bands in the parietal lobe ($p < 0.05$) and a clear negative correlation with the relative power of gamma frequency bands in the frontal and parietal lobes ($p < 0.05$). Under 36 h of sleep deprivation, for positive mood, VA showed a marked positive correlation with the relative power of theta frequency bands in the frontal, central, and parietal lobes ($p < 0.05$) and a convincing negative correlation with the relative power of alpha frequency bands in the frontal lobe ($p < 0.05$). The research findings furnish neurophysiological evidence of sleep's impact on mood, offering support for improving individuals' mental health and enhancing work performance, especially concerning soldiers operating in challenging combat environments.

Keywords: Mood · POMS · EEG · sleep deprivation · relative power

1 Introduction

The unique environment and high demands of modern warfare require soldiers to execute missions on irregular schedules and in extreme environmental conditions, leading to unprecedented physical and psychological challenges [1]. Prolonged duty, nighttime operations, intense combat, and evolving work requirements can reduce sleep duration and quality [2]. Additionally, battlefield noise and harsh environmental conditions contribute to difficulty falling asleep and maintaining sleep [3]. Consequently, many soldiers experience severe sleep deprivation during combat training, with some developing sleep disorders [2, 4].

Sleep is crucial to mood regulation and psychological well-being [5]. Sleep deprivation during military operations may lead to a range of adverse effects, including mood changes [6, 7]. Soldiers often experience fatigue, irritability, anxiety, and depression, which are closely associated with inadequate sleep [8]. Sleep deprivation weakens mood stability and diminishes the ability to cope with conflict and stress, posing potential threats to soldiers' mental health and operational effectiveness [7, 9, 10]. For instance, Lieberman et al. assessed the mood states of soldiers before and after a simulated 53-h combat training, during which they had a total sleep time of 3.3 h. The Profile of Mood States (POMS) results showed significant changes in every mood dimension (tension, depression, confusion, fatigue, anger, and vigor) before and after the training [8]. In a study by Dinges et al. [11], healthy participants subjected to sleep restriction of only five hours per night for a week showed significant increases in negative mood states such as tension, fatigue, and confusion, along with a significant decrease in positive mood states like vigor.

Mood involves physiological and psychological states, significantly influencing an individual's thoughts and behaviors [12]. It is expressed through external manifestations like facial expressions and vocalizations and internal indicators such as electroencephalogram (EEG) and electrocardiogram (ECG) signals. With the advancement of brain research programs worldwide, there is a growing body of research on the intrinsic expressions of moods. EEG signals, a physiological data source from the brain cortex, have been confirmed to be closely related to moods [13].

The strong correlation between sleep deprivation and mood changes may be attributed to brain function and activity alterations. While numerous studies have confirmed the detrimental effects of sleep deprivation on cognitive functions such as alertness, working memory, and decision-making [14, 15], research on its impact on moods is relatively limited. Some studies suggest that sleep deprivation significantly impacts moods more than cognitive or motor performance [16]. Therefore, this study aims to investigate the influence of sleep deprivation on the moods of healthy participants by collecting corresponding positive and negative mood scores from the POMS scale and spontaneous EEG data under different durations of sleep deprivation. The research seeks to understand the relationship between sleep deprivation and moods and explore potential mechanisms, providing a basis for the parameter design and target selection of modal improvement methods such as transcranial physical intervention and neural regulation.

2 Method

2.1 Participants

Thirty healthy men (19–30 years, mean age 24.2 years) participated in this study. Participants were required to have good physical and mental health, with no history of neurological disorders, a habitual sleep duration of 7.27 ± 0.74 h, no sleep disorders or irregularities, and a habitual low intake of caffeine (average weekly consumption of tea and coffee ≤ 3 times). The Ethics Committee of Beihang University approved the experiment, and participants were provided with detailed explanations of the experimental procedures and instructions before the commencement of the study. All participants volunteered to participate in the experiment and completed informed consent forms.

2.2 Experimental Procedures

Participants were instructed to abstain from consuming alcohol, coffee, and other stimulating foods or beverages for one week before the commencement of the experiment and throughout the experimental process. They were also advised not to engage in vigorous or competitive physical activities to minimize factors that could induce mood fluctuations. Before the formal experiment, participants were required to complete the

Pittsburgh Sleep Quality Index (PSQI) questionnaire, and those with a score below five were considered to have good sleep habits, making them eligible for the subsequent experiment.

The experimental design employed a within-subject crossover design. Participants took part in a single session of total sleep deprivation. Participants arrived at the laboratory one day before the test and slept in the laboratory that night to ensure 8 h of sleep. On the second day, participants began sleep deprivation at 8 a.m., completed the POMS questionnaire, and recorded the participants' resting-state EEG data for 6 min, marking the completion of the first data collection and serving as the baseline measurement. Participants were required to maintain wakefulness for 36 h, with subsequent data collection occurring at 24 h and 36 h into the deprivation (SD24h and SD36h, respectively) and recording EEG data. The sleep deprivation experiment concluded at 8 p.m. on the third day (Fig. 1).

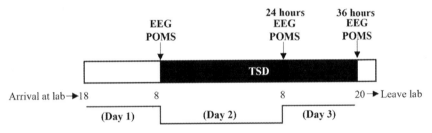

Fig. 1. Experimental Procedure Schematic

2.3 EEG Signal Acquisition and Preprocessing

The EEG data were recorded using the Neuroscan Products Scan 4.3 system, and electrode placement followed the international 10–20 system standard. Electrodes were configured with a sampling frequency of 1000 Hz, and electrode impedance was maintained within the range of no more than 10 kΩ.

In order to eliminate the interference of potential non-steady states on the data at the beginning and end of the experiment, the stable signals in the middle 5 min were selected for subsequent analysis. In order to improve the data signal-to-noise ratio, the EEG signal was divided into 2-s periods for analysis after passing through a 0.1–40 Hz non-recursive (finite impulse response, FIR) band-pass filter. Bilateral mastoids TP9 and TP10 were selected as reference electrodes, spike data segments and abnormal lead signals were manually removed, and the independent component correlation algorithm (ICA) algorithm was applied to repair blink or motion drift data segments.

2.4 Statistical Analysis

The statistical analysis of experimental data was conducted using SPSS 22.0 software. One-way repeated measures analysis of variance (ANOVA) was employed to analyze the behavioral and resting-state EEG relative power data under different sleep conditions, specifically to identify the main effect of time (Baseline, 24h-SD, 36h-SD). Pearson correlation analysis was used to explore the degree of correlation between changes in mood factors and spontaneous EEG data. Corrections were applied using the Greenhouse-Geisser test when sphericity assumptions were violated. The chosen significance level for all analyses was set at $P < 0.05$.

3   Results

3.1   Mood-Behavioral Analysis at Different Stages of Sleep Deprivation

The POMS includes six subscales: Anger-Hostility (12 items), Confusion-Bewilderment (7 items), Tension-Anxiety (9 items), Depression-Dejection (15 items), Fatigue-Inertia (7 items), and Vigor-Activity (8 items) [17]. Participants must rate 65 adjectives on a 5-point scale (0 = not at all, 4 = extremely). The positive mood score is equivalent to the Vigor-Activity subscale score, while the negative mood score is the sum of the scores from the remaining five subscales.

Table 1. Analysis of Scores (x ± s) for Different Duration of TSD on the POMS Factors

Mood factor	Baseline	TSD		F value	P value
		24h	36h		
CB	6.83±1.7	9.00±4.48	9.17±4.67	9.18	0.000*
TA	10.47±2.7	10.77±4.12	9.47±4.17	1.00	0.372
DD	16.37±4.87	18.40±6.44	16.00±7.67	1.21	0.302
AH	6.40±4.50	10.90±6.53	9.83±5.83	4.86	0.010*
FI	5.77±2.61	9.30±4.94	10.83±6.71	5.44	0.006*
VA	18.7±5.98	10.87±5.64	10.83±6.71	16.41	0.000*
TMD	61.1±12.98	69.23±19.82	65.43±20.39	1.53	0.223

Based on the results of the repeated measures analysis of variance presented in Table 1, significant differences ($p < 0.05$) were observed in the CB (Confusion-Bewilderment), AH (Anger-Hostility), FI (Fatigue-Inertia), and VA (Vigor-Activity) scores between the sleep-deprived groups and the baseline group. Further post-hoc comparisons revealed a significant increase ($P < 0.001$) in CB, AH, FI, and VA scores for participants after 24h and 36h of total sleep deprivation compared to the baseline. Additionally, there were no significant differences in CB, AH, and FI levels between 24 h and 36 h of total sleep deprivation.

These findings suggest that participants' mood states undergo significant changes under different conditions of sleep deprivation, particularly in terms of confusion, anger, fatigue, and vigor. These results are of significant importance in understanding the impact of sleep deprivation on mood well-being.

3.2   Analysis of EEG Relative Power Under Different Sleep Deprivation Durations

Analyzing the relative power of different frequency bands in the EEG allows for a better understanding of the activity characteristics of specific brain regions under different states. Among the 32 electrodes, we focused on the frontal region (F3, Fz, F4), central region (C3, Cz, C4), parietal region (P3, Pz, P4), and occipital region (O1, Oz, O2) to conduct region-specific data analysis. Since EEG signals are non-stationary, to avoid signal attenuation and distortion at the edges, each data segment was multiplied by an equally long Hamming window (50% overlap) for power spectral estimation using the Welch algorithm. The power spectrum was divided into five frequency ranges, including δ (0.5-4Hz), θ (4-8Hz), α (8-14Hz), β (14-30Hz), and γ (30-40Hz). The average absolute power spectrum for each frequency band was calculated, and to eliminate differences in power baselines under different conditions, the absolute power for each frequency band was divided by the total power across the entire target frequency range, resulting in the relative power for each frequency band.

Figure 2 displays the relative power in different frequency bands across various brain regions under different sleep conditions. From the figure, it can be observed that different conditions of sleep deprivation lead to inconsistent changes in relative power across frequency bands. For instance, in the θ band, there is a significant increase in relative power after 24 h of sleep deprivation, followed by a substantial decrease at 36 h. Regarding the α rhythm, there are significant differences between brain regions after 24 h of sleep deprivation. However, after 36 h, the α wave relative power in all brain regions noticeably decreases.

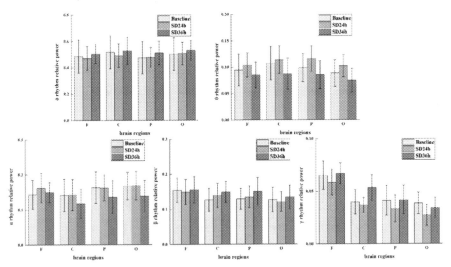

Fig. 2. Relative Power of Different Rhythms in Various Brain Regions Under Different Sleep Conditions

To further analyze the changes in EEG rhythms in different brain regions under conditions of sleep deprivation, one-way repeated measures analysis of variance was conducted separately for the relative power data of resting-state EEG at different durations of sleep deprivation, as shown in Table 2. From the results of repeated measures analysis of variance, significant changes ($p < 0.05$) were observed in θ and α waves across various brain regions compared to the baseline values before sleep deprivation, indicating a significant impact of sleep deprivation on θ and α waves. Significant changes ($p < 0.05$) in the γ band were also observed in the frontal and parietal lobes. However, δ and β bands did not show significant changes in any brain region. These results highlight the differential effects of sleep deprivation on various EEG rhythms, contributing to a more comprehensive understanding of the impact of sleep deprivation on EEG activity.

Under conditions of sleep deprivation, an increase in θ wave activity and a decrease in α wave activity were observed, which is associated with decreased cognitive function and attentional decline [18, 19]. The impact of sleep deprivation on γ waves may vary depending on the study and conditions. Some studies suggest that sleep deprivation may lead to decreased γ wave activity, associated with decreased cognitive function and mood instability [20]. However, other studies propose that γ wave activity may increase, especially in tasks related to attention and perception.

Table 2. Results of Significance Analysis for Relative Power Differences in EEG Rhythmic Waves

	F		C		P		O	
	F	P	F	P	F	P	F	P
δ	0.691	0.504	0.986	0.377	0.479	0.621	0.483	0.618
θ	7.552	0.001	12.727	0.000	11.622	0.000	5.660	0.005
α	3.420	0.037	3.879	0.024	3.911	0.024	4.529	0.013
β	1.655	0.197	1.862	0.162	0.633	0.534	0.966	0.385
γ	4.277	0.017	2.718	0.072	5.080	0.008	1.369	0.260

3.3 Correlation Analysis Between Mood and EEG Relative Power

Performing Pearson correlation analysis between the relative power changes of EEG rhythm waves and the changes in various factors of POMS, the results are presented in Tables 3 and 4.

The results of the Pearson correlation analysis show that under the condition of 24 h of sleep deprivation for negative moods, there is a significant positive correlation ($p < 0.05$) between CB and the relative power of the θ frequency band in the parietal lobe and a significant negative correlation ($p < 0.05$) between CB and the relative power of the γ frequency band in both the frontal and parietal lobes. Under the condition of 36 h of sleep deprivation for positive moods, there is a significant positive correlation ($p < 0.05$) between VA and the relative power of the θ frequency band in the frontal, central, and parietal lobes and a significant negative correlation ($p < 0.05$) between VA and the relative power of the α frequency band in the frontal lobe. These results indicate

Table 3. Correlation Analysis Between POMS Factors and EEG Relative Power at SD24h

Mood factor	Frequency band	Brain region			
		F	C	P	O
CB	θ	.282	.276	.371*	-.183
	α	-.120	-.143	-.184	-.077
	γ	-.368*	——	-.597**	——
AH	θ	.019	.156	-.010	-.084
	α	-.142	-.020	-.048	-.046
	γ	-.049	——	.007	——
FI	θ	.033	.176	.049	-.097
	α	-.200	-.175	-.137	.042
	γ	-.054	——	-.047	——
VA	θ	.088	-.118	.088	-.032
	α	.018	.059	.058	.004
	γ	.032	——	-.146	——

Note: *Significantly correlated at the 0.05 level (two-tailed). **Highly significantly correlated at the 0.01 level (two-tailed).

Table 4. Correlation Analysis Between POMS Factors and EEG Relative Power at SD36h

Mood factor	Frequency band	Brain region			
		F	C	P	O
CB	θ	.119	.079	.101	-.093
	α	-.110	-.158	-.211	-.161
	γ	-.205	——	-.163	——
AH	θ	-.039	-.039	-.061	-.273
	α	.049	.076	.060	-.205
	γ	-.147	——	.133	——
FI	θ	-.129	-.092	-.133	-.344
	α	-.035	-.091	-.052	-.266
	γ	.073	——	.292	——
VA	θ	.487**	.415*	.487**	.063
	α	-.416*	-.318	-.326	-.281
	γ	-.359	——	-.215	——

Note: *Significantly correlated at the 0.05 level (two-tailed). **Highly significantly correlated at the 0.01 level (two-tailed).

that under different conditions of sleep deprivation, there are some correlations between mood factors and spontaneous EEG, providing valuable information for understanding

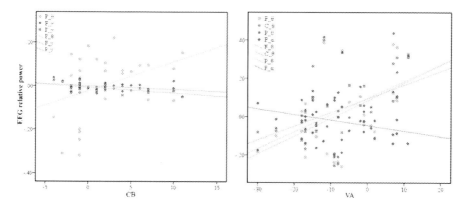

Fig. 3. Correlation Analysis Between POMS Factors and EEG Relative Power

the impact of sleep deprivation on moods and EEG activity, which helps further explore the complex relationship between sleep and moods (Fig. 3).

4 Discussion

In this study, we conducted a 36-h total sleep deprivation experiment, administered the POMS questionnaire, and simultaneously recorded spontaneous EEG data. We analyzed the behavioral data of moods and changes in the relative power of resting-state EEG under three sleep conditions (baseline, SD24h, and SD36h), attempting to elucidate their correlations. Sleep deprivation led to a deterioration of subjective mood states in healthy participants, characterized by increased negative moods and decreased positive moods. Significant changes were observed in the θ, α, and γ rhythms before and after sleep deprivation. Correlation analysis between mood factors and resting-state EEG revealed that the enhancement of negative moods in individuals due to sleep deprivation was related to frontal and parietal lobes changes. In contrast, the attenuation of positive moods was associated with changes in the frontal, central, and parietal lobes.

Regarding mood state scores, the study results indicated a worsening of subjective mood states under sleep deprivation conditions, manifested by increased confusion, irritability, decreased vigor, and increased fatigue, with a reverse trend in energy levels consistent with previous research findings [8, 10]. Different factors of mood states exhibited varying susceptibility to sleep deprivation, with CB and VA being more sensitive than AH and FI. The POMS scores after 36 h of total sleep deprivation showed no significant difference from those after 24 h, suggesting that mood changes primarily occur in the first circadian rhythm of sleep deprivation. That highlights the importance of early monitoring of mood changes during prolonged military tasks, emphasizing improving mood experiences and reducing fatigue. It is crucial for minimizing errors, enhancing efficiency, and guiding the development of corresponding equipment and techniques.

The θ wave activity, generally associated with pre-sleep or deep meditation states, increased in different brain regions after SD24h, indicating that sleep deprivation inhibited cortical activity, leading to fatigue and an increased tendency to sleep [19]. However, after 36 h of sleep deprivation, θ wave power decreased compared to 24 h, highlighting the significant role of circadian rhythm regulation. The reduction in α wave activity in the frontal, central, and parietal regions after 36 h of sleep deprivation indicated a restless and confused brain state, accompanied by decreased attention and impaired cognitive function [21]. After 36 h of sleep deprivation, an increase in γ wave relative power in the frontal lobe and a decrease in the parietal lobe reflected adaptive changes in brain activity under sleep deprivation conditions associated with alertness and cognitive function.

Most notably, our correlation analysis results demonstrated a specific correlation between changes in mood states and spontaneous brain activity. Specifically, after SD24h, there was a significant positive correlation between the relative power of the θ frequency band in the parietal lobe and negative mood CB and a significant negative correlation with the relative power of the γ frequency band in both the frontal and parietal lobes. That indicates a clear impact of sleep deprivation on mood states and brain activity, potentially leading to mood instability and cognitive decline. Although θ wave activity is typically more associated with the frontal lobe [22], the relative power of the θ frequency band in the parietal lobe also plays a role in mood regulation. For positive mood VA, there was a significant positive correlation with the relative power of the θ frequency band in various brain regions under sleep deprivation conditions, suggesting a crucial role of θ wave activity in positive mood regulation. Positive mood was also significantly negatively correlated with the relative power of the α frequency band in the frontal lobe, reflecting an adaptive response of frontal lobe activity to the decline in positive mood. These research findings emphasize the complex relationships between sleep deprivation, mood regulation, and brain oscillations, providing insights into the intricate interplay between moods and EEG activity.

This study employed EEG technology to explore the neural mechanisms behind changes in individual mood states caused by sleep deprivation. The experiment recorded only two critical time points of total sleep deprivation, possibly not fully reflecting the changing trends of mood factors throughout the entire process of sleep deprivation. Future research should refine the experimental design to analyze the dynamic effects of mood changes over time. Additionally, the study sample included only healthy individuals, and the results may not be generalizable to specific clinical populations, such as individuals with sleep disorders. Further research can expand the sample range to consider differences in different populations. Finally, the study can be further deepened, for example, by using brain imaging techniques to explore the functional connections between brain regions and their relationship to mood states.

In conclusion, this study provides preliminary empirical evidence for the relationships between sleep deprivation, mood states, and spontaneous brain activity. However, further research is needed to understand these complex interactive mechanisms better. These research findings hold significance for improving the mood states and work efficiency of military personnel and guiding the development of relevant equipment and technologies.

References

1. Xiao, H., Li, J., Yan, P., et al.: The mediating effects of psychological stress and psychological resilience on the relationship between sleep quality and work stress in soldiers performing major tasks. J. Third Mil. Med. Univ. **43**(04), 354–358 (2021)

2. Troxel, W.M., et al.: Sleep in the military: promoting healthy sleep among US servicemembers. Rand Health Q. **5**(2), 19 (2015)

3. Vermetten, E., Germain, A., Neylan, T.C. (eds.): Sleep and Combat-Related Post Traumatic Stress Disorder. Springer, New York (2018). https://doi.org/10.1007/978-1-4939-7148-0

4. Gehrman, P., Seelig, A.D., Jacobson, I.G., et al.: Predeployment sleep duration and insomnia symptoms as risk factors for new-onset mental health disorders following military deployment. Sleep **36**(7), 1009–1018 (2013)

5. Walker, M.: Why We Sleep: Unlocking the Power of Sleep and Dreams. Simon and Schuster (2017)

6. LoPresti, M.L., Anderson, J.A., Saboe, K.N., et al.: The impact of insufficient sleep on combat mission performance. Mil. Behav. Health **4**(4), 356–363 (2016)

7. Samadi, A., Gaeini, A., Bazgir, B.: Sleep and combat readiness: narrative review. J. Mil. Med. **22**, 141–153 (2020)

8. Lieberman, H.R., Bathalon, G.P., Falco, C.M., et al.: Severe decrements in cognition function and mood induced by sleep loss, heat, dehydration, and undernutrition during simulated combat. Biol. Psychiat. **57**(4), 422–429 (2005)

9. Paterson, J.L., Dorrian, J., Ferguson, S.A., et al.: Changes in structural aspects of mood during 39–66 h of sleep loss using matched controls. Appl. Ergon. **42**(2), 196–201 (2011)

10. Short, M.A., Louca, M.: Sleep deprivation leads to mood deficits in healthy adolescents. Sleep Med. **16**(8), 987–993 (2015)

11. Dinges, D.F., Pack, F., Williams, K., et al.: Cumulative sleepiness, mood disturbance, and psychomotor vigilance performance decrements during a week of sleep restricted to 4–5 hours per night. Sleep **20**(4), 267–277 (1997)

12. Zhang, G.H., Yu, M.J., Chen, G., et al.: A review of EEG features for emotion recognition (in Chinese). SCIENTIA SINICA Inform. **49**(9), 1097–1118 (2019)

13. Hagemann, D., Naumann, E., Lürken, A., et al.: EEG asymmetry, dispositional mood and personality. Personality Individ. Differ. **27**(3), 541–568 (1999)

14. Durmer J S, Dinges D F. Neurocognitive consequences of sleep deprivation[C]//Seminars in neurology. Copyright© 2005 by Thieme Medical Publishers, Inc., 333 Seventh Avenue, New York, NY 10001, USA., 2005, 25(01): 117–129

15. Banks, S., Dinges, D.F.: Behavioral and physiological consequences of sleep restriction. J. Clin. Sleep Med. **3**(5), 519–528 (2007)

16. Pilcher, J.J., Huffcutt, A.I.: Effects of sleep deprivation on performance: a meta-analysis. Sleep **19**(4), 318–326 (1996)

17. Mcnair, D., Lorr, M., Droppelman, L.: Profile of mood states. Educ. Ind. Test. Serv. (1971)

18. Drummond, S.P.A., Brown, G.G., Gillin, J.C., et al.: Altered brain response to verbal learning following sleep deprivation. Nature **403**(6770), 655–657 (2000)

19. Finelli, L.A., Baumann, H., Borbély, A.A., et al.: Dual electroencephalogram markers of human sleep homeostasis: correlation between theta activity in waking and slow-wave activity in sleep. Neuroscience **101**(3), 523–529 (2000)

20. Saletin, J.M., Goldstein-Piekarski, A.N., Greer, S.M., et al.: Human hippocampal structure: a novel biomarker predicting mnemonic vulnerability to, and recovery from, sleep deprivation. J. Neurosci. **36**(8), 2355–2363 (2016)

21. Klimesch, W.: EEG alpha and theta oscillations reflect cognitive and memory performance: a review and analysis. Brain Res. Rev. **29**(2–3), 169–195 (1999)
22. Luu, P., Collins, P., Tucker, D.M.: Mood, personality, and self-monitoring: negative affect and emotionality in relation to frontal lobe mechanisms of error monitoring. J. Exp. Psychol. Gen. **129**(1), 43 (2000)

Effects of Individual Factors and Recall Direction on Working Memory Span

Mufan Zhao and Chengqi Xue[✉]

School of Mechanical Engineering, Southeast University, Nanjing 211189, China
ipd_xcq@seu.edu.cn

Abstract. Recently, working memory span has received much attention from researchers. Memory materials in previous studies are usually in the form of text or pattern to explore people's working memory capacity and duration, with few researches on working memory span. Thus, this article aims to explore the impact of individual factors and recall direction on one's working memory span. In this study, two sets of digital memory materials were presented randomly, and 12 participants were invited to memorize the numbers and retell the numbers they remembered in required orders: forward recall and backward recall. At the same time, the BD-II-407 Memory Span Tester was applied to record the indicators of participants' working memory span such as "score", "time", "number of errors" and "number of digits memorized", then statistical methods was used to analyze the data. The results show that individual factors and recall direction both have a significant effect on working memory span, and the participants' performance during the backward-recall task was superior to that during the forward-recall task, especially when the memory materials become too long. Findings of this study will help people have a better learning of working memory span. Besides, follow-up studies need a more rationally structured sample and more scientific memory materials to further explore the effects of individual physiological factors and types of memory techniques on working memory span.

Keywords: Working Memory Span · Individual Factor · Recall direction

1 Instruction

In recent years, working memory has attracted a lot of attention from researchers, which not only serves as an important measure of cognitive resources, but also has significant influence on cognitive behaviors [1]. Working memory is a cognitive system which is responsible for temporarily maintaining and manipulating information during complex cognitive processes such as reading, counting, and reasoning, differing from the traditional concept of short-term memory which only refers to the temporary storage of information. It is now widely acknowledged that working memory consists of short-tern memory and interference control. To measure these two main components, researchers developed various tasks, such as working memory span, change detection, and n-back tasks, which have also provided the basis for computerized adaptive cognitive training to improve working memory [2].

© The Author(s), under exclusive license to Springer Nature Switzerland AG 2024
D. Harris and W.-C. Li (Eds.): HCII 2024, LNAI 14692, pp. 125–134, 2024.
https://doi.org/10.1007/978-3-031-60728-8_11

Working memory span, the maximum length of a series of stimuli that the subject can retell immediately and correctly after the stimuli presented one by one in a fixed order, is one of the most widely used methods when measuring one's short-term memory capacity. Within the span task, the stimuli can be presented in the form of letters or numbers, visually or auditorily. According to recent studies, the forward memory span task is commonly used as the working memory training task, which requires the subjects to recall the memory materials in the same order as presented [3]. Some studies have also combined the forward span task with the backward span task, which is much more challenging because it requires the subjects to recall the memory materials in reverse order as displayed [4]. Some researchers believed that forward span represents short-term memory and backward span represents working memory, which means that there is only the maintenance part of working memory works during the forward span tasks. However, researchers have rarely compared the effect of the forward span task and that of the backward span task on subject's working memory span directly. To understand whether the recall direction has any effect on subject's working memory span, subjects will be invited to participate in both forward and backward span tasks in this study, and relevant metrics will be recorded and analyzed.

The influence of individual factors on working memory span also deserves to be explored. A review of the literature shows that working memory span will be influenced by many factors, including background environment, the form of the memory materials, antecedent interference, and even the complex interactions between these variables [5]. It is the complexity that ensures working memory span tasks continue to play a key role in the development of working memory theory. However, current researchers mostly paid their attention to the effect of individual differences in the aspect of working memory span itself on the subject's performance during certain tasks, only few researches make individual differences as variables affecting working memory span. For example, Naveen et al. considered working memory span as an independent variable and pointed out that higher working memory span does not favor children's auditory learning in conditions with background noise interference [6]. Farzaneh et al. studied the working memory capacity or structure differences in monolingual and bilingual adults and the results suggest that there is greater specialization in working memory modality among bilinguals [7]. Takako et al. proposed that the backward digital span task may be an effective screening measure for dementia signs in the elderly [8]. Based on the foundation of previous studies, the other purpose of this paper is to investigate the effects of individual factors such as personality and memory techniques on subjects' working memory span.

Previous studies related to working memory span mostly used memory materials in the form of text or patterns to explore people's working memory capacity and duration. In this study, digital memory materials will be employed to reduce the interference that different subjects may have different understandings of the same verbal or picture-based memory materials. Memory Span Tester will also be used to record the data related to individual's working memory span under the requirements of different recall directions, and then analyze the data in order to investigate the effects of individual factors and recall direction on the working memory span of the subjects. Here are the hypotheses of this study:

- Hypothesis 1: Individual factors have a significant effect on subjects' working memory span.
- Hypothesis 2: Recall direction has a significant effect on subjects' working memory span.
- Hypothesis 3: Subjects' backward span is superior to forward span under the same conditions.

2 Experiment Preparation

2.1 Environment

The experiment was conducted from 8:00 a.m. to 12:00 p.m. in the Human Factors Laboratory at Southeast University, in a room with good lighting and temperature of 25 °C. The purpose of choosing the same time and place to conduct the experiment was to ensure that all the subjects involved in the experiment were exposed to similar independent variables such as temperature, noise, and lighting, minimizing the interference of external factors on the experimental results. The size of the desktop used for the experiment was 1200 mm × 600 mm, which was selected according to the office building design standard JGJ/T 67-2019 and the conditions achievable with the experimental equipment.

2.2 Apparatus

Experimental Equipment. In this experiment, the BD-II-407 Memory Span Tester (see Fig. 1), a commonly used psychological measuring instrument, was applied to record the indicators of participants' working memory span. This instrument can be used to test numerical memory span or to help improve user's memory in psychological experiment and has the function of measuring the subjects' ability to combine vision, memory, and reflection speed simultaneously. The device consists of a microcomputer controller, a main panel, a test panel, a keyboard, and other components, with a timing range of 0–99 min and 59 s. Besides, the device also has a self-check function, which is used to check whether the controller, the display or other components work. The main panel is equipped with six digital tubes for real-time display of the indicators of participants' working memory span, such as "scoring", "timing", "number of errors" and "number of digits memorized". The test panel is equipped with one large digital tube for displaying the memory material and each digit will be displayed on the digital tube for 0.7 s. The participants need to remember the digits displayed and input the answer through the keyboard in the right order.

The instrument has two response modes, namely, "forward mode" and "reverse mode". The former mode requires the subjects to recall the memory materials in the same order as presented, while the latter one requires the subjects to recall the memory materials in reverse order as displayed. The subjects should input the answer according to the automatic prompts of the answer lamp, the instrument will automatically ring the beep when the subject answered the wrong answer and the wrong answer indicator light. At this time, the subject should press the enter key to continue with the experiment. During the experiment, if the subject failed to enter the right answer eight times in a row

Fig. 1. The BD-II-407 Memory Span Tester

or completed the whole memory task, the instrument would automatically stop and ring the long beep, indicating that the test is over.

Memory Materials. In this experiment, memory materials will be displayed in the form of digits to reduce the interference caused by subjects' different comprehension of verbal or picture-based memory materials. Two sets of digital code, called code I and code II, will be displayed by the instrument, with the number digits increasing from 3 to 16. The three-to-sixteen-bit digits are randomly composed of the numbers 0–9 and every fourteen three-to-sixteen-bit digits form a set of codes. The digital memory materials will be presented on the test panel.

Additionally, noise-cancelling headphones were prepared to avoid the interference of ambient noise on the subjects' working memory span.

3   Methodology

3.1   Participants

Based on previous researches, 12 subjects were enrolled from school of mechanical engineering in Southeast University and each subject received a payment at the end of the experiment. Subjects included 5 males and 7 females between the ages of 22 and 26 years (M = 23.25), all of whom had normal vision or corrected vision and normal intellect. Besides, subjects were chosen to be bilinguals, even though Farzaneh et al. pointed out that there was almost no difference in working memory capacity between the bilingual and the monolingual [7]. Subjects all had basic knowledge of computer operation and were trained to be familiar to the tester applied in the experiment. To ensure the normal conduct of the experiment, subjects were required to avoid staying up late on the night before the experiment. All the subjects gave their written informed consent for this study.

3.2   Experimental Design

In order to investigate the effects of subjects' individual factors and recall direction on working memory span, a two-factor within-subjects design was used in this experiment. Independent variable I is the recall direction that the subjects should follow when entering the answer. Independent variable II is the subjects' individual factors, which can be categorized into two levels according to the personality of the subject (self-confident group and self-doubting group) or into three levels based upon the memory techniques that the subjects employed during the experiment (no-skill group, read-out group and encoding group). Each subject was asked to participate in the forward span task and the backward span task twice respectively, with 48 trials in total. The response values of the experiment were provided on the main panel once the subject finished the task.

Two sets of digital memory materials, code I and code II, were used in the experiment. In this experiment, each subject was required to complete four pre-designed span tasks (forward span task with code I, forward span task with code II, backward span task with code I, backward span task with code II). Since the purpose of this study is to investigate the effects of recall direction and subjects' individual factors on the working memory span, the code sets can be considered as an irrelevant variable and should be randomly assigned to the subjects in order to reduce the impact of irrelevant variables on the experimental results. After excluding the irrelevant variables, the experiment would adopt a balanced design in respect of the independent variable I, the recall direction, which means two forward span tasks and two reverse span tasks should be arranged rationally before being assigned to the subjects. In this study, the subjects were arranged to conduct the experiment in the following order: (f1, f2, b1, b2), (f1, b1, f2, b2), (f1, b1, b2, f2), (b1, f1, f2, b2), (b1, f1, b2, f2), and (b1, b2, f1, f2), and each combination of tasks would be assigned to two subjects. In the above series, f1 and f2 represent the first and the second forward span task respectively, while b1 and b2 represent the first and the second backward span task respectively. With the balanced design, time and effort costs can be saved to a certain extent, and proactive interference on the experimental results due to the fixed order of tasks with different recall directions can be reduced as well. For example, if the first two tasks are both forward recall tasks, subjects will have a general idea of the codes in advance, which may cause proactive interference to the subsequent reverse recall tasks, making the recorded value of the backward span higher than the real value. Likewise, if the first two tasks are both backward recall tasks, subjects will be frustrated due to the reverse recall tasks, which may also cause proactive interference to the subsequent forward recall tasks, making the recorded value of the forward span lower than the real value.

At the end of each trial, subjects should be allowed to take sufficient rest to relieve brain fatigue before next trial. During the experiment, factors that may affect the subjects' working memory span should be recorded in detail. After each trial, the subjects should tell the memory techniques they adopted in the task they have just completed. After the whole experiment, paired t-test was applied to analyze the data, and the results were analyzed and discussed in conjunction with the subjects' subjective reports.

3.3 Experimental Procedures

The experiment was conducted according to the following procedures with irrelevant variables under control.

– Set up the Experimental Environment. Place the instrument on the desktop within the comfort range of the subject's operation. Turn on the power.

- Prepare for the Experiment. Introduce the equipment to the subjects and allow the subjects to try it out. Attention should be paid to avoiding the influence of the learning effect on the experiment.
- Introduce the Experiment tasks. Inform the subjects of the experiment tasks and ask them to wear noise-canceling headphones.
- Conduct the Experiment. Press the reset button, select the target set of code and response mode, and signal the subject to start the experiment. After the tester stops and beeps, keep the record of the values displayed on the main panel. Let the subject take a full rest to relieve the brain fatigue before beginning the next trial. Repeat the steps for four times until the whole experiment finishes.
- Interview the Subject. Ask the subjects about the memory techniques used in each trial and keep a record.

4   Results

According to the interview results, subjects were categorized into self-confidence group (7 subjects) and self-doubting group (5 subjects) based on their personality and into no-skill group (3 subjects), read-out group (4 subjects), encoding group (5 subjects) based on the memory techniques they used to finish the tasks. As shown in Table 1, individual factors were significantly correlated with the four metrics of memory span, while recall direction was significantly correlated with three metrics. The results of the experiment suggest that individual factors and recall direction do have a significant effect on memory span. However, there is no significant interaction between the two variables.

Table 1. Paired t-test results of independent variables and working memory span, (a) number of digits memorized, (b) score, (c) number of errors, (d) time.

Independent Variable	P-value (a)	P-value (b)	P-value (c)	P-value (d)
Individual Factors	<0.001	<0.001	<0.001	<0.001
Recall Direction	<0.001	/	<0.001	<0.001

Figures 2, 3 and 4 illustrates the effects of individual factors and recall direction on memory span. As can be seen, confident subjects' working memory span was better than that of the self-doubting subjects. Performance of the subjects who employed memory techniques was superior to that of the subjects with no strategies, and encoding was more conducive to improving memory span than reading the materials, considering the same amount of time spent on the tasks. The difficulty of the backward span task was significantly higher than that of the forward task and, in the backward task, only the number of memorized digits was slightly higher than that of the forward task. Besides, it suggested that memory span was more vulnerable to individual factors during the reverse recall process.

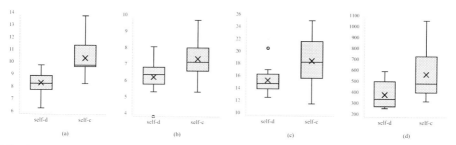

Fig. 2. The relationships between individual factor I-individual personality and working memory span, (a) number of digits memorized, (b) score, (c) number of errors, (d) time.

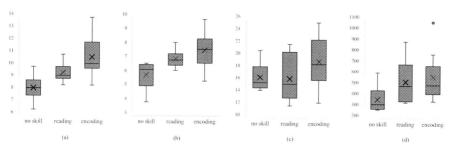

Fig. 3. The relationships between individual factor II-memory techniques and working memory span, (a) number of digits memorized, (b) score, (c) number of errors, (d) time.

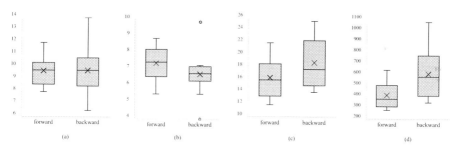

Fig. 4. The relationships between recall direction and working memory span, (a) number of digits memorized, (b) score, (c) number of errors, (d) time.

5   Discussion

5.1   Individual Factors

According to the experimental results, individual factors do have a significant effect on working memory span, which confirms Hypothesis 1, differing from Hye ryeong's conclusion that differences in individual factors have nothing to do with memory span [9]. Reasons for the divergence may be that Hye ryeong mainly explored the differences in individual physiological factors such as age and gender, whereas in this study personality and memory techniques were the key points. This speculation is consistent with the conclusion of Gerald Teha et al.'s experiment [5].

Individual Personality. The subjects can be separated into self-confident group and self-doubting group according to their subjective report and task performance. As can be seen from Fig. 2, subjects from the self-confident group got higher scores and remembered more digits in both forward and backward span tasks, though they made little more mistakes to some extent. After interviewing the subjects, it can be speculated that the subjects of the two groups may have different levels of anxiety during the execution of the tasks, contributing to the above phenomenon. This speculation is based upon Wang's findings that positive emotions can help expand working memory span [10]. As mentioned earlier, the experimental equipment will emit a beep sound when the subjects input the wrong number, which can be seen as an interference factor. Most of the subjects from the self-confident group thought that the beep sound had no effect on their performance, while most self-doubting subjects believed that the noise increased their anxiety to a certain extent and the negative feelings deepened along with the time, leading to a decrease in their concentration and in the accuracy rate. Similarly, Trezise and Reeve showed that anxiety has a significant influence on working memory span and the affected memory span will deepen the feelings of anxiety, exacerbating the effects on working memory span over time [11]. Noritake argued that worrying has a negative effect on the visuospatial working memory capacity [12]. Jintao pointed out that test anxiety will affect subjects' working memory processing efficiency to some extent [13]. All these findings are consistent with the phenomenon observed in this study. In addition, just as Hunter's findings said [14], some of the subjects with lower self-confidence even indicated that when the frequency of errors increased, they just wanted to end the irritating and humiliating tasks instead of focusing on it.

Memory Techniques. The subjects can be categorized into three groups: the no-skill group, the read-out group, and the encoding group based upon their subjective report and task performance. As can be seen from Fig. 3, subjects from the read-out group and the encoding group got higher scores and remembered more digits in both forward and backward span tasks. The encoding group got the highest working memory span scores, which can be attributed to the fact that the subjects in the encoding group encoded the digits presented to keep the number of groups to be memorized at a reasonable level based on Miller's theory, reducing the difficulty of the tasks. The best performer was from the encoding group, and his subjective report showed that, in addition to using the technique of encoding information in groups, he gave each group of digits a specific meaning, such as commemorative dates, page numbers of books and door numbers. John Dunlosky demonstrated that applying right memory strategies can help improve one's memory span significantly [15] and Tahira Yasmin also concluded that phonological articulation can aid memory after administering memory span tests to children with speech disorders [16]. All the findings show a positive effect of aids on memory span.

5.2 Recall Orientation

According to the results of paired t-tests, recall direction has a significant effect on working memory span, and the backward memory span is slightly better than the forward one under the same conditions in terms of the "number of digits memorized" (Fig. 4), which is positively correlated with working memory span, indicating that Hypothesis 2 and Hypothesis 3 are both valid. This conclusion is in line with the results of a memory span study conducted by Katherine Guérard with verbal memory materials [17]. Related studies have shown that forward recall has a priority effect, which means the subjects will preferentially remember the memory material that appeared first, while backward recall has a novelty effect, which means the subjects will remember the memory material presented at the end more deeply [18]. Meanwhile, Saito S pointed out that individuals' working memory span is also affected by the duration of the task. Accordingly, as the number of digits of the memory materials increased, the duration of the working memory task increased, weakening the priority effect of the forward span. However, the novelty effect of the backward span was not affected by the time factor, especially in terms of the "number of digits memorized". Therefore, the backward span is superior to the forward span. In addition, Hale argued that executive control is only related to the backward span instead of the forward span [19] and Vandierendonck put forward a similar conclusion [20]. Thus, it seems reasonable that forward span training and backward span training will have different effects on working memory.

6 Conclusion and Outlook

In conclusion, individual factors and recall direction both have a significant effect on working memory span, but there is no significant interaction between these two independent variables. Additionally, the subjects' performance during the backward recall was superior to that during forward recall in terms of the number of digits they could memorized, especially when the memory materials become too long. People can use strategies such as encoding or reading out the memory materials to enhance working memory span during the process.

There are still some limitations in this study. For example, the sample size of the experiment is limited. The following studies could design a more rationally structured sample and more scientific memory materials to further explore the effects of individual physiological factors and types of memory techniques on working memory span. Besides, in this experiment, all the subjects are bilingual or multilingual users, researchers can make comparisons between multilingual and monolingual holders' working memory span in future studies.

Acknowledgments. This work was supported jointly by National Natural Science Foundation of China (No. 72271053, 71871056) Joint fund. And I would like to express my sincere gratitude to the volunteers who participated in the data collection experiment.

References

1. Zhang, H.: The impact of working memory capacity on lane changing decisions under auditory-verbal cognitive load. J. Saf. Environ. **24**(1), 195–205 (2024)
2. Li, Y.: Effects of forward and backward span trainings on working memory: evidence from a randomized controlled trial. Psychophysiology **60**(1), 14154 (2022)

3. Melby-Lervag, M.: Working memory training does not improve performance on measures of intelligence or other measures of "far transfer": evidence from a meta-analytic review. Perspect. Psychol. Sci. **11**(4), 512–534 (2016)

4. Takeuchi, H.: Neural plasticity in amplitude of low frequency fluctuation, cortical hub construction, regional homogeneity resulting from working memory training. Sci. Rep. **7**(1), 1470 (2017)

5. Tehan, G.: Individual differences in memory span: the contribution of rehearsal, access to lexical memory, and output speed. Q. J. Exp. Psychol. Sect. A-Hum. Exp. Psychol. **53**(4), 1012–1038 (2000)

6. Nagaraj, N.K., Magimairaj, B.M., Schwartz, S.: Auditory distraction in school-age children relative to individual differences in working memory capacity. Atten. Percept. Psychophys. **82**(7), 3581–3593 (2020). https://doi.org/10.3758/s13414-020-02056-5

7. Farzaneh, A.: Working memory capacity and structure in monolinguals and bilinguals. J. Cogn. Psychol. **33**(4), 393–402 (2021)

8. Takako, Y.: The classical backward digit span task detects changes in working memory but is unsuitable for classifying the severity of dementia. Appl. Neuropsychol. **30**(5), 1–7 (2021)

9. Hye-ryeong, H.: Korean Wh-Island sentences: individual differences in acceptability judgments and working memory. Lang. Res. **55**(2), 379–412 (2019)

10. Wang, A.: A study on the relationship between emotional fluctuation and working memory breadth of flight students based on civil aviation English. J. Civil Aviat. **8**(1), 130–134 (2024)

11. Trezise, K.: Worry and working memory influence each other iteratively over time. Cogn. Emot. **30**(2), 353–368 (2016)

12. Noritake, Y.: Effects of pressure-induced worry and negative thoughts on verbal and visuospatial working memory capacity. Kawasaki J. Med. Welfare **23**(2), 43–50 (2018)

13. Jintao, S.: Effect of test anxiety on visual working memory capacity using evidence from event-related potentials. Psychophysiology **59**(2), 13965 (2021)

14. Hunter, B.: Individual differences in working memory capacity predict benefits to memory from intention offloading. Memory (Hove, England) **30**(2), 11–15 (2021)

15. John, D.: The contributions of strategy use to working memory span: a comparison of strategy assessment methods. Q. J. Exp. Psychol. **60**(9), 1227–1245 (2006)

16. Tahira, Y.: Working memory span and receptive vocabulary assessment in Urdu speaking children with speech sound disorder. Acta Psychol. **231**, 103777 (2022)

17. Katherine, G.: Revisiting backward recall and benchmark memory effects: a reply to Bireta et al. (2010). Mem. Cogn. **40**(3), 388–407 (2012)

18. Satoru, S.: Exploring the forgetting mechanisms in working memory: evidence from a reasoning span test. Q. J. Exp. Psychol. **62**(7), 1401–1419 (2009)

19. Hale, J.B.: Analyzing digit span components for assessment of attention processes. J. Psychoeduc. Assess. **20**(2), 128–143 (2002)

20. Vandierendonck, A.: Working memory components of the Corsi blocks task. Br. J. Psychol. **95**(Pt1), 57–79 (2004)

The Experiment Study on EEG Characteristics of Different Personality Errors Under Consequence Stress

Qianxiang Zhou[1,2], Tangqian Liu[1,2], and Zhongqi Liu[1,2(✉)]

[1] School of Biological Science and Medical Engineering, Beihang University,
Beijing 100191, China
Lzq505@163.com
[2] Beijing Advanced Innovation Centre for Biomedical Engineering, Beihang University,
Beijing 102402, China

Abstract. In this study, the subjective score, behavioral performance and EEG data of 41 subjects were collected and analyzed under two experimental conditions (no stress and consequence stress). According to the Big Five Personality Scale, the personality characteristics of the subjects were divided into five categories (i.e., Neuroticism, Openness, Conscientiousness, Pleasantness, and Extraversion). It was found that neuroticism personality and pleasantness personality were significantly correlated with stress perception, but neuroticism personality was more sensitive to stress. The higher the level of neuroticism, the higher the subjective questionnaire score. The results of behavioral performance analysis showed that the error rate under the condition of no consequence stress was greater than that under the condition of consequence stress. The results of event-related potential analysis found that Pe was significantly affected by different experimental conditions, and was greater under consequence pressure, while ERN was not significant difference between different experimental conditions. Time-frequency analysis results found that weaker α and β band oscillations were induced under consequence stress. Under the stressful conditions, there was a significant negative correlation between conscientiousness score and α-band energy. In summary, this study showed that the impact of consequence pressure on human error could be characterized by the changes in error-related ERP components and time-frequency characteristic indicators.

Keywords: Consequence Stress · Human Error · Big-five Personality · EEG · Event-related Potential

1 Introduction

When faced with an emergency, human physiology and psychology undergo major changes and are prone to errors that can lead to accidents. Major accidents tend to occur in emergencies, which puts operators under consequence stress due to failure of tasks. On the other hand, each person has certain individual differences due to the moderating effect of personality traits.

© The Author(s), under exclusive license to Springer Nature Switzerland AG 2024
D. Harris and W.-C. Li (Eds.): HCII 2024, LNAI 14692, pp. 135–150, 2024.
https://doi.org/10.1007/978-3-031-60728-8_12

Consequence stress is the psychological and physiological stress caused by the participant's concern about the consequences of the task (mainly failure) that may affect society, others, and the individual, triggering the individual's concern about the consequences of the task. Consequence stress is a significant cause of human error accidents. The study of human error under consequence stress can provide a basis for operator selection and help in effectively predicting the occurrence of human error.

There has been less research on the correlation between consequence stress and human error, and the present study focuses on the use of rewards and punishments as triggers for consequence stress. The researchers found that after the presentation of implicit reward and punishment cues, the heart rate of introverts increased, and introverts showed shorter reaction times to reward-convexed cue stimuli. During the non-dominant response phase, compared with extroverts, introverts showed higher inhibitory response error rates [1]. Through eye movement experiments, the researchers examined the effects of individual attentional control processing induced by monetary rewards and punishment. The results found that both rewards and punishments promoted individuals' attentional control; only the processing was different [2].

The researchers combined stress factors with THERP [3] to classify human errors, analyzed space-specific tasks, obtained quantitative relationships between task segments and probabilities, and completed analyzing risk assessment from qualitative to quantitative [4]. Although these methods have strong practicality, most start from human operational behaviors and do not recognize human error from cognition. Thus, they cannot fundamentally solve the problem.

Many researchers have used event-related potential (ERP) techniques for neurocognitive studies of error processing under stress, but the results of these studies have been inconsistent. A study by Meyer et al. using electric shock as punishment found that high-anxious individuals had increased ERNs when punished after an error [5]. This conclusion was supported in the study by Riesel et al., and this effect persisted after the punishment ceased, suggesting that punitive learning increased anxiety in individuals [6].

A study of the relationship between extraversion, conscientiousness and performance concluded that extraversion and conscientiousness were associated with hit rates under the condition of job stress [7]. A study of personality traits and stress among ICU nurses found that openness and extraversion were associated with less stress perception and that conscientiousness was negatively associated with "work stress" and lack of "self-confidence and competence" stress [8]. Conscientiousness has been found to be more sensitive to rules and norms of social obligation, and lower extraversion and openness may be associated with a more remarkable ability to focus on tasks, leading to fewer driving errors [9]. Sociable people are less likely to be involved in accidents, while those who are more anxious, expressive and risk-taking are more likely to be involved in accidents [10]. In a study, it was noted that extraversion, easygoing, and dutifulness of the Big Five Personality were negatively correlated with feelings of stress, while the neuroticism dimension was positively correlated with stress perception [11]. A study of university teachers found that research performance was higher among teachers with pleasantness, extraversion and pioneering personality traits [12]. Operator's conscientiousness had a predictive effect on task performance, and pleasantness, conscientiousness, extraversion and openness were moderately correlated with task performance [13].

Human error research aims to reduce the incidence of human error and improve the reliability of human-machine systems [14]. Therefore, this study analyzed the mechanism of human error in different personalities under consequence stress, explored the EEG characteristics of errors, and provided methods of personnel selection, training and task planning for emergency tasks, which can reduce the probability of human error and improve the safety and reliability of human-machine systems from the root cause.

2 Method

2.1 Subject

A total of 41 people were recruited (22 men and 19 women). Their ages ranged from 20 to 35 years old, and they were all postgraduate students. All of them were in good health, without cognitive dysfunction or other psychiatric diseases. The subjects were required to get enough sleep the day before the experiment, eat normally on the day of the experiment, and prohibit the consumption of stimulating beverages such as alcohol, tea, coffee, and functional sodas.

2.2 Experimental Tasks

This study utilized a modified EAT (Error Awareness Task) paradigm as an experimental task. The task was a response inhibition task combining the Go/NoGo and Stroop tasks. In the task, participants were presented with a series of colored words, and there were both matches and mismatches between word meanings and colors. When there was a mismatch between word meaning and color, the participant was required to press the space bar as quickly as possible. When the words were repeated on two consecutive trials (Repeat NoGo) or when there was a match between the word's meaning and the color (Concordance NoGo), subjects did not need to make any response. The experiment consisted of 4 blocks; the former 2 blocks were no-consequence stress experiments, and the latter 2 blocks were consequence stress experiments. Each block contained 180 trials. There was a 2-min break for each block completed.

At the beginning of each experiment, a white cross gaze point "+" was first presented on the screen for 500 ms, followed by a colorful Chinese character stimulus. Participants were required to respond by pressing the space bar as soon as possible after a Go trial; when a NoGo trial was presented, participants were not required to make any response. In the no-consequence stress condition, the Chinese character stimulus presentation interface disappeared immediately after the participants pressed the key and then proceeded to the subsequent trial. In the experimental condition with consequence stress, when the subject made a mistake (Go trial not pressed, NoGo trial pressed), the subject was penalized by hearing a short, pure tone of 8000 Hz, 50 dB, lasting 500 ms. At that time, the screen was black for 500 ms, and then proceeded to the subsequent trial.

2.3 Experimental Equipment

The hardware part of the experimental system mainly included a set of EEG acquisition equipment (Brain Products GmbH, Germany), a stimulation computer and an EEG recording computer.

The stimulation computer contained experimental software to present stimulation to the subjects and record behavioral data such as keystrokes; the EEG recording computer contained the EEG recording software Recorder, which was used to record EEG data.

2.4 Experimental Procedure

Each subject was required to follow the process below to complete the experiment.

1. The principal experimenter explains the experimental task and procedure to the subject.
2. Subjects completed an informed consent form and the Big Five Personality Questionnaire.
3. Subjects practiced the experimental task for 20 trials.
4. Subjects were given EEG creams.
5. Subjects were subjected to a no-consequence stress experiment, performing the experimental tasks of the EAT paradigm, which lasted approximately 20 min.
6. Subjects completed the stress scale and then rested for 5 min.
7. Subjects performed a consequence stress experimental task that lasted approximately 20 min.
8. Subjects completed the stress scale.
9. The experiment was over.

2.5 Data Collection

Subjective Score Collection for Stress. Consequence stress measures an individual's response to the severity of possible consequences. A modified self-rated stress scale was used in this study [15].

Behavioral Collection. In this study, behavioral performance indicators were collected using E-Prime (Ver. 3.0) software.

1. Total error rate (total errors/total number of attempts).
2. Consistent false alarm error rate (number of consistent NoGo error keystrokes/number of consistent NoGo attempts).
3. Repeat false alarm error rate (number of repeat NoGo error keystrokes/number of repeat NoGo attempts).
4. Number of error keystrokes (NoGo trial keystrokes).
5. Number of omissions (number of Go attempts not keyed).
6. Correct response time (the interval between Go trial stimulus presentation and making a key press response).
7. False report response time (the interval between NoGo trial stimulus presentation and making an incorrect key press response).

8. Consistent false alarm response time (the interval between the presentation of a consistent NoGo trial stimulus and the making of an incorrect keypress response).
9. The repetition of the false alarm response time (the interval between the repetition of the NoGo trial stimulus presentation and the making of the false key press response).

Electroencephalographic (EEG) Acquisition. EEG data were acquired using Brain Vision Recorder from Brain Products, Germany, with a sampling frequency of 500 Hz. The electrode positions were in the standard international 10–20 lead expansion system layout. The ground electrode (GND) was placed at the forehead AFz lead position and the reference electrode (REF) was placed at the head FCz lead position.

3 Results

3.1 Big Five Personality Data

Using the Big Five Personality Lite Scale, the Big Five Personality data were collected from the subjects participating in the experiment, and the SPSS software was used to statistically analyze the means, standard deviations, minima, and maxima of the subjects after the Big Five Personality traits were analyzed. The statistical results were shown in Table 1.

Table 1. Subjects' Big Five personality score statistics (N = 41)

Index	Average	Standard deviation	Minimum	Maximum
Neuroticism	31.61	8.13	12	50
Extraversion	41.20	6.69	24	53
Openness	43.51	7.56	24	59
Pleasantness	41.12	5.92	27	56
Conscientiousness	43.31	4.56	34	55

Figure 1 showed the distribution of subjects in the low, medium, and high-scoring bands for each dimension of the Big Five Personality characteristics. The distribution of Table 1 and Fig. 1 showed that all subjects scored moderately and evenly in each personality dimension.

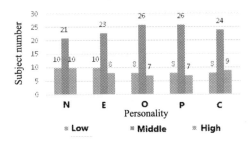

Fig. 1. Personality distributions

3.2 Subjective Stress Data

The mean and standard deviation of the stress of self-assessment scale scores in the two experimental conditions were calculated separately, and the results are shown in Table 2. It can be seen that the stress self-assessment scale scores showed more significant consequence stress than no stress ($p < 0.001$).

Table 2. Results of self-rating stress scale (N = 41)

Statistic	No stress	Consequence stress
Average	18.366	19.415
Standard deviation	3.701	5.250
P	<0.001**	

Note: * p < 0.05, ** p < 0.01

3.3 Behavioral Performance Data

The z-score test was performed on all data to exclude outliers. Then, the mean and standard deviation of each performance result under the two experimental conditions were calculated separately, after which the ANOVA was performed on each index under the two pressure conditions, and the results are shown in Table 3.

Table 3. Statistics of performance results (Average ± Standard deviation, P value)

Performance index	No stress	Consequence stress	P
Total error rate	9%(±3%)	7%(±3%)	<0.001
Consistently misreporting error rates	25%(±10%)	22%(±9%)	<0.001
Repeated false error rate	22%(±10%)	20%(±9%)	<0.001
Number of error keys	83.71(±32.19)	74.95(±30.44)	<0.001
Missing number	17.28(±14.82)	4.73(±4.02)	<0.001
Correct reaction time	534.96(±78.50)	439.66(±56.18)	<0.001
False response time	536.56(±85.94)	452.64(±72.36)	<0.001
Uniformly false response time	517.05(±79.88)	438.15(±65.44)	<0.001
Repeated false response	561.53(±100.21)	468.76(±87.74)	<0.001

Notes: * p < 0.05, ** p < 0.01

As can be seen from Table 3, compared with the two experimental conditions, the total error rate of no stress was significantly greater than consequence stress ($p < 0.001$), and the error rate of consistent false alarms, the error rate of repetitive false alarms, the number of incorrect keystrokes, and the number of omissions all showed that no stress was significantly greater than consequence stress ($p < 0.001$). For the other three metrics, there was a significant difference between the two experimental conditions ($p < 0.05$). Correct response time, false alarm response time, consistent false alarm response time, and repeated false alarm response time all showed no stress greater than consequence stress ($p < 0.001$).

3.4 ERP Data

Figure 2 showed the brain region distribution of ERN and Pe under the two experimental conditions. As can be seen from the figure, the amplitude of both ERN and Pe showed more consequence stress than no stress; ERN mainly showed prefrontal distribution, while Pe mainly showed Parietal-occipital cortex distribution.

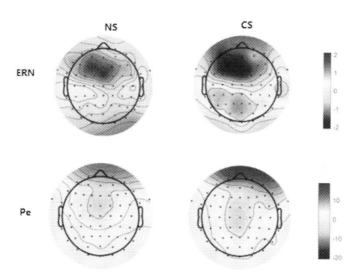

Fig. 2. The distribution of ERN and Pe of brain regions

According to the brain area distribution of ERN and Pe, the average peak of ERN in Fz and FCz leads was selected as the ERN amplitude. The average peak of Pe in CPz and Pz leads was selected as the Pe amplitude. The average and standard deviation of ERN and Pe amplitudes in the experimental conditions were calculated respectively, and the results were shown in Table 4.

Table 4. Amplitude and P value of ERN and Pe (Average ± Standard deviation, μv) (N = 31)

EEG index	No stress	Consequence stress	p
ERN	-1.41(±2.34)	−1.81(±3.23)	0.223
Pe	3.27(±4.08)	5.16(±5.48)	<0.001

Notes: * p < 0.05, ** p < 0.01

As shown in Table 4, the difference in ERN amplitude between the two experimental conditions was not significant (p = 0.223), while there was a significant difference in Pe amplitude (p < 0.001).

According to the Big Five Personality scores, all participants were divided into high and low-level groups according to the mean of each personality score (as shown in Fig. 2).Independent samples T-tests were performed on the ERN and Pe amplitude in

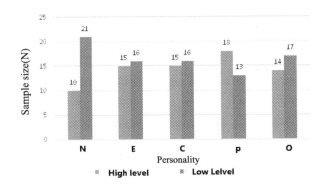

Fig. 3. High and low level group distribution of five kinds personality

Table 5. Independent sample T test results of high and low level Big Five personality (N = 31)

Personality	ERN		Pe	
	No stress	Consequence stress	No stress	Consequence stress
Neuroticism	0.272 (0.787)	0.462 (0.648)	−0.633 (0.532)	0.604 (0.551)
Extraversion	1.376 (0.179)	2.589* (0.015)	−0.743 (0.464)	−1.395 (0.174)
Openness	0.300 (0.768)	0.434 (0.668)	−0.486 (0.630)	−0.604 (0.551)
Pleasantness	−1.197 (0.241)	−0.967 (0.362)	−2.153* (0.040)	0.906 (0.372)
Conscientiousness	0.875 (0.389)	−0.733 (0.470)	−2.338* (0.026)	0.168 (0.868)

the two experimental conditions, with the groups being high and low levels of each personality, respectively. The results were shown in Table 5 (Fig. 3).

The results of Table 5 illustrated that there is a significant difference in Pe amplitude between the pleasantness personality and the low level of conscientiousness personality in the no-stress condition, respectively, and that the high pleasantness group is higher than the low pleasantness group and the high conscientiousness group is higher than the low conscientiousness group; and that there is a significant difference in ERN amplitude between the high-extraversion personality and the low-extraversion personality in the condition of consequence stress and that the high-extraversion group is higher than the low-extraversion group.

3.5 Time-Frequency Data of EEG

The amplitude of the β-band energy (β-ERD) and the amplitude of the α-band energy (α-ERD) of the two regions of interest, ROI1 and ROI2, were extracted for all subjects in the FCz lead and the PO3 lead. The mean and standard deviation of the two under the two experimental conditions were calculated and then analyzed by ANOVA, and the results are shown in Table 6. It can be seen that there is a significant difference between the β-band energy and the α-band energy between the two experimental conditions (β-band: $p = 0.001$; α-band: $p = 0.002$). The band oscillations are enhanced without pressure for both β- and α-band energies.

Table 6. Energy Of α band β band (Average ± Standard deviation, μV^2/Hz) (N = 31)

EEG index	No stress	Consequence stress	P
β-ERD	0.062 (±0.030)	−0.027 (±0.022)	0.001**
α-ERD	0.007 (±0.058)	−0.178 (±0.038)	0.002**

Notes: * $p < 0.05$, ** $p < 0.01$

3.6 Big Five Personality Correlations with Subjective Stress Results

The Big Five Personality characteristics scores were correlated with the Stress Self-Rating Scale scores in the two experimental stress conditions, and the results were shown in Table 7.

Table 7. Correlation between Big five personality and self-rating scale of stress (Correlation coefficient (significance)) (N = 41)

Personality	No stress	Consequence stress
Neuroticism	0.436** (0.004)	0.341* (0.029)
Extraversion	−0.106 (0.511)	0.052 (0.749)
Openness	0.140 (0.383)	0.081 (0.613)
Pleasantness	−0.168 (0.292)	−0.249 (0.116)
Conscientiousness	−0.243 (0.125)	−0.271 (0.086)

Notes: * p < 0.05, ** p < 0.01

The results of Table 7 showed that the stress self-assessment scale scores (r = 0.436, p = 0.004) were positively correlated with the neurotic personality scores under the condition of no consequence stress; the stress self-assessment scale scores (r = −0.387, p = 0.013) were all negatively correlated with the pleasantness personality scores; and the stress self-assessment scale was positively correlated with the neurotic personality scores under the condition of no consequence stress (r = 0.341, p = 0.029).

3.7 Big Five Personality Correlations with Performance Results

The results of the correlation analysis between the Big Five Personality and the behavioral performance metrics (Total Error Rate, Correct Response Hour and False Alarm Response Hour, Consistent False Alarm Error Rate and Repeated False Alarm Error Rate, Consistent False Alarm Response Hour and Repeated False Alarm Response Hour,

Table 8. Correlation between Big five personality and Total error rate (Correlation coefficient (significance)) (N = 41)

Personality	No stress	Consequence stress
Neuroticism	0.31 (0.847)	0.114 (0.476)
Extraversion	0.129 (0.423)	0.159 (0.322)
Openness	(0.307) (0.051)	0.155 (0.332)
Pleasantness	0.000 (1.000)	−0.018 (0.913)
Conscientiousness	−0.103 (0.520)	−0.186 (0.244)

Number of Erroneous Keystrokes, and Number of Missed Keystrokes) were shown in Tables 8, 9, 10, 11 and 12.

Table 9. Correlation between Big five personality and Consistently misreporting error rates and Repeated false error rate (Correlation coefficient (significance)) (N = 41)

Personality	Consistently misreporting error rates		Repeated false error rate	
	No stress	Consequence stress	No stress	Consequence stress
Neuroticism	0.016	0.187	−0.072	0.114
	(0.922)	(0.242)	(0.655)	(0.476)
Extraversion	−0.003	−0.025	0.127	0.217
	(0.986)	(0.876)	(0.427)	(0.172)
Openness	0.249	0.037	0.262	0.156
	(0.117)	(0.816)	(0.098)	(0.330)
Pleasantness	−0.030	0.009	0.014	−0.035
	(0.854)	(0.955)	(0.932)	(0.829)
Conscientiousness	−0.140	−0.242	−0.074	−0.145
	(0.384)	(0.127)	(0.645)	(0.365)

Table 10. Correlation between Big five personality and Correct reaction times and False response time (Correlation coefficient (significance)) (N = 41)

Personality	Correct reaction time		False response time	
	No stress	Consequence stress	No stress	Consequence stress
Neuroticism	0.123	−0.168	0.032	−0.298
	(0.443)	(0.293)	(0.845)	(0.059)
Extraversion	−0.059	−0.314*	0.021	−0.238
	(0.715)	(0.046)	(0.897)	(0.134)
Openness	−0.057	0.136	−0.074	0.167
	(0.725)	(0.398)	(0.647)	(0.297)
Pleasantness	0.081	−0.082	0.087	−0.120
	(0.613)	(0.609)	(0.588)	(0.457)
Conscientiousness	0.191	0.136	0.237	0.093
	(0.233)	(0.396)	(0.135)	(0.562)

Notes: * $p < 0.05$

Table 11. Correlation between Big five personality and Uniformly false response time and Repeated false response (Correlation coefficient (significance)) (N = 41)

Personality	Uniformly false response time		Repeated false response	
	No stress	Consequence stress	No stress	Consequence stress
Neuroticism	0.068	−0.154	0.048	−0.293
	(0.671)	(0.336)	(0.765)	(0.063)
Extraversion	−0.005	−0.296	−0.002	−0.199
	(0.977)	(0.060)	(0.988)	(0.212)
Openness	− 0.122	0.218	− 0.094	0.111
	(0.447)	(0.172)	(0.558)	(0.490)
Pleasantness	0.125	− 0.228	0.068	− 0.070
	(0.436)	(0.152)	(0.674)	(0.663)
Conscientiousness	0.237	0.001	0.232	0.122
	(0.136)	(0.995)	(0.144)	(0.446)

Table 12. Correlation between Big five personality and Number of error keys and Missing number (Correlation coefficient (significance)) (N = 41)

Personality	Number of error keys		Missing number	
	No stress	Consequence stress	No stress	Consequence stress
Neuroticism	−0.019	0.148	0.232	−0.202
	(0.907)	(0.356)	(0.150)	(0.205)
Extraversion	0.043	0.121	0.054	0.173
	(0.788)	(0.453)	(0.740)	(0.281)
Openness	0.270	0.118	0.140	0.049
	(0.088)	(0.462)	(0.388)	(0.762)
Pleasantness	−0.012	0.003	−0.159	−0.092
	(0.943)	(0.984)	(0.328)	(0.569)
Conscientiousness	−0.137	−0.198	−0.061	−0.092
	(0.393)	(0.215)	(0.709)	(0.569)

Notes: * $p < 0.05$, ** $p < 0.01$

The results of Table 8 indicated that none of the Big Five Personality scores correlated with the total error rate in both experimental conditions; the results of Tables 9, 10, 11 and 12 indicated that none of the performance measures correlated in both experimental conditions, except for when responding correctly which was negatively correlated with the Extraversion Personality scores in the Consequence Stress Condition ($r = -0.314$, $p = 0.046$).

3.8 Big Five Personality Correlations with ERP Results

The Big Five Personality trait scores were correlated with ERN magnitude and Pe mag-

Table 13. Correlation between Big five personality and ERN amplitude and ERN amplitude (Correlation coefficient (significance)) ($N = 41$)

Personality	ERN amplitude		Pe amplitude	
	No stress	Consequence stress	No stress	Consequence stress
Neuroticism	−0.202 (0.275)	−0.177 (0.342)	0.230 (0.214)	0.361* (0.046)
Extraversion	−0.156 (0.402)	−0.309 (0.091)	−0.031 (0.87)	−0.281 (0.125)
Openness	0.118 (0.527)	0.001 (0.999)	−0.066 (0.723)	−0.01 (0.959)
Pleasantness	0.052 (0.78)	0.21 (0.257)	0.233 (0.208)	−0.04 (0.831)
Conscientiousness	−0.094 (0.614)	0.052 (0.783)	0.345 (0.057)	−0.13 (0.485)

Notes: * $p < 0.05$, ** $p < 0.01$

nitude in the two experimental stress conditions, respectively, and the results are shown in Table 13. The results showed that Pe magnitude ($r = 0.361$, $p = 0.046$) was significantly and positively correlated with neurotic personality scores in the consequence stress condition.

3.9 Big Five Personality Correlations with ERSP Results

The Big Five Personality characteristics scores were correlated with beta-band energy and alpha-band energy in the two experimental stress conditions, respectively, and the

Table 14. Correlation between Big five personality and β-band energy and α-band energy (Correlation coefficient (significance)) ($N = 41$)

Personality	β-ERD		α-ERD	
	No stress	Consequence stress	No stress	Consequence stress
Neuroticism	0.286 (0.118)	−0.030 (0.871)	0.301 (0.100)	−0.005 (0.978)
Extraversion	−0.048 (0.796)	−0.059 (0.753)	0.048 (0.798)	0.219 (0.237)
Openness	0.168 (0.368)	−0.186 (0.315)	0.221 (0.232)	0.028 (0.88)
Pleasantness	0.015 (0.935)	−0.187 (0.314)	−0.041 (0.825)	−0.094 (0.651)
Conscientiousness	−0.095 (0.609)	−0.091 (0.626)	−0.234 (0.206)	−0.359* (0.047)

Notes: * $p < 0.05$, ** $p < 0.01$

results are shown in Table 14. The results showed that alpha band energy ($r = -0.359$, $p = 0.047$) was significantly negatively correlated with conscientiousness personality scores in the consequence stress condition.

4 Discussion

There was a trend of consequence stress > no stress in ERN amplitude, suggesting that error monitoring ability is affected by consequence stress to some extent. It indicated that the brain's error detection ability is more vital under consequence stress, activating the corresponding brain regions and presenting greater ERN, which may be caused by participants' aversion to or fear of severe consequences. It has been shown that participants under the influence of negative emotions show greater ERN [16].

The difference in Pe amplitude between the two experimental conditions was significant, with consequence stress > no stress, suggesting that the ability to be aware of errors can be affected by consequence stress.

Response times in the two conditions showed no stress > consequence stress, the opposite trend of Pe amplitude. The theory of error consciousness suggested that Pe was related to the degree of awareness of the erroneous response during error processing and that the higher the degree of awareness, the higher the amplitude of Pe, thus suggesting that the shorter the response time, the higher the subject's level of error consciousness in the shorter the experimental condition, which may be because of the participant's reaction to the response made in the presence of stress. Lack of self-confidence. It has been established that ERN and Pe reflect two stages of error processing, respectively, where ERN represents the early stage associated with error detection, and Pe represents the late stage associated with error awareness recognition. In the presence of stress, cognitive load increases, and error detection decreases in the early stages of error processing.

The correlation analysis between Big Five Personality and ERP results revealed that the ERP amplitude of certain personality characteristics was affected to some extent by different stresses and that there was variability in the ERP amplitude. Highly neurotic personalities were more prone to nervousness, anxiety, and impulsivity, and therefore, the effect of stress on highly neurotic personalities would be greater, i.e., the higher the level of neuroticism, the greater the Pe amplitude. On the one hand, this may be because under the condition of stress, high-neurotic personalities were more impulsive due to their own personality characteristics and produced more errors, resulting in higher levels of error awareness; on the other hand, it may be because high-neurotic participants were more nervous and anxious under stress and were more skeptical of the accuracy of the responses they made, resulting in higher levels of awareness.

For the beta band, the statistical analysis of the beta band energy amplitude under the two experimental conditions showed that there was a significant difference between the no-stress condition and the stress condition; the β band oscillation amplitude was enhanced under the no-stress condition, and the β band oscillation amplitude was significantly weakened under the stress condition, and the intensity of the beta band oscillation was related to the behavioral inhibition of the error response, and the stronger the behavioral inhibition was, the stronger the β band oscillation was, and the higher the energy amplitude was. In the present study, it was found that the β-band energy value decreased and the oscillation showed attenuation under consequence stress, indicating that the behavioral inhibition of error response was weakened by stress, and the β-band was more sensitive to the presence or absence of stress.

The results for the alpha band were similar to those for the beta band, and again the alpha band energy amplitude statistics between the two experimental conditions showed a significant difference between the two experimental conditions, with the α band oscillation amplitude being enhanced in the no-stress condition. It has been found that the strength of α-band oscillations is related to alertness, cognitive load, and false consciousness; the higher the internal alertness, the higher the cognitive load, and the higher the level of false consciousness, the weaker the α-band oscillations and the lower the energy value. In the present study, it was found that the α-band energy value decreased and the oscillations showed attenuation under consequence stress, indicating that stress caused participants to be more alert in error responses and to increase the level of error awareness, but also took up too much attentional resource, increasing the cognitive load.

Correlation analysis of the Big Five Personality with the ERSP results in the four experimental conditions revealed that certain personality characteristics affect specific frequency band energy amplitudes to some extent. The results of the present study showed that the conscientiousness score showed a significant negative correlation with the α-band energy in the consequence stress condition, i.e., the higher the scores of conscientiousness, the lower the α-band energy, the higher the α-ERD amplitude, and the weaker the α-band oscillations in the consequence stress condition, which was also related to high conscientiousness personality characteristics.

5   Conclusion

The present study showed that changes in error-related ERP components and time-frequency characteristic indicators could characterize the effect of consequence stress on human error. Highly neurotic personalities were the most sensitive to stress perception. In contrast, extraversion, openness, and conscientiousness personalities were affected by changes in only one of the indicators in a given stress condition. Therefore, in the future practical application, after personnel screening through the Big Five Personality Scale, targeted stress management and adaptive training can be conducted for each type of personality and evaluated through relevant indicators to improve the stress tolerance ability of the target personnel and the accuracy of task completion under stress.

References

1. SvensonBai, X.J., Zhu, S.H., Shen, D.L., Liu, N.: Autonomic nervous arousal and behavioral response of punishment and reward in extroverts and introverts. Acta PsychologicaSinica **06**, 26–34 (2009)
2. Zhang, K., He, L.Y., Zhao, Y., Wang, J.X.: Optimization and asymmetry effects of reward and punishment on control attention: evidence from eye movements. Acta PsychologicaSinica **51**(11), 1207–1218 (2019)
3. Ostrom, L., Gertman, D., Blackman, H.: Assessing human reliability in space-what is known, what still is needed. In: Space Programs and Technologies Conference, p. 1532 (1992)

4. Leonard-Hood, D., Rogers, C.: Methodology for space station freedom crew-machine interface risk assessment. In: Space Programs and Technologies Conference and Exhibit, p. 4194 (1993)
5. Meyer, A., Gawlowska, M.: Evidence for specificity of the impact of punishment on error-related brain activity in high versus low trait anxious individuals. Int. J. Psychophysiol. **120**, 157–163 (2017)
6. Riesel, A., Kathmann, N., Wüllhorst, V., et al.: Punishment has a persistent effect on error-related brain activity in highly anxious individuals twenty-four hours after conditioning. Int. J. Psychophysiol. **146**, 63–72 (2019)
7. Schell, K.L., Reilley, S.P.: Quality control pharmacy tasks: big five personality model and accuracy of error detection. Psychol. Rep. **94**(3 Pt 2), 1301–1311 (2004)
8. Burgess, L.I.F., Wallymahmed, A.: Personality, stress and coping in intensive care nurses: a descriptive exploratory study. Nurs. Crit. Care **15**(3), 129–140 (2010)
9. Sârbescu, P., Maricuțoiu, L.: Are you a "bad driver" all the time? Insights from a weekly diary study on personality and dangerous driving behavior. J. Res. Pers. **80**, 30–37 (2019)
10. Landay, K., Wood, D., Harms, P.D., et al.: Relationships between personality facets and accident involvement among truck drivers. J. Res. Pers. **84**, 1–10 (2020)
11. Tang, P.S., Wang, L.: Perceived stress and depression among seven-year program medical students: mediating role of Big Five personality. Chin. J. Public Health **31**(9), 1188–1190 (2015)
12. Xu, C.P.: The Influence of Five-Factor Model on the Performance of College Teachers' Scientific Research. Hunan Normal University (2019)
13. Wei, S.M.: Personality measures as predictors of job performance: a meta-analytic review. Beijing Jiaotong University (2018)
14. Chen, S.G., Jiang, G.H., Wang, C.H.: Advancement in space human factors engineering. Manned Spaceflight **21**(2), 95–105 (2015)
15. Xu, L.L., Qu, L.M., Geng, Q.S.: The reliability and validity of the administrator work stress scale. Chin. J. Health Psychol. **20**(01), 153–154 (2012)
16. Hajcak, G., Mcdonald, N., Simons, R.F.: Anxiety and error-related brain activity. Biol. Psychol. **64**(1–2), 77–90 (2003)

Decision-Making Support
and Automation

Neural Correspondence to Environmental Uncertainty in Multiple Probability Judgment Decision Support System

Yoo-Sang Chang, Younho Seong[✉], and Sun Yi

North Carolina Agricultural and Technical State University, 1601 East Market Street, Greensboro, NC 27411, USA
ychang@aggies.ncat.edu, {yseong,syi}@ncat.edu

Abstract. With artificial intelligence (AI) technology development, decision support systems (DSS) supporting human judgment are applied to multi-agent systems (MAS) as an interactive automated system. Despite the development of automation in systems, human judgment is important to prevent system failures due to impaired situational awareness under uncertainty. In human judgment, uncertainty can affect neural correspondence which induces cognitive bias, resulting in distorted judgment. Therefore, neural correspondences under uncertainty for appropriate judgments should be considered. This paper suggests understanding neural correspondence with multiple information judgments under uncertainty. For uncertainty, we used expected and unexpected uncertainty concepts influencing trustworthiness for the system performance. We used electroencephalogram (EEG) to measure neural correspondence in the multiple information judgment system. Based on the analysis of neural correspondence, we found that the cognitive process is based on linguistic and mathematical processing. With having trust in the system, humans can experience a strong incongruent situation by observing poor system performance. This study will give insights into cognitive process improvements of the multiple probability information judgment system through understanding neural correspondence under uncertainty.

Keywords: Cognitive task analysis · Decision making and decision support · Electroencephalogram (EEG) · Multi-agent system (MAS) · Decision support system (DSS) · Expected uncertainty · unexpected uncertainty

1 Introduction

Human decision-making plays an essential role in MAS. With the development of technologies, multi-agent systems (MAS) have been applied to various industry fields, such as transportation, the Internet of Things (IoT), healthcare systems, and defense systems. MAS is an automated system based on interaction with multiple agents to deal with problems [1]. In the defense system, as the military domain, MAS is operated as a cooperative system with unmanned robots such as unmanned ground vehicles (UGV) and unmanned aerial vehicles (UAV) [2]. MAS can be operated as automated systems by

© The Author(s), under exclusive license to Springer Nature Switzerland AG 2024
D. Harris and W.-C. Li (Eds.): HCII 2024, LNAI 14692, pp. 153–164, 2024.
https://doi.org/10.1007/978-3-031-60728-8_13

unmanned robots. Still, the human agent role is essential in high-performance systems because human decision-making can prevent impaired situational awareness as a pit-fall in automated systems causing failure [3]. For this reason, decision support systems (DSS) can be applied to MAS to facilitate human judgment through supporting data analysis from agents based on artificial intelligence (AI) [4, 5]. Therefore, humans are crucial to building high-level systems in MAS.

It is necessary to understand the human cognitive process for facilitated human decision-making in MAS uncertainty situations. Humans cannot always make an optimal decision under uncertainty. The uncertainty can affect human decision-making because of a characteristic of the neural system. Uncertainty can be defined as risk probability by ambiguous information [6] and it can cause the non-optimal human decision-making by two characteristics of human neural system as a process of neural correspondence. First is the variation of neural circuitry, which means the human neural states are always changing when humans receive the information for every trial disregarding situation sim-ilarity. Second is the reception input in noise with cognitive bias (e.g., fatigue or mood) [7]. These neural system characteristics can happen in MAS with specific information type reception. Generally, in military domain, defense system is operated by multiple cue judgment as the cognitive model based on multiple information from cooperative agents in the combat environment [8]. In terms of agents, robot agents are also operated based on multiple cues during interaction in MAS [9]. Thus, we focused on capturing neu-ral correspondence to understand how to deal with uncertainty during decision-making based on multiple cues in MAS.

Uncertainty can affect not only human decision-making but also MAS as exter-nal uncertainty. In MAS, uncertainty can be defined as the effects on specific actions of agents by dynamically varied environments (e.g., sensor errors or network errors) causing poor system performance with many failures [1]. The uncertainty can cause the noise of input reception with distorted information that can affect trust, which can cause misuse or disuse, resulting in accidents in terms of human-automation interaction [10]. Thus, MAS should have policies to deal with uncertainty for high-level system per-formance. To implement uncertainty, we used the concept of expected uncertainty and unexpected uncertainty [11]. Expected uncertainty is knowing the unreliable environ-ment for the prediction, such as low anticipation for the automated system performance by experiencing many invalid performances. (e.g., five out of ten observations of when their prediction and system performance differ). In contrast, unexpected uncertainty can give a strong violated experience for the prediction when humans meet invalid predic-tions from a reliable environment. It means they can observe intensive experiences from a reliable environment built by a lot of reliable experience from the system (e.g., one out of ten observations of when their prediction and system performance differ). Through the concept of these uncertainties, we designed the experiment focusing on giving the visual stimuli as experiences of these uncertainties.

Neural correspondence measurement is a method to understand human decision-making behavior in the human cognitive process. We used electroencephalography (EEG) to measure neural correspondence for this study. EEG is one of the brain activity measurement methods based on minute electric signals from the human scalp. There are EEG analysis methods according to specific analysis domains, such as time or frequency domains. The time domain analysis is for brain activity analysis based on the event-related stimulus. The representative time domain analysis is event-related potential (ERP) through understanding human behavior of cognitive process by finding specific potential patterns from the start point of an event such as stimulus presentation. The frequency domain is the brain distribution activity based on mathematical transformation from time to frequency domain, such as fast Fourier transformation (FFT). The frequency domain can show the brain states, such as sleep, relaxation, or anxiety [12]. We used ERP analysis as time domain analysis to measure neural correspondence on a multiple cue judgment system such as MAS environment with DSS.

In sum, this study was performed for understanding human behavior based on neural correspondence after decision-making under uncertainty in a multiple cue judgment system with a decision support system like MAS with DSS. In this case, the cue is provided as probability. We used the concepts of expected and unexpected uncertainties to implement uncertainty for the experiment design of a multiple cue judgment system. For analysis after the experiment, we used EEG with ERP analysis, as time domain analysis, to measure neural correspondence after their decision-making. We expect this study to give insights into cognitive process improvements on a multiple cue judgment system such as MAS under uncertainty.

2 Literature Review

We discussed the importance of understanding human decision-making in a multiple cue judgment system with a decision support system under uncertainty. There are studies related to decision-making under uncertainty, multiple cue judgment, or MAS.

There are studies related to decision-making with uncertainty in business and economy fields [13–15]. Multiple cue judgment can reduce information integration strain by treating non-linear cues related to linear cues under multiple cues [16]. There are studies for understanding the effects when classification is performed by probability cue judgment [17, 18]. One study tested the hypothesis of labor division based on multiple cue information [19]. For the study of decision-making in MAS, game theory modeling is developed to improve human autonomy interaction using long short-term memory (LSTM) neural networks for human decision-making prediction [20]. One study suggests a theoretical utility function model including human cognitive bias during decision-making in MAS [7].

EEG is usually used in neural correspondence to understand cognitive processes underlying human behavior. In human decision-making, EEG analysis is performed with an artificial grammar learning paradigm to understand the intuitive cognition process [21]. There are studies related to trust and decision-making with EEG. The typically used EEG method is ERP analysis. Generally, ERP analysis is based on a positive or negative peak of potential from the onset, showing an event starting in ERP analysis. Studies show how trust can affect decision-making [22] and decision-making under expected and unexpected uncertainties with positive or negative compensation [23]. These studies show occurrence of feedback-related negativity (FRN), which has a negative peak around 200 ms to 300 ms, and P300, which has a positive peak around 300 ms after the onset.

The EEG analysis for trust by decision-making is used in human-automation interaction. Based on multiple cues for decision-making, human brain activity based on observational error-related negativity (oERN) having a negative peak after about 44 ms from the onset and observational error positivity (oPe) as showing a positive peak after about 150 ms after the onset was detected and analyzed [24]. These patterns can reflect the mismatch between expected and actual action outcomes. The convolutional neural network (CNN), a machine learning technique, is used for trust state classification based on time-frequency analysis for collected EEG data from human-automation interaction experiments [25]. In the supervised machine learning model, reducing the number of electrodes (channels) of EEG device can be used for trust classification efficiency, considering the reduction of accuracy loss [26]. A study about trust state for chatbots in e-commerce showed P2 (showing positive peak after about 200 ms from onset) and LLP (having a positive peak after 600 ms from onset) [27]. P2 and LPP can reflect emotional experience evaluations. There is a study about considering selfish agents in human-automation interaction experiment, and N170, having a negative peak potential around 170 ms after the onset, was detected [28].

As discussed above, it is difficult to find the research of understanding human's neural correspondence by decision-making on a multiple probability judgment system, such as MAS, with decision support under uncertainty. Thus, this research would be a meaningful neurological analysis of human decision-making process under uncertainty on MAS environment with DSS.

3   Methodology

3.1   Cognitive Process Model

We designed an experiment based on the theoretical cognitive mechanism including uncertainty. The information flow is from each agent in the system to humans. The information provides multiple probability cues for specific situations, such as the existence of enemies. The decision support system also includes probability information by data analysis based on information of agents. Humans will accept the information of the multiple probability judgment system with decision support and get the system performance experiences through comparison between their judgment and real-world result as output. These experiences will affect every human judgment in the system.

The expected and unexpected uncertainty results in good or poor system performance due to uncertainty in the environment. Expected uncertainty results in an experience of poor performance of the system by relatively more observation of invalid performance against human prediction by judgment. In contrast, unexpected uncertainty results in an experience of good system performance by less observation of invalid system performance against the prediction by judgment. In this case, the example of poor performance in expected uncertainty is observation for five out of ten inconsistent observations between decision-making and real-world result. The good system performance example is that one out of ten observations for inconsistency between judgment and real-world result. Those uncertainties will affect the reliability of the system usage environment, resulting in neural correspondence. Then, this neural correspondence will induce human judgment by feedback from the real-world result of the system under uncertainty. This study focuses on understanding neural correspondence based on the cognitive mechanism of the multiple probability judgment system.

3.2   Experiment Design

The experiment was designed based on the cognitive mechanism of the multiple probability judgment system with the decision support system. Figure 1 shows an example of a trial for judgment in the experiment.

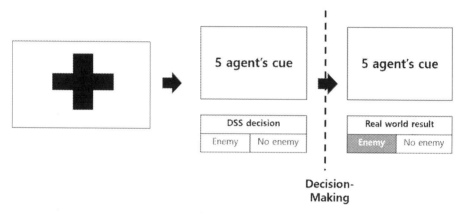

Fig. 1. Experiment design for one trial.

Participants saw the cross fixation in the display for 2 s. After 2 s of cross fixation, the cue provided information about the multiple probability system with decision support for 5 to 15 s. There were five agent probability cues for the existence of an enemy with the information of the decision support system. The decision support system (DSS) showed the decisions with the probability of enemy existence based on data analysis for the information of five agents. Logistic regression analysis was used for data analysis to implement AI in the decision support system. Participants decided on enemy existence according to their judgment by cue information. After judgment, the stimulus provided real-world result with the cue for 2 s. The real-world result was based on DSS to give good or poor system performance by expected and unexpected uncertainties.

The experiments were comprised of the number of poor system performance situation for each block for expected and unexpected uncertainties. The expected uncertainty was comprised of 50% poor performances for which cues and real-world results were different for enemy existence in System A. In contrast, unexpected uncertainty was comprised of 90% good performances for which cues and the real-world results were the same for enemy existence in System B. The experiment was performed in two blocks by expected uncertainty scenario (System A) and unexpected uncertainty scenario (System B). We experimented by PowerPoint, and the judgment was marked as onset when they pressed the number keyboard for 1 (Enemy) and 2 (No enemy).

3.3 Data Acquisition

The neural correspondence was collected by EEG. The used EEG device was Emotiv EpocFlex saline kit with 31 electrode channels as a 10–20 system for the location of the lobes of the brain [29] (see Fig. 2). The number of participants was two participants with male and female, and the age is over 18 years.

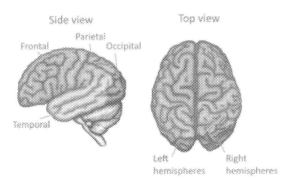

Fig. 2. Brain lobe for side and top view [29].

3.4 Data Preprocessing

EEG data preprocessing is necessary for more accurate data through noise and artifact removal in raw EEG signals. We followed the specific steps for EEG data preprocessing (see Fig. 3).

Fig. 3. Procedure of EEG data preprocessing.

The raw EEG data were filtered at 30 Hz as low-pass band and performed averaged reference from channels of electrodes for noise removal. After filtering and channel referencing, the epoch was produced based on the segment from 200 ms before to 1000 ms after onset as the starting point of showing the real-world result. The baseline was removed 200 ms before the onset for each epoch. We used independent component analysis (ICA) to remove channel noise, muscle, and eye movements after those artifact classifications to remove artifacts. The extreme high or low voltage was discarded, like less than 75 μV to over 75 μV and over 50 μV voltage drift [23]. EEGLAB in MATLAB was used for EEG data preprocessing [30].

3.5   Data Analysis Based on ERP

The representative analysis of the time domain we used was event-related potential (ERP) through finding positive or negative peak potential at a specific time from the onset. For example, P300 is a positive peak after 300 ms from the onset as an occurring stimulus or event. This pattern occurs for lying or a specific mental state. If the amplitude of P300 is higher, it can be diagnosed as mental performance is superior; in contrast, if the amplitude is lower, the mental state is weak, such as alcohol dependence [31]. There are a variety of other ERP patterns, as well as P300. We analyzed neural correspondence to understand human behavior in the multiple probability system based on the captured peak amplitude after onset. We performed ERP analysis according to each block, such as grand average ERP analysis for data from the expected uncertainty situation (System A) and unexpected uncertainty situation (System B).

4   Result

We found N400 to have a negative peak around 400 ms from 150 to 450 ms (ms) after the onset. N400 occurred around the front lobe (Fp1, Fp2, Fz, and Cz), the parietal lobe (CPz), and the occipital (O2) regions in terms of the averaged ERP plot. Figure 4 shows ERP plot of Fz.

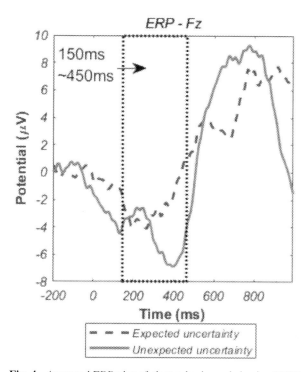

Fig. 4. Averaged ERP plot of electrode channels having N400

In terms of distribution for negativity, which means a higher negative amplitude value or negative distribution, a larger negativity distribution in topography was shown in unexpected uncertainty for 150 to 450 ms (see Fig. 5).

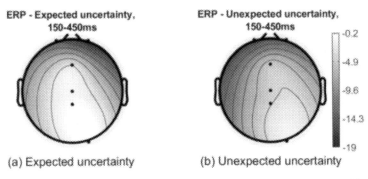

Fig. 5. Averaged ERP topography plot for electrode channels having N400

The averaged negative potential value was also shown in the averaged ERP plot (see Fig. 6). In terms of the numeric value of averaged potential as negative amplitude value for 150 ms to 450 ms, we found that the unexpected uncertainty scenario showed more averaged negative amplitude value (-7.631 μV) than the expected uncertainty scenario (-6.641 μV) from 150 ms to 450 ms (see Table 1). Thus, we can conclude that the negativity of N400 is increased under unexpected uncertainty.

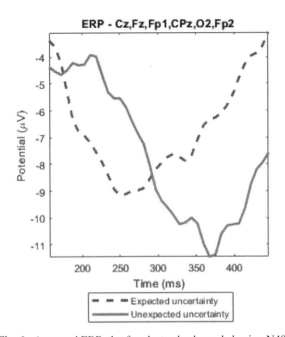

Fig. 6. Averaged ERP plot for electrode channels having N400

Table 1. Basic statistics for the averaged potential of selected channels from 150 ms to 450 ms (Cz, Fz, Fp1, CPz, O2, Fp2). Times is the point when maximum or minimum potential is shown.

	Expected uncertainty		Unexpected uncertainty	
	Potential (μV)	Time about potential (ms)	Potential (μV)	Time about potential (ms)
Min	− 9.168	250	− 11.459	367.188
Max	− 3.084	445.312	− 3.924	210.938
Mean	− 6.641	–	− 7.631	–
std	1.876	–	2.565	–

5 Discussion

The N400 occurred on the specific lobe, generally parietally maximal, of the brain in the multiple probability judgment system with the decision support system under expected and unexpected uncertainty. Generally, N400 occurs around 400 ms after onset and when they are processing linguistic or mathematical stimuli [32]. The probability judgment system provides mathematical cues so humans can think mathematically for decision-making. Regarding linguistical interpretation, humans can make a decision based on linguistic summary for the received cues with mathematical thinking (e.g., there was a higher probability for enemy existence from agents, and DSS decision also showed enemy existence, so they can decide that there is an enemy). Thus, we can conclude that the cognitive process follows the linguistical interpretation based on mathematical thinking in the multiple probability judgment system with decision support under uncertainty.

The negativity is increased under unexpected uncertainty for the N400 amplitude value. The increasing negativity can occur in incongruent situations. For example, when "eagle" is given as the prime word, and "pigeon" is shown as the target word after the prime word, the incongruent segment is reduced because these words are under the same category like bird or animal. However, if the target word is "stone," it makes it harder to associate "eagle" and "stone" because "stone" is an inanimate object, and it results in an incongruent segment. The negativity of N400 is increased when it is harder to associate prime and target words as incongruent [33]. If this phenomenon is applied to this study, the prime is the constructed reliability for the system performance by the experiences, and the target is the real-world result in comparison with judgment.

In expected uncertainty, the trustworthiness for system performance is constructed by an unreliable environment for performance with relatively more experience of poor system performance as prime. It can be associated with less assurance for system performance because the system performance environment is unreliable. So, the negativity can be decreased by less incongruent situation occurrence for unreliable system performance prediction when they observe poor performance under expected uncertainty.

In contrast, in an unexpected uncertainty scenario, the prime is a more reliable system performance with less observation for poor performance. Thus, humans can have assurance of system performance. If they observe poor system performance, it would not be an associated situation under a reliable system performance environment.

So, they can have an impactful experience with the incongruent situation if they observe a rare number of poor performances (10% poor performance) under the environment as having the trust for system performance. Thus, we can interpret that humans can feel a strong incongruent situation under unexpected uncertainty by rare observation of poor system performance.

6   Conclusion

We discussed the analysis of neural correspondence in multiple probability systems as MAS with decision support under uncertainty to understand human behavior. N400 occurred in frontal and parietal lobe regions and the negativity was increased under unexpected uncertainty. It can be interpreted that the cognitive process is performed as linguistic interpretation based on mathematical thinking in the multiple probability judgment system. In terms of the negativity of N400, we can interpret that the feeling of a strongly incongruent situation occurs when they meet poor system performance under unexpected uncertainty, as a reliable system environment with good system performance.

This study is a preliminary study, so more experiments with more participants are needed for valid analysis. The information type was probability in this study, so it would be a more practical study if the experiment is performed based on the MAS user interface used in the real world, such as the cooperative system with multiple agents. We expect that this study will give insight into the improvement of the cooperative system based on MAS in terms of effective cognitive processes in the user interface.

Acknowledgments. This research is based upon work supported by the ONR (Award No. N00014-22-1-2724). The views and conclusions contained herein are those of the authors and should not be interpreted as necessarily representing the official policies or endorsements, either expressed or implied, of the U.S. Government.

References

1. Balaji, P., Srinivasan, D.: An introduction to multi-Agent systems. In: Studies in Computational Intelligence, pp. 1–27 (2010)
2. Khan, A., Gupta, S., Gupta, S.K.: Cooperative control between multi-UAVs for maximum coverage in disaster management: review and proposed model. In: 2022 2nd International Conference on Computing and Information Technology (ICCIT) (2022)
3. Tweedale, J.W., Ichalkaranje, N., Sioutis, C., Jarvis, B., Consoli, A., Phillips-Wren, G.: Innovations in multi-agent systems. J. Netw. Comput. Appl. **30**, 1089–1115 (2007)
4. Khemakhem, F., Ellouzi, H., Ltifi, H., Ayed, M.B.: Agent-based intelligent decision support systems: a systematic review. IEEE Trans. Cogn. Dev. Syst. **14**(1), 20–34 (2022)
5. Gupta, S., Modgil, S., Bhattacharyya, S., Bose, I.: Artificial intelligence for decision support systems in the field of operations research: review and future scope of research. Ann. Oper. Res. **308**, 215–274 (2021)
6. Hsu, M., Bhatt, M., Adolphs, R., Tranel, D., Camerer, C.F.: Neural systems responding to degrees of uncertainty in human Decision-Making. Science **310**(5754), 1680–1683 (2005)

7. Geng, B., Brahma, S., Wimalajeewa, T., Varshney, P.K., Rangaswamy, M.: Prospect Theoretic utility based human decision making in multi-Agent systems. IEEE Trans. Signal Process. **68**, 1091–1104 (2020)
8. Sokolowski, J.A.: Enhanced decision modeling using multiagent system simulation. Simulation **79**(4), 232–242 (2003)
9. Guedea-Elizalde, F., Karray, F., Soto, R., Song, I., Basir, O.: Multi-agent CORBA-based robotics vision architecture for cue integration. In: IEEE International Conference on Systems, Man and Cybernetics (2003)
10. Dzindolet, M.T., Peterson, S., Pomranky, R.A., Pierce, L.G., Beck, H.P.: The role of trust in automation reliance. Int. J. Hum Comput Stud. **58**(6), 697–718 (2003)
11. Yu, A.J., Dayan, P.: Uncertainty, neuromodulation, and attention. Neuron **46**(4), 681–692 (2005)
12. Firoz, K.F., Seong, Y., Oh, S.: A neurological approach to classify trust through EEG signals using machine learning techniques. In: 2022 IEEE 3rd International Conference on Human-Machine Systems (2022)
13. Dijkstra, N., De Groot, K., Rietveld, C.A.: Entrepreneurial orientation and decision-making under risk and uncertainty: experimental evidence from the Columbia Card Task. Appl. Psychol. **72**(4), 1577–1592 (2022)
14. Johnson, J., Busemeyer, J.R.: Decision making under risk and uncertainty. WIREs Cognit. Sci. **1**(5), 736–749 (2010)
15. Heal, G., Millner, A.: Reflections: uncertainty and decision making in climate change. Rev. Environ. Econ. Policy **8**(1), 120–137 (2014)
16. Brehmer, B., Slovic, P.: Information integration in multiple-cue judgments. J. Exp. Psychol. Hum. Percept. Perform. **6**(2), 302–308 (1980)
17. Mata, R., Von Helversen, B., Karlsson, L., Cüpper, L.: Adult age differences in categorization and multiple-cue judgment. Dev. Psychol. **48**(4), 1188–1201 (2012)
18. Juslin, P., Olsson, H., Olsson, A.-C.: Exemplar effects in categorization and multiple-cue judgment. J. Exp. Psychol. Gen. **132**(1), 133–156 (2003)
19. Juslin, P., Karlsson, L., Olsson, H.: Information integration in multiple cue judgment: a division of labor hypothesis. Cognition **106**(1), 259–298 (2008)
20. Heintzman, L.: A predictive autonomous decision aid for calibrating Human-Autonomy reliance in multi-Agent task assignment. https://arxiv.org/abs/2112.10252
21. Firoz, K.F., Seong, Y.: A Neural study of intuitive mode of cognition while decision-making using Artificial Grammar Learning paradigm. In: Proceedings of the IISE Annual Conference & Expo 2023 (2023)
22. Long, Y., Jiang, X., Zhou, X.: To believe or not to believe: trust choice modulates brain responses in outcome evaluation. Neuroscience **200**, 50–58 (2012)
23. Kogler, L., Sailer, U., Derntl, B., Pfabigan, D.M.: Processing expected and unexpected uncertainty is modulated by fearless-dominance personality traits – an exploratory ERP study on feedback processing. Physiol. Behav. **168**, 74–83 (2017)
24. De Visser, E.J., et al.: Learning from the slips of others: neural correlates of trust in Automated agents. Front. Hum. Neurosci. **12**, 1–16 (2018)
25. Choo, S., Nam, C.S.: Detecting human trust calibration in automation: a convolutional neural network approach. IEEE Trans. Hum.-Mach. Syst. **52**(4), 774–783 (2022)
26. Firoz, K.F., Seong, Y., Chang, Y.-S.: A preliminary study on human trust in pseudo-real-time scenario through electroencephalography and machine learning based data classification. In: 1st International Conference on Smart Mobility and Vehicle Electrification (2023)
27. Wang, C., Li, Y., Fu, W., Jin, J.: Whether to trust chatbots: applying the event-related approach to understand consumers' emotional experiences in interactions with chatbots in e-commerce. J. Retail. Consum. Serv. **73**, 103325 (2023)

28. Dong, S.-Y., Kim, B.-K., Lee, K.-H., Lee, S.Y.: A preliminary study on human trust measurements by EEG for human-machine interactions. In: HAI 2015: Proceedings of the 3rd International Conference on Human-Agent Interaction, pp. 265–268 (2015)

29. Lim, S.H., Nisar, H., Thee, K.W., Yap, V.V.: A novel method for tracking and analysis of EEG activation across brain lobes. Biomed. Signal Process. Control 40, 488–504 (2018)

30. Delorme, A., Makeig, S.: EEGLAB: an open-source toolbox for analysis of single-trial EEG dynamics including independent component analysis. J. Neurosci. Methods 134, 9–21 (2004)

31. Sur, S., Vk, S.: Event-related potential: an overview. Ind. Psychiatry J. 18(1), 70–73 (2009)

32. Kutas, M., Federmeier, K.D.: Thirty years and Counting: finding meaning in the N400 component of the Event-Related Brain Potential (ERP). Annu. Rev. Psychol. 62, 621–647 (2011)

33. Daltrozzo, J., Wioland, N., Kotchoubey, B.: The N400 and late positive complex (LPC) effects reflect controlled rather than automatic mechanisms of sentence processing. Brain Sci. 2(3), 267–297 (2012)

Situational Awareness and Decision-Making in Maritime Operations: A Cognitive Perspective

Markus Hansen[1] and Salman Nazir[2(✉)]

[1] Training and Assessment Research Group, Department for Maritime Operations, University of South-Eastern Norway, Vestfold, Norway
[2] Department of Maritime Operations, University of South-Eastern Norway, Vestfold, Norway
Salman.Nazir@usn.no

Abstract. The vulnerable part of our ever-changing socio-technical challenges in a dynamic environment such as maritime berthing operations is frequently the human and our intrinsic cognitive limitations. Human factors and human error have historically been, and still are, attributed as contributing factors to accidents and incidents in the maritime domain [1]. This study utilizes Goal-directed task analysis (GDTA) along with a qualitative research framework to explore complex situational awareness (SA) and decision-making during maritime berthing operations. Many theoretical frameworks have been developed by researchers to understand how human cognitive functions in a dynamic and constantly changing environment [2–5]. Endsley's research framework was selected for this study based on its suitability, superiority, and applicability. Secondary research questions were also modeled and investigated to complement a more holistic understanding of the complex phenomena of situation awareness in the maritime domain. Utilizing non-probabilistic sampling, five experienced deck officers were interviewed using a semi-structured framework interview guide. The interview transcripts were analyzed using NVivo software. Findings showed 117 level 1 (perception), 32 level 2 (comprehension) and 15 level 3 (projection) information requirements. Secondary research showcased the top 3 factors negatively impact an individual's SA are noise, wrongfully assessing external factors, and distractions. Effective communication, mutual understanding of tasks, and sharing of relative information were identified to be crucial factors in ensuring cooperation within the ship's bridge team and improving situation awareness. The navigator's reliance on information varies based on factors like experience, task clarity, and familiarity with equipment. The findings reinforce available literature, while the secondary research questions justify need for further research. Overall, the theory of individual and shared SA is not only reinforced but also subtly broadened by this study, proving its applicability in maritime operations.

Keyword: Situation Awareness · Human Factors · Maritime domain · Process Safety · Berthing operations · Goal-directed task analysis

1 Introduction

The shipping industry stands as a vast and intricate sociotechnical system. As approximately 90 percent of all goods transportation occurs via sea routes. This massive operation facilitates the annual transfer of billions of dollars' worth of commodities across the world's oceans. Maritime accidents such as collisions and groundings are a longstanding problem globally. In 2021, the European Maritime Agency reported more than 21,000 sea vessels were engaged in maritime accidents from which more than 490 fatalities were found. Moreover, with about 90% of worldwide trade being dependent on sea routes and ship vessels, maritime accidents have severe consequences on countries economy [6]. Around 80% of sea accidents were attributed to human factors [7]. Additionally, some research questions these figures and the role of human factors in these sophisticated socio-technical systems [8].

2 Historical Background

The success of maritime seafarers before the time of mechanically propelled ships was based on their physical strength, fortitude and the ability to navigate ships with poor ergonomic comfort in operating the vessels. After the invention of steel ships, it brought a paradigm shift to the maritime industry, requiring seafarers to adapt to advanced learning methods along with the use of sophisticated navigational tools. Hands-on experience became essential in operating sea ships in the changing maritime landscape [1]. The capsizing of the Titanic in 1912 made the international community able to admit the need for regulations, leading to the establishment of international laws and conventions towards safety of life at sea such as the SOLAS act [9]. After the second world war, researchers started a scientific approach to understand human factors in maritime domain. One side the advancement of technology and equipment in socio-technical systems and on the other hand it triggered intrinsic human limitations. One such example is the grounding of the Torrey Canyon in 1967, which led to the spilling of 100,000 tons of crude oil. A subsequent investigation highlighted the contributing factors of acute time demands, inadequate communications and poor judgment by the crew [10, 11]. Although most of the scientific leaps and understanding was a result of extensive war time research. Situation awareness (SA), as a term, was first used extensively by the Douglas Aircraft Company. In the 1970s, global accident statistics exposed the disturbing loss of at least one merchant vessel at sea every day, sparking a rekindled interest in human factors research [1]. The result of this newfound interest initially increased mariners' efficiency by 15% to 35%, was further fueled by financial motivations. The digital age brought a focus on navigation bridge designs and layouts, initiating ergonomic research. These changes revealed the need for a new specialist mariner who would rely on cognitive- and specialized technical skills rather than physical strength and endurance as before.

In modern times, overseeing the safety navigation and execution of critical operations aboard ships has become a profession that been established throughout across Europe and the US to discover, examine, and implement their research [1]. However, the vulnerable link in this study remains the human operators as the most common cause for these accidents was the result of human errors and the multiple challenges faced by mariners in road traffic accidents. The modern operator who is trained for these situations has to navigate through an influx of information, requiring swift perception, comprehension of the information, categorizing and processing before making any critical decisions at sea [12]. The historical evolution of seafarer's reliance on physical strength and fortitude to the modern era's advanced learning methods and complex navigation tools lays the foundation for understanding the important role of SA in modern maritime operations.

2.1   Situational Awareness (SA) in Maritime Domain

Situation awareness (SA) is the understanding of a person's environment, its surrounding elements and how they change with time or other factors. It is crucial for effective decision making under different scenarios. It was defined by Endsley as "the perception of elements in the environment within a volume of time and space, the comprehension of their meaning and the projection of their status in the near future" [2]. Ship operations and navigations have highlighted the importance of situation awareness (SA) multiple times to ship bridge team members in complex maritime environments [13]. The International Maritime Organization cites as stated by Cordon, "the key to maintaining a safe shipping environment and to keep our oceans clean lies in all seafarers to follow high standards of competence and professionalism in the duties they perform onboard" [13]. It was also emphasized in a study about the prevalence of humans, attributing them to poor decision-making and overconfidence by the seafarers rather than technical difficulty. Furthermore, it was observed that the total ratio of sea accidents attributed to human factors are 75% but 82–83% of cases arise due to the cargo and passenger ships [14]. Accidents due to pilot error accounted for 43% of the total cases with that type of ship. Another factor for ship accidents was the improper integration of the pilot into a bridge team due to poor or ineffective Bridge resource management [15]. It was also observed that those individuals with low personality scores, and high levels of extroversion and diligence could predict both subjective and observer-rated situational awareness. Moreover, situation awareness was found to be associated with diverse physiological response patterns, such as an aptitude to suppress heart rate variability (HRV) from baseline from the seafaring period and recovery [16]. Therefore, accurately measuring and understanding situation awareness is important for enhancing maritime safety and decision-making. Understanding the factors that influence situation awareness including ineffective bridge communication and human errors highlights the need for accurate SA assessment. Ultimately, ensuring a comprehensive understanding of SA contributes to the overall competence and professionalism of seafarers, reinforcing the need to preserve a safe and environmentally secure maritime domain. Therefore, it is important to explore methods to assess situation awareness.

2.2 Goal-Directed Task Analysis (GDTA)

The authors have utilized Goal-directed task analysis (GDTA), which is a cognitive task analysis (CTA) exercise that can determine the pilot's decision, goals and required SA about the pilot's multifaceted environmental surroundings, systems and domains [17]. There are several techniques to measure SA in complex environments such as GDTA, SAGAT and SART. For this study, the applicability and suitability of the GDTA was found to be most effective and relevant, thus selected. Furthermore, it seamlessly integrated with the selected theoretical framework employed when investigating this subject. A goal-directed task analysis creates a hierarchy of objectives and forms initial or primary steps in a human-centered design process where the end-objective is to assist and enhance overall human performance in advanced and complex socio-technical environments. Furthermore, it is believed that human-centered design can both mitigate and resolve the aforementioned challenges (Table 1).

Table 1. Overview of the GDTA utilized as inspiration in this study [18]

Subject	Reference	Scope
Goal directed task analysis (GDTA)	(Bolstand et al., 2002)	Using GDTA to obtain situational awareness requirements, goals for multiple army brigade officers with importance on team SA
	(Endsley & Jones, 2011)	Outlining principles and methodology to execute a GDTA, also includes an example on commercial airline pilots
	(Humphery & Adams, 2011)	Augmentation of the GDTA by including a team-based system in CBRNE incident response domain
	(Sharma et al., 2019)	Determination of situation awareness information required for maritime navigations using GDTA method
	(Haffaci et al., 2021)	Establishment of SA information requirements and goals during docking of the shipping compulsory pilotage area

2.3 Research Questions

The aim of this study is to identify and describe situation awareness information require-ments during maritime operations using goal-directed task analysis by Endsley and Jones [17]. The study focuses on individual navigator and bridge team members. Other assets and supporting maritime roles were excluded such as shore-side workers, tugs, pilots and highly-specialized operational procedures. Moreover, the scenario is "mar-itime berthing operations" and were restricted to the final approach to portside, maneu-vering and berthing as this is where it was reported that numerous accidents occurred during critical phases of operation [19]. Hence, an augmented understanding of SA is required during critical operations, which can help reduce maritime accidents. In order to dig deeper, secondary research questions were also developed to further enhance the already existing body of knowledge while also demonstrating the usage of Endsley & Jones proposed GDTA methodology [17]. The primary research question was:

> "Determining individual SA information requirements during maritime berthing operations using Endsley's GDTA methodology"

The secondary research questions (SQR) were as follows:

- **SQR 1 (SA requirements):** Which factors negatively affect SA?
- **SQR 2 (Shared SA):** How do the members of the bridge team work together to ensure a good overall situation awareness and proficient cooperation?
- **SQR 3 (Validity and reliability):** How certain are the members of the bridge team that the information displayed or received is correct, and how does it affect their decisions.

3   Research Framework

The primary source of research literature is the Oria academic search engine from the University of Southeast Norway (USN) library resources, extended by Google Scholar for older, specific, or specialized literature. Additionally, the snowball technique and citation search are used to find more relevant research. The main theoretical framework is based on Endsley's [2, 17, 20] models and theory of individual and team situation awareness (TSA). Endsley's research framework is the most cited and widely used in the research literature and envelops most of this research [4]. This also includes her work on SA in dynamic situations; its link to decision-making and performance; its underlying human properties; and some of its core challenges. The primary focus of this study is individual's situation awareness (SA). Theoretical framework regarding team or shared SA is primarily used to provide context and understanding for the secondary research question and is not within the scope of this studies primary function. Despite Endsley's models and frameworks initially being used in aviation; its standards are used in different domains. These domains also include the maritime industry, with distinguished and effective results [16].

3.1 Individual Situation Awareness

Multiple theories have been developed by researchers to understand how human cognitive functions in a dynamic and ever-changing environment [2–5]. Although there has not been any consensus about which model and theoretical framework is best, most applicable, and descriptive. Although, the most widely used to understand SA is Endsley's (1995) model. Endsley's work on the topic is extensive in-depth, precise and is commonly used to understand and describe individual situation awareness (ISA). These three levels resolve around (1); perceiving elements in the environment, (2); comprehending the elements based on their disjointed nature, and (3); the ability to project the imminent future status of the elements in the operator's environment [2].

The first level emphasizes the perception of the elements in the individual's surroundings. Situation awareness begins with the individual's aptitude to observe his surroundings using sensory inputs such as visual, auditory, tactical, and more. Failure to perceive these elements by the individual, such as misinterpreting the situation is linked to accidents. The second level includes comprehending the environmental surroundings of the individual. It requires an understanding of the significance of each element considering relevant operator goals, and how they interact with each other. It depends on pattern recognition and cognitive paradigms based on experience and previously cumulative knowledge. A study of comprehension linked to collision between ships and offshore facilities found that 4 out of 18 incidents are related to loss of level 2 situation awareness [19]. This phenomenon is universal, as in case of road traffic incidents, reduced level 1 SA due to lack of attention or vigilance does contribute to a driver's ability to detect hazards while driving [21]. The third level of SA emphasizes the projection of the future status around an individual. It requires a highly developed mental model, and the process itself requires significant cognitive capacity. Level 3 SA rarely causes accidents in the maritime environment but remains critical for decision-making [19].

SA must be understood in the context of a dynamic and ever-changing situation rather than a static frame. Also, a person must acquire SA over time, thus emphasizing the temporal aspects. Endsley also suggests that SA is spatial, and that certain pieces of information in the element can be used extensively as important environmental markers [2]. An example would be the utilization of improvised range markers to determine ship speed, course or position. A well-experienced and seasoned operator will use predefined markers in the environment and divide them into subsets to allow for easier incorporation of information that is relevant to current goals and tasks. Finally, it is crucial to understand that there is no such thing as complete total SA, or contrary a complete lack of. Individual SA must be understood as being on a spectrum [2].

Endsley (1995) states that a person's ability to recognize the situations based on environmental cues will greatly affect their problem-solving abilities, and positively impact the decision-making process [2]. The ability to adapt and deploy sufficiently effective problem-solving strategies and mental models will also greatly increase their ability to solve and operate in complex environments. An underdeveloped mental model reduces the person's capacity to resolve new and slightly different obstacles, even when applying similar logic [2]. Other factors that will affect how a person performs is; capacity for simultaneous processing of objects in the pre-attentive sensory stores; both long- and short-term working memory; and mechanisms such as mental models, schemata, and scripts. Endsley and Jones (2011) explained that pattern-recognition and action-selection sequences can become overly routinized to the point of automaticity which is a true double-edged sword when developing SA [17]. This is why aviation, and to a lesser extent, maritime domain, use checklists to protect against processes becoming too automated. Lastly, a combination of experience, mental models, schema, and different goal-directed processes are required by the operator who seeks to fully understand the operational environment and continuously improve own SA.

3.2   The Challenges of Situation Awareness

In addition to temporal and spatial components, establishing and maintaining individual SA is a difficult task due to its various challenges termed "SA demons" [13]. These challenges include attention tunneling, overloading of data, requisite memory traps, misplaced salience, complexity creeps and WAFOS i.e., workload anxiety, fatigue and some other stressors. SA relies on the person's ability to swiftly shift attention and focus on the information that is relevant to the objective. Many times, several information sources have to be monitored and attended simultaneously by the operator, this is called attention sharing. It occurs only up to a limited degree. Attention tunneling refers to the failure of the individual to shift its focus or perform scanning techniques, leading to accidents. The requisite memory trap includes a focus on short-term memory, demanding active refreshing of information. WAFOS elements induce stress, affecting scanning patterns and resulting in premature closure in decision-making [2]. It was discovered that 35% of flight accidents which are related to SA fall under this category [22].

It was observed that 44% of accidents examined related to situation awareness was due to the inability to monitor and observe data [19]. The contributory causes were planning failures, interaction failures, distracting components, and lack of training. Data overload occurs when the rate of information surpasses the cognitive capacity, leading to outdated situation awareness. Complexity creep involves increased complexity in technological systems, undermining operators' trust and interpretation of information. Misplaced salience occurs when attention-grabbing but irrelevant elements overshadow pertinent information. Erroneous mental models, stemming from a lack of accurate mental models, impact comprehension and projection in SA. Out-of-loop syndrome shows how automation can destabilize SA by taking the operator out of the loop, leading to misinterpretation and late response [19]. These challenges highlight the challenges in sustaining situation awareness and emphasize the importance of addressing these issues for effectual decision-making in multifaceted operational environments.

3.3   Individual Situation Awareness (SA)

Individual situation awareness as a standalone concept is simple, however not particularly functioning, or applicable. Situation awareness on an individual level must be understood as a part of a dynamic environment of both external factors regarding tasks and environment, but also internal individual factors such as goals and objectives, cognitive ability, experience, and training. There are multiple known pitfalls related to human cognitive limitations and over-reliance on technical systems and states that would significantly reduce the overall SA, and that should be pro-actively avoided (Fig. 1).

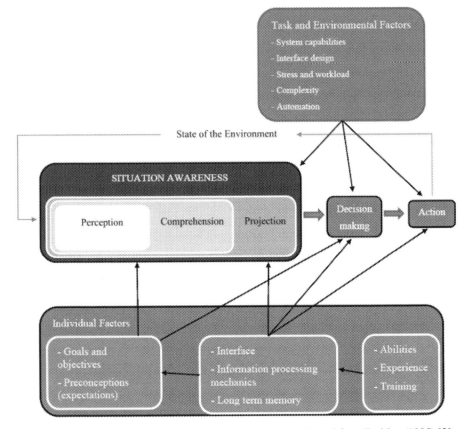

Fig. 1. Situation Awareness in dynamic decision making. Adapted from Endsley (1995) [2]

3.4   Team and Shared Situation Awareness

The magnitude of understanding that distributed SA is not just the combination of different crew members individual SA. Team situation awareness has a unique inherent abstract complexity that necessitates research and is not merely dependent on individual situation awareness theory [23]. It was further explained that team- and shared situation awareness is different in some ways from her proposed three-level model, as it includes unique activities such as team coordination and communication sharing. Each team member should acquire situation awareness that is related to their tasks, such as effective communication, shared vision or display and collective awareness [2]. From Endsley and Jones (2001) definition of TSA, the critical identified features are (1); a common goal, (2); interdependence, (3); specific roles [24].

In well-functioning teams, each member manages tasks independently while creating shared SA, depending on effective communication, proper equipment usage, and crew resource management techniques to address shared SA challenges on effective communication, proper equipment usage, and crew resource management techniques to address shared SA challenges. The information transfer for shared SA occurs through communication, shared display and environmental cues. However poor functioning crew identified group thinking, reluctance to share novel information as opposed to information that is commonly available, false consensus about another team member, rejection of information or utter disregard of information coming from lower ranked team members, shared misconception on similar incorrect experience, poor coordination and communication [24] (Fig. 2).

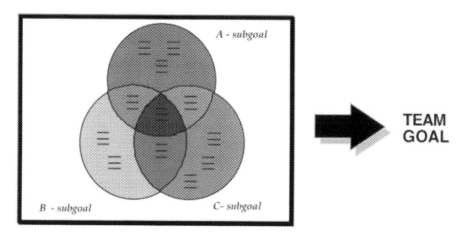

Fig. 2. Team SA as adopted from (Endsley and Jones 2001) [24]

Team SA Requirements. Team Situation Awareness (SA) requirements, integral to their goals, encompass diverse functions that may vary across domains and roles [24]. These requirements will vary depending on the domain and different function, although they can be understood as basic, comprehension and projection: Basic information about the system and additional information about each member must be shared. This could include status and capabilities such as training, injuries, levels of stress and fatigue. Information such as this is important to include and share with members of a team. Comprehension is focused on the interdependencies of team members goals and tasks. Bridge team members need to know the progress of different members goals that affect their own goal. All must know how their own tasks and actions impact the other members so that coordination can take place. Finally, members of the team must not only understand and project what will happen with their own goals and external events, but also what the other team members will do. This predictability and reliability allow other members to plan their course of action and lets the team work efficiently [24].

Team SA Devices. Endsley and Jones stated that there are multiple ways to how transmission of information occurs that is used when achieving SA [24]. This can be through communication, shared displays, or a shared environment. Communicating task or goal-relevant information can be conducted through simple verbal exchange, which is the most common, either directly or through devices such as radios or telephone. Non-verbal communication plays a significant role and is performed by gesturing, finger-pointing or facial expression.

Shared display information is also a source of achieving SA across a team. Information that is available on a screen can be accessed by multiple members of the same team and would contribute to a more common and shared understanding of the situation. This can be system instrumentation, displays, written materials, and audibles such as alarms and annunciator, or tactile instrumentation. A large part of the shared SA comes from the sharing environment. Navigators on the bridge of a vessel can feel the same vibrations, smell, and external cues within the operational environment. Other indicators such as pitching movements, roll changes, and observation of task performance among others, are important to the teams overall SA [24].

Team SA Mechanism. To achieve higher levels of SA (comprehension and projection) teams often rely on internally developed mechanisms rather than exclusively rely on external devices [24]. Newly established teams must use external devices such as verbal communication. As the team develops a mutual understanding and shared mental models, then higher levels of SA can be achieved without utilizing devices. Mental models of functioning systems are important to interpret observed environmental information, and help the operator gain an understanding of the current situation, and allow for projections of future actions [2, 22].

Team SA Process. When looking at both civilian and military aircrews, Endsley and Jones found noticeable processes and behaviors that were characteristic of well performing and effective teams [24]. Effective crews do: (1), engage in contingency planning during periods with low workload; (2), have captains who create a democratic work environment and share plans, strategies, and intentions, as well as consider options and provide explanations; (3), develop a shared understanding of the problem before looking for solutions.

It also showed characters that are considered poorly functioning ship crews. These characters are; (1), presence of "group thinking" which is characterized by a reluctance to query information and discuss with a leader who often override the team; (2), reluctance to share novel information as opposed to information that is commonly available; (3), a false consensus among the team members that other member shares a specific opinion without asking; (4), rejection of information coming from "lower" ranking members; (5), shared misconceptions based on similar incorrect experiences. Also, poor communication and coordination [24].

4   Research Method

This section explains the research methodology used in this study. It starts with a brief overview of the techniques adapted, an explanation of qualitative research framework and adherence to intellectual standards. The research methodology provides a thorough investigation of the chosen research design, Goal directed task analysis (GDTA) approach, and the method adopted for collecting data and its analysis.

4.1 Methodology Overview

Qualitative research is characterized by accessibility, flexibility, and relevance. It is deemed suitable for understanding scientific events in-depth, exploring reasoning and background, and adapting to evolving insights. While useful, qualitative research also presents challenges such as resource-intensiveness, oversimplification, and potential biases. Despite these drawbacks, qualitative methods prove invaluable when seeking to develop new theories or hypotheses, particularly in areas with limited existing information. Goal-directed task analysis (GDTA) from Endsley & Jones framework is used in this study [17].

The research framework identifies information required for complex environments like maritime berthing operations. Associated with a qualitative, descriptive research design, the study aims for an in-depth understanding. Since GDTA has its framework, no new research design is developed; instead, it is integrated into existing knowledge, relying on a predefined method [25]. The GTDA approach does not take into consideration how the operator is currently gaining situation awareness, but rather a skeptical approach to regulate dynamic operational situation awareness information [2]. Furthermore, this approach aims to detect what the operators ideally would like to grasp within the decision-making process of each decision, their sub-goals, and subsequently achieving the main objective and overall goal.

The methodology involves developing a goal-directed task analysis (GDTA) through interviews with experienced maritime navigators serving as subject matter experts (SMEs). The process includes unstructured interviews with SMEs concentrating on main objectives and SA information requirements. The preliminary goal structure is identified, representing pertinent goals without sequential, priority, or procedural aspects. GDTA validation involves multiple interview sessions, with 3–10 sessions recommended depending on environment intricacies. Subjectivity is acknowledged, and efforts are made to reduce it. Subsequent interviews use the initial GDTA as an instrument, allowing maritime navigators to review and modify the structure based on their knowledge.

4.2 Data Collection

Data collection involves interviews with participants selected through suitability sampling and snowball technique. Five subjects, including SMEs, participated, with interviews conducted via Microsoft Teams and one in person. The interviews were semi-structured, and conducted in the Norwegian language. For better legitimacy and reliability, they were later translated into English. The data collection procedure was permitted by the Norwegian Center for Research Data.

Participant's overview table provides details on each participant, including their age, experience, interview platform, date of interview, and duration of the interview. The data collected was analyzed using NVivo qualitative data analysis software. The participants had a mean age of 39,4 years, with an average of 12,6 years' experience as deck officers. All participants had at least a D3 deck officer license which permits "officer in charge of watch" duties irrespective of gross tonnage and trade area. The author placed an emphasis on experience, areas of operation, time spent conning, and an overall assessment, when selecting participants. The author does also possess the same aforementioned qualifications and works as a deck officer (Table 2).

Table 2. No. 2 Participant's overview and interview summary [18]

Participants	Age	Experience	Interview Platform	Date	Duration
SME-1	63Y	32Y	Microsoft Teams	05-10-2022	31 Min
Participant no. 2	26Y	3Y	Microsoft Teams	12-10-2022	52 Min
Participant no. 3	37Y	12Y	Microsoft Teams	18-10-2022	50 Min
Participant no. 4	27Y	4Y	Face to Face	19-10-2022	2 × 90 Min
Participant no. 4	44Y	12Y	Microsoft Teams	21-10-2022	30 Min

4.3 Data Analysis

It is important to classify and reduce qualitative data to gain a holistic understanding of an experimental phenomenon and data set [26]. Furthermore, it is important to simplify and assemble qualitative data to reduce complexity and avoid saturation in collected materials. The questions related to the SRQ were organized into 3 groups; factors affecting individual's situation awareness, strengths and weaknesses of shared and team SA, and a section on the reliability of information and its effect on decision-making.

This method was found to be effective for formulating qualitative data, enabling the analysis process [27]. Despite the advantages of the study, a drawback was acknowledged in the non-mutually exclusive coding of sentences, as outlined by [25]. For information relevant to the creation of the GDTA and determining SA information requirements, the study adopted the method outlined by [2]. Given the dynamic nature of maritime berthing operations, the highest priority goal constantly changes based on the existing environmental conditions. It cannot be a closed-ended question that could be answered with either yes or no, but an open-ended one, which requires a synthesis of information and SA requirements [2].

Goals were categorized based on priority of objectives crucial for successful job completion were taken as a priority with emphasis on descriptive labels explaining the nature of each hierarchy branch. Decisions were linked to sub-goals, and if significant overlap in SA requirements existed, multiple decisions were combined. Situation awareness information requirements, which were the foundation for decision-making, were outlined by focusing not only on level 1 SA elements but also on how each information supports task performance and corroborates level 2 SA requirements. For example, a change in wind direction and speed might affect a ship's performance and ability to follow its course. By associating this with SME's input, level 2 SA requirements will be established.

5   Results

This section describes the findings observed, based on the theoretical framework, GDTA and research methods. The section first represents a GDTA hierarchy as finalized; then methodically goes through level 1 to level 3 SA information requirements with suitable examples, answering the primary research questions. Finally, findings related to secondary research questions 1–3 are presented.

5.1 SA Information Requirements and Their Respective Levels

There was an agreement on the hierarchy structure of the objectives and goals. Although a few subjects proposed changes that were considered by the author to be too specific to their area of operation such as military procedures and vessels-specific operational procedures. The main objective identified was designated as "Navigate the ship safely to selected berthing". Primarily, six main goals were identified, but due to some repetitiveness in goals combined with instructions from GDTA guidelines, it was finally reduced to 3 main goals as follows:

- Maintaining control of the vessel and navigating according to the voyage plan
- Ensure appropriate information exchange.
- Manage resources efficiently

The method involved 3 distinct levels of information requirements that navigators should address to ensure a comprehensive understanding of their environment and facilitate effective decision-making (Table 3).

Table 3. Overall goal, main goals and subgoals during berthing operation [18]

Navigating the vessel safely to designated berthing	
1	Maintaining control of vessel and navigate according to the voyage plan
1.1	Maintain status of the ship
1.1.1	Operate within ship limitations
1.1.2	Overviewing available resources
1.1.3	Overviewing the technical equipment
1.2	Navigate according to the ships plan within set parameters
1.2.1	Monitor and execute voyage plan
1.2.2	Overviewing voyage plan
1.2.3	Adapt to navigational challenges
1.3	Maneuvering the vessel according to voyage plan within set parameters
1.3.1	Overview of available technical resources and equipment
1.3.2	Safe, secure and adequate mooring
1.3.3	Overview of harbor, basin, and berthing
1.4	Avoiding accidents and unwanted incidents
1.4.1	Grounding
1.4.2	Collison (Resolve)
1.4.3	Blackouts
1.4.4	Minimizing weather and external factors effect

(continued)

Table 3. (*continued*)

Navigating the vessel safely to designated berthing	
2	Ensure appropriate information exchange
2.1	Keep everyone informed at appropriate levels
2.1.1	Coordinate with deck members
2.1.2	Communicate with other vessels
2.1.3	Advise bridge team of berthing plans and intentions
2.1.4	Inform and communicate with VTS and port authorities
2.2	Ensure sharing of relevant information about planned operation
2.3	Ensure continuous flow of updated information about environment
3	Management of resources
3.1	Adjust operations to suit crew competence and reliability
3.1.1	Determine crew competence
3.1.2	Ensure sufficient availability of human resource
3.1.3	Ensure dynamic workload distribution among bridge team
3.1.4	Determine crew suitability to task
3.2	Configure ship for mooring and maneuvering
3.2.1	Configure ship for berthing
3.2.2	Configure ship ready for maneuvering
3.2.3	Configure anchors to be ready for drop
3.3	Minimizing Impact for unforeseen events
3.3.1	Loss of steering
3.3.2	Loss of propulsion
3.3.3	Blackout
3.3.4	Collision
3.3.5	Grounding
3.4	Perform a checklist
3.4.1	Prior to arrival at destination
3.4.2	Arrival
3.4.3	Post Arrival

5.2 Level 1 SA Information Requirement: Perception

In this level, ship navigators focus on perceiving elements close to their surroundings. The information includes real-time data such as the ship's status, navigational equipment, bridge team personnel and environmental conditions like weather. They gather information about the ship's features, limitations, and the availability of berthing equipment. Additionally, factors such as climate conditions, waters/fairway characteristics, and regulations play a central role in perception (Table 4).

Table 4. Level 1 SA information requirements [18]

Level 1: Perceptions information requirements	
Status of the ship i.e., (Heading, speed, steering, drift, gyro heading, UKC, XTD etc.)	**Weather Conditions** (Visibility, wind speed and direction, precipitation, current speed and direction, barometer, tide range, current tide)
Navigational equipment's status (GPS, S-band radar, doppler log, depth sounder, ballast and stability computer, list gauge, wind gauge and navigation system)	**Weather forecast** **Waters or fairway characteristics** (Location of grounds, islets, reefs, objects of navigation and interest, depth, narrow waters, available space for maneuvering the ship)
Vessel's equipment status (Hydraulic pumps, thrusters, available engine power, steering)	**Water fairway regulations** (EFS, VTS instructions, no-go zones, local area regulations, COLREG, SOLAS, MARPOL)
The ship's characteristics (stopping ability of the ship, windage area, comfort in sea state, maneuverability, turning radius)	**Harbor/berth/quay** (Berth length, bottom conditions, available bollards, planned safety margins, maneuvering space)
The ship's limitations (Clearance of height, width, length, draft)	**Route** (Distance, planned course, distance speed planned, alternative routes, bearing of objects)
Availability and status of ship's mooring equipment (Mooring lines, chains, anchors winches, deck lighting, gangways, communications equipment)	**Expected time for layover** (Planned layover, cargo, cars, passengers)
Personnel Overview (Certificates, experience, qualifications, background and suitability to task)	**Traffic** (Position of other ships, course size and speed, relative speed and distance, TCPA, CPA, Size, limitations, TSS and the ability to maneuver)
Readiness of crew **Status of communication equipment** (UHF, VHF, MF/HF)	**Emergencies** (hull status, watertight compartments and their structure personnel status and fire or waters intrusion in the compartments) **Port Restrictions**
Human Factors (rested, stress, productivity, functional capacity, responsiveness, toleration of workload alertness and attitude)	

5.3 Level 2 SA Information Requirement: Comprehension

The second level is comprehension of knowledge perceived at level 1. It includes methods on how the navigators use level 1 information to understand and assess the environment around them. Information is assessed regarding the suitability of tasks, strengths and weaknesses of the bridge team, the complexity of the task, and its impact on team functionality and safety. Assessing limitations, the need for evacuation, and the impact of deviations between expectations and reality are key aspects. Navigators also consider the impact of various factors, such as lack of resources, equipment performance, and weather conditions on their ability to follow the planned route (Table 5).

Table 5. Level 2 SA Information requirements [18]

Level 2: Comprehension Information requirements	
Assessments: –Suitability to allocated task –Bridge team weakness –Bridge team strength –Watertight integrity –Impact on safety –CPA and TCPA of other vehicles –Impact of bridge team performance –Ability to contain damage –Probability of regaining vessel power –Complexity of task	**Deviation:** –Between current crew resources and expectations –Between operational systems and expectations –Between functioning equipment and expectations –Between ship limitations and weather conditions –Between ship limitations and fairway characteristics –Between the current speed of the vessel, its course and position and planned speed, course and position
Determination –Need for evacuation –Emergency –If a person is qualified –Probability of collision or grounding –If the ship complies with local laws or maritime regulations	**Impact of:** –Current equipment on ability to follow route –Lack of human resource on safety –Weather impact on ship performance –Alteration of speed or heading –Loss of propulsion on ability of maneuver –Weather's impact on safety

5.4 Level 3 SA Information Requirement: Projection

At level 3, the ship navigators use information from the first two levels and predict the upcoming state of the environment. The navigators predict the changes in traffic congestion, potential conflicts, and the best method for ship berthing. Projections extend to changes in weather conditions, the need to use anchors, and the impact on ship traffic. Navigators also consider the future stability of the vessel, its position, route taken, and momentum according to the changes in the sea tide. In summary, these 3 levels of situation awareness information requirements give a systematic approach for ship navigators. They start by perceiving the nearby elements, later comprehending the implications of these perceptions, and eventually project and predict the future situation of the environment. This holistic approach makes sure that navigators are well-equipped for sound decision-making during maritime operations (Table 6).

Table 6. Level 3 SA information requirements [18]

Level 3: Projection information requirements	
Predict:	**Projection:**
–Impact of wrongfully or erroneously completed task	–Changes in weather condition
	–Need to use anchor
–Best suitable mooring setup	–Future target ship position, speed and course
–Engine power and equipment needs	–Future ship stability
–Ability to solve task	–Changes in the tide
–Areas of potential conflict	–Ship's own ability to follow route
–Changes in traffic congestion	–Need to use anchor
–Impact of lack of knowledge and experience with task	

5.5 SRQ1: Factors Negatively Affecting Navigators' Situation Awareness

To answer the question on which factors negatively affect navigators SA, 2 interview questions were structured:

1. Normally, when you fail in maritime operations, what is the thing that one usually misjudges or not pay attention to?
2. What will negatively affect your situation awareness?

The most common element that is observed to have a detrimental impact on SA was noise. All five of the SMEs had cited it 11 times. Expectedly, the most common complaint was that the other crew members working on the ship visited the navigation bridge during critical operations such as berthing or piloting narrow fairways. Talking, phone usage, interfering and questioning is the most common thing reported by the participants. The second factor was distraction of the navigator by other crew members or external factors. Surprisingly many note that people on shore or in other vessels try to get their attention. People do occasionally direct their high-beam headlights directly at the vessel. Likewise cited are personal problems such as financial uncertainty and troubles at home. The third common factor was assessment of external factors. Almost all answers related to misjudging wind strength and currents, and its effect on ships performance. So, in general the wind speed and direction, as well as wind currents (Table 7).

Table 7. Factors negatively affecting situation awareness [18]

Ranking	Factors	Sources	References
1	Noise	5	11
2	Distractions	3	9
3	Wrongful Assessment of external factors	5	7
4	Lack of trust among colleagues	4	6
5	Poor Communication	3	6
6	Uncertain or Incomplete Information	3	5
7	Misunderstandings	2	5
8	Overestimation of own abilities or skills	3	4
9	Unrest or Overwork	3	3
10	Unexpected technical Errors	2	3

5.6   SRQ2: How Members of Bridge Crew Cooperate to Ensure Good SA

The secondary research questions are regarding cooperation of the crew members on bridge "How do the members of the bridge team work together ensuring a good overall situation awareness and proficient cooperation.

The structured interview questions were as follows:

1. In what way does the bridge-teams cohesion and cooperation strengthen or weaken the shared SA?
2. How do the members of the bridge team use each other to maintain good SA?
3. What negatively affects shared SA between the bridge team?

It was suggested that effective communication among team members helps ensure good SA and team cooperation. A few SME's and interview participants also suggested that the maritime operations should have a flat hierarchy of their officers on deck. This should be implemented so that lower ranked officers are not afraid to ask questions or criticize decisions on a factual basis without the fear of reprimand or consequences. It was also stated that sharing of relevant information among deck members is important to keep the crew engaged and increase SA. Also, allowing lower ranked officers to be involved in decision making will be a good step. If the crew members do not have a shared understanding of the goals, then it becomes apparent when some unanticipated event occurs. Strategies, intentions, and objectives need to be openly addressed before any operation so that every member stays vigilant and ready (Table 8).

Table 8. Methods and Factors Sea navigators use to assess shared and ensure team cooperation [18]

Ranking	Factors	Sources	References
1	Effective Communication	4	10
2	Sharing relevant information	4	9
3	Mutual understanding of goals and tasks	4	8
4	Dynamic distribution of workload	4	7
5	Building trust	3	7
6	Include members in decision-making	4	6
7	Continuous learning	4	5
8	Freedom to report deviations or abnormalities	4	4
9	Monitor each other	2	4
10	Follow the plan and predictability	2	4

5.7 SRQ3: Information Reliability and How It Affects Decision-Making

To determine the information reliability and validity as the basis of decision-making, final secondary question was structured i.e., "How certain are the members that the information received or displayed is correct and how does it affect their overall decision-making?".

SME-1 stated this when asked about this question "To have good SA, you need a shared understanding of plans and goals. High levels of concentration and vigilance… and of course communication… You need to be observant and have your antennas tuned and be receptive to information. The ability to process information while sharing this information with the rest of the crew. Experience is often underrated, having been out in a cold night before, and bringing that knowledge is invaluable. I don't talk about lacking experience, but just having some experience."

Participant no.2 stated on being asked this question that "If I know that a certain data receiver on the vessel is defective or erroneous then of course I will be uncertain of the information received at first. But… that is a continuous assessment on our part about how reliable is the information that we are given. When it comes to information given by other crew members on deck [navigators], then I usually trust that information." The SME continues to talk about data reliability and adds that: "If we receive faulty critical information, then of course it would affect our trust in the system's information. But, if we have a known issue with a system regarding critical information, then we will have that fixed before leaving docks".

Participant no. 3 had a different philosophy on this question as he stated that "It has minimal effect on me. All the relevant information needed when I am maneuvering can be verified visually. Information given to me by others is only for backup - if I can call it that. You need to trust yourself and your instincts. Everything else is secondary information".

Participant no. 4 said that "It really depends on the ship. It becomes stressful if wrong or faulty information is received… I become more vigilant and attentive… Generally, I would ask for more frequent updating of needed information. To adapt, typically we increase safety measures."

Participant no. 5 states that "If you are not satisfied with the reliability of the information given, that you always have other methods to have it verified. And of course, it would affect decision-making with regards to how close we would navigate to certain objects. Safety margins increase with the level of uncertainty in the information."

6 Discussion

The main goal of safely navigating a ship to its designated docking position emerged from GDTA study and interviews of SMEs. Supporting these principal objectives were three crucial categories: (1) maintaining control of the ship and adhering to the traveling plan, (2) ensuring appropriate information exchange, (3) managing resources effectively. The required SA was categorized using Endsley's model. The level-1 of Endsley's model focused on ships surroundings, ships status, route, weather, regulations and sea traffic. Level-2 focused on comprehending those surroundings, assessing the impact of these elements and locating abnormalities. Level-3 involves using the information from the first 2 stages and predicting the future states. Moreover, 11 factors were identified in the secondary phase of the study that negatively impact SA. Among those factors noise, distraction and wrongful assessment by external factors were suggested as the main source of poor SA. Information reliability notably affected SA and decision-making. Trust between members of the bridge team also played a pivotal role for improved SA. A call for further research was advised to explore different leadership methods on distribution and team SA. This encapsulates the exploration of maritime SA, highlighting both its intricacies and the potential for future investigation.

6.1 SRQ 1 SA Requirements

The secondary research emphasizes on factors that are negatively affecting an individual's situation awareness. Participants of the interview highlighted wrongful assessment of external factors, lack of trust, and poor communication as significant contributors, which are mainly associated with shared situation awareness and team performance. On an individual level, participants identified wrongful assessment of external factors, overestimation of personal abilities, and being unrested or overworked as factors reducing overall situation awareness. These findings align partially with Endsley's challenges of individual SA including complexity, WAFOS, data overload, requisite memory trap, and attentional tunneling. Interestingly, participants consistently identified wrongful assessment of external factors during ships maneuvering and berthing as a common cause, suggesting potential areas for future research.

Several factors negatively affecting individual's SA were identified, with noise and distractions being the most frequently reported. However, the lack of classification based on literature and the absence of mutual exclusivity during coding introduce some confusion. The study suggests a need for a more unified approach to factor classification, emphasizing the origin of disturbances or distractions. The constant nature of factors like uncertainty or missing information, misunderstanding, and poor communication also calls for a more cohesive thematic analysis.

In conclusion, the study provides valuable insights into the factors affecting individual SA, offering implications for future research in human factors, technology integration, and the potential shift towards augmented reality and remote operation in maritime contexts.

6.2   SRQ 2 (Shared SA)

The second research question establishes a connection between factors contributing to shared SA and those negatively affecting it, highlighting the opposite sides of the same issues, such as building trust versus lack of trust, mutual understanding versus misunderstanding, effective communication versus poor communication, and sharing relevant information versus uncertain or missing information. The study highlights the complexity of shared SA, confirming Endsley's theoretical framework to be true that it goes beyond combining individual SA. The concept of shared SA involves not only sharing only information relevant to common goals but keeping information requirements for individual goals private.

The key factors identified to achieve good SA include sharing relevant information, mutual understanding of tasks, and proficient workload distribution. The conclusion suggests that factors ensuring good cooperation leans more towards cultural and personality factors rather than individual's SA alone, highlighting the need for further investigation into this connection. The study aligns with existing literature, emphasizing the importance of leadership styles in creating a democratic work environment and involving all members in decision-making for successful bridge teams. It means to create a uniform hierarchy of posts so that the bridge staff is not afraid to question their superior officers during maneuvering or berthing.

6.3   SRQ3 (Reliability and Validity)

The final secondary question delves into the validity and reliability of the information received by the bridge team and its impact on decision-making. The study shows that an individual's ability to adapt to a sufficient mental model is determined by their experience, which aids in identifying misinformation. The participants with greater experience tend to account for any misinformation by increasing safety margins. They adjust distances to objects or vessels and decrease their own ship speed based on their own mental models. Increased information update frequency is suggested as a strategy to identify validity of information, reflecting the vigilance and attentiveness of experienced navigators.

Trust emerges as a key factor influencing the reception of information This aligns with the findings related to well-functioning bridge teams and supports the literature on teamwork and shared Situational Awareness (SA). The study emphasizes that incomplete or inaccurate SA can lead to average performance, citing an example of misinformation comprehension and projection ultimately affecting ship performance. An interesting insight is provided by one of the participants if a critical system is known to have a fault or reads out erroneous information. In such cases, the problem will be fixed prior to leaving the berth. This approach is similar to that of the aviation industry where all equipment shall be fully functioning and tested prior to leaving to ensure a safe and proficient voyage, and a testament to the increased focus on safety.

6.4 Summary of Findings

Overall, the findings related to the GDTA hierarchy and information requirements are consistent with the literature. Suggesting that the literature and Endsley's framework is adequately descriptive and broad to describe and understand individual situation awareness in the maritime domain. Moreover, this study is a testament to the literature's universal applicability and provides a view for which situation awareness can be probed and understood. These findings add significant insights to the challenges seafarers encounter in maritime operations. The methods can be used for improving decision-making, creating effective teamwork and relationship building.

6.5 Limitations of the Study

The research paper's theoretical framework and literature are primarily based on well-known papers, articles, and books related to situation awareness, with a disproportionate focus on Endsley theoretical framework, and Gretch's summary and understanding of maritime history. This one-sided approach in the introduction, framework, and theory chapter limits inclusivity and comprehensiveness. Only literature available on Google Scholar and ORIA search engine was included, excluding potentially relevant source material. A goal-directed task analysis is a CTA and has some issues regarding biases and inherent failings. As the author was not able to have a subject matter expert validate the hierarchy, and only interviewed one SME. Biases from the author also became apparent through the analysis of material and during the interviews. It was suggested by GDTA guidelines to have at least 3–10 SMEs during the interview, but the author was only able to have one subject matter expert. Due to an insufficient understanding of more than 60 guidelines and frameworks, the author unintentionally used parts of the GDTA as interview guide. Lack of time and focus on secondary research questions may have also limited the size and scope of the hierarchy. Personal relationships with participants may have influenced responses, and limitations exist in the selected sampling method. Endsley and Jones do not recommend audio recording while interviewing subjects to minimize the effect of participants "treading carefully" to not upset their employer or something similar. The decisions to record interviews were exclusively to aid the subsequent qualitative analysis of interview transcripts. This could have slightly affected the results and outcome. Finally, during analysis, the author extrapolates answers to align with hierarchy goals, adds elements for information requirements, and establishes categories for easier participant reference. Poor planning and time management also affected the quality and comprehensiveness of interviews and subsequent analysis.

7   Conclusion

In conclusion, this study's goal was to identify the situation awareness (SA) requirements in maritime berthing operations without the help of pilotage, utilizing the Goal-Directed Task Analysis (GDTA) methodology. By using qualitative research analysis of five semi-structured interviews of 1 SME and 4 deck officers, it was observed that level 1 perception, level 2 comprehension, and level 3 projection information requirements are required for achieving and maintaining situational awareness. The top 3 factors negatively affecting situation awareness were found to be noise, distraction, and wrongful assessment of external factors. Effective communication, sharing of relevant information, and a mutual understanding of the goals among bridge crew were also highlighted to be an important aspect for better decision-making. The findings enhance the existing theoretical models of Endsley and its frameworks, emphasizing the applicability of Endsley's SA theory to the maritime domain. Additionally, it is also crucial to highlight the limitations in this study including reliance on limited sample size for interview, some potential biases in the semi-structured interviews and flaws in the GDTA guidelines. During the data analysis phase of this research the author's extrapolation of answers to align with hierarchy goals is acknowledged, as is the addition of elements to enhance information requirements. The introduction of categories for participant reference is seen as a necessary but challenging element. These factors may impact the generalizability and depth of the findings, warranting cautious interpretation and consideration in future research endeavors. Future research can explore how specific parts of the hierarchy are distributed among bridge team members and whether a better GDTA exercise can be developed for different maritime operations. Investigating the active goals or decisions during operations, potential limitations, and specific techniques used can provide valuable insights.

Acknowledgement. This article is based on the thesis titled "A Goal-Directed Task Analysis (GDTA) of Maritime Berthing Operations", written by the first author; Markus A. Hansen, accessible at the university of southeastern - USN archives. The second author would like to acknowledge the support of the project "Enhancing Human Performance in the Complex Socio-technical Systems (ENHANCE)" funded by the European Union's Horizon 2020 research and innovation program under the Marie Skłodowska-Curie grant agreement No. 823904.

References

1. Grech, M.R., Horberry, T.J., Koester, T.: Human Factors in the Maritime Domain, 1st edn. Taylor & Francis Group, New York (2019)
2. Endsley, M.R.: Toward a theory of situation awareness in dynamic systems. Hum. Factors J. Hum. Factors Ergon. Soc. **37**(1), 32–64 (1995). https://doi.org/10.1518/001872095779049543
3. Smith, K., Hancock, P.A.: Situation awareness is adaptive, externally directed consciousness. Hum. Factors **37**(1), 137–148 (1995)
4. Stanton, N.A., Salmon, P.M., Walker, G.H., Jenkins, D.: Genotype and phenotype schemata and their role in distributed situation awareness in collaborative systems. Theor. Issues Ergon. Sci. **10**(1), 43–68 (2009). https://doi.org/10.1080/14639220802045199

5. Wickens, C.D.: Situation awareness and workload in aviation. Curr. Dir. Psychol. Sci. **11**(4), 128–133 (2002). https://doi.org/10.1111/1467-8721.00184

6. Coraddu, A., Oneto, L., de Maya, B.N., Kurt, R.: Determining the most influential human factors in maritime accidents: a data-driven approach. Ocean Eng. **211**, 1 (2020). https://doi.org/10.1016/j.oceaneng.2020.107588

7. Xue, J., Van Gelder, P.H.A.J.M., Reniers, G., Papadimitriou, E., Wu, C.: Multi-attribute decision-making method for prioritizing maritime traffic safety influencing factors of autonomous ships 'maneuvering decisions using grey and fuzzy theories'. Saf. Sci. **120**, 323–340 (2019). https://doi.org/10.1016/j.ssci.2019.07.019

8. Wróbel, K.: Searching for the origins of the myth: 80% human error impact on maritime safety. Reliab. Eng. Syst. Saf. **216**, 107942 (2021). https://doi.org/10.1016/j.ress.2021.107942

9. Tikkanen, A.: Titanic—Aftermath of Titanic sinking | Britannica. Britannica (1999). https://www.britannica.com/topic/Titanic

10. Hetherington, C., Flin, R., Mearns, K.: Safety in shipping: the human element. J. Safety Res. **37**(4), 401–411 (2006). https://doi.org/10.1016/j.jsr.2006.04.007

11. Smith-Solbakken, M.: Torrey Canyon-ulykken. In: Store norske leksikon. (2022). http://snl.no/Torrey_Canyon-ulykken

12. Sharma, A., Nazir, S., Ernstsen, J.: Situation awareness information requirements for maritime navigation: a goal directed task analysis. Saf. Sci. **120**, 745–752 (2019). https://doi.org/10.1016/j.ssci.2019.08.016

13. Cordon, J.R., Mestre, J.M., Walliser, J.: Human factors in seafaring: the role of situation awareness. Saf. Sci. **93**, 256–265 (2017). https://doi.org/10.1016/j.ssci.2017.01.001

14. Sánchez-Beaskoetxea, J., Basterretxea-Iribar, I., Sotés, I., Machado, M.de lasM.M.: Human error in marine accidents: is the crew normally to blame? Marit. Transp. Res. **2**, 1–16 (2021). https://doi.org/10.1016/j.martra.2021.100016

15. Baker, C.C., McCafferty, D.B.: Accident database review of human element concerns: what do the results mean for classification? Abs technical papers 2005, pp. 1–8 (2005)

16. Saus, E.-R., Johnsen, B.H., Eid, J., Thayer, J.F.: Who benefits from simulator training: personality and heart rate variability in relation to situation awareness during navigation training. Comput. Hum. Behav. **28**(4), 1262–1268 (2012). https://doi.org/10.1016/j.chb.2012.02.009

17. Endsley, M.R., Jones, D.G.: Designing for Situation Awareness: An Approach to User-Centered Design, 2nd edn. CRC Press, Boca Raton (2011)

18. Hansen, M.A.: A Goal-Directed Task Analysis (GDTA) of Maritime Berthing Operations (Master's thesis). University of South-Eastern Norway Faculty of Technology, Natural Sciences and Maritime Sciences (2022)

19. Sandhåland, H., Oltedal, H., Eid, J.: Situation awareness in bridge operations – a study of collisions between attendant vessels and offshore facilities in the North Sea. Saf. Sci. **79**, 277–285 (2015). https://doi.org/10.1016/j.ssci.2015.06.021

20. Endsley, M.R.: Design and evaluation for situation awareness enhancement. Proc. Hum. Factors Soc. Ann. Meet. **32**(2), 97–101 (1988). https://doi.org/10.1177/154193128803200221

21. Tan, X., Zhang, Y., Wang, J.: Assessing the potential impacts of connected vehicle systems on Driver's situation awareness and driving performance. Transp. Res. F Traffic Psychol. Behav. **84**, 177–193 (2022). https://doi.org/10.1016/j.trf.2021.11.016

22. Jones, D.G., Endsley, M.R.: Sources of situation awareness errors in aviation. Aviat. Space Environ. Med. **67**(6). https://www.questionpro.com/blog/research-design/

23. Salas, E., Prince, C., Baker, D.P., Shrestha, L.: Situation awareness in team performance: Implications for measurement and training. Hum. Factors J. Hum. Factors Ergon. Soc. **37**(1), 123–136 (1995)

24. Endsley, M.R., Jones, W.M.: A Model of Inter and Intra-team Situation Awareness: Implications for Design, Training and Measurement. New Trends in Cooperative Activities: Understanding System Dynamics in Complex Environments (2001)

25. Frankfort-Nachmias, C., Nachmias, D., DeWaard, J.: Research Methods in the Social Sciences, 8th edn. Worth Publishers, New York (2015)
26. Jacobsen, D.I.: Hvordan gjennomføre undersøkelser? 3rd edn. Cappelen Damm Akademisk (2018)
27. Dalland, O.: Metode og oppgaveskriving, 6th edn. Gyldendal Akademisk (2017)

Report of the Working Group to Identify Future Challenges Faced by the Implementation of Resource Management in Remote and Distributed Teams

Don Harris[1]([✉]) [ID], Wesley Tsz-Kin Chan[2], Anna Chatzi[3], Hannes Griebel[4], Wen-Chin Li[2], Ting-Ting Lu[5], Pete McCarthy[6], Miwa Nakanishi[7], Tassos Plioutsias[1], and Dimitrios Ziakkas[8]

[1] Coventry University, Coventry, UK
{don.harris,ad3903}@coventry.ac.uk
[2] Cranfield University, Wharley End, UK
{wesley.chan,wenchin.li}@cranfield.ac.uk
[3] University of Limerick, Limerick, Ireland
anna.chatzi@ul.ie
[4] CGI Ltd., Leatherhead, UK
hannes.griebel@cgi.com
[5] Civil Aviation University, Tianjin, People's Republic of China
[6] Cathay Pacific Airways, Hong Kong, China
pete_mccarthy@cathaypacific.com
[7] Keio University, Tokyo, Japan
miwa_nakanishi@ae.keio.ac.jp
[8] Purdue University, West Lafayette, USA
dziakkas@purdue.edu

Abstract. Crew Resource Management (CRM) was introduced on the commercial aircraft flight deck to promote pilots acting in a well-coordinated manner. This was a result of several accidents where aircraft with no, or minor technical faults, crashed from a failure to utilize effectively the human resources available on the flight deck. CRM draws upon the disciplines of management science, organizational and social psychology. It originated in civil aviation, but its practices have now been adopted in other high-risk, high-performance industries where staff work in coordinated teams, e.g. Air Traffic Control, surgery, nuclear power operations and shipping. CRM is now facing new challenges to promote effective, coordinated teamwork. Teams are often now distributed across many locations but are still required to coordinate their activities in real time. CRM now must evolve to support the actions of remote and distributed teams. At the 2023 HCI International Conference in Copenhagen, a working group formed from subject matter experts to identify application areas and describe the key challenges faced in promoting CRM for remoted and distributed teams both during normal and non-normal operations. This paper describes the workings and initial findings of this working group. The results show that process areas, such as such as promoting Team Situation Awareness, workload management, coordination, and monitoring of the cognitive and affective states of others are more important for developing remote and distributed team CRM than are addressing the limitations imposed by the underpinning technology.

Keywords: Crew Resource Management · Remote Teams · Distributed Teams

1 Introduction

Crew Resource Management (CRM) is ubiquitous in the aviation industry. Although having its origins on the flight deck, CRM now permeates all aspects of airline operations [1]. The CRM concept evolved following several accidents where the principal cause was attributed as a failure to utilize all the human resources available on the flight deck appropriately, and in particular on accident-involved flights where there was also no major preceding technical failure. CRM-type practices are now commonplace in other high-risk industries which require teamwork, such as medicine [2–4]; nuclear power plant operations [5, 6]; the fire services [7]; Air Traffic Control [8] and shipping [9].

CRM is based upon the disciplines of applied social psychology and management science. Several authors have suggested that in aviation, CRM has progressed through several distinct eras [10]. In its first instantiation, as Cockpit (not Crew) Resource Management, it focused on improving the management style of just Captains. Emphasis was on improving communication, attitudes and leadership. By third generation CRM, the concept extended across the airline as a whole and by fourth generation its principles were being absorbed into all aspects of training and the development of procedures. In the following generation it was suggested that the CRM philosophy had instigated organizational culture changes, emphasizing that error is pervasive because humans are fundamentally fallible, especially when under stress; emphasis was placed on managing error rather than attempting to eliminate it entirely. MacLeod [11] however, argues that these generation apply only to the evolution of CRM in the USA and not elsewhere in the world. CRM practices are instructed in both the classroom and in the simulator and form an essential part of pilot non-technical training.

IATA [12] and ICAO [13] describe CRM in terms of a set of individual and team-related non-technical skills relating to observable descriptions of the knowledge, skills, abilities and personal attributes supporting effective crew performance [14]. These are defined by the job requirements for safe, effective and efficient operations, formulated using evidence collected from accidents, incidents, operations and training (Evidence Based Training - EBT). Mastery of these core CRM competencies are assumed to be effective countermeasures to error and underpin the ability to manage unsafe events.

ICAO [13] defines eight core non-technical skill competencies: Application of Procedures (APK); Communication (COM); Aircraft Flight Path Management using automation (FPA); Manual Aircraft Flight Path Management (FPM); Leadership and Teamwork (LTW); Problem Solving and Decision Making (PSD); Situation Awareness (SAW) and Workload Management (WLM). IATA [14] added a further competence: Knowledge (KNO). Mansikka et al. [15] undertook a principal components analysis of CRM performance scores and extracted four factors, which when incorporated into a path analysis described CRM as an input–process–output (IPO) model of team performance. This was further developed into CRM-DyMo (CRM Dynamic Model) [16, 17] integrating this model of CRM with threats identified during Line Oriented Safety Audits using the Threat and Error Management framework [18]. CRM DyMo demonstrated how performance in one competency was affected by performance in other competencies and illustrated the link between CRM and operational threats.

Distributed teams are not new and are relatively commonplace in many modern operations, for example military C4ISTAR (Command, Control, Communications, Computers, Intelligence, Surveillance and Reconnaissance) involves many networked assets in a distributed team. Airline Operational Control Centers functions include scheduling of aircraft; management of passenger and cargo loads; meteorological support; real-time monitoring of engineering data (often with embedded engineers from the manufacturers); aviation support for in-flight re-routing, and coordination of ground-based resources at the destination airports, etc. It can be argued that distributed teamwork has its roots in Computer Supported Collaborative/Cooperative Work from the 1980s and 90s [19, 20].

Perhaps the most famous example of a remote and distributed team was during the Apollo missions, and in particular the recovery of Apollo 13 after its in-flight emergency during its transit to the moon [21]. In more recent years, operational circumstances have effectively created remote and distributed teams even when all members are contained within a small physical distance. The advent of locked cockpit doors subsequent to the terrorist attacks of 9/11 and the advent of large modern aircraft (e.g. the Airbus A380) where crew members may be separated across two separate floors, create circumstances where flight deck and cabin crews operate as remote and distributed teams even when they are physically on the same aircraft.

However, with increasing interconnectivity and high-speed data links, remote and distributed teams are now becoming more common. Ad hoc teams may also be formed for short periods of time to perform specific tasks (e.g. coordination of multiple agencies during disaster relief). However, such remote and distributed teams pose special problems in terms of the dynamic management of their teamwork.

The working group was tasked to describe the key future scientific and operational challenges for the effective implementation of CRM in remote and distributed teams and identify current and future application areas.

1.1 Overview of Approach

In July 2023 a Working Group was established at the HCI International conference to identify the research and development challenges for remote and distributed CRM. Work progressed in two phases. Phase One identified implementation challenges for CRM in remote and distributed teams and associated target application areas. Phase Two prioritised these challenges.

Working Group members comprised subject matter experts who attended 2023 HCI International in Copenhagen, Denmark and who also participated as Board Members in the Engineering Psychology and Cognitive Ergonomics Conference.

2 Phase One

2.1 Method

In Phase One, Working Group members were asked to make e-mail submissions to address two issues:

- Describe the three main challenges for remote and distributed CRM with a short justification for each issue suggested, and
- To identify the main application areas for remote and distributed CRM both currently and projected areas for its future application.

2.2 Results

Challenges. Working Group members responses describing the main challenges for remote and distributed CRM were collated and grouped into seven overarching categories. These were:

- **Link Quality:** Latency and sound/vision quality. For this application area are these important to permit communication, coordination and decision making, etc.?
- **Reduced Interaction Quality**: Modality may be limited to sight/sound/maybe and maybe in advanced cases, haptic interactions.
- **Team Situation Awareness**: Does everyone need to be on the same page all the time or do team members mainly need to be aware of their local responsibilities?
- **Recognition of others cognitive and affective states** (non-verbal/poor interpersonal cues): If human interaction relies on non-verbal cues, how important is it if these are missing or degraded).
- **Coordination**: Leadership and Followership behaviors
- **Teambuilding**: Including team/work culture, speed of team formation and attitudes to remote partners. Teams may have to form quickly for specific purposes and may operate only for relatively short periods.
- **Learning and Training**: Opportunities, effectiveness and appropriateness of the medium.

Application Areas. Seven current and prospective areas for remote and distributed CRM were identified. These were:

- Space operations
- Motor sports
- Aviation (single crew, multi crew and across operational aspects)
- Air Traffic Control
- Telemedicine (including healthcare and surgery)
- Multi-agency search and rescue (including disaster relief)
- Complex military operations

2.3 Discussion

Several of the challenges identified were similar in nature to those for normal CRM, however for remote and distributed CRM they pose particular challenges. These challenges were in part a result of the technological limitations identified, the quality of the data links and reduced quality of interactions (restricted to sound, limited visual field and which may also involve some latency).

Communication and coordination are central to the success of CRM. Communication is closely linked with interpersonal trust, as it is the basis for efficient communication [22, 23]. Building trust is an active process, inspired and promoted within the team. The challenge that remote teams face is to build on their teamwork trust by keeping their team cohesion and members' familiarity at a high level [23, 24]. Remote CRM needs to work when certain non-verbal interpersonal cues are missing. Sharing certain types of data (e.g. a piece of paper) and physical experiences is difficult through remote connections. Communication drives CRM and promotes coordination but this depends very much on the nature and extent of communication [25]. Kanki and Palmer [26] described five ways that communication facilitates CRM. It provides information; establishes interpersonal relations; promotes predictable behavior patterns; maintains crews' attention on the task and is a management tool. These are challenging issues for remote and distributed teams working with limited link quality.

Adopting an Input-Process-Output approach, Team Situation Awareness (TSA) is one of the key processes for promoting CRM. However, the relationship between communication and TSA is complex. Many studies have found that increasing levels of communication promote coordination, Situation Awareness (SA) and decision making [27–30]. However other investigations have observed the opposite. During air combat it was observed that an increased rate of communication was related to decreases in TSA: it was symptomatic of a flight trying to regain SA [31]. TSA was initially predicated upon a common mental model held by all team members developed during air combat training. It was not developed during the engagement itself. In a similar manner, in civil aviation Orasanu and Fisher [32] observed that high performing crews used the low workload flight phases to plan ahead and discuss options but during an emergency they communicated less.

This begins to demonstrate the role of training in general (not just that in non-technical skills) in the development of CRM. It makes a case for the implementation of CRM concepts across all aspects of training (cf. Fourth generation CRM [10]. Learning and training was identified as a particular challenge for remote and distributed teams and will be a particular issue for multinational teams and/or those formed on an ad hoc basis to address a particular issue (e.g. military operations or disaster relief). Training, including group training, prior to operations may serve to negate some of the technology limitations identified (link and interaction quality) by providing an underpinning mental model upon which to build [31]. Leadership and followership behaviors are also developed during such training. These are in place before the operational implementation of CRM.

Most of the target application areas identified are of little surprise. Multi-national military and disaster relief operations are relatively commonplace (but still pose challenges). Telemedicine is also a rapidly developing area [33] but in this context it is perhaps the capability to undertake robotic surgery, where several of the surgical team are remote from the nursing staff, anesthetists and perfusionists, where remote and distributed CRM becomes of greater importance.

With the potential for extended duration space missions using multiple components (e.g. Artemis: NASA 2020) and the potential introduction of single crew commercial aircraft in the mid-2030s [34] there will be increasing impetus to develop remote and distributed CRM concepts in the Aerospace sector. Even with two crew on the flight deck, in emergency and abnormal situations pilots can easily end up task saturated, and remote assistance would offer the potential to reduce workload [35].

Motor racing, and in particular Formula One, provides a new application area and challenge. Teams are distributed along the pit wall, pit garages and back at team operating bases, monitoring the performance of the cars and the race context, and making real time strategic and tactical decisions under time pressure and with data links placing priority on data flows. Although not high jeopardy risk operations, Formula One is a very fast-paced, highly dynamic application of CRM with high data loads, so is particularly challenging.

3   Phase Two

3.1   Method

In a subsequent phase, Working Group members were asked to evaluate the importance of each of the challenges identified for remote and distributed CRM in each of the application areas. Ratings were completed as a matrix using an Excel spreadsheet emailed out to all members (see Tables 1 and 2).

Ratings used a five-point Likert-type scale running from a Very Important (challenge for developing remote and distributed CRM in this application area); through Important; a neutral OK rating; Not Really Important; and finally, Not at all Important (challenge for remote and distributed CRM in this application area).

Ratings were required for each application area in two general scenarios: during normal operations and during non-normal/emergency operations ('emergency' situations were not regarded as applicable for areas such as motor sports).

Subject matter experts were asked to be as discriminatory as possible when making their ratings.

3.2   Results and Discussion

Both Table 1 (normal) and 2 (non-normal/emergency) show that 'teambuilding' was only rated as being an important concept in aviation and complex military/disaster relief operations. In all other application areas it is likely that teams had already formed and may have spent time training and operating together in person before operating in a remote and distributed manner (the exception, to some extent, potentially being telemedicine). It was only in aviation and military operations where ad hoc teams would be rapidly formed. In contrast, learning and training for CRM in remote and distributed teams was seen as being of utmost importance for normal and non-normal/emergency operations. As previously suggested, prior team training could enhance team familiarity and trust, with the potential to circumvent some of the communication shortcomings imposed by the data bandwidth, promoting the basis for TSA and decision making [31]. It is unlikely remote connections will ever be 100% reliable so remote and distributed CRM practices need to be robust enough to survive a certain level of deterioration or break-down in link quality and potentially with communication latencies (e.g. space operations). However, perhaps surprisingly, overall link and interaction quality were not as highly rated as may initially be expected (particularly during normal operations) suggesting that CRM was not highly dependent on the quality of the link but was more dependent on the nature of the exchanges using the link.

Table 1. Modal values describing the importance of each challenge for remote and distributed CRM for the application areas identified during normal operations.

	Space operations	Motor sports	Aviation (Single crew, multi crew and across operational aspects)	Air Traffic Control	Telemedicine (incl. Healthcare)	Multi-Agency Search and Rescue (incl. Disaster Relief)	Complex Military Operations
Team Situation Awareness	Very Important	Important	Very Important	Very Important	Important	Very Important	Important
Link quality	Important	OK	Important	Very Important	Very Important	Important	OK
Reduced Interaction Quality	Important	Not Really Important	Important	Not Really Important	Very Important	OK	Very Important
Recognition of others cognitive and affective states	Very Important	Not Really Important	Important	Important	OK	Important	OK
Coordination	Very Important	OK	Very Important	Very Important	Very Important	Very Important	Very Important
Teambuilding	Not At All Important	Not Really Important	Important	Not Really Important	OK	Not Really Important	Very Important
Learning and training	Very Important	Very Important	Very Important	Very Important	Very Important	Very Important	Very Important

In contrast, coordination was seen as a very important challenge both in normal and in abnormal operating conditions (see Tables 1 and 2). Only in motorsport applications was it not regarded as being very important. Coordination is a product of team management and leadership [12, 13, 36] but is also dependent upon personnel adopting a followership role, as required. Establishing leadership and followership roles will be more difficult in distributed teams, particularly those formed quickly on an ad hoc basis, and may also require cultural sensitivity when operating in multi-national teams [37, 38] or in cross-profession teams with diverging levels of loyalty to the organization or other team members [39, 40].

Table 2. Modal values describing the importance of each challenge for remote and distributed CRM for the application areas identified during non-normal operations.

	Space operations	Motor sports	Aviation (Single crew, multi crew and across operational aspects)	Air Traffic Control	Telemedicine (incl. Healthcare)	Multi-Agency Search and Rescue (incl. Disaster Relief)	Complex Military Operations
Team Situation Awareness	Very Important	Important	Very Important	Very Important	Important	Very Important	Important
Link quality	Very Important	OK	Very Important	Very Important	Very Important	Important	Important
Reduced Interaction Quality	Important	Not Really Important	Important	Important	Very Important	OK	Very Important
Recognition of others cognitive and affective states	Very Important	Not Really Important	Very Important	Important	Very Important	Important	OK
Coordination	Very Important	Not Really Important	Very Important	Very Important	Very Important	Very Important	Very Important
Teambuilding	Not At All Important	Not At All Important	Not Really Important	Not Really Important	Important	Not Really Important	Very Important
Learning and training	Very Important	Very Important	Very Important	Very Important	Very Important	Very Important	Very Important

The inability to 'read' body language as a result of interactions being based solely upon limited visual and auditory channels may provide particular challenges. Follower behavior is also more difficult to establish than leader behaviors.

Recognizing the affective state of personnel was regarded as extremely important in normal space operations, where crews are very isolated and confined [41]. Space station crews may be in orbit for six-eight months. Managing both workload and morale are important for safe and efficient operations. Long duration missions to Mars will also be subject to degraded communication quality, with real-time, two-way communication becoming impossible as a result of transmission delays. Link quality is also likely to be quite poor, with just basic data flows. Support from ground-based elements to manage any non-normal situations will also become increasingly difficult with distance from the Earth. The impact simply of the remoteness of air vehicles, spacecraft or submersibles, and its influence on the relationships between the human operators (together or dispersed) will be an area requiring further attention in the future.

Looking across other application areas, sensitivity to affective and cognitive states of other personnel tends to increase in importance with the longevity of the team. However, being aware of the cognitive status of other team members increases in importance in non-normal/emergency situations, and in particular being sensitive to the management of workload [42, 43]. While remote team members do not have the immediate sense of shared fate (or incentive) imparted by being in the same submersible, aircraft or spacecraft as the other team members, this may be advantageous as a result of lowered stress and arousal levels.

The motorsports application area was notable in that it received few important ratings. Most CRM areas were regarded as unimportant. This is not to say that they are not challenging or vital for efficient and effective operations. What these ratings probably reflect is the low level of jeopardy risk to participants.

4 Conclusions

Opinion would suggest that the technological underpinnings supporting remote and distributed teams seem to be less important in developing effective CRM than the process areas, such as TSA, workload management, coordination, and monitoring of the cognitive and affective states of others. Teambuilding would not seem to be such a high priority, especially in application areas where teams may have had the opportunity to train face-to-face, gaining familiarity and building trust, before operating in a dispersed manner. Learning and training may be the key area to develop, providing the basis for operating effective distributed teams by promoting strategies and procedures to develop CRM in these types of operation.

References

1. Harris, D.: Human Performance on the Flight Deck. Ashgate, Aldershot (2011)
2. Yule, S., Paterson-Brown, S.: Surgeons' non-technical skills. Surg. Clin. **92**(1), 37–50 (2012)
3. Flin, R., Patey, R., Glavin, R., Maran, N.: Anaesthetists' non-technical skills. Br. J. Anaesth. **105**(1), 38–44 (2010)
4. Flin, R., Maran, N.: Identifying and training non-technical skills for teams in acute medicine. Qual. Saf. Health Care **13**(Suppl 1), i80 (2004)
5. O'Connor, P., O'Dea, A., Flin, R., Belton, S.: Identifying the team skills required by nuclear power plant operations personnel. Int. J. Ind. Ergon. **38**(11–12), 1028–1037 (2008)
6. Crichton, M.T., Flin, R.: Identifying and training non-technical skills of nuclear emergency response teams. Ann. Nucl. Energy **31**(12), 1317–1330 (2004)
7. Hagemann, V., Kluge, A.: The effects of a scientifically-based team resource management intervention for fire service teams. Int. J. Hum. Factors Ergon. **2**(2–3), 196–220 (2013)
8. Andersen, V., Bove, T.: A feasibility study of the use of incidents and accidents reports to evaluate effects of team resource management in air traffic control. Saf. Sci. **35**(1–3), 87–94 (2000)
9. Hetherington, C., Flin, R., Mearns, K.: Safety in Shipping: the human element. J. Safety Res. **37**(4), 401–411 (2006)

10. Helmreich, R.L., Merritt, A.C., Wilhelm, J.A.: The evolution of crew resource management training in commercial aviation. Int. J. Aviat. Psychol. **9**(1), 19–32 (1999)
11. MacLeod, N.: Crew Resource Management Training: A Competence-Based Approach for Airline Pilots. CRC Press, Boca Raton (2021)
12. International Air Transport Association: Evidence-Based Training Implementation Guide. International Air Transport Association, Montreal, Quebec (2013)
13. International Civil Aviation Organization: DOC 9995, Manual of Evidence Based Training. International Civil Aviation Organization, Montreal, Quebec (2013)
14. European Centre for the Development of Vocational Training: Changing Qualifications: A review of Qualifications Policies and Practices. Publications Office of the European Union, Luxembourg (2010)
15. Mansikka, H., Harris, D., Virtanen, K.: An input–process–output model of pilot core competencies. Aviat. Psychol. Appl. Hum. Factors **7**(2), 78–85 (2017)
16. Mansikka, H., Harris, D., Virtanen, K.: Pilot competencies as components of a dynamic human-machine system. Hum. Factors Ergon. Manuf. Serv. Ind. **29**(6), 466–477 (2019)
17. Harris, D., Mansikka, H., Virtanen, K.: The relationship between the dynamic model of crew resource management and line operational safety audits. Int. J. Hum. Fact. Ergon. **8**(4), 319–330 (2021)
18. Helmreich, R.L., Klinect, J.R., Wilhelm, J.A.: Models of threat, error, and CRM in flight operations. In: Jensen, R.E. (ed.) Proceedings of the Tenth International Symposium on Aviation Psychology, pp. 677–682. The Ohio State University Press, Dayton (1999)
19. Clegg, C., Waterson, P., Carey, N.: Computer supported collaborative working: lessons from elsewhere. J. Inf. Technol. **9**(1), 85–98 (1994)
20. Olson, J.S., Olson, G.M.: Computer-supported cooperative work. In: Bidgoli, H. (ed.) Encyclopedia of Information Systems, pp. 243–253. Elsevier, Oxford (2003)
21. National Aeronautics and Space Administration: Report of the Apollo 13 Accident Review Board. Author, Washington DC (1970)
22. Chatzi, A.V., Martin, W., Bates, P., Murray, P.: The unexplored link between communication and trust in aviation maintenance practice. Aerospace **6**(6), 66 (2019)
23. Tseng, H.W., Yeh, H.T.: Team members' perceptions of online teamwork learning experiences and building teamwork trust: a qualitative study. Comput. Educ. **63**, 1–9 (2013)
24. Dubé, L., Robey, D.: Surviving the paradoxes of virtual teamwork. Inf. Syst. J. **19**(1), 3–30 (2009)
25. Vorobeychik, Y., Joveski, Z., Yu, S.: Does communication help people coordinate? PLoS ONE **12**(2), e0170780 (2017)
26. Kanki, B.G., Palmer, M.T.: Communication and crew resource management. In: Weiner, E.L., Kanki, B.G., Helmreich, R.L. (eds.): Cockpit Resource Management, pp. 99–136. Academic Press, San Diego (1993)
27. Prince, C., Salas, E.: Situation assessment for routine flight and decision making. Int. J. Cogn. Ergon. **1**(4), 315–324 (1997)
28. Stout, R.J., Cannon-Bowers, J.A., Salas, E., Milanovich, D.M.: Planning, shared mental models, and coordinated performance: an empirical link is established. Hum. Factors **41**(1), 61–71 (1999)
29. Sorensen, L.J., Stanton, N.A.: Keeping it together: the role of transactional situation awareness in team performance. Int. J. Ind. Ergon. **53**, 267–273 (2016)
30. Huddlestone, J.A., Harris, D.: Student performance modelling using grounded theory techniques. Hum. Factors Aerosp. Safety **6**(4), 371–382 (2006)
31. Mansikka, H., Virtanen, K., Harris, D.: What we got here, is a failure to coordinate: implicit and explicit coordination in air combat. J. Cogn. Eng. Decis. Mak. **17**(3), 279–293 (2023)

32. Orasau, J., Fisher, U.: Distributed cognition in the cockpit: linguistic control of shared problem solving. In: Proceedings of the 14th Annual Conference of the Cognitive Science Society, pp. 189–194. Lawrence Erlbaum Associates, Hillsdale (1992)
33. Picozzi, P., Nocco, U., Puleo, G., Labate, C., Cimolin, V.: Telemedicine and robotic surgery: a narrative review to analyze advantages, limitations and future developments. Electronics 13(1), 124 (2024)
34. Aerospace Technology Institute: Accelerating Ambition: Technology Strategy 2019. https://www.ati.org.uk/wp-content/uploads/2021/08/ati-technology-strategy.pdf. Accessed 1 Feb 2024
35. Griebel, H.S., Smith, D.C.: DART – providing distress assistance with real-time aircraft telemetry. In: Harris, D., Li, W.C. (eds.) HCII 2023. LNCS, vol. 14018. Springer, Cham. (2023). https://doi.org/10.1007/978-3-031-35389-5_6
36. van Avermaete, J.A.G.: NOTECHS: Non-Technical Skill Evaluation in JAR-FCL. NLR-TP-98518. National Aerospace Laboratory (NLR), Amsterdam NL (1998)
37. Stoeller, W.: Global virtual teams. In: Dunne, E.S., Dunne, K.J. (eds.) Translation and Localization Project Management: The Art of the Possible, pp. 289–325. John Benjamins Publishing Company, Netherlands (2011)
38. Morrison-Smith, S., Ruiz, J.: Challenges and barriers in virtual teams: a literature review. SN Appl. Sci. 2(1), 1–33 (2020)
39. Merritt, A., Maurino, D.: Cross-cultural factors in aviation safety. In: Cultural Ergonomics (Advances in Human Performance and Cognitive Engineering Research), vol. 4, pp. 147–181. Emerald Group Publishing Limited, Leeds (2004)
40. Metscher, D., Smith, M., Alghamdi, A.: Multi-cultural factors in the crew resource management environment: promoting aviation safety for airline operations. J. Aviat./Aerosp. Educ. Res. 18(2), 6 (2009)
41. Kanas, N., et al.: Psychology and culture during long-duration space missions. Acta Astronaut. 64(7–8), 659–677 (2009)
42. O'Neill, T.A., McNeese, N., Barron, A., Schelble, B.: Human–autonomy teaming: a review and analysis of the empirical literature. Hum. Factors 64(5), 904–938 (2022)
43. Handke, L., Klonek, F., O'Neill, T.A., Kerschreiter, R.: Unpacking the role of feedback in virtual team effectiveness. Small Group Res. 53(1), 41–87 (2022)

Plan and Goal Recognition System for Adaptive Pilot Assistance in Tactical Helicopter Operations

Dominik Künzel$^{(\boxtimes)}$ and Axel Schulte

University of the Bundeswehr Munich, Neubiberg, Germany
{dominik.kuenzel,axel.schulte}@unibw.de

Abstract. In our contribution, we present an approach to an adaptive assistant system that supports pilots of a future military helicopter in dynamic missions by determining their intents on a tactical level. In a highly dynamic military mission environment, a pre-defined mission plan can quickly deteriorate due to unpredicted situational changes. To assist proactively and cooperatively, the assistant system needs an understanding of the currently pursued task and the corresponding course of action. This article describes an approach for a pilot assistant system that adapts its support to the momentary tactical plan to assist in the mission execution by observing the pilot interactions and probabilistic reasoning. For that, a plan and goal recognition system, based on hierarchical task networks, is integrated to generate partial-order sequences of observable actions. To derive the specifications of the observation and assistance demand a single-subject case study was conducted. To provide adaptive assistance the functions for an online intent recognition need to be developed and integrated into our mission and cockpit simulation environment.

Keywords: Adaptive Pilot Assistance · Plan and Goal Recognition · Intent Recognition · MUM-T · Human-Autonomy-Teaming · Helicopter Operations

1 Introduction

There is a considerable scientific effort to advance intelligent assistant systems in various domains. These include applications ranging from assistive technologies (Hoey et al. 2011), and robotic control (e.g. Pushp et al. 2017), up to complex military flight missions (e.g. Brand and Schulte 2021; Schwerd and Schulte 2021). There is a great aspiration, that these systems behave cooperatively and assist the human operator adaptively. In more complex applications, like military missions, assistant systems often depend on a mission plan describing the sequence of discrete tasks. This plan is usually pre-planned by the cockpit crew and establishes a shared understanding between pilots and assistant systems. However, a mission plan can quickly deteriorate due to unpredicted situational changes within a military mission. If the pilot rapidly adapts to the new mission constraints before re-planning, the assistance – still based on the obsolete plan – is no longer effective and could disturb or even work against the pilot's current intent. Therefore, it is useful that the system implicitly understands the pilot's momentary intent to establish a shared understanding and enable adequate support, even if the intention is not explicitly communicated (cf. Fig. 1).

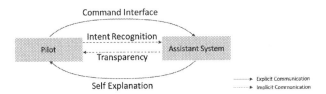

Fig. 1. Explicit and implicit information flow between pilot and assistant system

For this purpose, we are developing a system that infers the pilot's goal and the underlying tactical plan based on the tactical situation and the observed pilot's activities. This requires instrumenting the pilot and the mission system to monitor the pilot's performed tasks, activities, and interactions with the system. These observations must be interpreted as related to the tactical situation and mission plan to perform the inference.

2 Background and Related Work

2.1 Pilot Assistant System

Advanced pilot assistant systems can be described as a cooperative agent with a heterarchical relationship to the pilot, intending to improve the pilot's performance and safety (Schulte et al. 2016). Hence, the agent shall be able to understand the situation, the environment, the aircraft systems, and the pilot's mental situation. Assistant systems can be focused on flight deck operations (e.g. Onken and Prévot 1994; Estes et al. 2016; Suck and Fortmann 2016) or mission management and onboard re-planning (e.g. Brand and Schulte 2021; Schwerd and Schulte 2021). For the intervention, there are different kinds of triggers considered, which are either related to the pilot or the task and plan situation. Examples are the pilot's mental workload (Brand and Schulte 2021), the pilot's awareness of relevant information (Schwerd and Schulte 2021), or information related to the flight phase (Estes et al. 2016). Further, there exists research on using the pilot's intent related to flight plan changes (Strohal and Onken 1998) or phases and tasks concerning a current flight plan (Estes et al. 2016).

Mostly, assistance is related to flight execution or flight planning in very structured domains, such as instrument flight. With our contribution, we want to support the pilot in the overall mission execution and the currently pursued tactical course of action, in highly dynamic environments, based on their intent.

2.2 Plan and Goal Recognition

Han and Pereira (2013) define goal recognition "[…] as the problem of inferring an agent's intention through its actions and their effects on the environment". Complementary to this, plan recognition means the understanding of "the set of actions that have been or will be performed [...] to reach that goal" (Van-Horenbeke and Peer 2021). There are different approaches for plan and goal recognition (PGR), which can be categorized as plan library-based and domain theory-based (Van-Horenbeke and Peer 2021). Since we are focused on the domain theory approach, the plan library approach will not be further considered. Based on the domain theory approach (also known as plan recognition as planning), off-the-shelf-planning algorithms are used to create candidate plans of the observed agent. An algorithmic approach for that is to use hierarchical task networks (HTN) as described by Höller et al. (2018), which the authors are using for an empirical evaluation of typical planning problems. Jamakatel et al. (2023) applied this approach to recognize the pilot's intention in general aviation. Most research in the field of plan and goal recognition systems is in an environment with a well-structured pre-defined plan. In comparison, Hammarbäck et al. (2023) performed a work domain analysis to model intent for future manned-unmanned teaming (MUM-T). In their study, the authors examine how to model intent in the MUM-T domain so that a synthetic wingman understands the pilot's situated intent.

With our work, we present a concept for a plan and goal recognition system for adaptive pilot assistance for military helicopter operations on a tactical level. Thereby, we approach the complexity of recognizing the tactic-driven course of action based on pilot observations and the situation at hand, in a highly dynamic mission environment.

3 Pilot Assistant System Design

3.1 Architecture of the Adaptive Assistance

We envisage a system design that will infer the pilot's intent by using a domain theory approach (Künzel and Schulte 2023). The system is subdivided into four information processing stages: tactical situation detection, situation and pilot assessment, diagnosis, and intervention generation based on the pursued tactical plan. Figure 2 shows these essential functional modules of the adaptive assistant system. All available information (such as environment, aircraft capabilities, durations, mission goal, and obligatory tasks) is gathered and analyzed to deduce the tactical goals to achieve the overall mission objective. For each goal (e.g., tactical behaviors such as: protecting ground forces, investigating objects, etc.), a plan hypothesis is generated that describes the tactical course of action. Based on that, the pilot's intent is defined as the tactical goal and its corresponding plan (sequence of activities). Due to the inaccuracy of the sensor data and other uncertainties, it is necessary to use a probabilistic approach, to conclude the features, activities, and thus the pursued tactic from the observational data. For the concept and the system design, we have looked at following scenarios, according to the MUM-T helicopter domain: *support ground troops, area defense, reconnaissance, surveillance of an area, object investigation, and simultaneously attack multiple targets.*

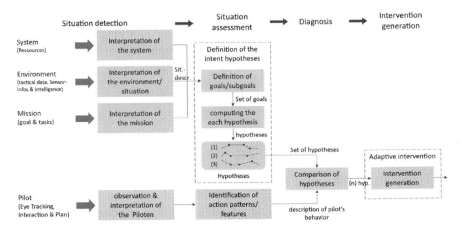

Fig. 2. The modular architecture of the assistant system (Künzel and Schulte 2023)

3.2 Defining the Plan and Goal Recognition Problem

Helicopter missions can be structured into different mission phases and activities within a specific phase. This hierarchical structure of helicopter missions is also taken up for our planning problem. Using hierarchical task networks (HTN) allows us to subdivide the mission at different hierarchical levels to move from high-level planning to low-level detailed action sequences. The starting point is the overall goals of the relevant tactics (related to the situation) for accomplishing the mission objective. For that, the required tasks are organized in a task network and decomposed into three levels: (1) mission phases, (2) individual tasks for each mission phase, and (3) actions for conducting the task. The following example is intended to demonstrate the structure based on the mission objective of "Object investigation". Each level is as follows: (1) "Target confirmation" describes the process of finding and identifying each target. (2) This can be decomposed into "Preliminary transfer close to T1" and "Confirm T1". (3) For the confirmation task the pilot has to perform the actions "Take position with helicopter for observing T1", "Align EO sensor of helicopter on T1", & "Classify T1 as NEUTRAL".

Those phases and sequence of activities differ according to the tactical approach and current situation. Often, the sequence of individual actions within a mission task (hierarchical levels 2 and 3), is not subject to a predefined order. Since the courses of action for one tactic can differ (such as prioritizing the tasking of the ownship instead of UAV), without having an impact on the overall goal, it can be defined as a **partial-order planning problem**. Additionally, for assisting the pilot in our case, no optimal plan is necessary and enables us to recognize several (interleaving) plans. Inferring the intent relies on the observations that are in real-world scenarios often not fully observable. Thus, our system must deal with a **partially observable environment**.

A HTN planning problem is described by a tuple $P = (D, s_0, t_{nI})$. D defines the domain D, initial state s_0, and initial task network t_{nI}. The domain D is defined by the tuple (L, C, A, M, δ). L refers to the preconditions and the propositional environment facts, which defines the state-based part of the problem (Höller et al. 2018). C is the set of compound tasks (abstracts), which refers here to mission phases and subphases.

The set of actions A (primitives) defines the lowest level of the hierarchical task network (e.g. "EO on Target"). M is the set of methods, which are used for the decomposition. $\delta = (prec, add, del)$ defines the preconditions (prec), as well as the positive (add) and negative (del) effects, that result from the successful execution of a task. For plan recognition as HTN planning, the planning problem needs to be extended by the initial state s_0, a set of observations $\bar{o}$, and the set of possible goals $\mathcal{G} = \{G_1, G_2, \ldots, G_n\}$, , defined as task networks (Höller et al. 2018). Each goal describes a task network $t_{nTactic}$, and refers to the tactical mission goal of the considered scenarios. An example for the task network for the goal "support ground troops" is given in Fig. 3. The observations $\bar{o}$ are the observables which are related to the derived features (see Sect. 3.3) that describe one or more actions, which the pilot needs to perform for reaching a specific goal. Thus, the HTN planning problem is extended and results in the **PGR planning problem** $P_{PGR} = (D, s_0, \bar{o}, \mathcal{G})$. The solution of our PGR planning problem is a sequence of actions to accomplish the mission objective, based on the initial state s_0. The primitive task usually represents the observable activities, cf.

Höller et al. (2018). In our case, the activities cannot be observed directly since they describe the sequence of actions within a tactical approach. Thus, all activities and observations must interpreted from a situational point of view, as described in Sect. 3.3.

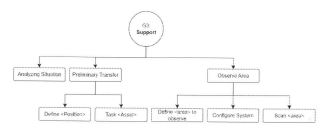

Fig. 3. Part of the hierarchical task network for supporting ground troops.

3.3 Situation Detection and Feature Extraction

To determine the pilot's intention, the activities carried out by the pilot must be identified based on the observations. It is not sufficient to use the observations directly to infer the pilot's intent, as an observation can imply different actions. For example, depending on the objects at the destination after the transfer, as well as the capabilities of the asset, a supportive, defensive, or even offensive objective may be considered. To recognize the tactic-specific activity, all observations must be interpreted from a situational and tactical point of view. Thus, the action (respectively task of the plan) is described by different features, such as the related asset, explicit task, geometrical and geographical reference, related target object, and the objective on the target. The features were categorized into three groups based on the accessibility:

- **Basic and geometric features**

    Basic and geometric characteristics can be determined directly from the measure-ment data, observations, or the tactical position. Examples: utilized asset, distance between assets and targets, absolute and relative positions, sensor alignment, clusters, area, and status of entities.

- **Simple features**

   A simple feature can be deduced from the basic and geometric features, but also by observing the interactions in the cockpit. Simple features generally occur in different situations and tactics. Examples: tasking, sensor usage, and tactical map interactions.

- **Situational features**

   To recognize the intention-related characteristics, the simple characteristics must be interpreted as related to the context and the tactic. This also includes the parallel or sequential execution of action from a temporal perspective. Examples: underlying direction of movement, focus and orientation related to the situation, the relation between tactical elements and situation, and specific objective on target.

Once the actions can be described by these features, the pilot needs to be observed to determine the performed actions.

3.4   Pilot Observation

Based on the obtained information from the situation analysis and observed measurement data of the pilot's activities the pursued goal can be inferred. The pilot is observed related to the following information:

- **Interactions with the system and tactical map**

   This includes selecting a page, setting a parameter, map interactions, and interactions with system functions like the sensor system. Additionally, the pilot can add tactical and structural elements to the map, which are also considered.

- **Tasking of UAVs and ownship**

   The tasks issued to the UAV or the ownship are also monitored. This includes the parameterization of these tasks (e.g. flight level or behavior) and reference to the situation, targets, or terrain.

- **Sensor usage (for target classification)**

   The observations related to the sensor usage are made up of the interactions with the sensor, orientation and zoom, sensed object, sensor source (UAV or ownship), and whether the sensor is used (based on gaze-tracking).

- **Automation and situation monitoring through gaze-tracking**

   Based on gaze-tracking, the automation and situation monitoring behavior is observed. Through that, areas of interest (AOI) in the overall tactical situation and relevant automation functionalities for achieving the tactical goal, can be identified.

Figure 4 shows the tactical map including the sensors stream (which is displayed to the pilot on the multifunctional cockpit display) during a scene, in which the pilot supports ground troops. Additionally, the figure shows the gaze-tracking (incl. Fixations; blue indicator), touch interaction (white dot) as well as the contextual interpretation of the pilot's control and visual interactions with the cockpit (as textual information on the top). The observation information is only shown to the supervisor (online or in replay).

Next, the data must be processed to identify the performed activities of a pursued tactical approach.

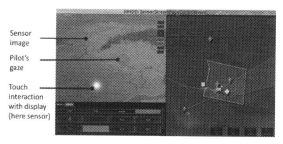

Sensor image

Pilot's gaze

Touch interaction with display (here sensor)

Fig. 4. Multifunctional display including the gaze track (current and past fixations in blue) and touch interaction (white). The semantic information of the last interaction is shown at the top. (Color figure online)

3.5 Intervention Generation

The process of intervention generation is subdivided into three steps: decision to intervene, planning of the intervention, and implementation of the intervention. The pilot observations, the identified intentions, and the tactical situations serve as the basis for the decision to intervene. The overall idea of the intervention is to simplify the situation for the pilot to achieve better mission performance and improve safety. Subsequently, the planning of the intervention needs to be performed to obtain the assistance plan. This plan includes the moment, type, and strategy of the intervention. Since the pilot should be supported in the mission execution and handling of the full situation, different kinds of assistance are considered:

- **Synchronize and respond to the pilot's activities.**
  Based on the inferred plan and the pilot observation, responsive assistance behavior is possible. For example: responsive execution of (simultaneous) actions or performing follow-up actions (as intended by the pilot), while he is focused on a sequence of actions related to another asset or AOI.
- **Support tactical planning.**
  This refers to suggestions related to the plan. For example, suggesting the usage of available assets, open tasks, or improvements (related to time and capability constraints) as well as configurations (e.g., for positioning and sensor management).
- **Suggest follow-up activities and perform those to execute a tactical plan.**
  As soon as the pursued tactical plan is inferred, the assistant can take over plan-related activities. Since we want the pilot to be the decision maker, we aspire an assistant behavior in which the pilot must accept or decline a suggestion. For example, monitoring an area, performing battle damage assessment after an attack, and suggesting new positions for follow-up activities.

The intervention is implemented in two different ways: dialog/output on the interface (such as hints, current status, upcoming activity) and tasking of the automation (assign follow-up task, if approved by pilot). The HTN approach as described in Sect. 3.2 allows to offer assistance based on the hierarchical levels. Therefore, the assistance can be related to the mission phases, tasks, or specific actions. Since the exact sequence of actions is in partial order at the beginning, but is getting more detailed based on the observations, the assistance can be increasingly more specific at the lowest level.

3.6   Modular Description of the Assistant System Components

Figure 5 shows the modular description of our integrated planning pipeline into our simulation environment. The scenario analyzer creates a description of the current situation as an input and initial state for the HTN planning. The planning problem is then defined based on the input and the stored tactical knowledge. For each tactical approach, a specific task network is generated. Based on the observational data and the generated task networks, the intention is inferred. Then, the intervention is generated (cf. Sect. 3.5).

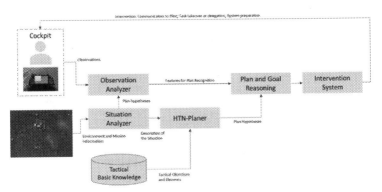

Fig. 5. Modular description assistant system integration incl. HTN-planning software pipeline

4   Case Study

4.1   Description

For structuring our problem and adapting the described method to our application domain, we conducted a single-subject case study. The purpose of the case study was to observe the pilot's behavior performing different tactics (and the underlying courses of action). That allows us to distinguish between explicitly and implicitly communicated information and define the intent in this domain. We focused on recognizable behavior patterns and observable characteristics. Additionally, identifying the need and type of intent-specific assistance in such scenarios was also assessed.

The single-subject case study was conducted with an experienced test pilot of the German army (approximately 2500 flight hours) in our helicopter research mission and cockpit simulator.

4.2   Mission and Cockpit Simulation Environment

Our helicopter research mission and cockpit simulator is shown in Fig. 6. The cockpit is equipped with hands on collective and stick (HOCAS) flight controls and three multitouch displays to display the interfaces, which are developed for our research. The system is instrumented with a fully integrated eye-tracking system and a context-aware display to generate observations. The main display shows the tactical map and simulated electro-optical sensor stream. System information and a timeline for tasking the assets are displayed on the side screens. The simulator allows us to simulate MUM-T military scenario missions.

Fig. 6. Cockpit of the helicopter research mission and cockpit simulator. The center display shows the tactical map. Both side displays are used for planning or system information. The eye-tracking cameras incl. Infrared pods (red) are mounted to the cockpit. (Color figure online)

4.3 Procedure

In our case study, the subject had to perform four different scenarios. Three of the scenarios are closely related to a specific tactic, and the fourth scenario demands a switch between two different tactical approaches.

Before the experiment, the eye tracking system was calibrated. The test pilot also received extensive training on the simulator to get familiar with the system functions (and commanding UAVs). During that time, the pilot did not encounter any specific tactical operation, which means, he had to perform the experimental task without specific training on the tactical task. The experiment began with a general briefing in which the overarching situation and the underlying tactics were discussed. A situation-specific briefing took place before each scenario, afterwards the subject was then asked to describe the tactical procedure again in a debriefing. All scenarios were designed in a way, that the pilot was demanded to use his helicopter and the available unmanned aerial vehicles (UAVs). In the scenarios, the subject had to achieve different objectives that required a certain tactical plan which aimed to "support ground troops", "simultaneously attack multiple targets", or "defend area".

4.4 Results

Through the study, we have been able to acquire knowledge to describe the PGR problem in this domain and to verify the assumptions for each component. It has become apparent, that the intent in this use case is the overall pursued tactical goal and the corresponding plan. The collected observational data has been analyzed to determine the features for recognizing the pursued tactical goal and the demand for assistance.

Interactions, Observations, and Features for Intent Recognition. The tactical situations were analyzed corresponding to the features and unambiguous characteristics. To this, the performed missions were divided into subphases and analyzed related to the feature (described in Sect. 3.3). Below, five subphases are described in detail: *Preliminary transfer, Positioning, Defending territory,* and *Reconnaissance* (by tasking and manually).

In the *Preliminary transfer* subphase, the **sequence of activities** was analyzed in detail. The challenge is that different sequences indicate different tactics, but at the same time, the sequence for one tactic (depending on the situation) is not always identical. Figure 7 shows the tactical situation and timeline of the ingress phase of a tactical approach. Here, different assets are transferred to different targets. This phase is similar for each tactical approach but already implies the most possible one.

Fig. 7. Section of the tactical map with the corresponding timeline of the activities.

The next subphase, *Positioning,* was analyzed regarding the **geographical positioning**. Figure 8a shows a tactical situation in which the pilot transferred each asset close to a potential target (the asset target pair is encircled in orange). The dashed marking shows the second target which is equally important to the white UAV from a geometrical point of view. Here, considering the geometry alone is not sufficient, since two targets are equally distant. For a more precise interpretation, the sensor usage and (as the mission continues) the underlying direction of movement a distinct interpretation. Compared to that, Fig. 8b shows a scene, in which the assets are transferred to a potential AOI instead of a specific object. In that case, only considering the distance/position can be deceptive since the reference object can also be a specific target.

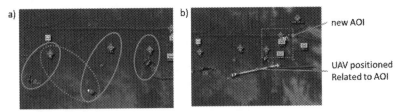

Fig. 8. Assets are positioned related to relevant objects or areas. In (**a**) each asset is close to a specific object which is emphasized by the orange circle. (**b**) shows a scene, in which the asset is probably positioned related to the AOI. (Color figure online)

Below, the subphase *Reconnaissance* as shown in Fig. 9 and Fig. 10 is analyzed. Figure 9 shows the process of searching for unknown objects in a distinct area by tasking a UAV. Different interactions were observed, e.g. defining the area, creating the SCAN task[1], and assigning the task to the UAV. Through the explicitly assigned task, the underlying actions (to recon the designated area) are apparent to the assistant.

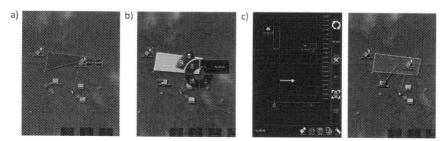

Fig. 9. Pilot scans an area for unknown objects. **(a)** Definition of the area to be scanned, **(b)** create a task for that area, **(c)** assign *SCAN* task to UAV via tasking timeline.

Figure 10 shows the scene, in which the pilot manually scans an area for unknown objects. For that, he uses the sensor of the UAV. This involves a comparison between the sensor image and the tactical map, which is emphasized by the gazes indicated by the blue dot and line. As soon as he recognizes an object of relevance, he performs a visual inspection. Here, different features can be considered to infer the tactical action: focus on a distinct AOI using the sensor, investigation of (until then) unknown objects, and position of own units.

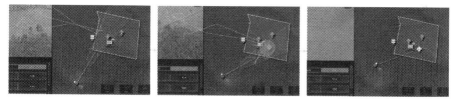

Fig. 10. Pilot manually scans an area for unknown objects with the UAV sensor (green sensor footprint). The blue dot and line indicate the gazes of the pilot. (Color figure online)

The described observations depict the different kinds of necessary features to reason about the pilot's activities. The features can be subdivided into the categories as described in Sect. 3.3 which allows to structure the module for analyzing the scenario.

Assessment of Intent-Specific Assistance. To improve the overall mission performance the pilot was observed while performing the missions. Different situations were considered to identify the demand for intent-specific assistance. The analysis showed

---

[1] A SCAN task describes a task, in which a previously specified area is scanned, to detect unknown targets.

that especially in complex scenarios (with high dynamic) it is barely possible for the pilot to use all assets to the same extent, which results in a poorer overall mission performance. Different scenarios (especially with rapid situational changes) occurred in which an *asset ingests an idle behavior* because the pilot was busy with managing another asset. This includes situations in which the pilot has to task individually sequences of actions that are (depending on the situation) similar for different assets. The same applies to logical sequences (e.g. transfer to a target and subsequent investigating), which is time-demanding and increases the workload. In situations that *require a joint or simultaneous approach*, it is necessary to react related to the associated asset.

It was also observed, that in large scenarios with highly dynamic and urgent situations, *planning optimal resource consumption and impact* can be a challenging task. For example, in scenarios, that demand very quick reactions and unplanned situations that arise, the consumption of onboard resources or fuel creates a complexity that is difficult to manage, especially with several tasked assets with different capabilities. Based on the described observations, three types of assistance were identified:

1. Planning support and plan execution (e.g. responsive execution of tasks; proposing follow-up activities or a sequence of actions including parametrization)
2. Plan optimization (e.g. optimal sequence of actions or resource-optimized asset planning)
3. Impacts estimation and projection of future state (e.g. estimated time and consumption of resources; scope of possible follow-up actions considering resources usage)

The observed situations proved our assumption about the demand for the different kinds of assistance. Since the proper utilization of all assets especially in highly dynamic situations with great urgency is a challenging situation, we will focus on *planning support and plan execution*. This includes supporting the pilot in the sense of responsive task execution and proposing possible sequences of actions (for assets), to fully utilize the available resources for higher overall mission performance.

Consequently, the collected data and the described analyses allow us to systematically define our functions and features for determining the pursued intent and support the pilot.

5   Conclusion

In our contribution, we presented our approach to a pilot assistant system that supports the pilot of a future military helicopter based on the inference of tactical intent. We addressed the architectural design, the PGR planning problem, the situation and pilot observation, and the assistant behavior. The performed single-subject case study was described, which allowed us to test our initial assumptions of the concept, obtain feedback from a pilot, and validate our experimental procedure. For that, we addressed the case study design and significant findings, which determine our overall system design. The authors are aware, that the described case study is a single-subject case study. To prove the reliability and functionality of our findings and the system, a detailed validation study has to be carried out after the completion of the implementation.

The concept will be integrated into our mission and cockpit simulation environment at the Institute of Flight Systems. This allows us to investigate by means of human-in-the-loop experimentation whether our system helps to enhance assistance in highly dynamic environments by inferring the pilot's intent without communicating it explicitly thus improving the performance and cooperation of pilot-assistant teams.

References

Brand, Y., Schulte, A.: Workload-adaptive and task-specific support for cockpit crews: design and evaluation of an adaptive associate system. Hum.-Intell. Syst. Integr. **3**(2), 187–199 (2021). https://doi.org/10.1007/s42454-020-00018-8

Estes, S.L., Burns, K.J., Helleberg, J.R., Long, K.M., Pollack, M.E., Stein, J.L.: Digital copilot: cognitive assistance for pilots. In: 2016 AAAI Fall Symposium Series, Cognitive Assistance in Government and Public Sector Applications (2016)

Hammarbäck, J., Alfredson, J., Johansson, B., Lundberg, J.: My synthetic wingman must understand me: modelling intent for future manned–unmanned teaming. Cogn. Tech. Work **26**, 1–20 (2023). https://doi.org/10.1007/s10111-023-00745-3

Han, T.A., Pereira, L.M.: State-of-the-art of intention recognition and its use in decision making. AI Commun. **26**, 237–246 (2013). https://doi.org/10.3233/AIC-130559

Hoey, J., Poupart, P., Boutilier, C., Mihailidis, A.: POMDP models for assistive technology. In: Decision Theory Models for Applications in Artificial Intelligence: Concepts and Solutions (2011). https://doi.org/10.4018/978-1-60960-165-2.ch013

Höller, D., Behnke, G., Bercher, P., Biundo, S.: Plan and goal recognition as HTN planning. In: 2018 IEEE 30th International Conference on Tools with Artificial Intelligence (ICTAI), pp. 466–473 (2018)

Jamakatel, P., Bercher, P., Schulte, A., Kiam, J.J.: Towards intelligent companion systems in general aviation using hierarchical plan and goal recognition. In: International Conference on Human-Agent Interaction (HAI 2023), Gothenburg, Sweden (2023)

Künzel, D., Schulte, A.: Concept of a goal and plan recognition system for adaptive pilot assistance in helicopter operations. In: Proceedings of the 22nd International Symposium of Aviation Psychology, Rochester, NY (2023)

Onken, R., Prévot, T.: CASSY - cockpit assistant system for IFR operation. In: ICAS proceedings 1994. 19th Congress of the International Council of the Aeronautical Sciences (1) (1994)

Pushp, S., Bhardwaj, B., Hazarika, S.M.: Cognitive decision making for navigation assistance based on intent recognition. In: Ghosh, A., Pal, R., Prasath, R. (eds.) MIKE 2017. LNCS (LNAI), vol. 10682, pp. 81–89. Springer, Cham (2017). https://doi.org/10.1007/978-3-319-71928-3_9

Schulte, A., Donath, D., Lange, D.S.: Design patterns for human-cognitive agent teaming. In: Harris, D. (ed.) EPCE 2016. LNCS (LNAI), vol. 9736, pp. 231–243. Springer, Cham (2016). https://doi.org/10.1007/978-3-319-40030-3_24

Schwerd, S., Schulte, A.: Operator state estimation to enable adaptive assistance in manned-unmanned-teaming. Cogn. Syst. Res. **67**, 73–83 (2021). https://doi.org/10.1016/j.cogsys.2021.01.002

Strohal, M., Onken, R.: Intent and error recognition as part of a knowledge-based cockpit assistant. In: Rogers, S.K., Fogel, D.B., Bezdek, J.C., Bosacchi, B. (eds.) Applications and Science of Computational Intelligence. Aerospace/Defense Sensing and Controls, Orlando, FL. SPIE (SPIE Proceedings), p. 287 (1998)

Suck, S., Fortmann, F.: Aircraft pilot intention recognition for advanced cockpit assistance systems. In: Schmorrow, D.D.D., Fidopiastis, C.M.M. (eds.) AC 2016. LNCS (LNAI), vol. 9744, pp. 231–240. Springer, Cham (2016). https://doi.org/10.1007/978-3-319-39952-2_23

Van-Horenbeke, F.A., Peer, A.: Activity, plan, and goal recognition: a review. Front. Robot. AI **8**, 1–18 (2021). https://doi.org/10.3389/frobt.2021.643010

Study on Collision Risk Assessment of Free Flight Based on CNS Performances

Jimin Liu[1], Ting-Ting Lu[2(✉)], Zhaoning Zhang[2], and Jinlong Wang[2]

[1] Strategic Development Department, East China Regional Air Traffic Management Bureau of CAAC, Shanghai 200335, China
[2] Air Traffic Management College, Civil Aviation University of China, Tianjin 300300, China
13681830403@163.com

Abstract. Free flight can improve the utilization of airspace, and the upgrading of communication, navigation and surveillance (CNS) systems has provided tremendous power to accelerate the realization of free flight. In this paper, directed towards the collision risk assessment under free flight environment, the three-dimensional coordinates of the aircraft random time were studied, and time variable were added to the three-dimensional reference system. The human intervention of automatic dependent surveillance (ADS) and aircraft position error caused by CNS performance were considered. Hereby, collision risk assessment model of free flight based on CNS performances was established. The computation formula of longitudinal overlap probability, lateral overlap probability and vertical overlap probability were deduced. At last, the effectiveness of the model was verified by the practical example, the computation results consistent with the standard.

Keywords: CNS Performances · Free Flight · Collision Risk · Safety Assessment

1 Introduction

With the constant improvement of CNS system, free flight has become the future trend of new navigation system. To ensure flight safety, collision risk research in the free flight environment based on CNS performance is imperative. Many scholars have achieved research results in this area. P.G.Reich established the classic Reich collision model and proposed the concept of a collision slab [1]. Based on the Reich model, some researchers have improved the model according to different applicable conditions [2, 3]. Other studies have used the probability calculation method, fault tree analysis method and Monte Carlo simulation method to evaluate the collision risk of the free flight environment of fixed airway structures [4–9]. However, in the free flight environment in its real sense, aircraft pilots can independently choose air lines. There will be no longitudinal, lateral and vertical safety separations, and flight is not constrained by fixed airway structures. Research in this environment mainly focuses on conflict detection and resolution techniques in the free flight airspace. Only a few scholars make researches on collision risk assessment in the free flight environment [10–16]. Yu describes the positioning error in the free flight environment by Brownian motion, and evaluates the collision risk [17]. Zhang used event tree theory, Bayesian network, and improved Event model to assess collision risk [18–20]. Lv considering human factors, research on collision risk, based on comprehensive analysis of CREAM and IDAC [21].

The above research still has the following two shortcomings: 1) the time factor of human intervention is not considered when establishing the 3D coordinate system in a free flight environment. 2) Although the impact of CNS performance on aircraft positioning errors has been considered in the collision risk assessment of fixed airway structures, integrated research on collision risk assessment in free flight environments based on CNS performance is still blank.

Therefore, this paper lifts the constraints of longitudinal, lateral, and vertical safety intervals and the constraints of airways structural, to establish a three-dimensional coordinate system of aircraft movement in a free flight environment, and adds time variables under human intervention into it. Otherwise, the impact of CNS performance on aircraft positioning errors was considered when constructing a collision risk model in a free flight environment. Finally, the constructed model is solved to obtain the collision risk based on CNS performance.

2   Model of Collision Risk

2.1   Establishing Coordinate System.

While literature [22] makes a position coordinate analysis of aircraft's 4D trajectory, it fails to consider aircraft's position error induced by CNS performance, the cycle of ADS position report, and the intervention of controllers and pilots. Hereby, supposing:

(1) Longitudinal, lateral and vertical positions of two aircraft are comparatively independent;
(2) $\overline{|\dot{x}|}$, $\overline{|\dot{y}|}$, $\overline{|\dot{z}|}$ refer to average speed in longitudinal, lateral and vertical directions respectively;
(3) Supposing the starting point of the leg being origin of coordinates O, type of aircraft A being i, type of aircraft B being j, v_i, v_j refer to the speed of i and j type of aircraft, $i, j = 1, 2, \cdots, n$, n being the number of aircraft type;
(4) Flight direction of aircraft A at the starting point is the positive direction on x axis, wingspan is a straight line on y axis, and with z axis perpendicular to surface xoy and downward in the positive direction, a right-angle coordinate system is established, aircraft B flies freely in 3-D space;
(5) α is the projection angle of speed v_j on xoy surface, $-90^0 \le \alpha \le 90^0$; β is the angle between the projection of speed v_j on xoy surface and y axis, $0^0 \le \beta \le 360^0$;
(6) $\varepsilon_x^i, \varepsilon_y^i, \varepsilon_z^i$ refer to CNS performance-induced position error of aircraft A on x,y,z axis; $\varepsilon_x^j, \varepsilon_y^j, \varepsilon_z^j$ refer to CNS performance-induced position error of aircraft B on x,y,z axis.

The 3-D coordinate system of aircraft position is shown in Fig. 1.

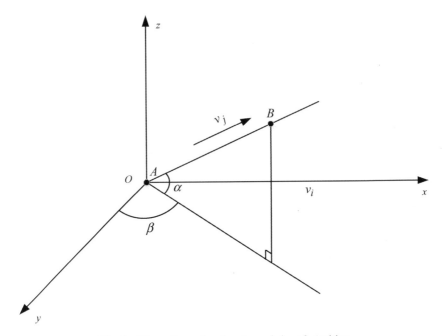

Fig. 1. Three-dimensional system of aircraft position

As Fig. 1 shows, if $t = 0$, the actual position coordinates of aircraft A and B are respectively $(t, x_0^i(t), y_0^i(t), z_0^i(t))$ and $(t, x_0^j(t), y_0^j(t), z_0^j(t))$, where

$$\begin{cases} x_0^i(t) = \varepsilon_x^i \\ y_0^i(t) = \varepsilon_y^i, \\ z_0^i(t) = \varepsilon_z^i \end{cases} \quad \begin{cases} x_0^j(t) = x_0^j + \varepsilon_x^j \\ y_0^j(t) = y_0^j + \varepsilon_y^j \\ z_0^j(t) = z_0^j + \varepsilon_z^j \end{cases} \tag{1}$$

In free flight, aircraft fly in ADS environment. Aircraft position is determined by ADS position reporting, and the cycle of reporting is T_r (Fig. 2).

Aircraft report position is obtained with every T_r, and predicted aircraft position can be obtained using extrapolation method of track. Position is indicated with certain time intervals. ADS position reporting starts form $t = 0$(separation between aircraft pairs being d_0^{ij}), and the next reporting time $t = T_r$. When separation reduces close to critical separation, intervention from controllers is necessary and avoiding clearance is to be issued. Supposing the delay time for clearance to reach pilot to start making avoiding actions is τ.

When $t = T_r + \tau$, the actual position coordinates of aircraft A and B are respectively $(t, x_{T_r+\tau}^i(t), y_{T_r+\tau}^i(t), z_{T_r+\tau}^i(t))$ and $(t, x_{T_r+\tau}^j(t), y_{T_r+\tau}^j(t), z_{T_r+\tau}^j(t))$, where

$$\begin{cases} x_{T_r+\tau}^i(t) = \varepsilon_x^i + \int_0^{T_r+\tau} v_i t \, dt \\ y_{T_r+\tau}^i(t) = \varepsilon_y^i \\ z_{T_r+\tau}^i(t) = \varepsilon_z^i \end{cases} , \quad \begin{cases} x_{T_r+\tau}^j(t) = x_0^j + \varepsilon_x^j + \int_0^{T_r+\tau} v_i t \cos\alpha \sin\beta \, dt \\ y_{T_r+\tau}^j(t) = y_0^j + \varepsilon_y^j + \int_0^{T_r+\tau} v_y t \cos\alpha \sin\beta \, dt \\ z_{T_r+\tau}^j(t) = z_0^j + \varepsilon_z^j + \int_0^{T_r+\tau} v_z t \cos\alpha \sin\beta \, dt \end{cases}$$

$$\tag{2}$$

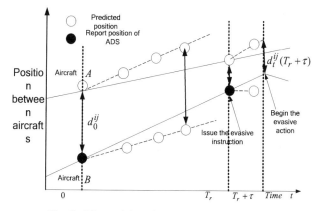

Fig. 2. The position changes of aircraft on ADS

2.2 Establishing Collision Risk Model

According to ICAO DOC 9689 [23], simple geometric shapes are used to indicate aircraft. Supposing A is a cylinder with radius d_{xy} and height $2\lambda_z$, another aircraft being proton B.

$$P_z^{ij}(t) \times (1 + \frac{|\dot{z}|}{2\lambda_z} \cdot \frac{\pi d_{xy}}{2V_{rel}^C}) \tag{3}$$

where, V_{rel}^C and $\overline{|\dot{z}|}$ are respectively the horizontal relative velocity and vertical relative velocity for B to enter cylinder A when two aircraft overlap.

Then collision probability of the two aircraft at random time t is:

$$P(t) = P_{xy}^{ij}(t) \times P_z^{ij}(t) \times (1 + \frac{\overline{|\dot{z}|}}{2\lambda_z} \cdot \frac{\pi d_{xy}}{2V_{rel}^C}) = P_x^{ij}(t) \times P_y^{ij}(t) \times P_z^{ij}(t) \times (1 + \frac{\overline{|\dot{z}|}}{2\lambda_z} \cdot \frac{\pi d_{xy}}{2V_{rel}^C}) \tag{4}$$

Let p_i be the percentage of type i aircraft in the whole fleet, p_j being the percentage of type j aircraft in the whole fleet. Since one collision is seen as two accidents, considering collision probability from $t = 0$ with minimum separation d_0^{ij} to $t = T_r + \tau$, collision times within $[0, T_r + \tau]$ is:

$$C_R = 2 \times NP \times \frac{1}{T} \int_0^{T_r+\tau} P(t)dt = \frac{2 \times NP}{T_r + \tau} \times \sum_{i=1}^n \sum_{j=1}^n (p_i p_j \times \int_0^{T_r+\tau_1} P_x^{ij}(t) \times P_y^{ij}(t) \times P_z^{ij}(t) \times (1 + \frac{\overline{|\dot{z}|}}{2\lambda_z} \cdot \frac{\pi d_{xy}}{2V_{rel}^C})dt) \tag{5}$$

3 Computing Method of Collision Risk

Supposing CNS performance-induced deviation error obeys normal distribution $N(0, \sigma^2)$, then deviation error in longitudinal, lateral and vertical directions respectively obeys $N_1(0, \sigma_x^2)$, $N_2(0, \sigma_y^2)$ and $N_3(0, \sigma_z^2)$, and: $\sigma^2 = \sigma_x^2 + \sigma_y^2 + \sigma_z^2$.

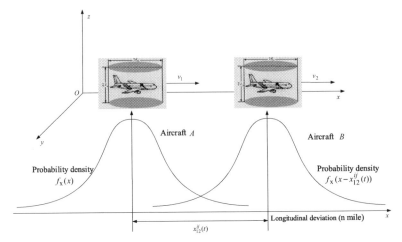

Fig. 3. The collision model and longitudinal overlapping probability density function

Longitudinal overlapping probability density function is shown in Fig. 3

At random time $t, t \in [0, T_r + \tau]$ overlapping probability of two aircraft is

$$P = \{|(x, y, z)| \ x^2 + y^2 \le d_{xy}, -2\lambda_z \le z \le 2\lambda_z\} \tag{6}$$

The position of two aircraft in longitudinal, lateral and vertical directions is mutually independent. From probability theory, at random time $t, t \in [0, T_r + \tau]$ longitudinal overlapping probability $P_x^{ij}(t)$, lateral overlapping probability $P_y^{ij}(t)$ and vertical overlapping probability $P_z^{ij}(t)$ are respectively:

$$P_x^{ij}(t) = P\{(|x_{ij}(t)|) \le d_{xy}\} \tag{7}$$

$$P_y^{ij}(t) = P\{(|y_{ij}(t)|) \le d_{xy}\} \tag{8}$$

$$P_z^{ij}(t) = P\{(|z_{ij}(t)|) \le 2\lambda_z\} \tag{9}$$

where $x_{ij}(t)$, $y_{ij}(t)$ and $z_{ij}(t)$ are respectively the longitudinal, lateral and vertical distance for two aircraft at time t.

Supposing the flight time for the aircraft on the whole route is T. T is equally divided into m time quantum $t(t = T_r + \tau)$. Within time quantum t, longitudinal distance of two aircraft $d_x^{ij}(t) = x_0^{ij} + X_i - X_j(x_0^{ij}$ being the initial longitudinal distance between the two aircraft). Hence,

$$d_x^{ij}(t) = x_0^{ij} + X_i - X_j = x_{ij}(t) - x_0^{ij} \sim x_0^{ij} + N(0, 2m\sigma_x^2) = N(x_0^{ij}, 2m\sigma_x^2) \tag{10}$$

At random time t, longitudinal overlapping probability of two aircraft is:

$$P_x^{ij}(t) = \int_{-d_{xy}}^{d_{xy}} f_x(x)dx = \int_{-d_{xy}}^{d_{xy}} \frac{1}{2\sqrt{m\pi}\,\sigma_x} e^{-\frac{(x_t^{ij} - x_0^{ij})^2}{4n\sigma_x^2}} dx \tag{11}$$

According to relevant references, during flight, once CNS performance environment in route is determined, the aircraft must stay in the specified precision range 95% of the flying time [11], hence the relation in longitudinal direction:

$$\sigma_x^2 = (\sigma_x^C)^2 + (\sigma_x^N)^2 + (\sigma_x^S)^2 = 0.2603(n_1^2 + n_2^2\overline{|\dot{x}|}^2 + n_3^2\overline{|\ddot{x}|}^2) \quad (12)$$

where σ_x^C, σ_x^N and σ_x^S indicate the longitudinal weight of deviation variance induced by communication, navigation and surveillance performance respectively.

By bringing form (12) into form (11), computational formula for longitudinal overlapping probability is obtained:

$$P_x^{ij}(t) = \int_{-d_{xy}}^{d_{xy}} \frac{1}{2\sqrt{m\pi}\sqrt{0.2603(n_1^2 + n_2^2\overline{|\dot{x}|}^2 + n_3^2\overline{|\ddot{x}|}^2)}} e^{-\frac{(x_{ij}(t)-x_0^{ij})^2}{4m\times0.2603(n_1^2 + n_2^2\overline{|\dot{x}|}^2 + n_3^2\overline{|\ddot{x}|}^2)}} dx \quad (13)$$

Similarly, computational formulae for lateral and vertical overlapping probability are respectively:

$$P_y^{ij}(t) = \int_{-d_{xy}}^{d_{xy}} \frac{1}{2\sqrt{m\pi}\sqrt{0.2603(n_1^2 + n_2^2\overline{|\dot{y}|}^2 + n_3^2\overline{|\ddot{y}|}^2)}} e^{-\frac{(y_{ij}(t)-y_0^{ij})}{4m\times0.2603(n_1^2 + n_2^2\overline{|\dot{y}|}^2 + n_3^2\overline{|\ddot{y}|}^2)}} dy$$

$$(14)$$

$$P_z^{ij}(t) = \int_{-2\lambda_z}^{2\lambda_z} \frac{1}{2\sqrt{m\pi}\sqrt{0.2603(n_1^2 + n_2^2\overline{|\dot{z}|}^2 + n_3^2\overline{|\ddot{z}|}^2)}} e^{-\frac{(z_{ij}(t)-z_0^{ij})}{4m\times0.2603(n_1^2 + n_2^2\overline{|\dot{z}|}^2 + n_3^2\overline{|\ddot{z}|}^2)}} dz \quad (15)$$

In free flight, the position of two aircraft in longitudinal, lateral and vertical directions is mutually independent, namely, longitudinal, lateral and vertical overlapping probability is to be taken into account when collision risk of two aircraft occurs. Hence collision times within $[0, T_r + \tau]$ is:

$$C_R = \frac{2 \times NP}{T_r + \tau} \times (1 + \frac{\overline{|\dot{z}|}}{2\lambda_z} \cdot \frac{\pi d_{xy}}{2V_{rel}^C}) \times \frac{1}{2\sqrt{m\pi}\sqrt{0.2603(n_1^2 + n_2^2\overline{|\dot{x}|}^2 + n_3^2\overline{|\ddot{x}|}^2)}} \times \frac{1}{2\sqrt{m\pi}\sqrt{0.2603(n_1^2 + n_2^2\overline{|\dot{y}|}^2 + n_3^2\overline{|\ddot{y}|}^2)}}$$

$$\times \frac{1}{2\sqrt{m\pi}\sqrt{0.2603(n_1^2 + n_2^2\overline{|\dot{z}|}^2 + n_3^2\overline{|\ddot{z}|}^2)}} \times \sum_{i=1}^{n}\sum_{j=1}^{n} P_i P_j$$

$$\times \int_0^{T_r+\tau}\int_{-d_{xy}}^{d_{xy}} e^{-\frac{(x_{ij}(t)-x_0^{ij})^2}{4m\times0.2603(n_1^2+n_2^2\overline{|\dot{x}|}^2+n_3^2\overline{|\ddot{x}|}^2)}} \times \int_{-d_{xy}}^{d_{xy}} e^{-\frac{(y_{ij}(t)-y_0^{ij})}{4m\times0.2603(n_1^2+n_2^2\overline{|\dot{y}|}^2+n_3^2\overline{|\ddot{y}|}^2)}} \times \int_{-2\lambda_z}^{2\lambda_z} e^{-\frac{(z_{ij}(t)-z_0^{ij})}{4m\times0.2603(n_1^2+n_2^2\overline{|\dot{z}|}^2+n_3^2\overline{|\ddot{z}|}^2)}} dxdydzdt$$

$$(16)$$

4 Example Evaluation

In the computation of collision risks, some parameters do not often change, and have little impact on the computation result, mean value here being adopted. If aircraft and are of the same type, the mean value of relevant parameters for the two types of aircraft is found according to aircraft ratio. By statistical analysis of vicinal aircraft number on certain flight leg, data in Table 1 can be obtained (length unit being nm, velocity unit knot and time unit min).

Table 1. Table of collision risk parameters.

d_{xy}	λ_z	$|\bar{x}|$	$|\bar{y}|$	$|\bar{z}|$	T_r	τ	V^C_{rel}
0.036	0.02	84.7	185.2	1.5	16	2	82.35
NP	m	α	β	n_1	n_2	n_3	
500	20	45^0	30^0	10	400	20	

By bringing parameters in Table 1 into form (16), collision risk under maximum combination (RNP10, RCP400, RSP20) is computed:

$$C_R = 2 \times NP \times \frac{1}{T} \int_0^{T_r+\tau} P(t)dt = \frac{2 \times NP}{T_r + \tau} \times P_x^{ij}(t) \times P_y^{ij}(t) \times P_z^{ij}(t) \times (1 + \frac{|\bar{z}|}{2\lambda_z} \cdot \frac{\pi d_{xy}}{2V^C_{rel}})dt)$$

$$= 2.58 \times 10^{-9} \tag{17}$$

5   Conclusions

The paper establishes 3D coordinates for aircraft on flight track at random time, and above that, time variable is added to the coordinates, with the impact of human intervention on collision risk under ADS taken into account. It also set up CNS performance-based collision risk assessment model in free flight. Computational formula for longitudinal, lateral and vertical overlapping probability is deduced. Safety assessment computation is conducted for collision risks in free flight through examples, and collision times 2.58 $\times 10^{-9}$ under maximum combination CNS performance (RNP10, RCP400 and RSP20), which satisfies the target level of safety(1.5×10^{-8}), and lays a basis for further research of safety assessment in free flight.

Acknowledgments. This work was supported in part by National Social Science Foundation (No. 22XGL001); Key Project of Civil Aviation Joint Fund of National Natural Science Foundation (No. 2233209); Civil Aviation Safety Capacity Building Fund (No. [2022]156).

Disclosure of Interests.   All authors disclosed no relevant relationships.

References

1. Reich, P.G.: Analysis of long-range air traffic systems-separation standards I II III. J. Navig. **19**(1): 88–98, 169–186, 331–347 (1966)
2. Hsu, D.A.: The evaluation of aircraft collision probabilities at intersecting air routes. J. Navig. **34**, 78–102 (1981)
3. Zhang, Z., Zhang, X., Li, D.: Computation model of lateral collision rate on parallel routes based on VOR navigation. J. Traffic Transport. Eng. **7**(3), 21–24 (2007)
4. Brooker, P.: Longitudinal collision risk for ATC track systems: a hazardous Event model. J. Navig. **59**(1), 55–70 (2006)

5. Paielli, R.A., Erzberger, H.: Conflict probability estimation for free flight. NASA Ames Research Center, Moffett Field, CA: NAS 1.15:110411; A-962310 (1996)
6. Shepherd, R., Cassell, R., Thapa, R., et al.: A reduced aircraft separation risk assessment model. In: AIAA Guidance, Navigation, and Control Conference, New Orleans (2003)
7. Everdij, M.H.C., et al.: Modeling lateral spacing and separation for airborne separation assurance using Petri nets. J. Simul. 83(5), 401–414 (2007)
8. Stroeve, S.H., Blom, H.A.P., Bakker, G.J.: Systemic accident risk assessment in air traffic by Monte Carlo simulation. Saf. Sci. 47(2), 238–249 (2009)
9. Huang, B.: Lateral collision risk model on parallel routes based on communication, navigation and surveillance performances. J. Southwest Jiaotong Univ. 47(6), 1075–1080+1091 (2012)
10. Li, Q.: The Design and Development of Multimodal Conflict Cues. Civil Aviation Flight University of China, Guang Han (2011)
11. Shi Wenxian. A cooperative MAS approach to conflict resolution [D].Nan Jing: Nanjing University of Aeronautics and Astronautics, 2008
12. Cheng, L.: Research on Technologies of the Conflict Detection and Resolution Among Multi-aircraft in Free Flight Airspace. Nanjing University of Aeronautics and Astronautics, Nan Jing (2005)
13. Guo, Q.: Study of Aircraft Conflict Resolution Method. Civil Aviation University of China, Tian Jin (2008)
14. Jiang, X., Wu, M., et al.: Application of ensemble learning algorithm in aircraft probabilistic conflict detection of free flight. In: 2018 International Conference on Artificial Intelligence and Big Data (ICAIBD). IEEE (2018)
15. Christodoulou, M.A., Kodaxakis, S.G.: Automatic commercial aircraft-collision avoidance in free flight: the three-dimensional problem. IEEE Trans. Intell. Transp. Syst. 7(2), 242–249 (2006)
16. Massink, M., Francesco, N.D.: Modelling free flight with collision avoidance. In: International Conference on Engineering of Complex Computer Systems. IEEE Computer Society (2001)
17. Yu, S., Zhang, Z.: Study on collision risk between multiple aircrafts under free flight condition based on brownian motion. Aeron. Comput. Techn. 45(4), 74–82 (2015)
18. Zhang, Z., Liang, Y., et al.: Assessment model of collision risk based on event tree in free flight. Sci. Technol. Eng. 15(2), 304–308 (2015)
19. Zhang, Z., Liang, Y.: Bayesian network-based study on collision risk in free flight. China Saf. Sci. J. 24(9), 40–45 (2014)
20. Zhang, Z., Shi, R.: Study on free flight collision risk based on improved event model. China Saf. Sci. J. 25(7), 35–40 (2015)
21. Lv, Z., Wang, S., Zhang, Z.: Collision risk in free flight based on CREAM and IDAC. Saf. Environ. Eng. 24(01), 111–114+120 (2017)
22. Qu, Y., Han, S.: Collision risk model of four-dimensional flight track on identical airway based on terminal arrivals. J. Nanjing Univ. Aeron. Astron. 42(5), 601–606 (2010)
23. Doc 9689-AN/953. Manual on airspace planning methodology for the determination of separation minima. Montreal: International Civil Aviation Organization (1998)

EBT Training Effectiveness and Evaluation

Qingyu Meng[1], Tong Li[1(✉)], and Hao Xie[2,3]

[1] Civil Aviation Management Institute of China, Huajiadi East Road 3, Chaoyang District, Beijing, China
ttlitong@163.com
[2] Fudan University, Handan Road 220, Yangpu District, Shanghai, China
[3] Air China Limited Southwest Branch, Airport North Road 3, Shuangliu District, Chengdu, China

Abstract. With the development of Evidence based training (EBT), more and more airlines realize this is a subsystem of SMS, which provides overarching tool from operation safety to training and vice versa. The analysis of instructor grading data and operation data allows the training manager analyze the whole system performance. In order to run through ADDIE (Analyze, design, development, implement, evaluation) process, evaluation is necessary to course design, instructor performance and the training system performance. This paper analyzes two airlines EBT training data from the competency grading, trainees rank, correlation perspectives, and also propose the possible way of analyzing competency from FOQA data.

Keywords: EBT training effectiveness · Training system evaluation · Competency · FOQA data · Correlation

1 Background

Since EBT training has been recognized by ICAO, IATA and IFALPA, aviation authorities and airlines around the world have gradually replaced the conventional airline pilot recurrent training by EBT training. In the process of implementing EBT, the training effectiveness as a key performance indicator of training has been closely monitored in civil aviation industry. The evaluation of training effectiveness and training system performance not only affects the rationality of EBT course curriculum arrangement and threat training topics, but also directly relates to the overall quality of EBT training.

Today, safety data integrates very limited amount of training data or training records for safety performance assessment. Additionally, under traditional task-based training, the quality of the training data and records does not provide sufficient visibility on the pilot's and instructor's abilities that contribute efficiently to safe operations. This limitation exists since traditional training focuses on a few technical skills, while human performance encompasses a broader set of non-technical skills and attitudes.

The current training evaluation of EBT still relies on the performance of airline pilots in specific training scenarios on CAT-D flight simulators. After the EBT instructor follows a standard evaluation pattern for observing, recording, categorizing, and evaluating, the behavior of the training pilot will be documented by an individual score from 1 to 5 that assigned to the pilot profile in each competency. Although the training courses and training topics of EBT is based on historical aviation accident or incident reports, but there is still a certain difference between the training scenarios and actual operational threat. Currently, no quantitative means have been established to reveal the relationship between the score of competency and actual operational performance. Hence, integrating actual operational data and EBT concept would comprehensively reflect the quality of EBT courses, as well as lay a solid foundation for improving civil aviation safety.

This study try to analyze the data from EBT training to accomplish the training effectiveness evaluation. Meanwhile, we need to consider how to evaluate the training system performance through operation data. FOQA data is elaborated as a source to reflect the possibility of evaluating competency performance. This paper uses recurrent training data of implement instructors(II), implement examiners(IE), pilot trainees and operation data of airlines. In recurrent training, nine competency of trainees are measured on a five-point scale.

When it comes to the effectiveness of training, instructor bias cannot be avoiding. There are a number of well-known biases [1–6] that can impact on the reliability of rating the non-technical performance of individuals and teams. The first group of biases that can negatively impact on rating non-technical skills all relate to situations in which one aspect of performance becomes the main focus of assessment, and in turn, that aspect of performance then influences other aspects of assessment. A second set of biases relate to general patterns in the way in which an assessor makes their ratings. The final set of biases relate to the influence of normative assessment instead of the criterion-referenced assessment at the heart of a competency-based training approach to non-technical skills development. Halo effect, central tendency, contrast effect, visceral bias, leniency and severity are the bias that the instructors usually show in evaluation. Feldman M, Lazzara EH, etc. [7], studied the rater training to support high stakes simulation-based assessments in medical area and proposed 4 methods for promote raters accuracy. Observational performance assessment is more complex than knowledge tests or attitude surveys in that the rater introduces an additional source of variance due to rater errors or biases that may weaken the quality of inferences one can make about physician competence.

Arthur etc. [8] try to use meta data to test training effectiveness by"reaction, learning, behavior and result". Barriers for assessment are studied, such as poor leadership support and existing standards of practice that remain fixed regardless of training may prevent certain skills from manifesting in actual clinical practice [9, 10].

Those characteristics from the data is worth noting in the data analysis and evaluation and interfere them in the design of the instructors training. Also, the data within or between fleet, airlines, ranks, with other or among IE, between different EBT modules are analyzed.

2 EBT Data Analysis

2.1 Sample Description

This paper collect EBT data from two airlines (A and B) with the same type of aircraft. Each trainee participated in 3 training sessions. The first session consists of a 2-h evaluation and a 2-h maneuver validation (MV) for a proficiency check. The second and third session are periodic training in full flight simulator. Three sessions are abbreviated respectively as FFS1, FFS2 and FFS3. There are 195 training sessions, 65 trainees, evaluating by 24 Implement Instructors(II) or Implement Examiners(IE), referred to as I/E (see Table 1).

Table 1. Sample composition

Airline	I/E	Trainee	Training Session	Grade
A	12	37	111	999
B	12	28	84	756
Total	24	65	195	1755

2.2 General Analysis

Overall Analysis. The ratio of grades 1–5 is 0%, 3%, 82%, 13% and 1% respectively (see Fig. 1)) in the total sample, the grade is concentrated in grade 3. The ratio of low scores and high scores are both low. The result conforms to the Asian idea of "the doctrine of the mean" and is related to a short time with the implementation of EBT. I/E are not familiar with the grading principle and word picture yet. So I/E cannot give the different grades well according to the different performance of the trainees.

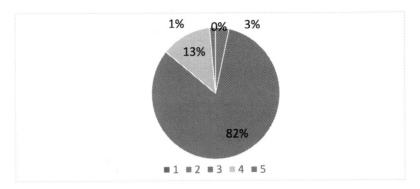

Fig. 1. Grade distribution: Total sample

Nine Competency Analysis. As shown in Fig. 2, the mean value of the total sample is 3.12. The lowest competency values of the nine competencies are PSD, PRO, FPM, WLM and KNO, while those higher than the mean of the nine competencies are LTW, SAW, COM and FPA. Further analysis of the ratio of nine competency grades find that the frequency of grade 2 is the highest in PSD and the frequency of grade 4 is the lowest in PSD, followed by PRO, resulting in the lowest mean value of these two competencies. The frequency of grade 4 is the highest in LTW and the frequency of grade 2 of SAW is 0, resulting in the highest mean of these two competencies. This is consistent with the EBT instructor training, which has stated that SAW is usually not a key competency, since it is usually combined with other competencies and usually the others are more efficient for improvement.

The frequency of grade 2 and grade 5 of FPM is high, and the distribution of grades is more distinct, indicating that FPM is observed easily by I/E. The frequency of grade 2 and grade 5 of FPA is low, and the grades are mainly concentrated in grade 3 and grade 4, indicating that I/E need to improve the identification of this competency in the subsequent calibration.

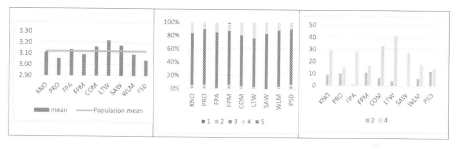

Fig. 2. Grade of Nine Competencies: Total sample

Training Type Analysis. As shown in Fig. 3, with the progress of sessions, trainees' overall performance become better and their scores become higher. The ratio of grade 2 in FFS1, FFS2 and FFS3 gradually decreased, and the ratio of grade 3 gradually increased. It is worth noting that the ratio of grade 4 is lower in FFS2 than FFS1. The ratio of grade 4 is also lower in the Scenario-Based Training Phase (SBT, FFS2 + FFS3) than the evaluation phase (FFS1), which indicates that IE are more daring to give low or high grade than II.

Trainee Rank Analysis. As shown in Fig. 4, in the total sample, the distribution of trainees of First Officer (FO), captain and instructor is relatively uniform. The mean of nine competencies of three kinds of trainees are drawn into the radar map. It is found that the score of KNO, PRO, FPM, LTW and PSD varies more than the other competencies when ranks of trainees are different. The higher the trainee's ability, the higher the mean score. However, the differentiation of FPA scores among different ranks trainees is not obvious, which is consistent with the above mentioned phenomenon that FPA scores are concentrated in grade 3 and grade 4. It is worth noting that the mean of SAW, WLM and COM of the instructors are lower than those of the captains. It may be related to the

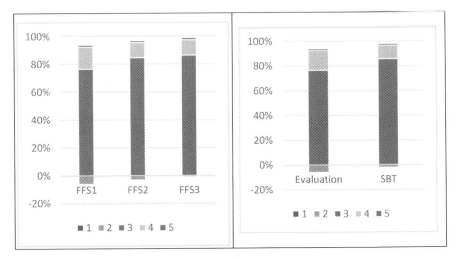

Fig. 3. Grading of different training type

higher expectations of I/E in these three non-technical competencies when trainees are instructors. FPM and WLM are the obvious shortcomings of FO trainees and PSD is the obvious shortcomings of captain trainees. Each competency of instructors is similar.

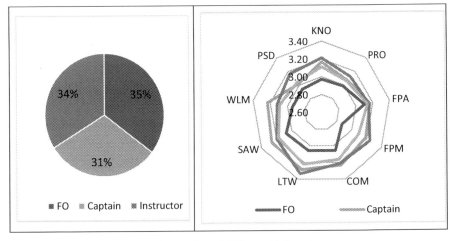

Fig. 4. Grading of different flight rating

Individual I/E Analysis. There are ten IE and thirteen II, with the exception of No. 8, who is both the IE and II. As can be seen from Fig. 5, there are 2 I/E (8%) who give only one grade, and they are all II. Further screening the I/E list of grading concentration, there are five I/E (21%) who score above 95% of a certain grade as shown in Table 2. All I/E give a concentrated score of grade 3, of which 2 I/E only give grade 3. There is only one IE on the list, the other four are II. Compared with the total sample, I/E who are inclined to give more grade 4 or 5 and less grade 1 or 2 are defined as lenient I/E. There are 4 lenient I/E (17%) as shown in Table 3. Lenient I/E are preferring to give grade 4 or 5 rather than grade 3. There is only one IE in the lenient I/E list, and the other three are II. On the other hand, the ratio of this IE scoring 5 is 11.1%, which is much higher than the average level, indicating that IE are more daring to give grade 5. Above all, IE are more likely to give the low or high grade than II. In the transition from legacy training to EBT training, IE work for the first day of Evaluation and MV check, they are learning to adapt the grading skill, II work on the continuous 2 days, they are learning to be more confident as IE to give more 1 or 5 as needed.

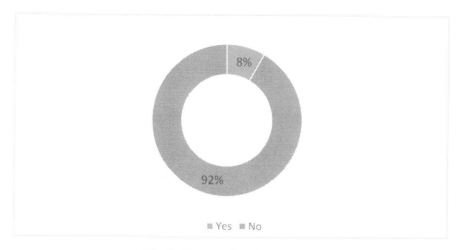

Fig. 5. The rate of grading one level

Table 2. I/E list of grading concentration

I/E	ID	Session	Score	1	2	3	4	5
IE	12	8	72	0.0%	2.8%	95.8%	1.4%	0.0%
II	13	12	108	0.0%	0.0%	99.1%	0.9%	0.0%
II	14	4	36	0.0%	0.0%	100.0%	0.0%	0.0%
II	16	8	72	0.0%	0.0%	100.0%	0.0%	0.0%
II	23	12	108	0.0%	1.9%	95.4%	2.8%	0.0%
Overall		195	1755	0.0%	3.4%	82.5%	12.7%	1.4%

In order to further analyze the grading situation at the individual level, the grading ratio of each I/E is plotted as a percentage accumulation histogram, as shown in Fig. 6. No. 15 I/E only scores grade 2 and 3, and the ratio of grade 2 is significantly higher than that of the total sample. No. 17 scores grade 2 and 4 more than the population. Table 4 shows the correlation coefficient between grading of each I/E and the total sample. The

Table 3. Lenient I/E list

I/E	ID	Session	Score	1	2	3	4	5
II	1	6	54	0.0%	0.0%	55.6%	42.6%	1.9%
IE	3	7	63	0.0%	1.6%	49.2%	38.1%	11.1%
II	11	12	108	0.0%	0.0%	79.6%	20.4%	0.0%
II	22	8	72	0.0%	2.8%	77.8%	19.4%	0.0%
Overall			195	1755	0.0%	3.4%	82.5%	12.7%	1.4%

greener color, the higher correlation, and the redder color, the lower correlation. Correlation1 is the correlation calculated based on the ratio of grade 1–5, and Correlation2 is the correlation calculated based on the mean of nine competencies. According to the Correlation1 value, the correlation coefficients of No. 17, 3, 1 and 15 are 17.83%, 81.28%, 82.22% and 95.70%, respectively. Among them, No. 1 and 3 are lenient I/E, and the ratio of No. 15 and 17 giving a certain grade is significantly higher than that of the total sample. No. 14 and 16 do not have the Correla-tion2 value. After analysis, it is found that these two I/E only give one level grade, which belong to over-centralized I/E.

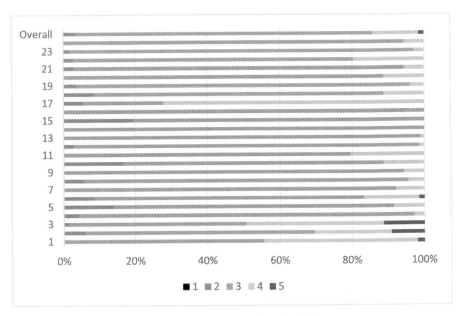

Fig. 6. Individual I/E grading distribution

Table 4. I/E grading correlation

I/E No.	Correlation1	Correlation2
1	82.22%	66.30%
2	98.25%	67.07%
3	81.28%	21.19%
4	99.24%	40.32%
5	98.61%	17.35%
6	99.72%	-17.52%
7	99.79%	73.05%
8	99.37%	69.97%
9	99.63%	71.94%
10	97.91%	16.77%
11	99.20%	22.67%
12	99.12%	32.32%
13	99.13%	-5.50%
14	99.01%	-
15	95.70%	42.92%
16	99.01%	-
17	17.83%	63.17%
18	99.71%	28.06%
19	99.38%	65.31%
20	99.93%	67.45%
21	99.61%	-12.82%
22	99.42%	25.77%
23	99.33%	73.80%
24	99.63%	-13.91%
Overall	100.00%	100.00%

2.3 Comparative Analysis by Airlines

This paper further analyzes and compares the EBT data of different companies. The mean score of each competency of Airline A is higher than those of Airline B (see Fig. 7). At the same time, as shown in Fig. 8, the ratio of grade 5 in Airline B is 0, and the ratio of grade 3 is higher, indicating that I/E of Airline B are not daring to give high or low grades than Airline A. This paper makes further statistics of the grade distribution of Airline A and Airline B in FFS1, FFS2 and FFS3. Table 5 shows that, with the pro-gress of session, the score of Airline A is getting higher and higher, while the score of Airline B is mainly manifested by the difference between evaluation phase and SBT. II give a concentrated score of grade 3, and IE are more daring to give grade 4. To sum up, the grade distribution of Airline A is more decentralized.

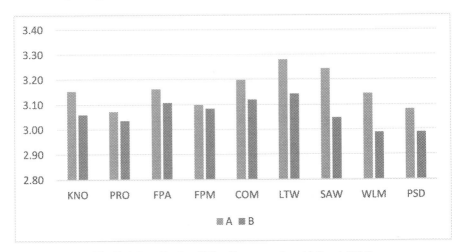

Fig. 7. Mean Grade of Nine Competencies: Airline A VS B

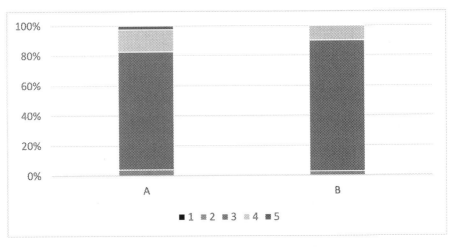

Fig. 8. Grade Distribution: Airline A VS B

Table 5. Grading of different sessions: Airline A VS B

Session	Airline A			Airline B		
	FFS1	FFS2	FFS3	FFS1	FFS2	FFS3
Grade 1	0%	0%	0%	0%	0%	0%
Grade 2	7%	3%	1%	5%	3%	1%
Grade 3	77%	79%	80%	76%	92%	94%
Grade 4	14%	15%	16%	19%	6%	5%
Grade 5	2%	2%	3%	0%	0%	0%
Total	100%	100%	100%	100%	100%	100%

3   Evaluation for Training System Performance

Training system performance is needed to evaluate after implementing EBT, however, due to the allocation of resource, it takes time to break the silos and merge data to form unified data analysis perspectives. We analyze from FOQA data perspectives for the possible evaluation without realistic data in this paper.

3.1   Competency Evaluation Based on FOQA Data

Before evaluating the EBT competency of flight crews with FOQA data, we need to consider the range of data types collected by FOQA, and map the relationship between available FOQA data and EBT competencies. It should be noted that due to the inability of FOQA data to accurately analyze the flight crew's decision-making or communication process, only actions or system status data can be identified. Therefore, the corresponding competency's observed behavior or performance indicator cannot be directly scored by FOQA data.

PRO refers to the flight crew's ability to use procedures during normal operations or encountering threats and errors. The evaluation objectives of this competency typically include standard operating procedures (SOP), abnormal procedures, and supplementary procedures for special situations. For the evaluation of routine SOP, a digital mapping relationship can be established between SOP and system statuses, those actions during standard operations can be produced as time-series data. By comparing actual FOQA data with standard time-series data, it can be identified whether incorrectly sequenced flight actions exist in normal flights, or whether the flight crew follows regulatory requirements such as instrument procedure speed limits and noise abatement procedure. Callantine T J. [11] has developed the Crew Activity Tracking System (CATS) based on FOQA data, by comparing the airline SOP with the actual FOQA data, CATS successfully identified threats and errors that occur during normal operation. Furthermore, typical scenarios include the selection of the Flight Management System (FMS) mode during descent, have been applied in airline training program.

The occurrence of aircraft malfunctions as well as related abnormal procedures is seldom happened during flight operation, the corresponding action and coping strategies for malfunctions is a key point in PRO evaluation. By establishing a set of evaluation criteria from FOQA data such as flight phase and abnormal procedure, the behavior or action applied by the crew can be scored. Sun has developed a wind shear control quality evaluation method based on FOQA data to quantitatively evaluate the crew's compliance and handling capabilities when encounter low level wind-shear.

Supplementary procedures for special situations, such as anti-icing or single-engine taxiing, directly affect flight safety and efficiency. Implementation errors in these procedures can pose a serious threat to safety. However, unlike SOP, which can be detected in every flight, or abnormal procedures, which always start with a malfunction, these types of procedures are not always applicable. Therefore, for the identification of such procedures, it is possible to identify the first action of the relevant procedure to analyze threats and errors in supplementary procedures.

Competency FPA is a critical competency in EBT. Good automation management can significantly reduce the workload of flight crews and enhance their ability to handle complex failures. However, improper automation management can lead to over-speed, stall, mid-air collision, or controlled flight into terrain. Since FOQA systems collect a large amount of aircraft system and status data, identification can be made based on parameters such as vertical speed in Reduced Vertical Separation Minimum (RVSM) areas, Instrument Landing System (ILS) signal acquisition sequence, and circular approach protect areas. Automation management is related to aircraft models, and even for aircraft from the same manufacturer, different options may lead to different automation management systems. Currently, there are only a small number of studies on FPA competency specific to aircraft models.

Competency FPM has always been a research focus of FOQA data. Multiple studies have evaluated the manual handling capabilities of flight crews from different dimensions using FOQA data. Li Daqing etc. [12] developed a three-level flight crew competency evaluation model and system based on FOQA data to quantitatively evaluate the various competencies of flight crews. Xie H etc. [13] identified precursors of heavy landing when the plane is about to land and classified landing loads, which can serve as indicators for evaluating flight crews' landing skills. Wang Lei etc. [14] used FOQA data to quantitatively evaluate pilot handling capabilities from both temporal and spatial dimensions. Lee H K etc. [15] studied threat precursors of go-around procedure based on FOQA data, and by applying neural networks and Long Short-Term Memory (LSTM) to predict parameters such as pitch angle, altitude, and engine thrust associated with dangerous precursors during go-around maneuvering.

Moreover, some research even has developed a method to transfer FOQA data into flight simulator, while could provide a vivid training scenario for trainees. This will help pilots learn to respond correctly when exposed to real flight threats. However, due to the limited types of data collected by FOQA, currently there is no research focus on competencies such as COM, LTW, PSD, SAW, WLM, KNO.

Under EBT, the training system performance is measured and evaluated through a feedback process in order to validate and refine the curriculum, and to ascertain that the organization's program develops pilot competencies and meets the training objectives. The typical EBT feedback process should use defined training metrics to collect data in order to:

- identify trends and ensure corrective action where necessary,
- identify collective training needs,
- review, adjust and continuously improve the training program,
- further develop the training system, and
- standardize the instructors.

We will continue our job on breaking the silos and merge the data, integrating the training system performance into Safety management system.

3.2 EBT Competency Evaluation

Flight Operations Quality Assurance (FOQA) and Line Operational Safety Audit(LOSA) are two kinds of key operation data in civil aviation, which make significant contributions in EBT development. FOQA data, which also refer as Quick Access Recorder(QAR) data in some research, is automatically collected dedicated parameters from the aircraft at a specific frequency. In EBT competency evaluation, the advantages of FOQA are its large data volume, standardized data, and full flight segment coverage, which makes it possible to quantitatively evaluate the aircraft's status. However, this also limits its application scope, which cannot comprehensively evaluate all the competences in line operation. In contrast, LOSA adopts a peer observation method, in which observers enter the cockpit to identify actual flight threats, errors, and coping strategies applied by the flight crew. In EBT competency evaluation, the advantages of LOSA are that qualified EBT instructors can use the same criteria in both simulation and real aircraft to consistently evaluate the flight crew's performance. However, this method has a large demand for LOSA obervors and cannot achieve standardized evaluation for every flight segment. This study aims to explore the possibility of combining EBT with FOQA data from a theoretical perspective.

References

1. Balzer, W.K., Sulsky, L.M.: Halo and performance appraisal research: a critical examination. J. Appl. Psychol. **77**(6), 975 (1992)
2. Croskerry, P.: The importance of cognitive errors in diagnosis and strategies to minimize them. Acad. Med. **78**, 1–6 (2003)
3. Croskerry, P.: Achieving quality in clinical decision making: cognitive strategies and detection of bias. Acad. Emerg. Med. **9**(11), 1184–1204 (2002)
4. Thomas, M.J.W.: Training and Assessing Non-Technical Skills: A Practical Guide (1st ed.). CRC Press (2018). https://doi.org/10.1201/9781315550336
5. Yeates, P., O' Neill, P., Mann, K., Eva, K. W.: 'You' re certainly relatively competent': Assessor bias due to recent experiences. Med. Educ. **47**(9), 910–922
6. Downing, S.M.: Threats to the validity of clinical teaching assessments: what about rater error? Med. Educ. **39**:350–355. [PubMed: 15813754] (2013)
7. Feldman, M., Lazzara, E.H., Vanderbilt, A.A., DiazGranados, D.: Rater training to support highstakes simulation-based assessments. J. Contin. Educ. Health Prof. 2012 Fall **32**(4), 279–86. https://doi.org/10.1002/chp.21156. PMID: 23280532; PMCID: PMC3646087
8. Arthur, W., Jr., Bennett, W., Jr., Edens, P.S., Bell, S.T.: Effectiveness of training in organizations: a meta-analysis of design and evaluation features. J. Appl. Psychol. **88**(2), 234–245 (2003)
9. Baker, D., Dismukes, R.: A framework for understanding crew performance assessment issues. Int. J. Aviat. Psychol. **12**(3), 205–222 (2002)
10. Beaudin-Seiler, B.M., Seiler, R.: A study of how flight instructors assess flight maneuvers and give grades: inter-rater reliability of instructor assessments. J. Aviation/Aerospace Educ. Res. **25**(1) (2015)
11. Callantine T J.: The crew activity tracking system: Leveraging flight data for aiding, training and analysis. In: 20th DASC. 20th Digital Avionics Systems Conference (Cat. No. 01CH37219). IEEE, 1: 5C3/1–5C3/12 vol. 1 (2001)
12. Li, D., Chen, X.: Method and system for pilot competency portrait based on large data of aviation QAR. Beijing: CN113298431B, 2023–04–21
13. Xie, H., Li, T., Lai, S.: Civil aircraft landing loads prediction based on flight data and oleopneumatic absorber behavior. In: 2021 IEEE 3rd International Conference on Civil Aviation Safety and Information Technology (ICCASIT). IEEE, pp. 227–231 (2021)

14. Lei, W., Ying, Z., Shuo, W.: Quantitative evaluation of pilot's unsafe operating behavior driven by QAR data. J. China Saf. Sci. **33**(5), 49 (2023)
15. Lee, H.K., Puranik, T.G., Fischer, O.P., et al.: Flight data driven system identification using neural networks for landing safety assessment. In: 2021 IEEE/AIAA 40th Digital Avionics Systems Conference (DASC), pp. 1–9. IEEE (2021)

Exploring Functionalities for an Intelligent Pilot Advisory System in Normal Operation

Sarah Ternus[1,2(✉)] [ID], Jakob Würfel[2] [ID], Anne Papenfuß[2] [ID], Matthias Wies[2] [ID], and Martin Rumpler[1]

[1] Trier University of Applied Sciences, 55768 Birkenfeld, Germany
sarah.ternus@dlr.de
[2] German Aerospace Center, Lilienthalpl. 7, 38108 Braunschweig, Germany

Abstract. This paper delves into the functionalities of an Intelligent Pilot Advisory System (IPAS) in normal aviation operations. Building upon the foundational work of "Intelligent Pilot Advisory System: The Journey From Ideation to an Early System Design of an AI-Based Decision Support System for Airline Flight Decks" by Jakob Würfel et al., which primarily focused on emergency scenarios, this study extends the IPAS's application to non-emergency contexts. Utilizing a user-centered approach, a workshop involving pilots, data scientists, and Human-Artificial Intelligence Teaming (HAT) experts was conducted to brainstorm and evaluate functionalities for this system in regular flight operations. The methodology combined creative and analytical techniques, including the 6-3-5 ideation method, mind mapping and design studio method, leading to rapid prototyping and iterative feedback. During the workshop, several key functionalities for the IPAS were identified, such as the Mission Monitoring and Advisory Function (MMAF), which provides real-time updates on flight-related factors, as well as the integration of pre-flight briefing and operational guidance. Based on the workshops results an early prototype was developed, showcasing a timeline-based presentation of information and interactive user interface elements. This prototype serves as the basis for initial feedback evaluation and ongoing refinement. By integrating AI and leveraging the amount of aviation data, this intelligent advisor aims to improve situational awareness, decision-making, and operational efficiency in normal flight operations. In this context, this paper highlights the need for extended pilot testing and integration with existing cockpit systems, emphasizing the importance of human-AI teaming aspects, customization, data security, and the system's impact on pilot skills, training and the environment.

Keywords: Aviation · Workshop · Human-AI Teaming · Decision Support System · Human-Centered Design

1 Introduction

At a time when the applications of Artificial Intelligence (AI) are expanding and research in this domain is developing at a remarkable pace, the integration of AI

D. Harris and W.-C. Li (Eds.): HCII 2024, LNAI 14692, pp. 235–247, 2024.
https://doi.org/10.1007/978-3-031-60728-8_19

into pilot advisory systems has emerged as a frontier with immense potential. The concept of an Intelligent Pilot Advisory System (IPAS) represents an important step in this direction [18]. This paper builds upon the foundational work laid out in "Intelligent Pilot Advisory System: The Journey From Ideation to an Early System Design of an AI-Based Decision Support System for Airline Flight Decks" by Jakob Würfel et al. [18]. Their research provides a comprehensive understanding of the ideation and early system design of Artificial Intelligence (AI) based decision support systems for airline flight decks.

Central to this exploration is the recognition of the critical role that pilots play in ensuring the safety and efficiency of flight operations. The demands on pilot decision making and situational awareness are high [5,6] and the integration of an IPAS into normal operations could provide an opportunity to enhance these capabilities. In the past, research on the IPAS has primarily focused on its use in emergency situations, as described in more detail in Sect. 3. However, since relying on the system only in emergencies may lead to a lack of familiarity and trust of pilots in the system, this paper explores the implementation of the IPAS for normal operations. Furthermore, our focus shifts from theoretical frameworks to practical applications, seeking to identify and evaluate specific functionalities that the IPAS can offer in the realm of everyday flight operations and applications that extend beyond emergency scenarios.

To address this critical issue, a user-centered approach was adopted. A group of seven experts participated in a comprehensive workshop to brainstorm and evaluate ideas for the IPAS in normal operations. The methodology used to explore this concept and brainstorm ideas were multiple creative and analytical techniques [17]. The active involvement of pilots in the ideation process allowed for valuable insights into their specific user needs and resulted in the conceptualization of extending the IPAS to be an omnipresent aid in the cockpit, offering continuous assistance and insights throughout all flight phases. From briefing to approach procedures, this system aims to provide comprehensive information and guidance, thereby enhancing the decision-making process, improving operational efficiency, and ensuring a higher standard of flight safety.

This paper first reviews related work and the basic concept of IPAS. It then discusses the rationale for the IPAS in normal operations. Next, the methodology used to brainstorm ideas for the IPAS in normal operation is described and the results are presented. Finally, a conclusion and opportunities for future research are provided. Through this exploration, we aim to contribute a novel perspective to the ongoing discourse on AI in aviation, emphasizing the benefits for the IPAS to become a trusted and routine part in flight operations.

2 Related Work

In the realm of aviation technology, the integration of AI has been a subject of extensive research and development [7,10,15,16]. Thereby, the potential of multiple applications for AI are identified [10], which could be merged in an intelligent pilot advisory system, as described in Sect. 3.

Pilot advisory systems have undergone significant evolution over the years. Already in 1981, Parks Jr. and Haidt [14] developed the Advanced Airport Safety System, aimed at increasing safety at busy, unregulated airports. This joint effort by NASA and the Federal Aviation Administration (FAA) equipped pilots with vital air traffic and weather data, enhancing the traditional methods of visual flight [14]. Similarly, in 2002, Bove and Andersen [1] investigated the effectiveness of a new Cockpit Advisory Take-Off Monitoring System (ATOMS). Designed to aid pilots in making critical take-off decisions, particularly in assessing acceleration and deceleration, this system aimed to improve safety during the crucial take-off stage of a flight [1]. In the development of advanced pilot advisory systems, the Cockpit Assistant System (CASSY) and the Crew Assistant Military Aircraft (CAMA) [13] represent significant milestones in the integration of decision support systems in aviation. These systems were designed to enhance situation awareness and reduce pilot workload through cognitive system engineering. Hereby, they marked a significant shift from traditional cockpit systems, focusing on complementing human pilot capabilities rather than just automating tasks [13].

While these systems are certainly important and beneficial, they have limitations in terms of adaptability and scope, which necessitate advancements for more comprehensive support in dynamic flight operations. The integration of AI, particularly in decision support systems, addresses these limitations. Hereby, a significant source to consider is the European Union Aviation Safety Agency's (EASA) Artificial Intelligence Roadmap 2.0 [7], which is a comprehensive document that emphasizes a human-centric approach to the integration of AI in aviation. This updated roadmap, which builds upon the initial version released in 2020, focuses on several key areas, including safety, security, AI assurance, ethical considerations and lastly human factors in the aviation industry, providing guidelines for the safe and effective implementation of AI in aviation. Hereby, the roadmap covers aspects such as AI explainability, which involves ensuring that human end users receive understandable, reliable, and relevant information regarding how an machine learning application produces its results. The concept of Human-Artificial Intelligence Teaming (HAT) is further elaborated within this context, emphasizing the importance of ensuring adequate cooperation or collaboration between human end users and AI-based systems to achieve specific goals [7].

3   Intelligent Pilot Advisory System

The German Aerospace Center (DLR) is currently developing the IPAS as a research platform to explore and demonstrate the implementation of AI-based assistance systems in the flight deck of commercial aircraft. It was first introduced in [18] and its purpose is to address several research topics, such as the practical implementation of user-centered explainability of AI-generated information, as required by the EASA in the AI Roadmap 2.0 [7], or the development of appropriate AI models. Therefore, the development of the IPAS is divided into two research areas, the development and research of the AI Crew Interaction System (AICIS) and the development and research of the AI Core Module (AICOM) [2,3]. Figure 1 further illustrates the systems concept. Large parts of the IPAS are developed according to an iterative development model called "Human System Exploration" [9] to explore, test and extend new ideas, user requirements and system designs in each iteration.

The IPAS was initially designed to assist flight crews by processing and providing data, as well as generating options and recommendations for decision making, both in emergency situations and during normal operations. To date, the focus has been on developing use cases for abnormal or emergency situations. One particular area of application examined was support in the selection of alternate airports in such a situation. Hereby, several prototypes have been developed and tested with commercial pilots in flight simulator studies. In these studies, pilots were confronted with a series of emergency situations, handling in-flight technical problems and resolving these using the IPAS to decide on suitable alternate airport options. In those scenarios the IPAS evaluates multiple criteria like weather conditions, wind, runway specifications, and assistance systems to suggest the best options, each with a calculated rating. Hereby, the IPAS not only offers recommendations but also presents all necessary information to pilots, allowing them to understand and potentially validate the system's decisions.

4   IPAS for Normal Operation

As discussed in the previous section the IPAS's prior development has been primarily focused on emergency scenarios, specifically aiding in identifying suitable alternative airports for emergency landings. However, since emergencies are rare in actual flight operations, pilots might lack practical experience interacting with the system, potentially leading to a lack of calibrating their trust regarding IPAS's capabilities. To address this, the plan is to extend the IPAS's application to non-emergency operation as well.

The benefits of implementing the IPAS in normal aviation operations becomes increasingly evident when considering the advancements in AI and the growing availability of aviation data. AI has reached a level of commercial viability, making it a potent tool for developing new data and AI-driven assistance systems in aviation. With platforms like Flightradar24[1], Flight Aware[2], and Meteoblue[3] providing extensive and detailed flight and weather data, the opportunity to utilize this wealth of information is close at hand. Such data, when integrated into systems like the IPAS, could significantly enhance situational awareness and decision-making processes for pilots. By leveraging AI algorithms that can analyze and interpret vast amounts of data in real-time, the IPAS could provide pilots with precise, actionable insights during all phases of

---

[1] https://www.flightradar24.com/ - Last accessed: 2024/01/11.

[2] https://flightaware.com/ - Last accessed: 2024/01/11.

[3] https://www.meteoblue.com/ - Last accessed: 2024/01/11.

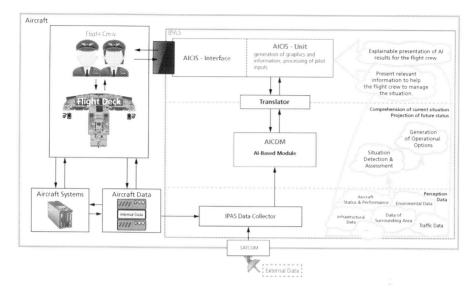

Fig. 1. The conceptual system model of the IPAS, first shown in [18]. The system model illustrates the system components and their tasks, as well as the flow of information. Thereby, the IPAS Data Collector collects data from the aircraft systems and the environment, which is analyzed by the AICOM. The AICIS serves as the interface between the crew and the AI system, for example, by processing input from the crew and displaying options and recommendations generated by the AI.

flight. This could not only improve flight safety and efficiency but also ensure that the operations are conducted with the most current and comprehensive information available. The result would be a more informed, responsive, and forward-thinking approach to normal aviation operations. Therefore, integrating the IPAS into routine operations could generally extend its benefits beyond emergency situations.

Furthermore, multiple studies highlight the important role of familiarity and experience with automation systems, to accurately evaluate it. Muir [12] highlighted the importance of competence of automation, with any sign of incompetence reducing trust. Hereby, regular use of the IPAS is crucial for pilots to accurately evaluate its recommendations, avoiding "automation bias" - a tendency to over-rely on or distrust automation due to unfamiliarity, which has been the subject of much research in the last decade and was summarized by Lee and See in "Trust in Automation: Designing for Appropriate Reliance" [11]. Frequent utilization of the IPAS in non-emergency scenarios could empowers pilots to calibrate their trust, therefore matching the systems capabilities.

It is worth noting that the commercial benefits of implementing IPAS in normal operations can be as significant as the technical and psychological benefits. The support provided by an IPAS, beyond just emergency situations, would make it an attractive investment for airlines. From a commercial standpoint, it is natural that airlines are continually seeking ways to optimize operations, reduce costs, and enhance the overall safety of their flights. The IPAS, with its capabilities to utilize AI and vast data resources, fits perfectly into this. By assisting in various flight processes it could make procedures more efficient. This efficiency translates into tangible cost savings for airlines, such as reduced fuel consumption, improved time management, and minimized delays.

5   Methodology

To explore new opportunities and gain diverse ideas a one-day workshop was held. Hereby, the workshops focus was to generate many ideas and then to group and categorize them in order to develop many different but also suitable functionalities for the IPAS in normal flight operations. The workshop brought together a diverse group of seven experts, three of whom were pilots. One of the pilots has a military background and previously operated military cargo planes for short and medium-haul flights. Presently, he is involved in flying commercial cargo operations covering the same distances. The second pilot focuses on long-haul cargo flights, and the third pilot is dedicated to civil aviation, particularly for short and medium-haul journeys. The other workshop participants consisted of data science and HAT researchers. This multi-disciplinary group has been selected to promote a broad understanding and to encourage innovative brainstorming.

The methodological approach combined several creative and analytical techniques that are mentioned in [17]. Initially, the 6-3-5 ideation method was used to generate a wide array of ideas. This was followed by mind mapping to visually organize and group these ideas, encouraging discussions around their interconnections. The next phase involved formulating 'How-Might-We' questions, focusing on practical applications and implications of the ideas. Lastly, the design studio method was employed, facilitating rapid prototyping and iterative feedback, thus refining the ideas further. The categorization and analysis of the ideas that followed the initial brainstorming was intended to give opportunity for identifying common trends. This systematic approach was instrumental in distilling the ideas into actionable insights and potential functionalities for the pilot advisory system.

6   Workshop Findings and Further Development

The conducted workshop on the development of an IPAS for normal operation generated many interesting ideas, which were discussed, expanded and categorized. In the following, the ideas are presented first, then a structure of the IPAS is outlined in which the ideas are incorporated in and finally a first design concept is discussed.

6.1   Identified Functionalities

The main idea that emerged during the workshop was the concept of a Mission Monitoring and Advisory Function (MMAF) as a central feature. Hereby, the

IPAS is imagined not just as a tool, but as an integral assistant throughout the flight, constantly informing pilots of any changes in conditions and events that might impact the flight plan or be of relevance to them.

The central functionality of the MMAF is conceptualized to assess a wide array of factors influencing flight trajectory, efficiency and safety. With this idea the IPAS is designed to provide real-time updates on aspects like NOTAMS, traffic and weather conditions, that might influence a planned flight. Thereby, the IPAS firstly assumes the role of an information source and secondly uses the information displayed to make recommendations on how to proceed or whether the route should be adjusted. This continuous monitoring ensures that pilots are always informed of the latest developments, allowing for more informed decision-making.

The brainstorming session also highlighted the IPAS's potential in the pre-flight briefing process. An idea was proposed where it could actively monitor the briefings, filter out the most pertinent information, and provide pilots with concise summaries. This integration could ensure that the pilots can align their mental model with the latest data and the data basis of the IPAS.

As the flight progresses into more critical phases like takeoff and landing, suggestions were made about the system providing guidance on operational limitations and technical constraints. Furthermore, an idea was presented that predictive analytics could enable the IPAS to forecast probable approach routes and track miles, further aiding with decision-making and ensuring a safer and more efficient approach and landing.

During the cruise phase, the workshop participants envisioned the IPAS, in addition to the functionality of the MMAF, to continuously update pilots with alternative airports, preparing them for any contingencies. The system could also offer recommendations for optimizing flight paths and speed, adhering to the 4D trajectory concept for efficient operations [8], thereby contributing to environmental sustainability through reduced fuel consumption.

Lastly, the IPAS was imagined to optimize pilot communication. By assisting in communication between aircraft, with airline operations centers and air traffic control, the system could streamline information exchange.

6.2   IPAS Structure

With all those brainstormed multifaceted functionalities the IPAS necessitates a well-organized structure to manage its diverse functions effectively. At the conceptual stage, three distinct operational modes were identified to encapsulate the extend of its functionalities: the Briefing Mode, the Mission Support Mode, and the Option Support Mode (see Fig. 2), which can further branch into various sub-modes tailored to the current flight stage or specific emergency scenario [18].

The Briefing Mode serves a foundational role, incorporating the IPAS into pre-flight briefings. This mode includes the briefing functionality that was brainstormed in the workshop and is designed to foster a better understanding of the system's information basis.

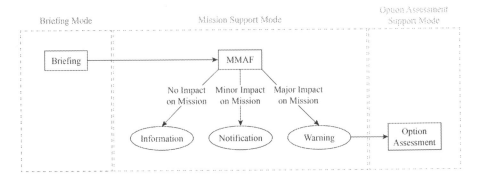

Fig. 2. Structure of the IPAS's Modes and Indications of Events in the Mission Support Mode. (Based on [4])

Transitioning from this preparatory phase, the Mission Support mode and therefore the introduced MMAF come into play during normal flight operation. This not only aids in proactive planning but also enables real-time, informed decision-making, with the IPAS classifying events based on their impact and suggesting appropriate responses for minor disruptions and giving alternate options if an event with major impact on the mission were to occur [4].

If this happens, the IPAS enables the pilots to switch to the Option Assessment Support mode. It is in this mode that its capacity to analyze emergent situations rapidly and present viable alternatives becomes indispensable, particularly in scenarios requiring significant deviations from the planned flight path [4].

The interplay between these modes - starting from the initial alignment in the Briefing Mode, through the continuous support in the Mission Support mode, to the decisive guidance in the Option Assessment Support mode - should ensure that pilots receive consistent, relevant guidance throughout the flight, enabling them to adapt seamlessly to both routine and emergency scenarios.

6.3   Design Concept

During the design studio, inspired by the concepts developed for the IPAS in normal oparation, several quick, low-fidelity paper prototype sketches were created with a particular focus on the design of the MMAF, which can be seen in Fig. 3. The presentation was envisioned as a timeline, where different kinds of information, notifications, and warnings are displayed using icons. Following the structure envisioned in the previous section, the events with no impact on the mission are simply displayed to ensure that pilots receive all necessary details clearly, thereby likely improving situational awareness. In the case of a notification, which occurs in instances of an event that might have a minor impact the system provides information about the event and offers advice on whether and how to respond. In the event of a warning, it is displayed prominently, and a

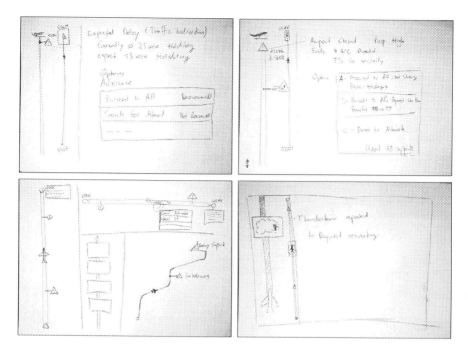

Fig. 3. Sketches from the 'Design Studio' method of the workshop depicting ideas for the MMAF and the IPAS Front Page in Normal Operation.

button is included to facilitate a mode switch to the Option Assessment Support mode.

Furthermore, the user interface of the IPAS for normal operation should be designed for maximum clarity and ease of use. It should feature large, easily readable fonts and high-contrast color schemes to ensure readability under various conditions, catering to the dynamic environment of a cockpit. Interactive elements are a core aspect of this design. By tapping or clicking on an icon, pilots can navigation through different layers of information. This interactive approach should allow pilots to access more data as needed, without overwhelming the primary display. Moreover, the system should be engineered to prioritize information based on its urgency and relevance. Critical warnings should be prominent, ensuring immediate attention, while less urgent notifications should be displayed less prominently. This hierarchy of information is supposed to help pilots to focus on the most pressing issues first, improving their decision-making process in critical situations. Ergonomics and accessibility should also be key considerations in the design of the MMAF. The placement and physical design of the system should be optimized for ease of access and visibility, ensuring that it is within easy reach and view of the pilot without causing strain. The focus on ergonomic design should take into account the typical cockpit environment, ensuring that the system is both functional and comfortable for the pilot to use over extended periods.

Fig. 4. First-Stage Prototype of the IPAS in Normal Operation.

In further advancing the design of the IPAS for normal operation, a first-stage prototype has been developed afterwards, embodying the ideas and concepts laid out in the workshop, as can be seen in Fig. 4. This prototype serves as a tangible representation of our vision, bridging the gap between theoretical design and practical application. The prototype demonstrates the timeline-based presentation of information, where icons are used to denote different types of notifications and warnings. It incorporates the interactive user interface elements, allowing pilots to delve deeper into specific notifications with simple taps or swipes. The prioritization of information is considered, with critical warnings prominently displayed and less urgent notifications placed in a more subtle manner. This prototype serves not only as a proof of concept but also as a platform for ongoing refinement. It allows for testing and feedback, which is invaluable in fine-tuning the design to better meet the needs and expectations of pilots. The iterative process of development, testing, and enhancement is key to achieving a final design that is both intuitive and effective in enhancing pilot situational awareness and decision-making in flight operations.

7   Conclusion and Future Research

The exploration of the IPAS in the context of normal flight operations has revealed a lot of potential. By integrating AI and leveraging vast data resources, the IPAS could enhance the pilots decision making processes and their information basis. The regular use of this system in non-emergency scenarios also has the potential to calibrate pilot trust and create familiarity with the system.

Based on this identified potential that the IPAS offers, a workshop was organized with seven experts, including three pilots, which resulted in many potential functionalities for normal flight operations. Hereby, the key functionality which was identified is a MMAF which offers information and guidance in all flight stages. The MMAF is envisioned to ensure continuous monitoring and informing of pilots about changes in conditions and events that might impact the flight plan, e.g. regarding NOTAMS, traffic, and weather conditions. Thereby it should also utilize predictive analytics, to forecast possible events. Furthermore, the MMAF functionality is extended by a pre-flight briefing integration function and includes functions for operational guidance, the integration of the 4D trajectory concept for more efficiency and the possibility to enhance communication. Based on those ideas and the first design concepts developed during the workshop, an early prototype was developed. This prototype gives an insight into a possible design of the MMAF functionality and provides the basis for initial feedback, evaluations and ongoing refinement.

Future research endeavors surrounding the IPAS should encompass a comprehensive spectrum of areas to ensure its effectiveness and integration in aviation operations. A critical aspect is the continuation of its development and refinement through extended pilot testing. This involves gathering feedback on the system's usability, effectiveness, and human-AI teaming aspects to ensure that the IPAS meets the practical needs of pilots in real-world scenarios. Hereby, it is also relevant to identify which information, notifications and warnings are relevant to pilots and need to be integrated into the system. Additionally, there is a need to explore the integration of the IPAS with current cockpit systems and technologies. This research should aim to establish seamless operational compatibility while preventing any redundancy or conflicts, thereby ensuring that the IPAS complements and enhances the existing environment.

Investigating the possibilities of customization and adaptability of the IPAS also represents an interesting field of research. Hereby, it could be investigated whether the IPAS should be tailored to various types of flights like long- and short haul flights and if it should be adjustable according to different pilot preferences. This adaptability could be a step forward to support a widespread applicability and acceptance. Moreover, given the data-intensive nature of the IPAS, future studies must rigorously address data security and privacy concerns. Ensuring that the system is not just effective but also safe and dependable in handling sensitive information is crucial.

Another vital area of research is the impact of regular interaction with the IPAS on pilot skills and training. It is important to understand how continual use of this system affects pilots' flying skills and decision-making capabilities, ensuring that the system supports rather than supplants these critical competencies. Lastly, the economic and environmental implications of the IPAS are aspects that warrant thorough investigation. Hereby, analyzing its potential to offer economic benefits to airlines, for instance in terms of fuel efficiency and reduced emissions, is essential. This analysis will play a crucial role in justifying the investment in the IPAS from both a commercial and environmental standpoint.

In summary, the brainstormed ideas for the IPAS portray it as a dynamic, integrated system focused on enhancing flight safety and efficiency through comprehensive mission health monitoring. By interweaving communication enhancement, briefing integration, and real-time advisory during all flight stages, an IPAS could become a transformative tool in the aviation industry and could mark a significant step forward in pilot assistance technology, but this necessitates further research.

Acknowledgments. We would like to show our gratitude to the workshop participants for sharing their knowledge and experience with us during the course of this research. Furthermore, we would like to thank our reviewers for their insights.

References

1. Bove, T., Andersen, H.B.: The effect of an advisory system on pilots' go/no-go decision during take-off. Reliabil. Eng. Syst. Saf. **75**(2), 179–191 (2002). https://doi.org/10.1016/S0951-8320(01)00093-X
2. Djartov, B., Mostaghim, S.: Multi-objective multiplexer decision making benchmark problem. In: Proceedings of the Companion Conference on Genetic and Evolutionary Computation, GECCO 2023 Companion, pp. 1676–1683. Association for Computing Machinery, New York (2023). https://doi.org/10.1145/3583133.3596360
3. Djartov, B., Mostaghim, S., Papenfuß, A., Wies, M.: Description and first evaluation of an approach for a pilot decision support system based on multi-attribute decision making. In: 2022 IEEE Symposium Series on Computational Intelligence (SSCI), pp. 141–147. IEEE (2022). https://doi.org/10.1109/SSCI51031.2022.10022076
4. Djartov, B., Würfel, J.: Navigating Decisions in the Cockpit - The Intelligent Pilot Advisory System. Lecture Notes in Computer Science (LNCS). Springer, Heidelberg (2024)
5. Endsley, M.R.: Supporting situation awareness in aviation systems. In: 1997 IEEE International Conference on Systems, Man, and Cybernetics. Computational Cybernetics and Simulation, vol. 5, pp. 4177–4181 (1997). https://doi.org/10.1109/ICSMC.1997.637352
6. Endsley, M.R.: Situation awareness in aviation systems. Handb. Aviat. Human Fact. **11**, 257–276 (1999)
7. European Union Aviation Safety Agency: Artificial intelligence roadmap 2.0: Human-centric approach to AI in aviation (2023). https://www.easa.europa.eu/en/document-library/general-publications/easa-artificial-intelligence-roadmap-20. Accessed 13 Dec 2023

8. Federal Aviation Administration (FAA): Trajectory Based Operations (TBO) (2022). https://www.faa.gov/air_traffic/technology/tbo. Accessed12 Jan 2023

9. Flemisch, F.O., et al.: Human systems exploration for ideation and innovation in potentially disruptive defense and security systems. In: Adlakha-Hutcheon, G., Masys, A. (eds.) Disruption, Ideation and Innovation for Defence and Security, pp. 79–117. Springer, Cham (2022). https://doi.org/10.1007/978-3-031-06636-8_5

10. Kulida, E., Lebedev, V.: About the use of artificial intelligence methods in aviation. In: 2020 13th International Conference "Management of large-scale system development" (MLSD), pp. 1–5 (2020). https://doi.org/10.1109/MLSD49919.2020.9247822

11. Lee, J.D., See, K.A.: Trust in automation: designing for appropriate reliance. Hum. Factors **46**(1), 50–80 (2004)

12. Muir, B.M., Moray, N.: Trust in automation. Part ii. Experimental studies of trust and human intervention in a process control simulation. Ergonomics **39**(3), 429–460 (1996)

13. Onken, R.: The cognitive cockpit assistant systems cassy/cama. SAE Technical Paper 1999-01-5537, SAE International (1999). https://doi.org/10.4271/1999-01-5537

14. Parks Jr., J., Haidt, J.: Automated pilot advisory system. Technical Memorandum NASA-TM-73296, NASA Wallops Flight Center, Wallops Island, VA, United States (1981). Accession number: 82N15027

15. Saraf, A.P., Chan, K.Y., Popish, M., Browder, J.H., Schade, J.: Explainable artificial intelligence for aviation safety applications. In: AIAA Aviation 2020 Forum, p. 2881 (2020)

16. Shmelova, T., Sterenharz, A., Dolgikh, S.: Artificial intelligence in aviation industries: methodologies, education, applications, and opportunities. In: Handbook of Research on Artificial Intelligence Applications in the Aviation and Aerospace Industries, pp. 1–35. IGI Global (2020)

17. Steimle, T., Wallach, D.: Collaborative UX Design: Lean UX und Design Thinking: Teambasierte Entwicklung menschzentrierter Produkte. dpunkt. verlag, Heidelberg, Germany (2022)

18. Würfel, J., Djartov, B., Papenfuß, A., Wies, M.: Intelligent pilot advisory system: the journey from ideation to an early system design of an AI-based decision support system for airline flight decks. In: AHFE (2023). https://elib.dlr.de/193112/

Predicting Runway Configurations at Airports Through Soft Voting Ensemble Learning

Xinglong Wang and Linning Liu[✉]

Key Laboratory of Internet of Aircrafts, Civil Aviation University of China,
Tianjin 300300 , China
357812315@qq.com

Abstract. The runway is a crucial area for airport operations, and air traffic controllers determine the current runway configuration by selecting a subset of available runways and their directions. As the number of runways at an airport increases, the complexity of choosing an appropriate runway configuration for the current weather conditions and traffic volume also increases. Establishing a runway configuration assistance decision-making system suitable for multi-runway airports is of significant practical importance. This paper utilizes actual historical data from Hartsfield-Jackson Atlanta International Airport, which has five runways. By processing meteorological data, runway configurations, and relevant operational data, the paper predicts runway configurations for twelve-time points in the next six hours, with predictions made every hour. A comparative analysis is conducted on the prediction results using three basic models: XGBoost, Random Forest, and CatBoost. Based on the results, the better model is selected and the optimal combination of weights is found for it to build the soft voter model. The research focuses on providing timely and accurate assistance decision-making recommendations for runway configurations based on meteorological and historical operational data. The aim is to enhance runway operational capacity, improve airport operational efficiency, and provide theoretical references for the development of operations at airports with multiple runways.

Keywords: Runway Configuration · Soft Voting · Machine Learning

1 Introduction

In the first two years following the end of the pandemic, the demand for air travel gradually recovered. According to the statistics from "China Civil Aviation Major Production Indicators in October 2023," the industry's total transport ton-kilometers reached 110.1 billion, a 158.6% increase compared to the same month of the previous year. The total passenger traffic turnover was 946.9 billion passenger-kilometers, showing a growth of 293.1% compared to the same month of the previous year [1]. With an increase in passenger travel and flight volume, airports face higher operational pressures, leading to inevitable flight delays. To alleviate congestion, there are two main approaches: constructing new airport facilities to increase capacity and implementing air traffic management measures to enhance the utilization of existing runway resources.

However, building new runways, taxiways, or terminals requires significant capital investment and rigorous feasibility studies, consuming time and resources. In contrast, effectively planning and predicting runway configurations to improve the utilization of existing runways is a timely and efficient solution to enhance airport operational efficiency.

Airport operational analysis primarily involves two key aspects: airport acceptance rate (AAR) and runway configurations. AAR refers to the number of flights that an airport can effectively accept and handle within a specific time, reflecting the airport's processing capacity. Runway configurations involve air traffic controllers selecting suitable runways and directions from the available set, forming effective runway combinations for inbounding and departing flights. These factors are influenced by various elements, including weather conditions, flight schedules, and air traffic flow. Accurate analysis and prediction are crucial for achieving efficient airport operations, as inaccurate predictions can lead to airborne and ground delays, as well as excessive waste of airport resources.

In the studies of airport acceptance rate by domestic and international experts, researchers have used different methods and data for model training and prediction. Proven et al. [2] and Cox and Kochenderfer et al. [3] used combined decision trees and Bayesian networks, respectively, to construct a prediction model to predict the AAR for the next 1–12 h using the Terminal Airport Forecasts (TAFs), the Local Aviation Model Outputs Statistical Program (LAMP) weather forecasts, and the AAR data of the previous hour to predict the AAR for the next 1–12 h. Wang et al. [4, 5] utilized more accurate multi-source weather forecast data for prediction to improve the accuracy of prediction. Meanwhile, some scholars analyze the factors affecting AAR in depth. Chung and Murphy [6] estimated AAR values using linear regression and other methods and studied several international airports, and found that runway configuration, weather data input by controllers, and adjustments to changes in AAR are key factors in AAR prediction, with the effect of wind being particularly significant. DeLaura et al. [7], by analyzing weather data, found that several wind-related metrics significantly affect AAR. In a study of New York metropolitan airports, a literature [8] used Gaussian process regression to predict AAR for three airports at the same time, which is a useful exploration to improve the accuracy of prediction.

In the study of runway operational configuration, scholars analyze the factors related to runway operational configuration and add the moment and various weather data to make predictions using machine learning or statistical models. Ramanujam et al. [9] predicted runway configurations by using a discrete choice model, and Houston et al. [10] predicted runway configurations by using logistic regression with the addition of airport operational information data, which was based on weather observation data. The above used weather observation data rather than weather forecast data, which lacked realism. Tien et al. [11, 12] proposed a method to quantify the uncertainty in airport capacity forecasts by using ensemble weather products and applied it to 35 airports for validation to improve the generalization of the airport capacity forecasting model, which efficiently captured the range of future airport arrival capacity. Wang Yuan et al. [13] proposed a deep learning-based data-driven framework for simultaneous prediction of airport runway configurations and airport receipts by employing a combined gridded weather forecast and considering operational interdependencies in operational parameter learning.

Despite these efforts, current research has some limitations: The input weather data mostly consists of real-time observational data rather than forecast data, lacking authenticity for model learning. And most studies focus on individual airports, lacking a universal model applicable to various airports.

Therefore, this study proposes a soft-voting model based on historical operational data and historical weather forecast data to help decision makers make optimal runway allocation decisions under different conditions by changing the model weights to accommodate different airport data. Through a comparison of XGBoost, Random Forest, and CatBoost models on two types of datasets, the superior XGBoost model and Random Forest model are weighted and integrated to form the Soft Voting model. By capturing the correlation between features and runway configurations, accurate predictions of runway configurations are made to assist decision-makers in improving airport operational efficiency.

2   Airport and Data Analysis

2.1   Airport Overview

Hartsfield-Jackson Atlanta International Airport (ICAO: KATL), abbreviated as "Atlanta Airport", is a 4F-level international airport and aviation hub, ranking as the world's busiest airport with over a billion passengers transported, holding the top global ranking in passenger throughput for 18 consecutive years [14]. The visual representation of the airport's layout is illustrated in Fig. 1.

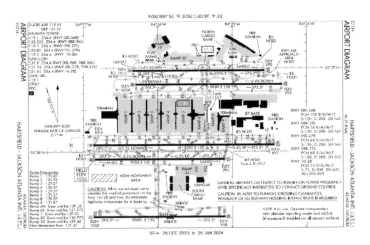

Fig. 1. Hartsfield-Jackson Atlanta International Airport layout

Atlanta Airport (KATL) has five parallel runways oriented in the north-south direction, namely 8L/26R, 8R/26L, 9L/27R, 9R/27L and 10/28. This parallel arrangement aims to efficiently meet the high-intensity flight operation demands of the airport, ensuring safe and efficient aircraft movements in different flight directions and weather conditions. The specific details of the runways are provided in Table 1.

Table 1. Hartsfield-Jackson Atlanta International Airport runway informations

Runway Designation	Length (meters)	Width (meters)	Surface Material
8L/26R	2743	46	Concrete/Asphalt
8R/26L	3048	46	Concrete/Asphalt
9L/27R	3776	46	Concrete/Asphalt
9R/27L	2743	46	Concrete/Asphalt
10/28	2743	46	Concrete/Asphalt

The magnetic heading divided by 10, rounded to the nearest integer and filled with two digits, serves as the runway code, ranging between 01 and 36. Each physical runway has two runway codes, with a difference of 18 representing the direction rotated 180°, such as 8 and 26. Parallel runways sharing the same runway code at the same airport generally use L (Left) and R (Right) suffixes to distinguish runways, for example, 8L/26R and 8R/26L. If there are three parallel runways sharing the same runway code, a C (Center) suffix is added for distinction. If there are more runways, unique code numbering is applied based on the actual situation of different airports.

Hartsfield-Jackson Atlanta International Airport (KATL) possesses five runways, allowing for the formation of various runway configurations for aircraft inbounds and outbounds. Based on on-site investigations, historical data analysis, and discussions with relevant experts and scholars, Table 2 lists the 25 primary runway configurations commonly used by the airport throughout the year.

Table 2. Hartsfield-Jackson Atlanta International Airport runway configurations

Runway Configuration	Inbound Runways	Outbound Runways
katl:D_26L_27R_A_26R_27L_28	26L, 27R	26R, 27L, 28
katl:D_8R_9L_A_10_8L_9R	8R, 9L	10, 8L, 9R
katl:D_26L_27R_28_A_26R_27L_28	26L, 27R, 28	26R, 27L, 28
katl:D_26L_27R_A_26L_27L_28	26L, 27R	26L, 27L, 28
katl:D_8R_9R_A_10_8L_9R	8R, 9R	10, 8L, 9R
katl:D_26L_28_A_26L_28	26L, 28	26L, 28
katl:D_26R_28_A_26R_28	26R, 28	26R, 28
katl:D_26L_27R_A_26R_27L	26L, 27R	26R, 27L

(*continued*)

Table 2. (*continued*)

Runway Configuration	Inbound Runways	Outbound Runways
katl:D_26L_27L_A_26R_27L_28	26L, 27L	26R, 27L, 28
katl:D_26L_27R_A_26L_27R_28	26L, 27R	26L, 27R, 28
katl:D_26L_27R_A_26R_27R_28	26L, 27R	26R, 27R, 28
katl:D_26R_27R_A_26R_27L_28	26R, 27R	26R, 27L, 28
katl:D_26L_27R_A_27L_28	26L, 27R	27L, 28
katl:D_10_8R_A_10_8R	10, 8R	10, 8R
katl:D_8R_9L_A_8L_9R	8R, 9L	8L, 9R
katl:D_26L_28_A_26R_28	26L, 28	26R, 28
katl:D_26L_28_A_26R_27L_28	26L, 28	26R, 27L, 28
katl:D_8R_9L_A_10_8R_9R	8R, 9L	10, 8R, 9R
katl:D_10_8R_9L_A_10_8L_9R	10, 8R, 9L	10, 8L, 9R
katl:D_26L_27R_A_26R_28	26L, 27R	26R, 28
katl:D_10_8L_A_10_8L	10, 8L	10, 8L
katl:D_8R_9L_A_10_9R	8R, 9L	10, 9R
katl:D_8L_9L_A_10_8L_9R	8L, 9L	10, 8L, 9R
katl:D_8R_9L_A_8R_9L	8R, 9L	8R, 9L
katl:D_26L_27R_A_26L_27R	26L, 27R	26L, 27R
katl:other	other	

2.2 Research Data and Processing Flow

In the process of ensuring efficient airport operations and safe aircraft control, the selection of runway configurations has become a crucial decision. This key decision requires controllers to consider multiple important factors comprehensively, to choose the runway configuration that best suits the specific flight demands during a particular time period. This section will delve into the two major data blocks used in the study: meteorological data and historical airport operation data, in order to gain an in-depth understanding of this complex decision-making process.

1. Airport Meteorology:

Weather information is crucial for aircraft flight and airport operations. METAR (Meteorological Aerodrome Report), TAF (Terminal Aerodrome Forecast), and LAMP (Localized Aviation MOS Program) are the primary sources of aviation weather information currently used. METAR provides routine weather reports for airports at fixed intervals (usually hourly or half-hourly), offering regular reports on current weather conditions. TAF is an airport forecast containing a brief description of expected weather conditions at the airport for a specific period and is released at specific times. For this study, LAMP historical weather forecast data is chosen to obtain more comprehensive historical weather prediction information. It includes forecasts for future weather conditions at a specific time point, providing more comprehensive weather information for model training and analysis compared to METAR and TAF.

2. Historical Airport Operation Data:

Historical operational data at airports encompass crucial information regarding terminals, airports, and runways. Among these, the runway, as one of the core facilities at the airport, directly indicates the operational efficiency of aviation traffic. This study aims to thoroughly investigate relevant operational data related to airport runways, with a specific focus on aircraft takeoff and landing situations, as well as the utilization of runway configurations.

Key inputs to this study include aircraft takeoff and landing data. Through detailed analysis of takeoff and landing data, insights can be gained into the operational busyness of the airport, characteristics during peak and off-peak periods, and the distribution of traffic at the airport. This is crucial for the model to understand the flow distribution of the airport, meet the demands during busy periods, and optimize strategies for resource adjustment accurately, providing substantial support for predicting future runway configuration choices and flight scheduling.

The usage of runway configuration is a key input and supervised label for this study. In-depth analysis of the runway configuration usage data allows an understanding of the relationship between runway configuration changes and corresponding meteorological conditions and airport traffic load. This is essential for the model to comprehend the runway configuration decisions of the airport under different operational environments, and it is crucial for enhancing the airport's adaptability to complex operational conditions. Accurate predictions can provide the airport with more flexible runway management strategies, ensuring efficient and safe operations under various operational conditions.

2.3 Data Preprocess

The selected time range for the data in this study covers the entire year of historical operational and meteorological forecast data for Hartsfield-Jackson Atlanta International Airport from X year November to X + 1 year October. The choice of prediction frequency and time span allows for a more comprehensive consideration of future operational conditions, enhancing the accuracy and practicality of the predictions. To achieve our prediction goals, we combine and preprocess data from multiple sources to form the initial training dataset.

The data processing details are outlined below, focusing on meteorological forecast data, aircraft traffic data and runway configuration data:

Meteorological Forecast Data. The LAMP data fields selected for this study include temperature, wind direction, wind speed, gust intensity, cloud base height, visibility, cloud types, lightning probability, precipitation status, and related information. In the identification and extraction of meteorological training data, it is crucial to select weather forecast information closest to the prediction time to provide the most accurate meteorological forecast data.

The following steps are involved in processing weather data:

Data Retrieval: Based on the prediction time, retrieve all weather forecast data before or at the same time as the prediction time. This ensures that the model considers only information known at the time of prediction, avoiding reliance on future weather data and ensuring the real-time accuracy of the predictions.

Time Point Matching: For the desired prediction time, obtain the most closely matching meteorological forecast detailed data from the retrieved data. Ensuring the selected data is closest to the target prediction time allows the model to use the most accurate and situationally relevant weather data for training and analysis.

Data Integration: Organize the selected meteorological data with a prediction frequency of once per hour, predicting twelve time points at a time, to ensure that the data is arranged in chronological order. This meets the temporal requirements of the training set, helping the model better understand the dynamic characteristics of meteorological changes and improving the accuracy of predictions for future time points.

Through these steps, it ensures that the LAMP data used for runway configuration selection is carefully filtered, matched, and refined. This provides the model with the most accurate and practical meteorological forecast information, enabling more precise predictions for airport runway configuration.

Aircraft Traffic Data. Airport aircraft traffic data is primarily extracted from actual inbound times and runways, as well as actual outbound times and runways. These detailed data are aggregated into the desired prediction time intervals (e.g., every fifteen minutes, every half-hour, every hour) to obtain the actual counts of inbound and outbound aircraft. Data fields include the number of inbound and outbound aircraft.

The following steps are involved in processing aircraft traffic data:

Data Retrieval: By parsing date and time, read the actual inbound and outbound aircraft data at the airport, transforming it into analyzable data frames. This step involves extracting key fields such as takeoff and landing times, runway information, and more.

Time Interval Segmentation and Counting: Using the date and time information in the data frame, segment and count the data at preset time intervals. Utilizing tools such as the resample function, segment the inbound and outbound aircraft traffic data into intervals such as every half-hour, every hour, etc., to obtain the number of aircraft for each time period.

Data Integration: Integrate the segmented and counted inbound and outbound aircraft numbers by time period to form a complete time series dataset.

Through these steps, we ensure the clarity and consistency of airport aircraft traffic data, providing the model with temporal information that enables more accurate predictions of aircraft traffic for future time periods.

Based on the actual analysis of the operational data for Hartsfield-Jackson Atlanta International Airport, the following Fig. 2. Schematic diagram of aircraft traffic average values over the day illustrates the average values at different times of the day throughout the year.

Runway Configuration Data. Airport runway configuration data primarily stems from the extraction and combination of inbound and outbound runway numbers. The runway usage is combined and counted based on descriptions like "D_10_8L_A_10_8L," where this string signifies that runway 10 and 8L are used for departing flights, and runway 10 and 8L are used for inbound flights. Data fields include the runway configuration at the predicted time and the runway configuration at the time point just before the prediction.

Generating Independent Configuration Data: Read the configuration file containing detailed information on airport runway configurations. Based on the analysis of experts,

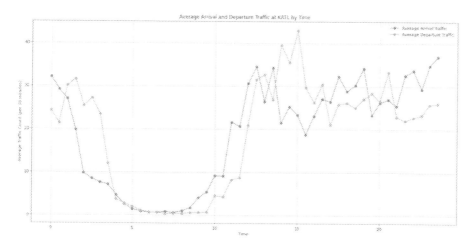

Fig. 2. Schematic diagram of aircraft traffic average values over the day

scholars, and actual operational data, establish common configuration data for Hartsfield-Jackson Atlanta International Airport (KATL) according to the frequency of occurrence, as outlined in Table 2. Store this information in the form of a unique value array to represent the independent configurations of the airport. All other runway configurations are grouped into the "katl:other" type. This helps simplify the configuration data, improve model prediction accuracy, and make it easier to understand and analyze.

Extracting Runway Configuration at the Predicted Time: By reading the actual label data for Hartsfield-Jackson Atlanta Airport, filter the labels based on timestamps to obtain the exact runway configuration used by the airport at the given time. This serves as supervised learning label data for the model.

Extracting Runway Configuration at the Previous Time Point: Through filtering and comparing the timestamps of runway configuration data, select the configuration information closest to the given timestamp as the runway configuration for the previous time period. This provides contextual information on runway configuration for each timestamp, enabling the model to incorporate temporal sequences.

Through these steps, we ensure the clarity and consistency of airport runway configuration data. The model is provided with information on runway configurations at the predicted time and the previous time point, enabling more accurate predictions of runway usage for future time periods.

Based on the actual analysis of operational data for Hartsfield-Jackson Atlanta International Airport, the following Fig. 3 illustrates the proportional representation of different configurations throughout the year.

In summary, the training set integrates diverse data sources from Hartsfield-Jackson Atlanta International Airport, including meteorological forecast data, aircraft traffic data, and runway operational configuration data. This comprehensive training set provides the model with comprehensive and temporally consistent inputs, laying the foundation for a more accurate prediction of future operations at Hartsfield-Jackson Atlanta International Airport. The format of the training set is illustrated in the following Table 3:

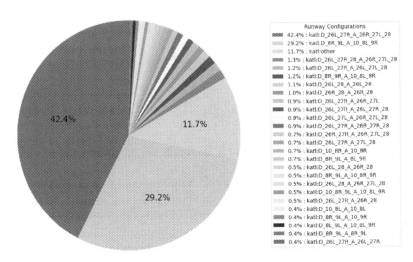

Fig. 3. Runway configuration utilization ratio

Table 3. Illustrative table of training set fields

Data	Field	Type	Min	Max
Runway Configuration	Current Runway Configuration	Categorical	26 types	
	Previous Runway Configuration	Categorical	26 types	
Time Difference	Time difference between prediction time and weather forecast time	Numerical	90	390
Weather	Temperature	Numerical	21	94
	Wind Direction	Numerical	0	36
	Wind Speed	Numerical	0	26
	Gust Speed	Numerical	0	38
	Cloud Base Height	Numerical	1	8
	Visibility	Numerical	1	7
	Cloud Type	Categorical	5 types	
	Lightning Probability	Categorical	4 types	
	Precipitation	Boolean	2 types	
Airport Traffic	Inbounding Aircraft Count	Numerical	0	58
	Departing Aircraft Count	Numerical	0	66

3   Ensemble Algorithm Construction

3.1   Principles of Machine Learning Algorithms

Random Forest. Random Forest is an ensemble learning method with decision trees as its basic unit, belonging to the ensemble learning branch of machine learning. The core idea of this algorithm is to construct multiple decision trees and integrate them to form a "forest" structure. The ensemble concept reflects the core concept of Bagging (Bootstrap Aggregating).

By randomly sampling subsets of training samples (with replacement) and constructing multiple decision trees based on these subsets, randomness of samples and features is introduced. In the splitting process at each node, only a portion of randomly selected features is considered. This randomness helps increase the diversity of the model, reduce the risk of overfitting, and form a more robust performance within the ensemble. In classification problems, the Random Forest algorithm selects the majority classification result as the final result, while in regression problems, it takes the average of multiple regression results as the final result.

XGBoost (eXtreme Gradient Boosting). XGBoost is an efficient gradient boosting tree algorithm, belonging to the boosting framework in ensemble learning. In the context of ensemble learning, the core idea of boosting trees is to construct multiple base learners and combine them into a powerful model. XGBoost draws inspiration from the essence of GBDT (Gradient Boosting Decision Trees) and adopts an additive model approach. It iteratively generates multiple base learners, with each iteration focusing on correcting the deviation between the results of the previous models and the actual values.

Specifically, XGBoost introduces gradient information, i.e., the gradient of the loss function, to guide the update of model parameters in each iteration. Simultaneously, by introducing a regularization term, XGBoost effectively controls the complexity of the model, preventing overfitting. This makes XGBoost excel in terms of performance, flexibility, and ease of use. The extremely gradient boosting strategy enables XGBoost to efficiently learn complex nonlinear relationships during the training process.

The objective function is represented as follows:

$$\tilde{y}_i^{(T)} = \sum_{j=1}^{T} f_j(x_i) = \sum_{j=1}^{T-1} f(x_i) + f_j^{(T)}(x_i) \tag{1}$$

where $\tilde{y}_i^{(T)}$ represents the predicted value for the i sample, (x_i) represents the feature values of the i sample, $\sum_{j=1}^{T-1} f(x_i)$ represents the cumulative value of the first $T-1$ trees, and $f_j^{(T)}(x_i)$ represents the prediction result of the T sample.

CatBoost. CatBoost is a gradient boosting decision tree (GBDT) framework based on oblivious trees. It is characterized by its few parameters, support for categorical variables, and high accuracy. The framework is designed to efficiently and effectively handle categorical features, as reflected in its name, which consists of "Categorical" and "Boosting." One of CatBoost's core advantages lies in its excellent handling of categorical features. Unlike other GBDT frameworks, CatBoost can directly handle categorical features during the training process without the need for cumbersome manual conversions. This feature provides significant convenience when modeling real-world datasets. Additionally, CatBoost reduces the risk of overfitting and enhances model stability by introducing oblivious trees.

Summary of Three Models. These three powerful machine learning models—Random Forest, XGBoost, and CatBoost—each demonstrate outstanding performance in different aspects. Random Forest cleverly reduces overfitting risks by constructing multiple randomly sampled decision trees, making it suitable for complex data structures and high-dimensional data. XGBoost is renowned for its efficiency and robustness in gradient boosting decision trees, enhancing generalization ability and training efficiency through regularization terms and parallel computation. CatBoost, designed specifically for handling categorical features, can automatically process category data without the need for one-hot encoding. It improves training speed through optimization strategies.

3.2   Voting Classifier Ensemble Algorithm Principles

Voting Classifier is an ensemble learning method that combines the predictions of multiple base models to make the final prediction through weighted averaging or probability averaging. Its uniqueness lies in the flexible balancing of predictions from each model. By cleverly assigning weights, considering the contribution of each model in detail, and merging opinions from multiple independent models, it significantly enhances overall predictive performance. It can reduce the risk of overfitting in individual models, improve the generalization ability of the overall model, and balance the weaknesses of each model. Voting Classifier is divided into two voting strategies: Soft Voting and Hard Voting.

Hard Voting is a simple voting strategy based on the principle of majority rule. In Hard Voting, each base model predicts the sample, and the class with the most occurrences is selected as the final prediction result. If a tie occurs, one of the classes is usually chosen as the result.

Soft Voting is a probability-based voting strategy. In Soft Voting, each base model provides probability or confidence estimates for each class. The models then average or weight these probabilities. The final prediction result is the class with the highest average probability (or weighted average probability).

The Voting Classifier allows better utilization of the strengths of each model, making model more flexible. It can provide more accurate and reliable predictions in complex and dynamic airport operational environments. The Fig. 4 illustrates the algorithmic principles of the Voting Classifier. Figure 5 shows schematic diagrams for both the Hard Voting Classifier and the Soft Voting Classifier.

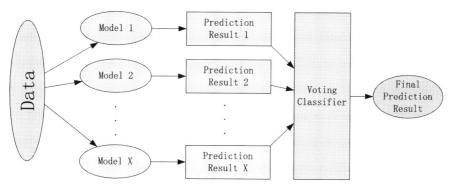

Fig. 4. Algorithmic principles of the voting classifier

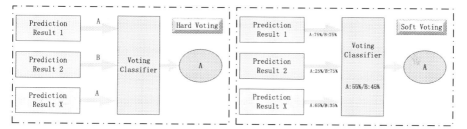

Fig. 5. Hard voting classifier and the soft voting classifier

4 Example Evaluation

To meet the complex requirements of predicting airport runway configurations, the dataset used in this study is divided into two categories based on input features: one includes meteorological forecast data, airport aircraft traffic data, and airport runway operation configuration data, while the other only includes meteorological forecast data and airport runway operation configuration data. These datasets undergo the same processing steps mentioned earlier and can be understood as grouped data, where each group covers the subsequent six hours starting from the respective time point, divided into half-hourly time intervals, totaling twelve time points. Each hourly prediction represents a one-hour time interval between groups. The data is stored and used in CSV format. The total data file contains 99,216 rows, with 79,117 rows in the training set and 19,776 rows in the validation set. Approximately 98,893 rows (about 99.7%) of the data do not contain missing values and are used for machine learning models.

The experimental environment for this study is as follows: the operating system is Windows 10, the processor is Intel® Core™ i5-8300HQ @2.30 GHz, the memory is 16GB, the development tool is PyCharm, and the programming language is Python.

In this study, we chose to perform a comparative analysis on the two types of datasets mentioned above. By comparing the performance results of the three models in predicting the runway configuration at Atlanta Airport, we determined the result weights for each model in the Soft Voting Classifier. We trained on both datasets, one containing

260   X. Wang and L. Liu

traffic data and the other without, and conducted a detailed comparison of two performance metrics: log loss and accuracy. Log loss is used to evaluate the accuracy of probability predictions in classification models, measuring the difference between the model's prediction and the actual labels for each sample. A smaller log loss value is better. Accuracy, on the other hand, represents the overall accuracy of the model in classification, indicating the proportion of correctly predicted samples out of the total samples. These metrics are important standards for assessing the accuracy and loss of model predictions. The results are shown in the Table 4:

Table 4. Model performance comparison on different data aspects

Model/Result	No Traffic Data		With Traffic Data	
	Log Loss	Accuracy	Log Loss	Accuracy
CatBoost	0.61	0.76	0.65	0.81
Random Forest	0.46	0.89	0.23	0.91
Xgboost	0.34	0.90	0.15	0.96

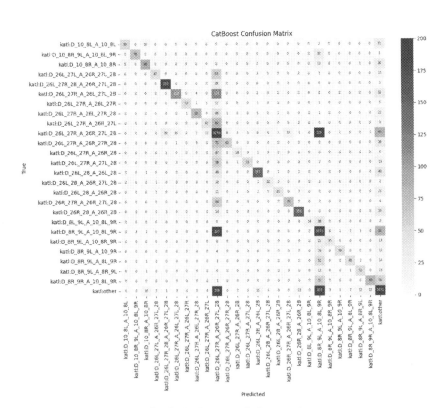

Fig. 6. CatBoost confusion matrix

As shown in the table above, when comparing two different datasets, the dataset without traffic data focuses on predicting based on meteorological and runway configuration historical information. On the other hand, the dataset with traffic data takes into account the actual traffic situation, including information about inbounding and departing flights. The predictive performance of the dataset containing traffic data is superior to that without traffic data. This is primarily attributed to the models incorporating actual traffic information, allowing them to have a more comprehensive understanding of the airport's operational environment.

The following figure illustrates the performance confusion matrices of the three different models on the training set that includes traffic data. The actual runway configurations are shown along the Y-axis, while the model-based predictions are shown along the X-axis. The diagonal of the matrix reflects accurate predictions, and the off-diagonal squares indicate errors between model predictions and actual values. The color in each square corresponds to the numerical value, with darker colors indicating larger values, reflecting a higher number of samples.

The following three figures represent the performance confusion matrices for each of the three models:

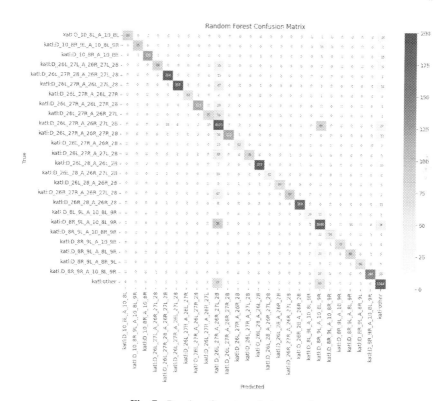

Fig. 7. Random forest confusion matrix

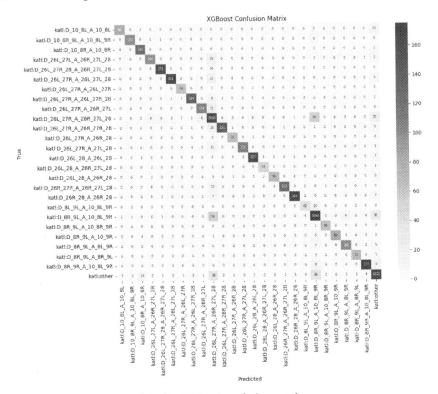

Fig. 8. XGBoost confusion matrix

As shown in the above figures, theXGBoost model and the Random Forest model generally perform well in accurately identifying the correct runway configurations compared to CatBoost in most scenarios.

The Voting Classifier is an ensemble learning method that combines the predictions of multiple base models using a weighted average or probability average to make the final prediction. Its uniqueness lies in the flexible balancing of predictions from each model, considering not only the majority decisions of the models but also the confidence levels of each model. By cleverly assigning weights, the Voting Classifier more finely considers the contribution of each model, combining the opinions of multiple independent models, significantly improving overall predictive performance. Its advantage lies in reducing the risk of overfitting from a single model and enhancing the generalization ability of the overall model. In practical applications, the Voting Classifier excels in handling complex tasks and multiple-source data, becoming an important technique in the field of ensemble learning (Figs. 6, 7 and 8).

In our study, we selected well-performing machine learning models, XGBoost and Random Forest, and seamlessly combined them into a powerful Voting Classifier. By introducing the Voting Classifier, we can better leverage the strengths of each model, making our model more flexible and providing more accurate and reliable predictions in the complex and dynamic airport operational environment. This offers robust support for airport operations and management decision-making. The results of the Voting Classifier are shown in the Table 5, the Fig. 9 represent the performance confusion matrices for voting classifier models:

Table 5. Result of the voting classifier

Model/Result	With Traffic Data	
	Log Loss	Accuracy
Voting Classifier	0.08	0.98

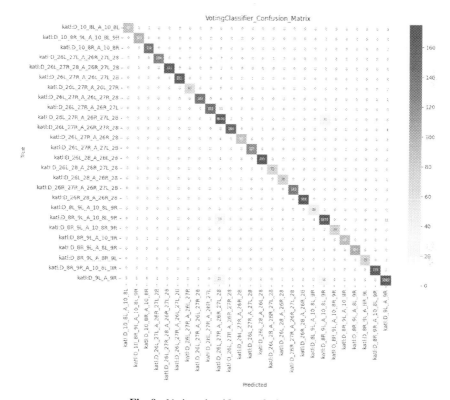

Fig. 9. Voting classifier confusion matrix

5 Conclusion

Runway configuration plays a crucial role in airport operational efficiency. Inappropriate runway usage can lead to the wastage of airport resources or ground and air congestion. Currently, air traffic control personnel rely on years of experience and rules for selecting and adjusting runway configurations in real-time, lacking scientifically effective tools for providing suggestions. Therefore, there is an urgent need for a data-driven runway configuration assistance decision system to enhance airport operational efficiency and alleviate the workload of air traffic controllers.

This paper proposes a Voting Classifier model that fully leverages the strengths of XGBoost and Random Forest models for predicting runway configurations at Hartsfield-Jackson Atlanta International Airport for the next six hours, with a time interval of half an hour for each of the 12 time points. The model takes LAMP data as input for weather forecast and utilizes historical airport operational data, including runway configurations at the prediction time, configurations at the previous time point, and inbound/outbound aircraft traffic values, involving a total of 14 features. Experimental results demonstrate a significant improvement in prediction accuracy using the Voting Classifier model, achieving an accuracy of approximately 98%.

The advantage of the Voting Classifier lies in its flexibility to adjust the weights of different models based on the actual operational data of different airports, enabling the application of the Voting Classifier model in any scenario for optimal prediction results.

Acknowledgments. This work was supported in part by National Natural Science Foundation of China (No. 62173332), the National Natural Fund Key Projects of China (No. U2133207), the Tianjin Multifund Project (No. 21JCYBJC00700) and the Special Funds for Basic Research Operations of Central Universities (No. 3122020052).

Disclosure of Interests.   All authors disclosed no relevant relationships.

References

1. Civil Aviation Administration of China. Statistics on Major Production Indicators for October 2023. Official website of the Civil Aviation Administration of China (2023). https://www.caac. gov.cn/big5/www.caac.gov.cn/XXGK/XXGK/TJSJ/202311/P020231120378501422678.pdf
2. Provan, C.A., Cook, L., Cunningham, J.: A probabilistic airport capacity model for improved ground delay program planning. In: Digital Avionics Systems Conference (DASC), 2011 IEEE/AIAA, 30th IEEE (2011)
3. Cox, J., Kochenderfer, M.J.: Probabilistic airport acceptance rate prediction. In: AIAA Modeling and Simulation Technologies Conference (2016)
4. Wang, Y.: Prediction of weather impacted airport capacity using ensemble learning. Digital Avionics Systems Conference (DASC), 2011 IEEE/AIAA, 30th IEEE (2011)
5. Wang, Y.: Prediction of weather impacted airport capacity using RUC-2 forecast. In: Digital Avionics Systems Conference (DASC), 2012 IEEE/AIAA 31st IEEE (2012)
6. Chung, S., Murphy, D.: Developing a model to determine called rates at airports. In: 10th AIAA Aviation Technology, Integration, and Operations (ATIO) Conference (2010)
7. DeLaura, R.A., et al.: Initial assessment of wind forecasts for Airport Acceptance Rate (AAR) and Ground Delay Program (GDP) planning. Massachusetts Inst. of Technology Lincoln Lab, Project Rept. ATC-414, Lexington, MA (2014)
8. Murça, M.C.R., John Hansman, R.: Predicting and planning airport acceptance rates in metroplex systems for improved traffic flow management decision support. Transp. Res. Part C: Emerg. Technol. **97,** 301–323 (2018)

9. Ramanujam, V., Balakrishnan, H.: Data-driven modeling of the airport configuration selection process. IEEE Trans. Hum.-Mach. Syst. **45**(4), 490–499 (2015)

10. Houston, S., Murphy, D.: Predicting runway configurations at airports, No.12-3682 (2012)

11. Tien, S., et al.: Evaluation of an airport capacity prediction model for strategizing air traffic management. American Meteorological Society 95th Annual Meeting (2015)

12. Tien, S.-L., et al.: Using ensemble weather forecasts for predicting airport arrival capacity. J. Air Transp. **26**(3), 123–132 (2018)

13. Wang, Y., Zhang, Y.: Prediction of runway configurations and airport acceptance rates for multi-airport system using gridded weather forecast. Transp. Res. Part C Emerg. Technol. **125**, 103049 (2021)

14. China Civil Aviation Network. Observations on Aviation Hubs: Hartsfield-Jackson Atlanta International Airport [EB/OL], 15 Mar 2017. http://www.caacnews.com.cn/zk/zj/liyanwei/201703/t20170315_1210575.html

Single Pilot Operations - Who Should Do What? Allocating Aviation Tasks to the Performing Cooperators

F. Zinn[1]([envelope]) [ORCID], L. Ebrecht[2] [ORCID], F. Albers[1] [ORCID], M. Wies[3] [ORCID], and D. Niedermeier[4] [ORCID]

[1] German Aerospace Center (DLR), Institute of Aerospace Medicine, Aviation and Space Psychology, 22335 Hamburg, Germany
Frank.Zinn@dlr.de
[2] German Aerospace Center (DLR), Institute of Flight Guidance, Department Pilot Assistance, 38108 Braunschweig, Germany
[3] German Aerospace Center (DLR), Institute of Flight Guidance, Human Factors Department, 38108 Braunschweig, Germany
[4] German Aerospace Center (DLR), Institute of Flight Systems, Flight Dynamics and Simulation, 38108 Braunschweig, Germany

Abstract. Single Pilot Operation (SPO) is increasingly discussed amongst pilots, airlines, aircraft manufacturers, authorities, and other committees. In EASA's safety domain "the feasibility of the implementation of SPO in the EU regulatory framework by 2030" is to be assessed. Opinions on SPO vary widely, especially when the focus is on safety. Some see flight safety at risk, while others see a possible increase in flight safety, particularly through the simultaneous use of artificial intelligence or highly developed automation. The SPO concepts used as a basis for forming individual opinions differ a lot and are therefore often not comparable. Regardless of this, it is very likely that SPO will start to get into operation and might become one of the standards in commercial aviation in the future, e.g., starting for cargo flights. The way of implementation depends on various factors. The most important should be safety. In order to approach a possible common basis for decision-making, the DLR project NICo developed a safety-centered SPO concept and a suitable allocation of tasks to the different actors in an SPO scenario in multiple iterative processes. The concept and task allocation as well as the evaluation by 40 airline pilots are presented here.

Keywords: single pilot operation · NICo · virtual co-pilot · remote pilot · onboard pilot · AI

1 Introduction

Technical progress in aviation has been enormous in recent years, helping to increase its efficiency and safety [1]. Automation became a lot more sophisticated, glass cockpits with flight management systems were developed. Monotonous monitoring tasks are increasingly covered by automation reducing pilot´s workload. Current and foreseeable technological developments could now make it possible for large commercial aircraft to be operated with just one pilot on board. At present, single pilot operation (SPO) is only authorized for small aircraft with a maximum of 19 passengers and maximum take-off weight of 8.618 kg (19.000 lbs) [2].

Despite high technical assistance and automation systems, the cognitive and other demand on pilots can even be high in multi-pilot operations (MPO). During take-off and landing, in bad weather and in unpredictable situations, and even in normal operations, the task share between the two pilots and related crew coordination is essential for the safety of a flight. How safely can it be done without one of the two pilots in the cockpit? The prerequisites for this type of operation must be set at an equivalent safety level compared to the requirements for current dual pilot operations. Nevertheless, it is most likely that SPO will become an option for next generation of large aircraft in commercial aviation. Manufacturers are heading towards to extend SPO [3, 4] and aviation authorities are also increasingly discussing the topic and focusing on it in research projects [5, 6]. The key questions are therefore how and when SPO will find its way into commercial aviation. An implementation of SPO will change the conditions for pilots and other aviation professionals considerably [4]. There are many questions about how SPO could be realized as safe and reliable as MPO [7]. With current automation and assistance systems in large aircraft many pilots anticipate problems. In an online-survey amongst 136 airline pilots we found out that the majority of pilots were very critical of and opposed to SPO [8]. The anticipated problems with SPO were identified in 5 factors: (1) interaction and responsibility, (2) overload of single pilot, (3) health of single pilot, (4) over-automation, and (5) data connection. In order to establish SPO, a lot of issues have to be solved and pilots need to participate in the development in order to gain acceptance. Due to the fact that only a sufficient level of detail guarantees a basis for a substantial assessment, further development steps will certainly lead to iterative conceptual adjustments. As we assume that the development and the realization of a decent concept will take several years of research and preparation (e.g. regulations), we would like to aim for a time horizon of 8–9 years and thus the year 2032. This is in line with the estimation illustrated in "The Human Dimension in Tomorrow's Aviation System" [9]. In our opinion, some fundamental prerequisites must be met by then: A robust, reliable and adaptive automation as well as a stable data link communication between the aircraft and ground control station has to be guaranteed if ground support takes part of future SPO concepts. Furthermore, aircraft must have highly reliable emergency autoland systems for the case of pilot incapacitation (Reliable Emergency Autoland Systems). Their predecessors have already been approved by the FAA for smaller aircraft (e.g. from Garmin for Piper M600, Cirrus Vision Jet and the Daher TBM 940) [10]. Apart from that, various SPO-concepts are conceivable [11–16].

It is expected that the task allocation will significantly change when moving from MPO to SPO. SPO will not be simply realized by taking one pilot out of the cockpit that supports the on-board pilot (OBP) remotely with the same task allocation as used in current dual pilot operations (DPO). In current DPO, depending on the flight phase, the tasks are either allocated according to the rank, i.e., Captain or First Officer, or to their role as pilot flying (PF) or pilot monitoring (PM). The tasks allocated to each crew member are clearly defined in the operating manual as part of the Standard Operating

Procedures. The impact of SPO on the procedures will be significant, so that the task allocation between the different cooperators has to be reassessed.

This contribution will present the basic outline of the DLR´s concept for upcoming SPO developed in the institutional funded project "Next Generation Intelligent Cockpit" (NICo) [17]. A sufficiently detailed allocation of aeronautical tasks to the co-operators involved in SPO will be introduced. Here we are guided by the established task categorization of Aviate, Navigate, Communicate, Manage Systems, and Manage Mission [18, 19]. In addition, the task allocation was carried out for the FORDEC decision model [20]. This task allocation had been presented to commercial pilots in order to provide a figure to a possible future SPO concept. The 41 pilots took part of one-to-one online interviews for the evaluation of the SPO-concept as part of a job requirement analysis for future single and remote airline pilots.

Here we will present the SPO-concept and the associated task allocations as well as a first evaluation of both, followed by a discussion of the concept and the results.

2   The 3C-SPO Concept

In this SPO-concept, there are three main cooperators: a *human onboard pilot*, a *human remote pilot* and a *virtual co-pilot*, which is mapped in an artificial intelligence. Since the concept includes three cooperators, we named it 3C-concept.

The onboard pilot (OBP) is always the pilot in command (PIC). He always has the responsibility, makes the decisions and is - during a normal operation - in charge of the task areas Aviate, Navigate, Communicate and Manage Mission and any necessary FORDEC. The OBP is continuously supported by the virtual co-pilot (VCP). A more detailed description of the VCP and its embedding in the concept follows in the next paragraph and the assignment of tasks is shown in the following chapter. During normal operation, the remote pilot (RP) does not intervene in the flight. In this scenario, the RP has a surveillance assignment: he is supposed to observe up to 8 aircraft and their visualized parameters. On the monitors of his RP workstation all important flight-parameters are displayed. His RP workstation is located on the ground [21]. A more detailed description follows in 2.2.

In the case of *abnormal operations,* the RP actively supports the flight operations. He takes over communication as far as possible, supports troubleshooting, is responsible for the Manage Mission area and becomes a partner in FORDEC. During *OBP incapacitation,* the RP takes over the tasks of the OBP and becomes pilot in command (PIC). However, it is not intended that the RP will work manually in the Aviate task area; instead, he would specify a flight path via digital interfaces, which would then be flown automated. If there is a *VCP failure,* the RP takes over its tasks. The allocation of tasks for abnormal operations and incapacitation is also described in the task matrix (Chapter 3). When the RP has to take over active tasks (abnormal operation, emergency, OBP-incapacitation, VCP-failure), the RP hands over observation of the other assigned aircraft and focusses on the one aircraft in need of assistance. In the case of difficult approaches and departures, it is also possible for the RP to provide dedicated support to the OBP during a normal operation. The OBP decides when support of an RP is needed. For a better understanding, the VCP and the RP should be explained in more detail.

2.1 Virtual Co-pilot

The VCP is an on-board assistance system based on AI methods and algorithms that can support the OBP in all tasks. The OBP communicates with the VCP via a combination of a graphical user interface with touchscreen and mainly voice control and voice output. It continuously performs complex monitoring tasks and signals detected anomalies to the OBP.

The VCP knows the system status of all aircraft systems and sensors and has a comprehensive picture of its environment (e.g. weather, air traffic, infrastructure on the ground such as airports and their special features). The VCP supports in normal operation by reading out checklists, reacting to the OBP's inputs and callouts and checking them (cross-checks).

In abnormal situations, the VCP offers further support: It applies the SOPs; in all other cases, the VCP generates and proposes evidence-based and well-founded solutions, alternative recommendations and it supports the OBP in the execution of his decisions, for example by modifying the flight plan in the flight management system after OBP's confirmation. On the basis of its comprehensive data and access to important systems, the VCP calculates the consequences of unforeseen events (e.g. system errors or special circumstances entered by the OBP, such as a medical emergency in the cabin) and their impact on a safe realization of the current flight mission. VCP's proposals must be derived from the facts in a way that is optimally comprehensible for the OBP. The OBP can either select a proposed solution generated by the VCP or interactively check proposed solutions based on his own observations, whereupon the proposed solutions are updated by the VCP.

2.2 Remote Pilot

The RP simultaneously monitors up to 8 aircraft and their parameters. Via its work station, the RP has a mental model of the current flight status, recognizes deviations from the target status and accordingly knows all the necessary information about the aircraft systems, fuel consumption, energy status and weather and all necessary inputs from the OBP. In case of deviations from normal status, RP will be informed by monitoring software. In normal operations, monitoring flight statuses is his only safety-related task. Tasks in the area of the Airline Operating Centre could be added.

The RP has the option of switching between surveillance view and a view for dedicated support via the Human Machine Interface (HMI) [21]. The surveillance view provides a list with the most relevant information of each aircraft under supervision (e.g. call sign, aircraft type, origin, destination, flight phase, aircraft state and system data). Besides, there is a map view comprising all aircraft. The second view "dedicated view" allows the detailed view of an aircraft. It comprises common electronic flight information system (EFIS) with its different displays, like Primary Flight Display, Navigation Display, Electronic Centralized Aircraft Monitor (ECAM)/Engine Indication and Crew Alerting System (EICAS), and other information (e.g. Quick Reference Handbook, Flight Crew Operations Manual, Charts, Traffic and Weather information).

If an OBP requires special support on his flight, the RP hands over the monitoring of his other flights to free RP colleagues and concentrates fully on his tasks on this one flight.

The HMI view is switched accordingly from surveillance view to the dedicated support view. The RP now has access to all the necessary functions. The entire cockpit activity is then displayed on the ground synchronized in real-time. As soon as the abnormal situation is pacified, the RP can go back into surveillance mode. Only in the case of OBP incapacitation the responsibility for the flight switches to the RP.

3   The Task Allocation

The shift from today's DPO to a SPO concept, such as the 3C-SPO concept as presented here, will be only feasible, if an equivalent level of safety can be guaranteed. Hence, safety was the most important factor that was considered for the task allocation. Risks that might arise from increased workload, missing crosschecks, lack of situational awareness or reduced decision-making capabilities have to be mitigated by the VCP and/or the RP. To maintain the level of safety these mitigation capabilities have to be sufficiently reliable. The future technical feasibility as well as the potential reliability were considered when tasks were assigned to the VCP and the RP. Specifically, the security, reliability and technical capabilities of the datalink required for all RP tasks was an important parameter. In addition to technical factors, human-machine interface considerations and the OBP's trust into technical systems were considered, too. Ethical and legal principles affected the task allocation with respect to decision-making and the related responsibility of the OBP.

   This task allocation proposition was developed jointly by flight engineers, aviation psychologists and commercial pilots from major airlines. The established categorization in aviation into the task groups Aviate, Navigate, Communicate, Manage Systems and Manage Mission was used as a grid. The FORDEC decision model was considered separately. In a second development step, all essential tasks of these task areas were identified and aggregated at a medium level. No large overlaps should occur and no essential tasks should be omitted [22]. Subsequently, it was discussed for each of the tasks which co-operators should be involved in the execution, whereby exactly one co-operator always has the final responsibility and at least one other co-operator assists in different ways, quality and quantity (see figures). As the allocation of tasks can vary under different flight conditions, the conditions of Normal Operations, Abnormal/Emergency, OBP Incapacitation and VCP Failure were considered separately. The task allocations shown in Tables 1, 2, 3, 4, 5, 6 were developed in many iterative discussion processes. In addition, brief descriptions of the activities for each task were included for the PIC and the assistant.

   In the course of the task allocation matrix´ development, some basic principles emerged, which can be deduced from the following tables. For example, the RP is not intended to be used as a PM for normal operation. Instead, the OBP will co-operate as PIC with the VCP as assistant. In Abnormals and Emergencies, the RP takes over some part of the communication, manages the entire mission and part of the aircraft system in joint responsibility with the other two co-operators. Only in the event of an OBP incapacitation does the RP become the PIC and takes over most of the tasks with the support of the VCP. Should the VCP and a backup system fail, the RP takes over its tasks.

As in DPO, the single pilot on board the aircraft bears the responsibility for the safety of the flight. The OBP has the final authority and is the final decision maker. Given this responsibility, the aviate task (see Table 1) with its substantial effect on safety is the primary and most important task of the OBP. The main focus of the OBP should be on this task and it is the task with the highest priority for the OBP. With the best overview of the situation, the OBP is the superior participator to execute this task. Unless the OBP is incapacitated, it is his responsibility to execute memory items which require immediate actions (for example stall recovery, initiation of an emergency descent or handling of unreliable indications), to manually control the flight path, to control the auto flight system, to control flaps, speed brakes and gear, to maintain mode awareness, to determine the aircraft performance, to monitor the flight parameters, and to crosscheck any aviate actions of the VCP. The VCP is supporting the OBP with the execution of this task whenever required. The VCP also monitors the OBP during execution of the aviate task. Only in case of an OBP incapacitation, the responsibility for the aviate task is transferred to the RP which is again supported by the VCP.

Similar to the aviation task, the OBP bears the responsibility for the execution of navigate task (see Table 2). The OBP is again supported by the VCP and only in case of an OBP incapacitation, the RP becomes the responsible actor supported by the VCP. This way the OBP is responsible for maintaining the flight path and for following the instructed taxi route. One exception exists: the navigate task "navigation accuracy" rests with the responsibility of the VCP, as the VCP has the best ability to continuously monitor required navigation accuracy and compare it so required navigation accuracy.

In DPO, the PM is responsible for the communication (see Table 3) with ATC in normal operation. This way, the PF can focus on his primary tasks aviate and navigate. With SPO and the omission of the know PF and PM division, this is changing. The OBP now becomes responsible for all communication in normal operation. This is due to the fact that this is the most efficient solution. The RP is not involved in normal operation and the VCP is technically not able to listen and act as a human PM today. Communicating the OBPs intentions to the VCP is not an easy solution.

Furthermore, a VCP which completely thinks along and is aware about the intentions of the OBP is technically not implemented yet and maybe technically not feasible today. Therefore, the OBP will become responsible for the communication task. However, the OBP is supported by the VCP in same tasks. The communication tasks of the OBP include communication with ATC, with the cabin crew members, with the RP, with the VCP, with the company or AOC, with the passengers, with the ground personnel, and with other aircraft. The OBP receives support by the VCP in the communication with ATC, with the company or AOC and with other aircraft. In abnormal and emergency situations, the OBP is released of some communication tasks which are taken over by the RP. This reduces the workload. The tasks include communication with the company, with the passengers and with the ground personnel. This way, the OBP can focus on his communication with ATC. In case of an OBP incapacitation, the RP becomes responsible for all communication tasks and is partly supported by the VCP.

Manage systems (see Table 4) is primarily the task of the PM in DPO. In SPO this will not become the task of the OBP as the distraction from the aviate, navigate and communicate tasks would be too big. In normal operation, the task will be handled by

Table 1. Allocation of Aviation task

OBP = Onboard Pilot
RP = Remote Pilot
VCP = Virtual Co Pilot

AVIATE	macht... bei NORMAL (incl. IRREG) operation			macht... bei ABNORMAL/EMERGENCY operation			macht... bei OBP INCAPACITATION			macht... bei VCP FAILURE			X = Performs in command	A = Assist
	OBP	RP	VCP	OBP	RP	VCP	OBP	RP	VCP	OBP	RP	VCP		
Execute memory items	X			X		A		X	A	X	A		Recognize the need to execute the applicable procedure (e.g. fire, or severe damage, etc) Decide about the correct time when to execute the memory items (e.g. not below 400ft AGL). Monitor execution of memory items and confirm irreversable actions.	Perform memory items.
Manual flight path control	X			X		A	No manual fpc -> Emergency Autoland			X	A		Use primary flight controls and thrust to maintain desired flight path.	Monitor flight path and primary flight parameters.
Reliable Emergency Autoland System (Future)			A			A		A	A		A			Autoland is activated automatically or can be activated by RP/VCP.
Automatic flight path control	X		A	X		A		X	A	X	A		Select appropriate level of automation to maintain desired flight path.	Monitor flight path and primary flight parameters. Monitor Autoflight System Limitations.
Second flight controls (flaps, speed, brake)	X		A	X		A		X	A	X	A		Use or command secondary flight controls as needed to maintain desired flight path.	Set or monitor secondary flight controls as needed to maintain desired flight path. Observe Secondary flight control limitations.
Check FMA (check autopilot modes)	X		A	X		A		X	A	X	A		Monitor selected modes of automation.	Monitor selected modes of automation.
Calculate weight and balance and performance	X		A	X		A		X	A	X	A		Define input parameters for performance/W&B computation. Verify Computation results.	X-check input parameters for plausibility and perform calculation. Present result to OBP/RP (OBP incapacitation) and transfer results to aircraft systems (thrust, speeds, CG, etc.).
Perform crosschecks on SP actions, Monitor primary flight parameters			X			X			X	X			Monitor all actions and check for plausibility. Supply cautions when system or flight parameters approach critical values. Supply warnings when system or flight parameters exceed critical values.	

Table 2. Allocation of Navigation task

OBP = Onboard Pilot
RP = Remote Pilot
VCP = Virtual Co Pilot

NAVIGATE	macht ... bei NORMAL operation			macht ... bei ABNORMAL/EMERGENCY operation			macht ... bei OBP INCAPACITATION			macht ... bei VCP FAILURE			X = Performs in command	A = Assist
	OBP	RP	VCP	OBP	RP	VCP	OBP	RP	VCP	OBP	RP	VCP		
Maintain flight path (speed, altitude, heading, position)	X		A	X		A		X	A	X	A		Position the airplane in accordance with applicable navigation procedure (departure, enroute, approach, taxi, etc.)	Monitor the airplane position in accordance with applicable navigation procedure (departure, enroute, approach, taxi, etc).
Navigation accuracy			X			X			X		X		Monitor position accuracy according route requirements.	
Taxi	X		A	X		A		X	A	X	A		Perform taxi according cleared routing.	Verify position vs. cleared routing and inform about high threat areas (e.g. RWY crossing).
Immediate evasive maneuvers (Traffic, Terrain, Emergency descent)	X		A	X		A		A	X	X	A		Monitor situation and perform avoidance action if needed. (Avoidance may be performed either by VCP or manual)	Monitor situation and provide information.
Plan environment-friendly route	X		A	X		A		X	A	X	A		Evaluate route changes and accept or reject them.	Update preplanned route according to latest information available and provide information (optimum level, modified routing) to OBP/RP (OBP incapacitation)

Table 3 . Allocation of Communication task

OBP = Onboard Pilot
RP = Remote Pilot
VCP = Virtual Co Pilot

COMMUNICATE	macht... bei NORMAL (incl. IRREG) operation			macht... bei ABNORMAL/ EMERGENCY operation			macht... bei OBP INCAPACITATION			macht... bei VCP FAILURE			X = Performs in command	A = Assist
	OBP	RP	VCP	OBP	RP	VCP	OBP	RP	VCP	OBP	RP	VCP		
with ATC	X		A	X		A		X	A	X	A		Perform ATC communication.	Provide information regarding communication requirements (e.g. entry clearances, position reporting, weather reporting).
with cabin	X			X	A			X		X			Perform standard cabin communication (cabin ready, additional information, minor irregularities).	Assist in standard cabin communication (cabin ready, additional information, minor irregularities).
with OBP			X		X	X						X	Perform standard communication with OBP E.g.: - standard callouts - deviations - alerts	
with RP	X			X		A		X		X			Decide and perform when, what and how to communicate with RP.	Assist OBP in communication with RP.
with VCP	X			X	A			X		X			Decide and perform when, what and how to communicate with VCP.	Assist OBP in communication with VCP.
with company/AOC	X		A	X	X			X					Decide and perform when, what and how to communicate with AOC.	Communicate standard reports (e.g. Out, Off, On, In).
with passengers	X			X	X			X		X			Decide and perform when, what and how to communicate with Pax.	
with ground personnel	X			X	X			X		X			Decide and perform when, what and how to communicate with ground personnel.	
with other aircraft	X		A	X	X	A		X	A	X	A		Decide and perform when, what and how to communicate with other aircraft.	After decision of OBP / RP /OBP (incapacitation) takeover standard communication. e.g. - IFBP (inflight broadcasting procedure) - distress messages to all stations

Table 4. Allocation of Manage Systems task

OBP = Onboard Pilot
RP = Remote Pilot
VCP = Virtual Co Pilot

MANAGE SYSTEMS	NORMAL (hw) operation			ABNORMAL/ EMERGENCY operation			OBP INCAPACITATION			VCP FAILURE			X = Performs in command	A = Assist
	OBP	RP	VCP	OBP	RP	VCP	OBP	RP	VCP	OBP	RP	VCP		
Monitor systems			X	X		X			X		X		Monitor system status in addition to system alerts.	
Operate systems normal			X	X		X			X		X		Configure systems according normal procedures (e.g. fuel pump configuration, anti-ice operation)	
Operate systems abnormal (reversible)						X							Configure systems according abnormal procedures (only reversable items).	
Operate systems abnormal (irreversible)				X	A	A							Perform abnormal system operation which is non-reversable or requires special monitoring with help of either RP or VCP.	Assist OBP during operation of aircraft systems which are non-reversable or require special monitoring. VCP: if RP not / not yet available.
Identify failures				X	A	A							Identify system failure with help of RP or VCP.	Assist OBP during identification of failure. VCP: if RP not / not yet available
Verify failures				X	A	A							Verify system failure with help of RP or VCP.	Assist OBP during verification of failure. VCP: if RP not / not yet available
Fuel management			X			X			X		X		Monitor fuel usage compared to flight plan.	
Present Technical status aircraft			X			X			X		X		Consolidate and present technical status.	

Table 5. Allocation of Manage Mission task

MANAGE MISSION	macht... bei NORMAL (incl. IRREG) operations			macht... bei ABNORMAL/EMERGENCY operation			macht... bei OBP INCAPACITATION			macht... bei VCP FAILURE			X = Performs in command	A = Assist
OBP = Onboard Pilot RP = Remote Pilot VCP = Virtual Co Pilot	OBP	RP	VCP	OBP	RP	VCP	OBP	RP	VCP	OBP	RP	VCP		
Weather	X		A		X	A		X	A	X	A		Define parameter relevant for operation.	Continuously monitor weather for relevant airports (departure, destination, alternate) and notify relevant changes.
Monitor Regulations - airport, company, flightcrew, aircraft, airspace/ATC	X		A		X	A		X	A	X	A		Receive and verify information by VCP.	Monitor all regulatory requirements and present current status. (e.g. flight duty time limitation, NOTAM changes, airspace closures, reporting requirements, etc).
Notams	X		A		X	A		X	A	X	A		Read and understand relevant NOTAM.	Monitor and consolidate NOTAM.
Initiate IDM (Inflight Decision Making)	X		A		X	A		X	A	X	A		Continuously monitor flight progress and verify a valid plan b is available at any given time.	Continuously monitor flight progress and present information that are relevant for current plan (e.g. weather deterioration, airport closure, etc).

Table 6. Allocation of FORDEC task

OBP = Onboard Pilot
RP = Remote Pilot
VCP = Virtual Co Pilot

FORDEC	macht ... bei NORMAL (incl. SEVERE) operation			macht ... bei ABNORMAL/EMERGENCY operation			macht ... bei OBP INCAPACITATION			macht ... bei VCP FAILURE			X = Performs in command	A = Assist
	OBP	RP	VCP	OBP	RP	VCP	OBP	RP	VCP	OBP	RP	VCP		
Initiate FORDEC	X		X	X		X	X			X			OBP: Recognize situation, where a structured decision making process (FORDEC) is needed. VCP: Notify OBP if due to a situation change (technical, operational, weather, etc) a decision might become necessary.	-
F: Collect facts	X		X	X	X	X		X	X	X	X		Collect and present relevant facts.	-
O: Generate and communicate options	X		X	X	X	X		X	X	X	X		OBP: Evaluate Options. RP/VCP: Collect and present relevant options. OBP incapacitation: RP evaluate options	-
R: Analyse and communicate risks	X		X	X	X	X		X	X	X	X		OBP: Evaluate risks and benefits of all options. RP/VCP: Present optimum solution from own point of view. OBP incapacitation: RP evaluate risks and benefits of all options.	-
D: Recommend decision			X		X	X		X	X		X		RP: Present optimum solution from RP point of view. VCP: Present optimum solution from VCP point of view.	-
D: Take decision	X			X			X			X			Decide about further action.	
E: Execute	X	A	A	X	A	A	X	A	A	X	A		OBP: Execute decision. OBP incapacitation: RP Execute decision.	Monitor Execution.
C: Check	X		X	X	A	A	X	X	A	X	A		Continuously monitor new facts and re-evaluate decision.	Continuously monitor and present new facts and re-evaluate decision.

the VCP. The VCP monitors the systems, operates the systems, manages the fuel, and consolidates and presents the technical status of the aircraft. This task allocation does not change in case of an OBP incapacitation. In abnormal and emergency situations, the OBP will be involved in the identification and verification of the technical failure and will operate systems with irreversible switching functions (switching of a system which cannot be switched back into the previous operation mode during flight).

Manage mission (see Table 5) is related to weather, to regulations (airport, company, aircraft, airspace and ATC), to NOTAMS, and to inflight planning and decision making. The OBP is responsible for all these tasks in normal operation and is supported by the VCP. In abnormal and emergency situations as well as during an OBP incapacitation the RP takes over the responsibility for the manage mission tasks. The RP is as well supported by the VCP.

Most airlines apply decision-making schemes that structure the decision-making process is airline cockpits to guarantee sound decisions. One of the most popular decision-making schemes is called FORDEC, which is short for Facts, Options, Risks, Decision, Execution and Check. Such schemes strongly rely on the interaction of two humans exchanging their views on the facts, option and risks. For future SPO (see Table 6) it is expected that especially the decision-making process will be supported by automated systems that are part of the VCP. Most of the steps of the FORDEC process are allocated to the OBP as well as to the VCP. It is expected that an automated VCP system is capable of collecting facts, generating options and deriving associated risks as well as exchanging them with the OBP to support the decision-making process. According to the basic principle of the task allocation matrix only in abnormal situations tasks are allocated to the RP. In this case the RP contributes to the decision-making process, too. However, the final responsibility for the decision remains always with the OBP, as he is, according to the basic task allocation approach, solely responsible for the safety of the flight.

4   Evaluation of the SPO-Concept by Commercial Pilots

As part of a research question, that was focusing a job requirement analysis for SPO the concept and the allocation of tasks were presented in detail to N = 41 commercial aircraft pilots in one-to-one online interviews. Prior to the survey, the participants had to familiarize themselves with the materials on the NICo-SPO concept and task allocation. In order to ensure that all subjects understood and internalized the SPO concept and the task allocations, all 41 participants were interviewed individually online. This allowed open questions to be clarified in advance. Only one respondent subsequently stated and expressed in the respective rating that he did not fully understand the concept (Fig. 1, rating = 3). This participant was excluded from all analyses, because a basic understanding of the concept is a prerequisite for valid data. The results from the 40 remaining participating professional pilots - 19 captains, 20 first officers and one senior first officer (SFO) - were therefore analyzed and included in the results (Table 7).

The data reported here is the evaluation of the considered task allocation for pilots and the SPO-concept. It was obtained via evaluative questions as part of the mentioned larger job requirement analysis. One online interview lasted approximately 3 h per participant.

Table 7. 3C-SPO concept evaluation

	AM	s
1. The concept is understandable[a]	5,37	0,70
2. The concept is well thought out	4,23	1,19
3. The allocation of tasks fits into the concept described	4,85	0,92
4. The allocation of tasks makes sense	4,88	1,02
5. I have concerns about the allocation of tasks	2,95	1,40
6. The concept is safe	3,48	1,40
7. The concept has a high probability of being implemented	3,75	1,35
8. The concept is accepted by pilots	2,07	1,14
9. The concept is accepted by passengers	2,58	1,20
10. The concept is accepted by airlines	4,77	1,00
11. The concept is accepted by aircraft manufacturers	4,98	0,80

Note. This table demonstrates pilot's evaluation of the 3C-SPO concept and the corresponding task allocation.

[a]The first rating was calculated on the basis of 41 participants. One participant was thereafter excluded from further calculations. All other ratings were subsequently calculated on the basis of 40 participants.

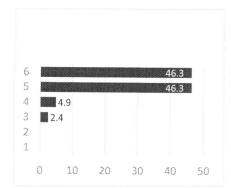

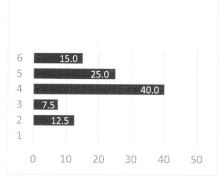

Fig. 1. Concept evaluation question 1. Percentages are presented on each dot of the scale from 1 = "strongly disagree" and 6 = "strongly agree".

Fig. 2. Concept evaluation question 2. Percentages are presented on each dot of the scale from 1 = "strongly disagree" and 6 = "strongly agree".

After questions about the SPO concept were clarified, 11 questions were presented to assess the concept. The participants were asked to give a value between 1 and 6, with the end of the scale 1 meaning "strongly disagree" and the end of the scale 6 meaning "strongly agree" (see Table 7). The scale levels in between were to be regarded as equally

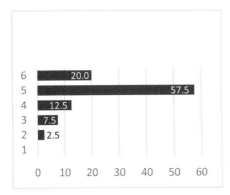

Fig. 3. Concept evaluation question 3. Percentages are presented on each dot of the scale from 1 = "strongly disagree" and 6 = "strongly agree".

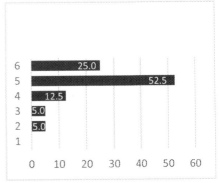

Fig. 4. Concept evaluation question 4. Percentages are presented on each dot of the scale from 1 = "strongly disagree" and 6 = "strongly agree".

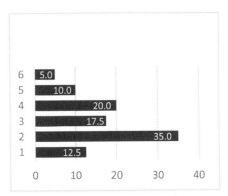

Fig. 5. Concept evaluation question 5. Percentages are presented on each dot of the scale from 1 = "strongly disagree" and 6 = "strongly agree".

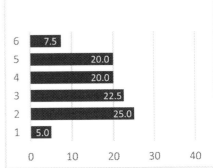

Fig. 6. Concept evaluation question 6. Percentages are presented on each dot of the scale from 1 = "strongly disagree" and 6 = "strongly agree".

spaced. The theoretical scale mean is therefore 3.5. It took one participant approximately ten minutes (of the whole online interview) to answer these evaluative questions.

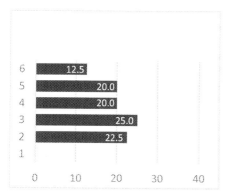

Fig. 7. Concept evaluation question 7. Percentages are presented on each dot of the scale from 1 = "strongly disagree" and 6 = "strongly agree".

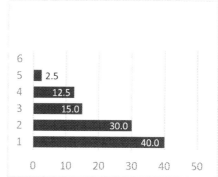

Fig. 8. Concept evaluation question 8. Percentages are presented on each dot of the scale from 1 = "strongly disagree" and 6 = "strongly agree".

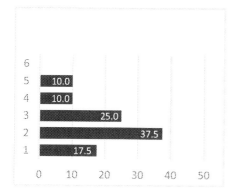

Fig. 9. Concept evaluation question 9. Percentages are presented on each dot of the scale from 1 = "strongly disagree" and 6 = "strongly agree".

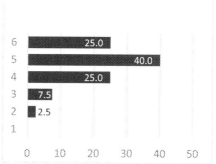

Fig. 10. Concept evaluation question 10. Percentages are presented on each dot of the scale from 1 = "strongly disagree" and 6 = "strongly agree".

A predominant proportion of respondents considers the concept to be well thought out ($AM = 4.23$, Fig. 2), only 20% of the respondents stated that the concept (still) lacks sophistication. 90% of the participating pilots stated that the allocation of tasks suits the concept described (Fig. 3; $AM = 4.85$) and an equivalently high proportion of the participants (90%; Fig. 4) say that the allocation of tasks makes sense ($AM = 4.88$). On the other hand, asked about concerns regarding the considered task allocation 35% of the subject revealed more or less concern (Fig. 5), if they were to share the tasks with the other co-operators in the manner described ($AM = 2.95$).

When asked about the safety of the concept, the arithmetic mean is again moderately high ($AM = 3.48$), with pilots' evaluations utilizing the entire range of the scale. There are participants who consider the concept to be not safe at all and participants who consider it to be absolutely safe (Fig. 6). With an arithmetic mean of 3.75, which is

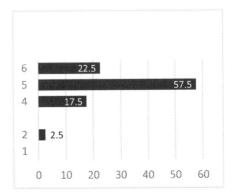

Fig. 11. Concept evaluation question 11. Percentages are presented on each dot of the scale from 1 = "strongly disagree" and 6 = "strongly agree".

located slightly above the scale center of 3.5 a high probability of implementing the described SPO concept is considered to be medium. No participant disagrees at all with a high probability of implementation (Fig. 7).

Nevertheless, pilots do rather not assume that pilots accept the SPO concept (*AM* = 2.07). That means, that even pilots who consider the concept as safe do not envision acceptance amongst their colleagues (Fig. 8). The pilots also anticipate that the acceptance of passengers would be clearly below scale center (*AM* = 2.59). Only 20% of the involved pilots assume the concept being accepted by passengers (Fig. 9).

Then again airlines are expected to be clearly in favor of the concept with an *AM* of 4.77. 90% of the participants assume the airlines would accept the given SPO concept (Fig. 10). A similar high estimate of acceptance is given when asked about the aircraft manufacturers (*AM* = 4.98). Only one participant (2.5%) does not see the considered concept to be accepted by aircraft manufacturers (Fig. 11).

In order to answer the question if cockpit position, respectively flying experience, has an influence on evaluating the SPO concept a one-factorial MANCOVA was conducted with position (CPT vs. F/O + SF/O) as a between-subjects factor and age as a covariate. Results show that both variables have no influence on the assessments of the various evaluation aspects with regard to the SPO concept presented and its corresponding allocation of tasks (combined dependent variables), $F(11, 27) = 1.354, p = .250$, *Wilk's* $\Lambda = .645$.

Which variables surveyed here have an impact on the probability of implementation of the SPO concept? A correlation analysis shows the connection between the perceived probability of implementation of the introduced 3C-Concept and other concept evaluation variables. The direction of impact is strictly speaking interpretative in a correlation analysis, but mostly one direction is more meaningful. The prerequisite for implementation is the safety of the concept ($r = .73$) and the associated allocation of tasks ($r = .59$) as well as the anticipated acceptance among passengers ($r = .50$) and pilots ($r = .49$) and, to a somewhat lesser extent, the anticipated acceptance among airlines ($r = .37$) and aircraft manufacturers ($r = .44$).

The evaluation of the task allocation matrix shows, that the concept is comprehended by the pilots. Furthermore, the task allocation matrix was evaluated predominantly positively by the experts -especially regarding the important aspect of safety- whereas ratings of possible acceptance of the concept by the most directly affected stakeholders, i.e. pilots and passengers, were not too optimistic.

5 Discussion

With this contribution we have succeeded in defining a concept for upcoming commercial SPO with large aircraft with a suitable task allocation as a framework and starting point for further developments. A future state of technical development will certainly entail further adjustments to the concept and its task allocation. The concept has to be investigated more in detail, this means, concrete developments for the implementation of the concept in order to investigate the potentials and efforts of AI and remote support for OBPs.

With a sample of 40 subject matter experts, i.e. professional airline pilots, we have evaluated the SPO concept and its task allocation which was developed in iterative steps by experts in aviation, aerospace engineering and aviation psychology. The evaluation has shown that the concept was seen as understandable, well-thought out and the described allocation of flight tasks between OBP, VCP and RP makes sense. The group of pilots also attested those manufacturers and airline will very likely accept this concept. The safety of the concept, however, was not rated that optimistic. The fact that the concept with its task allocation is rated as moderately safe in the group of airline pilots means, on the one hand, that further (developmental) research must be carried out together with pilots, particularly on the aspect of safety. On the other hand, SPO as a general idea and without defined cooperators and task allocation had been rated as far less safe by pilots in a past study [8]. This shows that the direction of our developmental framework is promising.

The probability of the implementation of the 3C-SPO concept with its task allocation as described here was only rated moderate. The acceptance of the concept by pilots as well as by future passengers was rated rather low, which fits to the moderate ratings in implementation probability and safety. An interesting follow-up question is whether there would be a different perspective on passenger vs. freight transport operations. However, the fact that the task allocation fits the concept and makes sense was a very encouraging result. Further research is needed to determine how even well-evaluated AI-supported concepts for upcoming SPO with large aircraft can gain more acceptance by users and customers. It has been shown that the evaluation was not dependent on the subjects´ flight experience. Therefore, all results must be seen and discussed as valid for the community of all pilots.

It should be noted that the task allocation proposed in this contribution does not represent the only possible solution. Depending on the assumptions on the basic role of the OBP, depending on the technological progress in the fields of AI and datalink capabilities, the task allocation might vary significantly.

This contribution is based on the principle that the responsibility for the safe conduction of the flight remains with the OBP. As a consequence, the OBP will always take the final decision. In addition to that, maintaining flight path remains always a task of the OBP. During the development of the task allocation the fact that the RP is not allowed to control the aircraft's flight path from ground even in the case of pilot incapacitation was controversially discussed. Security considerations finally led to the decision not considering any flight path control from ground. Based on the recent development of emergency autoland systems in smaller aircraft [10] it was decided that such a system will recover the aircraft in case of pilot incapacitation instead of relying on the RP.

However, in case of abnormal situations the responsibility for the failure and system handling remains with the OBP. The underlying assumption is that the OBP is supposed to have the best overview of the systems behavior and the state of the aircraft. For reversible actions the automation of the VCP performs the necessary tasks, however for irreversible actions, that are usually handled with dedicated crosschecks in current DPO, the OBP has to perform these tasks by himself. This task allocation is debatable because the OBP should put his main focus on the tasks required for the safety continuation of the flight - the aviate tasks. It is possible that the OBP's distraction with failure handling and the related increased workload will have a negative impact on safety.

Future work must definitely focus on generating convincing arguments for pilots and passengers in SPO per se, as we have seen that even a well-thought out concept of task allocation which also seems to provide a safe operation cannot generate sufficient acceptance at this point of time or development.

It must be taken into account at this point that the mere imagination of working with a technology that does not yet exist in a setting that does not yet exist either is difficult and is necessarily viewed with healthy skepticism. Confidence and acceptance in new technologies arise primarily in dealing with them (assuming that they are able to meet the requirements). A similar process has been observed in recent months with the rapidly spreading and improving large language models such as Chat GBT, Bing, Bard or Claude. The next step would therefore be to evaluate the task allocation or parts of it in realistic simulator scenarios in terms of safety level and feasibility.

References

1. Fatal accidents I Airbus Accident Statistics. https://accidentstats.airbus.com/statistics/fatal-accidents (2024). Accessed 19 January 2024
2. EASA: Easy Access Rules for Normal-Category Aeroplanes (CS-23) - CS-23 Amendment 6 and AMC & GM to CS-23 Issue 4 available in pdf, online & XML format I EASA (2024). https://www.easa.europa.eu/en/document-library/easy-access-rules/easy-access-rules-normal-category-aeroplanes-cs-23. Accessed 19 January 2024
3. Pinar, H.: Airbus and Dassault Pushe for Single-Pilot Operations Amidst Rising Automation. https://www.airlinerwatch.com, 6 September 2023. https://www.airlinerwatch.com/2023/09/airbus-and-dassault-advocates-single.html. Accessed 19 January 2024
4. Broderick, S., Flottau, J., Dubois, T.: Single-Pilot Operations Are Under Increased Scrutiny. Aviation Week Network, 4 October 2023. https://aviationweek.com/air-transport/safety-ops-regulation/single-pilot-operations-are-under-increased-scrutiny. Accessed 19 January 2024
5. Single pilOt Line Operations, 25 July 2023. https://cordis.europa.eu/project/id/101114589. Accessed 19 January 2024
6. EASA: eMCO-SiPO - Extended Minimum Crew Operations – Single Pilot Operations – Safety Risk Assessment Framework I EASA (2024). https://www.easa.europa.eu/en/res

earch-projects/emco-sipo-extended-minimum-crew-operations-single-pilot-operations-saf ety-risk. Accessed 19 January 2024

7. Stanton, N.A., Harris, D., Starr, A.: The future flight deck: modelling dual, single and distributed crewing options. Appl. Ergon. (2016). https://doi.org/10.1016/j.apergo.2015. 06.019

8. Zinn, F., Della Guardia, J., Albers, F. (eds.): Pilot's perspective on single pilot operation: challenges or showstoppers. In: Harris, D., Li, WC. (eds.) Engineering Psychology and Cognitive Ergonomics. HCII 2023. Lecture Notes in Artificial Intelligence, vol. 14018. Springer, Cham (2023). https://doi.org/10.1007/978-3-031-35389-5_16

9. Kirwan, B., Charles, R., Jones, K., Li, W.-C., Page, J., Tutton, W., BettigniesThiebaux, B: The human dimension in tomorrow's aviation systems. CIEHF - white paper (2020)

10. Garmin Autonomí® | Autonomes Fliegen. https://discover.garmin.com/de-DE/autonomi/ (2024). Accessed 19 January 2024

11. Bilimoria, K.D., Johnson, W.W., Schutte, P.C.: Conceptual framework for single pilot operations. In: Proceedings of the International Conference on Human-Computer Interaction in Aerospace. HCI-Aero '14: International Conference on Human-Computer Interaction in Aerospace 2014, Santa Clara California, 30 07 2014 01 08 2014, pp. 1–8. ACM, New York (2014). https://doi.org/10.1145/2669592.2669647

12. Bailey, R.E., Kramer, L.J., Kennedy, K.D., Stephens, C.L., Etherington, T.J.: An assessment of reduced crew and single pilot operations in commercial transport aircraft operations. In: 2017 IEEE/AIAA 36th Digital Avionics Systems Conference (DASC). In: 2017 IEEE/AIAA 36th Digital Avionics Systems Conference (DASC), St. Petersburg, FL, 17.09.2017 - 21.09.2017, pp. 1–15. IEEE (2017). https://doi.org/10.1109/DASC.2017.8101988

13. Matessa, M., Strybel, T., Vu, K., Battiste, V., Schnell, T.: Concept of Operations for RCO/SPO

14. Myers, P.L., Starr, A.W.: Single pilot operations IN commercial cockpits: background, challenges, and options. J. Intell. Robot. Syst. (2021). https://doi.org/10.1007/s10846-021-013 71-9

15. Vu, K.-P.L., Lachter, J., Battiste, V., Strybel, T.Z.: Single pilot operations in domestic commercial aviation. Hum. Factors (2018). https://doi.org/10.1177/0018720818791372

16. Comerford, D., et al.: NASA's Single-pilot operations technical interchange meeting: Proceedings and findings (2013)

17. Niermann, C.: Institute of Flight Guidance - NICo (Next Generation Intelligent Cockpit) (2024). https://www.dlr.de/fl/en/desktopdefault.aspx/tabid-1149/1737_read-69821/. Accessed 19 Jan 2024

18. Billings, C.: Aviation automation - the search for a human-centered approach (1997)

19. Ebrecht, L.: High-fidelity task analysis identifying the needs of future cockpits featuring single pilot operation with large transport airplanes. In: Harris, D., Li, W.-C. (eds.) Engineering Psychology and Cognitive Ergonomics, vol. 14018. LNCS, pp. 60–76. Springer, Cham (2023)

20. Soll, H., Proske, S., Hofinger, G., Steinhardt, G.: Decision-making tools for aeronautical teams: FOR-DEC and beyond. Aviation Psychol. Appl. Hum. Factors (2016). https://doi.org/ 10.1027/2192-0923/a000099

21. Niermann, C., Ebrecht, L., Küls, J., Sebastian Findeisen, M., Hofmann, T.: Development process for a remote co-pilot to support single-pilot operation in a next-generation air transportation system. In: Human-Centered Aerospace Systems and Sustainability Applications (2023). https://doi.org/10.54941/ahfe1003914

22. Friedrich, M., Papenfuß, A., Hasselberg, A.: Transition from conventionally to remotely piloted aircraft – investigation of possible impacts on function allocation and information accessibility using cognitive work analysis methods. In: Stanton, N.A. (ed.) Advances in Human Aspects of Transportation. In: Proceedings of the AHFE 2017 International Conference on Human Factors in Transportation, July 17–21, 2017, The Westin Bonaventure Hotel, Los Angeles, California, USA. International Conference on Applied Human Factors and Ergonomics, pp. 96–107. Springer, Cham (2017). https://doi.org/10.1007/978-3-319-60441-1_10

Author Index

Printed in the United States
by Baker & Taylor Publisher Services